Rebel Raider

Winner of the 1986
DOUGLAS SOUTHALL FREEMAN
HISTORY AWARD

Rebel Raider

The Life of General

JOHN HUNT MORGAN

James A. Ramage

THE UNIVERSITY PRESS OF KENTUCKY

Editorial and Sales Offices: Lexington, Kentucky 40508-4008

Library of Congress Cataloging-in-Publication Data
Ramage, James A.
    Rebel raider

    Bibliography: p.
    Includes index.
        1. Morgan, John Hunt, 1825–1864. 2. Generals—
United States—Biography. 3. United States—Army—Biography.
4. Confederate States of America. Army—Biography.
5. Kentucky—History—Civil War, 1861–1865—Campaigns.
6. Indiana—History—Civil War, 1861–1865—Campaigns.
7. Ohio—History—Civil War, 1861–1865—Campaigns.
I. Title.
E467.1.M86R35   1986   973.7'42'0924   86-1548
ISBN 0-8131-0839-X (pbk: alk. paper)

TO ANDREA

CONTENTS

Illustrations follow page 116

MAPS

PREFACE

The purpose of this book is to describe the life and career of John Hunt Morgan and to evaluate his role in the Civil War. I find it intriguing that even though Morgan harassed the Union for almost three years and won the adoration of the Southern people, historians have dismissed him as a romantic figure who made little impact on the war. I asked, why did Morgan succeed so greatly as a leader early in the war, then decline so dramatically? Why did he risk the raid in Indiana and Ohio? Why was he the only member of his staff harmed in the skirmish that took his life? In searching for answers I have endeavored to describe what happened in Morgan's life, but I have gone beyond the facts to interpret and explain, with particular emphasis on the influences of family and society that shaped his personality and career. I realize that some readers will disagree with my interpretations—the Morgan legend was born in controversy and his memory stirs powerful emotions. But as a teacher I will be gratified if my work stimulates discussion and further study.

When Morgan joined the Confederate war effort, he intuitively adopted the tactics of classic guerrilla warfare. Making his own rules, he terrorized Federal provost marshals in an independent campaign to protect Southern sympathizers in Kentucky. He killed pickets, masqueraded as a Union officer, and employed civilians in the fighting, setting off a cycle of escalating violence that led to an unauthorized policy of retaliation by his command on the property of Union civilians.

Morgan's small victories made him famous. The Southern people recognized him as the guerrilla par excellence of the Confederacy and identified with him as the primary model for a popular movement for guerrilla warfare culminating in the partisan ranger act. He represented the Southern ideal of the chivalrous knight, the cavalier of romantic literature come to life; and the tinge of deviltry in his reputation made him a folk hero unusually attractive to women, who thronged in large crowds to adore him.

But at the height of his career, as a widower, Morgan met a beautiful young woman and fell in love. He married and came to labor under excessive dependence on his bride. As long as he practiced guerrilla warfare, he was one of the most successful guerrilla chiefs in history, but after the wedding, his heart was with his wife and not beside his men. Meanwhile, the Union cavalry, which had been no match for Morgan's command, gained in strength and efficiency. And Morgan's independence and tendency to make his own rules—the same characteristics that set him apart as a larger-than-life hero—made him a maverick in his own army. The people loved him, but the Confederate high command considered him dangerous.

F. Scott Fitzgerald wrote: "Show me a hero and I will write you a tragedy," and thus it was with Morgan. Hated by the North because his guerrilla tactics threatened civilized warfare, when he was killed he was under investigation by his own government for depredations committed by his men in enemy territory. But the greatest pathos in his life was the intense mental conflict he suffered, the periodic bouts with severe depression. The illness furnished a wellspring of creativity before the marriage, but afterward it placed him in an extraordinary dilemma, which contributed to his controversial death.

I gratefully acknowledge the assistance of Burton Milward, who provided a sounding board for my ideas, suggested productive leads, arranged and accompanied me on visits to sites such as Morgan's boyhood home in Lexington, gave the use of his personal collection of papers on Morgan, donated his expertise, and inspired me continually. James C. Klotter contributed thorough and up-to-date familiarity with historiography, introduced me to archivists and local historians in far-flung regions, and provided friendly encouragement. Milward and Klotter read the manuscript and made valuable suggestions, but the interpretations are solely mine; I am responsible for my weaknesses.

Ralph A. Tesseneer read part of the manuscript and consulted on human motivation and personality conflicts. Frances K. Swinford conducted my tour of Christ Church Episcopal; Frank G. Rankin bestowed information and provided inspiration and encouragement; and Arville L. Funk furnished documents and a tour of the route of the Great Raid in Indiana, which gave me a sense of the terror experienced by the citizens when Morgan's men appeared.

Roy Cochran guided me through the court records of Huntsville and contributed to my comprehension of the burgeoning spirit of frontier Alabama. Richard H. Doughty acquainted me with Greeneville, Tennessee and advanced my knowledge of Morgan's death. John Marshall Prewitt loaned a valuable diary and took me for coffee in the restaurant that now occupies the bank Morgan's men robbed in Mount Sterling, Kentucky. Joel Sierra served as my guide and interpreter in Monterrey, Mexico.

I am grateful to Patricia Sterling for her careful editing, which greatly improved the manuscript. I thank Joseph Ruh, Mary S. Rezny, Charles B. Castner, Jill A. Harris, and Tauni Graham for assistance with illustrations, and Dan E. Pomeroy for preparing the maps.

Northern Kentucky University supported the work with a sabbatical leave and two faculty project grants. Many individuals contributed generously by inviting me into their homes, sharing documents, making suggestions, providing leads, and in several cases conducting preliminary research.

In particular I am grateful to the following: Michael C.C. Adams, A.D. Albright, Carl Anderson, L.C. Angle, Calvin Applegate, Gary Arnold, Marylin Bell Hughes, James R. Bentley, Leon Boothe, William S. Bryant, Kathleen Bryson, Jean Calvert, Frances Coleman, James F. Corn, Nelson L. Dawson, John Dobson, Samuel R. Flora, William Floyd, Lyle Gray, Lowell H. Harrison, Penny Harrison, Walter H. Hendricks, David M. Hilton, James J. Holmberg, Nicky Hughes, Roger Ihrig, John B. Jett, Alethia Hunt Woods Kelly, Mary Kelm, Frank Levstik, William J. Marshall, Mary-Morse Matthews, Patrick Michael McCoy, Frances McPeak, Edna Millikan, Thomas L. Owen, Mrs. Buddy Parker, David Payne, O. Walter Place, Darryl Poole, Shirley Raleigh, W. Michael Ryan, Richard V. Salisbury, Richard A. Shrader, Eugene H. Sloan, Kate Stansbury, W. Frank Steely, Raines Taylor, Sharon Taylor, Edison H. Thomas, Mrs. Reid Towler, H. Lew Wallace, Macel Wheeler, L. Clayton Willis, Robert J. Womack, and John D. Wright.

I thank the staffs of the following libraries and depositories: Bluegrass Trust for Historic Preservation, Cincinnati Historical Society, University of Cincinnati, Library of Congress, Duke University, The Filson Club, Huntsville Public Library, Indiana Historical Society, Indiana State Library, Kenton County Public Library, University of Kentucky, Kentucky Historical Society, Kentucky Library at Western Kentucky University, Kentucky Military History Museum, Kentucky State Library and Archives, University of Louisville, Louisville Free Public Library, Lawson McGhee Library, University of North Carolina, Northern Kentucky University Library and Oral History Archive, Ohio Historical Society, Stones River National Military Park, Tennessee State Library and Archives, University of Texas, and Transylvania University.

The book demanded a place in my family, and I thank my daughter Andrea for sharing my time with Morgan's men. Most important of all, I thank my wife Ann for always supporting the work, even during the many evenings when I excused myself to the solitude of the study to pound the keys of the portable typewriter. Ann typed the manuscript, assisted with proofreading, accompanied me on trips, and as my closest companion and best friend, shared in the excitement of historical endeavor.

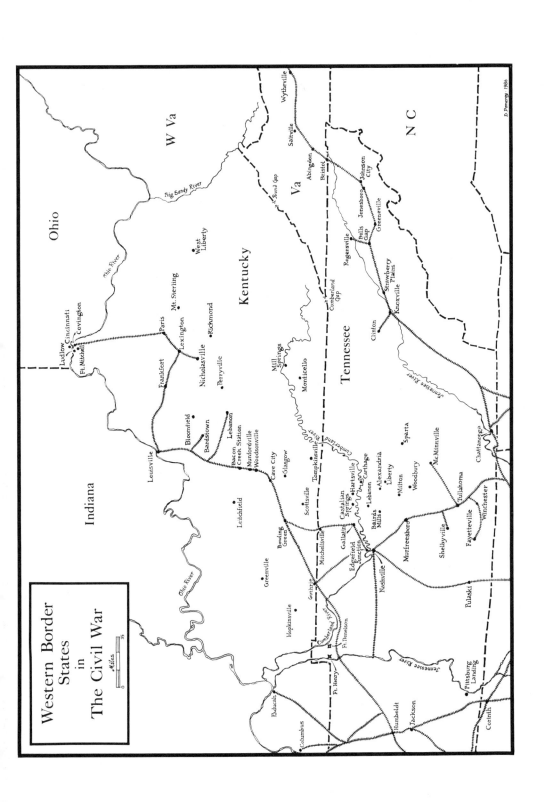

Western Border
States
in
The Civil War

Miles

0   35

Ohio

Indiana

W Va

N C

Kentucky

Tennessee

Va

Big Sandy River

Ohio River

Ohio River

Tennessee River

Cumberland River

Cumberland River

Tennessee River

Cumberland Gap

Pound Gap

Ludlow
Cincinnati
Covington
Ft. Mitchell

West
Liberty

Mt. Sterling
Paris
Lexington
Richmond
Nicholasville
Perryville
Frankfort

Wytheville

Saltville

Abingdon
Bristol
Johnson
City
Jenesboro
Greeneville
Bulls Gap
Rogersville
Strawberry
Plains
Knoxville
Clinton

Mill
Springs
Monticello

Bloomfield
Bardstown
Lebanon
Bacon
Creek Station
Munfordville
Woodsonville
Cave City
Glasgow
Louisville

Leitchfield

Scottsville
Tompkinsville
Castalian
Springs
Gallatin
Edgefield
Junction
Mitchellsville
Hartsville
Lebanon
Carthage
Bairds
Mills
Alexandria
Liberty
Milton
Woodbury
Sparta
McMinnville
Chattanooga
Tullahoma
Winchester
Fayetteville
Shelbyville
Murfreesboro
Nashville

Bowling
Green

Greenville

Hopkinsville

Guthrie

Paducah

Columbus

Ft. Henry
Ft. Donelson

Humboldt
Jackson

Pittsburg
Landing

Corinth

Pulaski

D. Pomeroy 1986

ONE

Folk Hero of the Revolution

It was the eighth day of January, 1864, and sleigh bells rang in the crisp morning air; two inches of fresh snow covered the roofs and sidewalks, and horsedrawn sleighs glided smoothly through the broad, level streets of Richmond, the Confederate capital. The freezing cold and glittering snow heightened the festive mood of the large crowd assembling in the sunshine outside the elegant Ballard House Hotel. Gen. John Hunt Morgan, the Kentucky cavalryman, and his wife Martha had arrived during the snowstorm in the night, and Mayor Joseph Mayo had invited everyone to a parade and public reception in his honor. Anticipation enlivened every countenance, and the presence of an unusual number of women, bundled up in coats and scarves, animated the throng with a lively cheerfulness. "There is a greater curiosity to see him," wrote a resident, "than any other Man in the South, Gen. Lee not excepted."[1]

By 11:00 A.M. the masses of citizens were filling the sidewalks; on Franklin Street they pressed around the military band and brigade of soldiers in dress uniform, standing in open ranks at present arms; they swarmed into the doorways and windows of the Exchange Hotel opposite the Ballard House. Toward noon they grew impatient and set up a clamor for Morgan. Finally he appeared, escorted by the mayor. He was thirty-eight years old, stood exactly six feet tall, weighed 185 pounds, had broad, square shoulders. He wore a civilian suit of black broadcloth, black cavalry boots and a black felt hat turned up on the right with a golden wreath-around-a-tree embroidery. His feet were small, his hands were small and white for a military man, and his complexion was fair. He had a well-trimmed black mustache and imperial beard, and dark auburn hair. His keen grayish-blue eyes were mirthful.[2]

Everyone agreed that Morgan was as fine a specimen of physical manhood as they had ever seen. He moved with manly strength and grace and was strikingly handsome. But what all observers noticed, and photographers and portraitists of the day were unable to capture, was his inimitable smile, a boyish grin that displayed a brilliant set of perfect white teeth; none who saw it could forget. "It comes over his face like the laugh over a child's countenance—having in it an innocence of humor which is very beautiful to me," recalled one of his women friends.[3]

All eyes turned on Morgan, and the crowd surged forward; the band struck up "La Marseillaise", the theme song of the French Revolution, and the people poured out their soul in the heartfelt cheer of the American Revolution: "Huzza! Huzza! Huzza!" Morgan was seated beside the mayor in a beautiful barouche (an open carriage with double seats) that led the way, followed by the band, marching soldiers, and about twenty carriages with members of the city council, Morgan's brother-in-law Gen. Ambrose Powell Hill, Gen. James Ewell Brown "Jeb" Stuart, and other dignitaries. (Morgan's wife had been invited to accompany him, but she was recuperating from a difficult childbirth and needed to recover from the journey.) More enthusiastic spectators greeted the procession as it moved west on Main Street and, turning north on Ninth, passed the famous Washington monument with its equestrian statue of George Washington, right hand raised, pointing the way to victory.[4]

At City Hall the parade halted, and Morgan was conducted to the southern portico where, under a brilliant blue sky in the January sunshine, an immense assemblage swelled out into Capital Square. When Morgan appeared at twenty minutes past twelve, they sent up a deafening cheer. He bowed debonairly and waved his hat, and the applause was tumultuous. Then Mayor Mayo stepped forward to repeat the well-known comparison of Morgan to Francis Marion, the most famous guerrilla leader in the American Revolution, and to decry Morgan's recent imprisonment in the North.

Fellow-Citizens: When I gaze upon the spectacle here presented this forenoon, my mind is carried back to the days of '76. Then we were engaged in a war with a civilized nation, and it pleased Providence to give us a Southern Marion, whose valor and prowess carried death and confusion into the ranks of the enemy. [Cheers.] Now we are engaged in a far deadlier war—if a savage crusade against our lives, our laws and institutions can be called such—with a nation whose acts are a disgrace to the age in which we live; and again it has pleased God to raise up to us another Marion from the Southwest, in the person of Gen. John H. Morgan—the hero who now stands before you, and whose name and fame, already bright in history, have been rendered doubly dear to us by the savage cruelty and indignity with which he has been treated by our savage foe. Fellow-citizens, I present to you General John H. Morgan, of Kentucky.[5]

After enthusiastic and prolonged cheering, Morgan responded:

Fellow-citizens: I thank you for this reception, and hope that my future career will prove that I am not unworthy of the honor you have done me. Not being accustomed to public speaking, I will give way to others who are. Again, I thank you for this manifestation of your regard.[6]

At the conclusion of the ceremony, the people crowded eagerly around the carriage. John B. Jones, a clerk in the war department, was astounded at the forwardness of the women; one even kissed Morgan's hand. The carriage moved slowly off, but the people were loath to let him go. One group of ladies and gentlemen followed the procession to the Ballard House and crowded into the hallway outside Morgan's suite, refusing to leave until Mayor Mayo brought the hero out and introduced him to everyone.[7]

Three days later, on Monday, January 11, Morgan attended a formal reception given in his honor by the Virginia state legislature. Usually the lawmakers met in tranquil solemnity before empty galleries, but by noon on this day—an hour before the ceremony—a throng of men, women, and children converged on the statehouse and packed the balcony of each chamber, with little boys hanging over the sides for a better view. Ladies rushed into the senate chamber, ousting the senators from their seats. It was most irregular, but the senators took it goodnaturedly, perching themselves in windows, on stools, and on the floor. At last Morgan was presented, and once each senator had been introduced to him, the women restrained themselves no longer— they rushed forward and swarmed around him, shaking his hand and blocking the aisles. With difficulty the House Committee of Arrangements rescued him and commenced escorting him through the multitude of women densely packed in the rotunda and on the stairway of the vestibule. Bright eyes and feminine forms besieged him on every hand, and he was frequently brought to bay by the pressure of hoop skirts and crinoline dresses: "It is the first time I have been surrounded without seeing a loop-hole of escape somewhere," he said. In the house chamber the ladies were even less restrained than those in the senate, forcing the delegates to adjourn in pandemonium.[8]

In their exhilaration at seeing Morgan in person, hearing his voice, touching him, the women were openly expressing an identification with a folk hero who had a special place in the hearts of the Southern people. The Confederacy had many heroes, among them great commanders such as Robert E. Lee, Thomas J. "Stonewall" Jackson, Albert S. Johnston, and Pierre G.T. Beauregard. But more than any other leader, Morgan, the revolutionary guerrilla, represented the Southern ideal of the chivalrous knight, the cavalier from the romantic novel come to life. He had given plain folk vicarious victory after victory over the despised Yankees, and on this larger-than-life, superhero level, he was without peer. As an editorial writer in Columbia, South Carolina, proclaimed:

When the future historian records the annals of this war—when the romancist seeks to discover amid its tangled threads a plot for his story—when the poet draws from its heroic chapter of events a theme on which to rhapsodise—when the soldier and the patriot desires an example that he may emulate and loom up grandly in some niche of his country's heart, no name will stand out more prominently from the brilliant galaxy by which it is surrounded, than that of plain John Hunt Morgan. . . .

[In every situation] he has combined those rare qualities which at once bespeak the true man and the honorable soldier. Winning fame wherever his blade has caught the sunlight, winning love amounting almost to veneration from those whom he has liberated, winning the respect and confidence of his superiors for his masterly ability as a commander—ever prompt, always alert, rarely failing to achieve success, the whole career of John Morgan has been a steady triumphal march toward a glorious end. As such we greet him as a type of the manhood of our Confederacy.[9]

The people were well aware that Morgan was only a brigadier general in command of fewer than 4,000 men, that he could not win a decisive battle or defend Richmond (Lee needed 70,000 and more to do that). Nevertheless, their romanticism sent their imaginations on flights of fantasy: an Atlanta newspaper, for instance, had once compared Morgan's small squadron of less than 200 to Albert S. Johnston's army of 45,000: "He is a perfect terror to the Yankees, and has inspired them with greater fear than all the army of General Johnston besides."[10]

For the Southern people, Morgan personified adventure and romance in combat in which they could not participate directly. He did what many Southerners would have liked to do themselves—make violent revolution. He gave them an outlet for their suppressed fear and aggression, bringing a release from tension and a renewal of dedication to the cause. Morgan anecdotes, with their aura of swashbuckling and derring-do, bravery and beauty, and victory against overwhelming odds, provided momentary deliverance from the frustration of war reverses; in his admirers' minds he took on fabulous, almost magical powers.

Since the Press Association of the Confederacy distributed news stories to members by telegraph, and many papers reprinted one another's articles and those of Northern journals, dispatches relating to the legend and the exploits of his command made the rounds. For instance, a news release announcing that Morgan's men had managed the explosion of a locomotive in Cave City, Kentucky, appeared first in Atlanta, then was reprinted in Richmond, Savannah, and Mobile. The papers might carry such reports several times per week; it was not unusual to have several in one issue.[11]

The public's identification with their "knight" was affectionate and familiar—news columns frequently quoted Morgan dialogue and described him for the readers. A Northern reporter commented, "We have been asked a thousand and one times what kind of man Morgan is, and how he looks." And there was continual expectation of repeat performances. He "will soon turn up again, the public may rest assured," one communiqué promised. "Before long we shall hear of him again," another concluded.[12]

In contrast to the Union's Gen. William T. Sherman, who eluded the press and feuded with reporters, Morgan cultivated friendly relations with war correspondents. He visited their offices in person and encouraged members of his staff to file dispatches as special correspondents. During one raid behind enemy lines, the officer left in charge at headquarters agreed to release any positive news to the press immediately.[13]

Morgan enthusiasts so reordered present fact into make-believe, and made the legend so much larger than life that one journalist felt compelled to remind everyone that their hero sometimes rested and ate food, "for, after all, 'Morgan and his men' are no more than flesh and blood." Nevertheless, when everything looked gloomy and few bright spots appeared on the horizon, his victories seemed to confirm the myth that Southerners were superior and their revolution preordained. The pride and honor of the people were interwoven with his achievements; he confirmed their worth, their belief in themselves, and their hope of victory.[14]

"Whenever we have met with disaster and the cruel foe has planted his poisoned fangs still deeper in our quivering heart, then I would turn to our gallant 'Marion,' and his brave and daring deeds would be as a soothing balm to our bleeding wounds. . . . I have watched his brilliant career, ever since he first shot out into our clouded sky, like a glorious meteor," wrote May Wheat-Shobus of Salisbury, South Carolina. "We know that Morgan and other compatriots are near and still strong to do battle, this revives our drooping spirits, energizes us and keeps our heads above the dark despondency," another woman observed. "We are hoping soon to hear of some more of your brilliant successes, indeed we almost look to you to deliver our country and prayers daily ascend to Heaven for your success," said a third. In Charleston, Emma Holmes recorded in her diary: "Morgan is one of my favorite heroes, & I am always delighted to hear of some new & brilliant exploit."[15]

All ages and all classes identified with the Morgan legend, but the adoration reached its zenith among Southern women. Wherever he went, his horse Black Bess had to be guarded to preserve her mane and tail from assault by young women with stars in their eyes and scissors in their hands. In Gallatin, Tennessee, when he gave Susan Alexander a ride around the square behind him on Black Bess, she vowed to marry no other than one of Morgan's men. A young maiden in Nashville announced that she would rather have a kiss from Morgan than a wedding proposal from the wealthiest officer in the Federal army. His wife was besieged for autographs, and he turned down requests for coat buttons by explaining that all he had left were Yankee buttons, and he did not suppose they wanted those.[16] A female poet in Knoxville published the poem "Morgan," one verse of which read:

> I bring no laurels to deck his brow—
>   A grateful nation will twine them there,
> But for our hero I offer now
>   A holier gift—a woman's prayer.[17]

A woman in Richmond offered even the life of her sweetheart, whom she recommended as a superior swordsman: "He would be too happy if the occasion came to interpose his sword to save your valued life tho it cost him his own."[18]

The war provided Southern women opportunities for self-realization and personal fulfillment that patriarchal society had denied them. Presenting a flag to Morgan's command, a committee of women in Gallatin pronounced: "We are ladies 'tis true but our hearts throb with the same sentiments that fire the souls and nerve the arms of the bravest men of our Southern armies." With the men gone, women made decisions, and gained in status and self-confidence by stepping into new roles. Women took over schoolteaching and plantation management; some went into milling, merchandising, and manufacturing. Yeomen wives plowed fields and mended fences; aristocratic ladies who had never held a needle joined sewing circles to make clothing and bandages. They established canteens at railroad stations and served refreshments to men on troop trains. A soldier traveling through Virginia was so frequently disturbed by attentive females that he placed a makeshift sign on his head: "Neither sick nor wounded, but sleepy." Women worked as clerks in government offices and served ably as hospital administrators: Kate Cumming in Mobile, for instance, and Sally Louisa Tompkins of Richmond, who was commissioned captain in the army for organizing and managing a hospital.[19]

Attitudes, values, and behavior patterns were altered as well, and women were liberated from some of the old taboos and restraints of the cult of "true womanhood." Stepping down from their pedestals, women in Richmond cut their hair short and sexually harassed the Confederate Congress by congregating in the balcony and ogling the members. Sentimentality became more open: young women in Richmond decked Jeb Stuart's horse with garlands of flowers and strewed roses in his path. It was a new, more extroverted expression of hero worship not seen before on this continent.[20]

With little apparent conscious effort, Morgan stirred his adorers to "perfect ecstasies" just by his presence—and a tinge of devilry. Like Robin Hood and Rob Roy, he was a bold outlaw, violating the limits of society and breaking the restraint of traditional practices and values. And he was a notorious libertine. Rumor held that before he married Martha, his second wife, he had taken advantage of several poor girls in his hometown of Lexington, Kentucky. George Prentice, editor of the Louisville *Journal*, explained the tendency of women to "admire and idolize a 'dashing hero,' especially if he has a strong spice of sin and the devil in him. A bold robber chief captivates their romantic fantasies sooner than a good and quiet Christian citizen, and a gloomy and desperate pirate like Byron's Conrad, takes a deeper hold upon their hearts and imaginations than any honest commander of a steam frigate or ship of the line."[21]

In the poem "The Federal Mother's Lullaby," printed in the newspaper of Morgan's command, the *Vidette*, a Northern mother pleaded with her baby to hush crying, for down the street she heard the clatter of hooves.

> Why, surely, 'tis the Morgan,
> Him whom I would not greet.
> For there's that in his glances

That makes my heart-strings thrill,
So darling, hush thy wailing,
And be for mother still.[22]

Beauty, romance, and roguishness came together in a powerful sexual attraction. With no annoying habits or negative characteristics to intervene, the mythical Morgan touched the souls of his women admirers in a manner which no actual man could emulate. Yet when they met him, the attraction grew stronger. In Charleston, Emma Holmes told her diary about an evening a friend spent with Morgan: "She said he was extremely different from what she had imagined. [He was] so mild & gentle in his manners that she would not have taken him for a soldier but for his boots & spurs, so unwarrior-like did he seem." A lady from Louisville dined with him, and "she, like all the ladies who see him, fell perfectly in love, was perfectly fascinated with his elegant and fine personal appearance."[23]

One day when Morgan was passing through Warren County, Tennessee, and stopped at the house of elderly Mrs. Livingston to ask directions, she became so flustered that she was speechless. Seeing her agitation, Morgan bowed and left. Recovering, Mrs. Livingston broke over to her neighbor's house; they hurried on their bonnets and went off to Dr. Armstrong's in McMinnville, the house Morgan had inquired for. There she was introduced.

"Madame, you are the lady I met a little while back on the road?"

"Yes," she exclaimed, throwing up her hands. "I'm the very one. But glory be to God! When I saw John Morgan I was so glad I couldn't say a word. I beg your pardon for not showing you the way to Dr. Armstrong's."[24]

In Richmond, Kentucky, Lucy Jennings said: "Oh! You can but poorly imagine what a joy it was to see what my eyes had so long desired *Morgan & his Men!* Morgan the Marion of the War! He whose name will live in the hearts of his Southern Brothers long years after they have gained that Independence for which he & his followers are making that noble & mighty struggle." In Harrodsburg, Elizabeth Hardin sighed: "At last I saw John Morgan! And was not disappointed. He was exactly my ideal of a dashing cavalryman."[25]

The Morgan legend seemed to confirm the mythical superiority of the Southern cavalier, the value of the cult of chivalry, and the worthiness of the Southern caste system. When he raided Northern towns, giving enemy civilians a sample of the bitter taste of invasion, Southern honor was to some extent restored. James M. Calhoun, mayor of Atlanta, told Morgan: "Your countrymen cannot but feel grateful to you, and do honor to themselves, by honoring you."

TWO

Patriarchs and Southern Honor

As a folk hero, John Hunt Morgan mirrored the people's belief in the Southern code of honor, a system of ethics with roots deep in mythology, literature, and civilization. A Southern gentleman's evaluation of himself was based upon the judgments of the community. His inner conviction of self-esteem was formed by the public assessment of his behavior. One element of honor was loyalty to forefathers. John Hunt Morgan's father, Calvin, taught his children to venerate the Morgan family tradition and exhibit traits of the Morgan lineage, whose patriarchs he brought parading forth after dinner in the parlor of their farm home near Lexington, and on carriage rides in the sunshine alongside green hemp fields. "Morgan blood is strong and virile; it dominates and individualizes," an observer noted. The men were generally tall, strong, and handsome; the women beautiful: "Our men are brave and our women virtuous," they boasted. "He is a Morgan from the crown of his head to the sole of his feet," they said of a cousin.[1]

Unhesitating in the defense of personal and family honor, Morgans served in the militia and were known for standing their ground and giving satisfaction. In 1811, John Hunt Morgan's grandfather Luther and Luther's brother Calvin were indicted, along with five other men, for fighting in a street brawl in frontier Huntsville, Alabama. On May 22, 1824, another Calvin Morgan—Luther's son and John's father—pleaded guilty to the same offense and was fined one cent by the county circuit court. In 1861 a cousin, George Washington "Wash" Morgan, exchanged pistol fire with Charles Douglas on the streets of Knoxville. The same year another cousin, St. Clair Morgan, fought a duel with a navy midshipman in the moonlight near Pensacola, using Sharps rifles at twenty paces. Seriously wounded in the right groin, he recovered—to give his life in battle in the Civil War. Morgan family tradition confirmed the tenets of Southern honor: members of the family were to display physical courage on all occasions and, when mortally wounded, to "die like a Morgan."[2]

The narrative of Morgan family tradition in America began with the immigration of James Morgan from England to Massachusetts in 1636. James eventually settled in Connecticut, where in a later generation John's great-grandfather Gideon Morgan (1751–1830) married Patience Cogswell, the daughter of an ingenious goldsmith who was experimenting with perpetual motion when he died. Gideon served as a corporal in a Connecticut regiment in the American Revolution and named one of his sons George Washington Morgan. He became a prosperous pioneer merchant, surveyor, and speculator, moving along the cutting edge of the frontier, establishing new towns and selling supplies to settlers. In 1806 he arrived in Knoxville, Tennessee and remained there until the population approached 1,000, then made his last move—a few miles westward to Kingston, where he opened a tavern.[3]

Gideon's son Calvin (b. 1773) and his brother Rufus became wealthy merchants and respected community leaders. Calvin established the first cotton gin in Knoxville and was prominent in banking; Rufus operated an iron furnace and had one of the finest mansions in the city; both were aldermen and trustees of East Tennessee College, today's University of Tennessee.

Another son, Gideon, Jr., married Margaret Sevier, who was the granddaughter of John Sevier, governor of Tennessee, and also a descendant of Chief Oconostota of the Cherokee remnant living in the mountains of North Carolina. Gideon, Jr., cultivated his wife's Indian relatives, and during the campaign against the Creek Indians in Mississippi Territory during the War of 1812, Gen. Andrew Jackson appointed him commander of a regiment of 400 Cherokee troops. On November 18, 1813, Gideon's regiment attacked a party of 310 Creeks at Hillabee Town, killing 61 warriors and taking 250 prisoners. "Will not shame redden the face & silence mute the tongue of those who have pretended to doubt the attachment of the Cherokee to our Country?" Gideon asked in his report. "They must now if they continue to murmur advance their real views, a thirst for their property and lives." Unfortunately, the fight lost its luster when Gideon learned that the tribe had surrendered to Jackson and that he had slaughtered men who had sued for peace. Indeed, the Hillabee massacre had the effect of prolonging the war: the remaining Creeks were determined to fight to the death.[4]

Jackson never condemned the atrocity; in fact, three months later the Cherokee regiment fought in the Battle of Horseshoe Bend, a decisive victory resulting in the Treaty of Fort Jackson, which ended the Creek War. The battle occurred when 1,000 Creek warriors made a last-ditch stand behind log breastworks in a bend in the Tallapoosa River. As Jackson closed on the enemy with a force of about 3,000, John Coffee's cavalry prevented their retreat by capturing the Creek canoes. Then Gideon's regiment used the boats to cross the river and enter the Creek village behind the Creek battle line. His Cherokee swiftly put the torch to the Creek huts and opened fire on the warriors from the rear, while the main body of Jackson's men stormed the parapet. Gideon's key diversion had contributed significantly to Jackson's great victory.[5]

More than any other member of the family in his generation, Luther Morgan (b. July 4, 1776), another son of Gideon, Sr., and grandfather of John Hunt Morgan, loved the outdoors. Wandering widely in the Tennessee Valley beyond the edge of the frontier, he discovered sulfur springs sixty-five miles south of Huntsville, Alabama. Foreseeing the day when the fertile soil of the region would support large cotton plantations, Luther purchased the springs, chained his pet bear to one of two giant birch trees, and erected a retail store made of bark and shaped like a wigwam under the other. Luther's great dream was to develop Blount Springs into the largest, most luxurious bathing resort in the Southwest. He had no way of knowing that Blount Springs would become a nightmare, bankrupting him as a businessman and creating emotional repercussions that would reverberate through future generations and have a profound influence on the life of his famous grandson.

Settlement in northern Alabama was sparse until the great wave of westward migration after the War of 1812. With cotton selling at 30 cents per pound, small farmers and planters from Virginia and other eastern states rushed to purchase new cotton land in Alabama. Peace with the Indians, prosperity, and a bouyant national mood contributed to a boom in land sales that reached its peak in 1818. A steady stream of immigrants came on the Great Valley Road running southwest from Virginia to Knoxville and branching west to Nashville and south to Huntsville. Families came in buggies, followed by slaves, livestock driven by field hands, and wagonloads of household goods.

Huntsville developed almost overnight from a small frontier village to a town with twenty-five cotton gins, a courthouse, two newspapers, and the Planters and Merchants Bank. The boom was on, based on 30-cent cotton delivered by slaves to the gin, where it was processed and pressed into large bales held together with bagging and bale rope produced in Kentucky hemp factories and imported to Huntsville by merchants in new buildings on streets named Cotton Row, Commercial Row, and Exchange Row. In 1817, Alabama became a territory, and two years later a state. Huntsville was the county seat for Madison County, in 1820 the most populous in Alabama with 19,619 people—9,323 of them slaves.

Luther Morgan was an early entrepreneur in Huntsville. As a wholesale merchant he imported whiskey, bacon, cotton bagging, and bale rope from Kentucky, and machine parts for cotton gins from the upper Ohio Valley. In 1812 he did $4,000 worth of business; by 1815, $15,000. During the boom years of 1815-19 he purchased several town lots, built a house, and began development of Blount Springs, where he constructed a large boardinghouse and thirty cabins, and advertised "the red, black and white sulphur water, adjoining each other . . . the great medicinal qualities they possess . . . have been made manifest by the many cures effected in cases of Rheumatic, Bilious and other affections." Planters opened thousands of acres of new cotton lands, and overproduction—more than the Panic of 1819—caused the price of cotton to plunge; by 1823 it was down to 11.4 cents. But it was assumed that the downturn was a temporary manifestation of the business cycle and that good prices would return. Immigration slowed in 1820, but by 1830 Madison County had grown to 27,990 of whom 13,977 were slaves.[6]

Luther entered partnership with his eldest son Samuel and twins Calvin and Alexander under the name Luther Morgan & Sons. They built a new warehouse and meathouse on Franklin Street and a brick store on Commercial Row facing the courthouse. In addition to wholesale merchandising, they exchanged money and invested in an iron foundry. The twins traveled to Lexington, Kentucky, to buy hemp products, and there in the Athens of the West they went courting. They were a tall and handsome set, proud representatives of the Morgan clan.[7]

Calvin, John's father, was a very unusual Morgan; he enjoyed reading and had attended Cumberland College in Nashville before entering the business world. Lacking the adventurous spirit common in the family, he apparently participated in the street brawl because of community expectations; it was uncharacteristic behavior. With a prominent chin and finely formed facial features, he was intelligent looking, but in his eyes there was vulnerability; when confronted he tended to give way. He was amiable and likable, and his friends elected him lieutenant colonel of the militia at the young age of twenty-one. Once a colonel of militia, a man had the title for life, and as a symbol of status the rank of "Colonel Morgan" proved particularly significant.

Calvin's greatest accomplishment in life, however, was winning the approval of his future father-in-law, John Wesley Hunt, whose every significant investment in merchandising, manufacturing, banking, and government securities had turned to gold; he was one of the wealthiest men west of the Allegheny Mountains. When banks failed all over the nation in 1819, his Farmers and Mechanics Bank in Lexington not only remained solvent but paid dividends to its stockholders.[8]

Everything about Hunt—from Hopemont, the beautiful Georgian mansion he constructed near Transylvania University, to the accomplished six sons and six daughters he and his wife Catherine filled it with—was animated with a spirit of success, accomplishment, and affluence. The aloof, broad-shouldered Hunt was a self-disciplined, righteous pillar of the Episcopal Church with no acknowledged weaknesses and little sympathy for impotence or ineptitude in others; his intense blue eyes seemed to sense their deepest shortcomings.

Calvin passed inspection, however; Hunt approved his marriage to the fifth child, Henrietta. She was a beautiful and slender seventeen-year-old with dark brown hair sweeping to stylish curls, a strong chin, small firm mouth, brilliant eyes, and a resolute expression that revealed the "very determined traits of character and positive convictions" she shared with her wealthy father. Hunt gave her the usual wedding gift for his daughters—a new carriage and team of fine horses. While Calvin was calling at Hopemont, Alexander, a major in the Huntsville militia, gave his attention to America Higgins, and on September 24 and September 25, 1823, they had matching wedding ceremonies at Christ Church Episcopal. In Huntsville, Cal and

Henrietta made their home in a beautiful new house on Franklin Street, a few blocks from the square; the deed was in the name of Luther Morgan & Sons.[9]

When the newlyweds came home, their reception was dimmed by increasing concern over the cotton market. In February, 1824, the price fell to 10 cents in Huntsville; partnerships dissolved; and merchants closed their doors and defaulted. Business was dropping off at Blount Springs, and it became clear that extensive investment in the springs had overextended the resources of the company. By January of 1825, Luther Morgan & Sons could not meet its obligations to wholesalers in New York, Baltimore, and Newark. Luther negotiated a deed of trust that mortgaged Blount Springs, the stores and houses in Huntsville, and five slaves. It provided that if the debts remained after three years, the property would be sold and the proceeds paid to the creditors. Luther and his wife, Ann, and each of his sons and their wives signed the agreement on January 17, 1825.[10]

Henrietta was nineteen, and three months pregnant. On June 1, 1825, she gave birth to a son, and in selecting a name she and Cal set aside one of the traditions of the antebellum South. Society was patriarchal, and in Huntsville the general pattern was to name the first male child for the paternal grandfather, the second male for the maternal grandfather, and the third for the father himself.[11]

By this tradition the newborn should have been Luther Morgan; instead, John Hunt Morgan was named for the *maternal* grandfather. Henrietta and Cal went on to have ten children, four girls and six boys, and none was named for Luther. The second son was given the father's name, Calvin, but the others were named for Hunt family members. Perhaps there was no conscious attempt to slight Luther. However, the pattern reflects an orientation toward the Hunts, and being the namesake of John Wesley Hunt proved a heavy burden for the eldest son.

As soon as the deed of trust was signed, Luther Morgan & Sons closed, and under the name Samuel D. Morgan & Co. the family continued the wholesale business. They improved Blount Springs, adding fifteen new cabins and a new wing of twenty rooms on the lodge. Rates were cut in half for children and servants. "Good music will be provided which will admit of Balls in the Evening," Luther announced, "in addition to the various other amusements of Billiards, Ninepins, Hunting, Fishing, &c. &c. Their liquors and other stores, are of the best quality, and such as to enable them (which they intend) to make this one of the most desirable watering places in the western country."[12]

Calvin opened a separate business, one more suitable to his quiet, studious personality. In an attractive brick building on Commercial Row he established Morgan's Apothecary Store; professional contact with physicians and the public appealed to him. In addition to selling such medicines as calomel, opium, and quinine, he offered oils, soaps, cologne, paint, and cigars. He tended the store himself and guaranteed a refund if customers were not completely satisfied. Also he handled shipments of merchandise from his father-in-law to the Morgan wholesale company, kept Hunt informed of market conditions, and settled Hunt's claims against individuals in Huntsville.[13]

Since virtually everything the Morgans owned was mortgaged, Hunt came to the rescue to insure the roof would not be sold from over his daughter's head; the Morgans' eastern creditors agreed to the transfer of Cal's house and lot to John Wesley Hunt for $700. The assistance freed Henrietta and Cal from concern about housing, but in that patriarchal society, such intervention threatened Calvin's manhood. Having failed to provide economic security for his family, he had become dependent upon his millionaire father-in-law.[14] And that was only the beginning. When Blount Springs and the other properties, including the drugstore, were sold at public auction, Calvin was unemployed.[15]

Again, Henrietta's family intervened. Her brother Charlton Hunt, a prominent Lexington lawyer, purchased Calvin's stock and employed Calvin as his agent to manage the store. Calvin reopened at a new location, now owing both his house and his job to the Hunt family. Moreover, three other drugstores opened in Huntsville, and the competition—plus continued depression in the cotton market—caused him to lose money. In 1829, a year after the sheriff's sale, Calvin's house was advertised for auction to satisfy unpaid taxes. He managed to pay up the back taxes but could not then afford servants to assist Henrietta with housekeeping and child care. In November, 1829, Hunt hired out two female slaves to Cal.[16]

Finally, in early 1831, Cal completely surrendered and humbly accepted his father-in-law's offer to employ him as manager of one of the Hunt farms in Fayette County. Cal purchased five horses for the trip and promised they would be in fine shape for farming afterward: "We shall travel with great economy and hope to get in without much expense. . . . I know I shall be contented and, hope to be happy, altho the pursuit is one with which I am unacquainted. However I come prepared fully, to give it all the industry and management I am capable of, together with feelings of utmost gratitude for all your kindness to me."[17]

Cal loaded his personal property on a new wagon and bundled his family in a carriage for the journey. There were now four children: John, five; Calvin, three; and babies Catherine and Ann. In Lexington they moved into a large two-story farmhouse that still stands on Tates Creek Road. Cal managed the farm as Hunt's agent, and in return Hunt furnished "a genteel and suitable support" from the proceeds of the farm.[18]

Today there are century-old scuff marks and well-worn places on the original hardwood boards of the stairs leading to the attic of the house where they lived. John and young Cal tramped up and down the stairs and chased across the dogtrot separating the kitchen-dining room and parlor. They caught tadpoles in the creek on the south lawn and watched with fascination as slaves cured bacon and hams in the smokehouse. If they soiled their knees playing Indian fortress in the cellar, they did not remain dirty for long. Henrietta saw to it that the slaves kept the children clean and the house immaculate. One of houseservant Phiola's regular tasks was sweeping the yard with a broom.[19]

The 300-acre farm was a bustling showplace for the latest varieties of livestock, machinery, and crops. Through the years Hunt improved the bloodlines of Kentucky thoroughbreds, harness horses, cattle, hogs, and mules by importing breeding stock from Pennsylvania, New York, and Virginia. Calvin supervised Hunt's slaves in raising hemp, grain, hay, and livestock. During a trip to England for medical treatment in 1839, he personally selected five shorthorn cattle for Hunt. The farm was one of the first in Fayette County to use a new wheat thresher and steam sawmill. Passersby noticed that the shutters of the house were painted, the windows cleaned, the fences well kept: everything was in order, and John Wesley Hunt approved.[20]

About a year after employing Calvin, Hunt renewed the contract for ten years. The arrangement provided security and acceptance in upper-class society, yet at times cash for personal expenses was scarce. When Calvin was in Europe in 1839, he calculated that the family would have cash from the sale of John and Cal's pigs and other products, "and then if there is any more wanting . . . we will all economize and make it up." The family lived an affluent life-style and Calvin was grateful to Hunt for saving his status as a gentleman of wealth.[21]

Another way Calvin established his reputation in the world of men was by having a successful marriage with many offspring. He and Henrietta had six more children after moving to Lexington; from age nineteen to thirty-nine she bore a child on an average of every two years. Catherine and Ann died as young children in the cholera epidemic of 1833. The fifth child, born in 1834, was named Catherine also (and nicknamed Kitty and Dolly); then came Richard in 1836, Charlton in 1838, Henrietta (nicknamed Tommy) in 1840, Thomas in 1844, and Francis Key in 1845.[22]

In the system of honor one's worth was enhanced also through titles and appearance. Everyone greeted and spoke of Calvin as "Colonel Morgan," in deference to his militia rank. He was well-dressed and attractive, had the affability and manners of a gentleman, and spoke in the soft, quiet tones of a man of learning. Aristocratic Southern society valued education, and he attempted to instill an appreciation for it in his children. In Europe, when he pictured the family in his mind, John and Cal were diligently studying in their Ma's room: "You and Cally seated at the candle stand. Charly & Dick in bed. Dolly frisking and ordering Betsy [Bouvette, the family's black mammy] about. Your Ma sewing and perhaps watching Phiola at her ironing. . . . You are good boys. . . . Oh how much I wish that you could know and feel the importance of education. What a pleasure and advantage it is to

[be] well informed. Without education you can never be any body. With it you may [be] the greatest in the land." He admonished that John "must allow himself full time to take pains with his writing or your Mother will beat him in Penmanship and that must not happen."[23]

There is no doubt that Calvin's honor was established in the Lexington community and among the Hunts; every reference to him is respectful. Hunt allowed people to assume that Calvin owned the farm; his name appeared in the state records as the person responsible for the taxes, and in the Lexington city directory as the owner. But when Calvin stood before the fireplace in his bedroom on the second floor and looked out over the bluegrass pastures and hemp fields, he knew the property he surveyed belonged to his wife's father—every acre, every fencepost, and every slave. Property ownership was the key to honor, and behind the facade Calvin was in reality a hired hand, an overseer paid for his work with room and board. It was not an honorable situation for a man of his background, status, and social standing.[24]

Furthermore, masculine honor required male headship of the family. Calvin agreed with society's designation of the wife as "the tender female given to man as an ornament & blessing, sheltered & protected" by distinctive Southern civilization. Henrietta, constrained from selfhood and self-expression by social conventions, was in a very ambivalent situation. As a mother she was responsible for the children, but as on many large Southern plantations, she shared their affection with a servant. Hunt had purchased Bouvette in Virginia and given her to Henrietta in Huntsville. She was a perfect houseservant—humble, kind, and loving, with a buoyant Christian spirit. In contrast to the stereotype, she was short and thin as a rail but made up for it in strength of character. A masterful teacher of young children, she knew when to be firm and when to be lenient.[25]

Bouvette nursed all ten children, and when they left home, they seemed to miss "Aunt Betty" almost as much as their mother. From prison camp Tom wrote: "Tell Aunt Betty she cannot imagine how very much I regret at [sic] not being able to see her since my arrival here at Camp Chase. She is never out of my mind." Richard's letters were so full of love for Bouvette that Henrietta's jealousy could not be restrained—she accused him of loving his black mammy more than his mother. He answered: "It is a singular notion which you have taken up, that from my frequent messages &c. to Aunt Betty, that I love her better than yourself. It is true that I love her and I think nothing more than natural that I should, but not before yourself do love her, but next."[26]

Forced by the customs of plantation slavery to share the affection of her children, torn between economic dependence on her father and love for her husband, Henrietta encountered confusion and irregularity in her relationship with Calvin. There was love and fidelity; but Hunt's well-intended intervention, Henrietta's own great strength of character, and Calvin's regressive tendencies gave her unusual power. In a patriarchal society, when the woman in reality becomes the head, ordinary familial tensions are intensified, and anarchy threatens. If Calvin admonished the older boys and Henrietta dissented, he would quietly retreat; indeed, he developed the habit of apologizing even when he had not transgressed:

> You say in your last letter you have been looking for some time for a storm from me. I cannot imagine to what you allude. I wrote incessantly at Paris hardly even looked over what I had written. Sometimes was sick and gloomy, often said much that was very foolish I warrant. I had nothing else to employ me. But as to complaining or much less scolding, I cannot at this moment bring to mind a single expression that could be construed into any such thing. I'll bet you my old standing wagon that you cannot show me in all my letters anything but lines of Love, pages of affection.[27]

In 1838, the fifteenth year of their marriage, Calvin began suffering from a lingering illness. Complaining of numbness in his legs, he said: "When I yet sit for any time I find them quite cold and dead, but when moving do not experience any serious inconvenience." He may have had diabetes or a spinal tumor or polyneuritis or pernicious anemia, but medical science had not advanced enough to render a diagnosis. After bathing at various mineral springs, he sought the opinion of the medical experts in Paris. Walking the streets six hours each day helped, but the professors told him that the disease "arises from causes so general that it requires a variety of applications & time to cure it. . . . My health . . . is so changeable that I now place no hopes in any occasional advantage I gain."[28]

Calvin fathered the last four children after the onset of the illness, and when able he still managed the farm. After Hunt died in 1849, however, Henrietta inherited Hopemont and other properties worth $65,013.78, and the family moved into the town mansion, where the taxes were paid in Calvin's name but the title was in Henrietta's.[29]

The love of Henrietta and the children comforted Calvin, and he compensated for ill health and loss of self-esteem by escaping into the literature of romance. In the popular *Waverley* novels by Sir Walter Scott, men were dominant, courageous, and brave; wives were subservient; honor was vindicated. He had made a pilgrimage to Scott's estate of Abbottsford in Scotland. The immortal Sir Walter, he professed, "has done more for the solace of the broken spirit, more for the happiness of the world and the honour of mankind than any other being who ever existed since the time of him who proved the sacred truth of God."[30]

Calvin died on May 1, 1854, at the age of fifty-two; Henrietta lived to age eighty-five and died in 1891.

In outward appearance Calvin Morgan was the head of a large family, owner of several slaves and a valuable plantation; in reality, he worked as a middle-class farm overseer for his wife's father, and Henrietta made the really significant decisions. Denied the fulfillment of paying homage to his forefathers by naming one of his six sons Rufus or Gideon, he praised the Morgans continually, emphasizing their military accomplishments. After sons John and Cal had displayed courage in battle in Mexico, Calvin informed his brother Samuel that they were fine Morgans and "would remind you very much of our noble and beloved Uncle Rufus, whose name I have taught them to reverence, and whose virtues I have endeavored to instil from infancy."[31] John Hunt Morgan was not only inculcated with the ethical system of honor and given the Morgan patriarchs as role models; he was expected to meet the standards of the grandfather whose name he bore. The weight on his young shoulders was burdensome indeed, and it remained to be seen how he would react to the challenge.

THREE

The Quest for Honor

In the antebellum South the great challenge of the adolescent was to establish an identity in the social order according to the accepted system of honor. For John Hunt Morgan, bridging the gap between childhood and adulthood was difficult. Not only was his father an inadequate role model, but he had to reconcile the unbridled militaristic tradition of the Morgans with the self-control and stability of the Hunts. Naming him after his grandfather had cemented family harmony, but now he was expected to live up to the name, and the family's economic dependence on Hunt added weight to the yoke. Some youths refused to accept such a challenge and responded by rebelling into waywardness.[1] Hunt's own namesake, his second son John Wilson, rejected his father's example and became a black sheep. The other (exemplary) eleven children said he was "wild & noisy," and "a bad, a very bad boy." At the age of twenty-six, he was killed in a duel, defending his name against charges that he drank excessively, used bad language, and had "loose sentiments" and Parisian manners.

Like all the Hunts and Morgans, John Hunt Morgan acquired by birth the status of membership in the aristocracy. He had the advantage of physical appearance, as well; he developed a tall, athletic body, strong and attractive. Another factor in honor was horsemanship. Mounted on some of the finest blood horses in the world, John and Cal cantered into town and galloped through the cane, wild rye and bluegrass, under the open, parklike forests of blue ash and bur oak in the savanna-woodland of Fayette County. John became an outstanding rider and good judge of horseflesh. On summer mornings, leaving the house before sunrise, they would take rifles to the oak-hickory woodlands outside Lexington. The rising sun glistened on the green leaves and the coves rang with the chirping of birds. Suddenly the trees would seem to come alive, stirring with gray squirrels leaping from one swaying bough to another, and the quiet would be broken by gunfire—the young hunters were developing marksmanship and familiarity with firearms. They bet on the races held regularly in Lexington and took their share of premiums at agricultural fairs.

John and Cal studied at home with their father and possibly others as tutors, and at a neighborhood school; John was seventeen when he enrolled in Transylvania University. Ascending the white steps of Morrison Hall, he passed between the stately Doric columns of the portico on his way to classes in Cicero's orations, Greek, Latin, algebra, and history. He joined the Adelphi Society, a literary fraternity that met on Friday nights to debate, read compositions, and practice parliamentary procedure—but the budding elocutionists were more interested in enjoying themselves than in improving their oratory. Several Adelphis were habitually absent; others came fortified by "Old Crow" whiskey and other ardent spirits, and interrupted the debates with "buffoonery." The night John joined, the secretary recorded in the large leatherbound minute book: "The President delivered his valedictory. By the way it was none of the longest consisting of about two lines and a half." Later in the year one of the rowdy members was fined $500 and suspended from the society for five months for "very disorderly conduct." Morgan was frequently absent, and every time he was assigned to debate an issue—such as "Which is more beneficial to a nation, warriors or statesmen?"—or to read a composition or critique a debate, he was not in attendance. He was not elected to any office, never served on a committee, and, as far as the record shows, spoke nary a word at regular meetings. His extreme bashfulness about speaking before a group made him uncomfortable in classes and fraternity sessions where rhetoric and oratory were stressed.[2]

John Wesley Hunt was disappointed with his grandson's performance as a college student, as were Calvin and Henrietta. Feeling out of place and finding it impossible to live up to the ideal, Morgan relieved inner distress by gathering with other students on the campus lawn to swear at passers-by, organizing boyish pranks in town, and encountering other young gentlemen on the field of honor. Although dueling was illegal in Kentucky, society recognized it as a test of personal valor and manliness, a means to demonstrate status as a gentleman and validate claims to leadership. Morgan had achieved recognition in no academic subject, but when he challenged Adelphi brother William L. Blanchard to a duel, he became the momentary hero of the Adelphi Society and the center of attention at the university.

The grievance is unknown; possibly Blanchard made an insulting remark about Morgan. In any event, like the chorus in an ancient Greek drama, John's Adelphi brothers arranged the duel, assisted in its execution (neither youth was seriously hurt), and celebrated the uproar it stirred in the community. On Friday night, June 21, 1844, they devoted their formal meeting to a mock trial of the two participants for "engaging in a single mortal combat." During the cross-examination Morgan stood and answered a question in his own defense—the only recorded statement he ever made in the fraternity. The society cleared both members by large majorities.[3]

The duel became such a *cause célèbre*, however, that the Board of Trustees feared it would lead to an outbreak of dueling in the student body. On July 4, therefore, they summoned Morgan and Blanchard to appear before them and explain their conduct. In special session at the law office of Madison C. Johnson, chairman of the board and prominent attorney, the trustees heard

the evidence and agreed that both students had violated the university regulation against dueling; the appropriate punishment was expulsion. Exercising
leniency, however they suspended Morgan for the remainder of the term and
only censured Blanchard. John left the university and never returned—the
duel, mock trial, and hearing before the board constituted for him an initia-
tion rite into the world of adult men, his personal "graduation" from the
university; it rescued him from a frustrating life as a college student and
established his honor. He had won the admiration of many of his peers by
being suspended for an act of personal courage and valor. He may not have
been conscious of it, but he had also made an important choice. He had
rejected Grandfather Hunt's reserve and wisdom—Hunt never fought a
duel—and embraced the Morgan tradition of frontier brashness and Southern honor. The details remain obscure, but he later participated—and was
severely wounded—in at least one other duel.[4]

With his reputation as a gentleman of valor established, Morgan's next
challenge was entrance into the world of adult responsibility. Business was
the most likely career, well accepted in the family traditions of both the
Hunts and Morgans, but John's parents had no capital for investment and no
means to offer a partnership. Grandfather Hunt was still very healthy (he
would live for five more years), and he never lent his grandchildren money
or entered into business with them. In Southern society the only activity
equal in status to plantation ownership was military service, and it seemed
the ideal alternative. A military career would fulfill the Morgan family tradition and provide the opportunity to defend personal, family, state, and
national honor.[5]

Therefore in September, 1845, when he was twenty, Morgan applied for
a commission as lieutenant in the United States Marine Corps. Richard M.
Johnson, veteran of the War of 1812 and Vice-President under Martin Van
Buren, recommended John as "a young man of high reputation for honor,
integrity & chivalry." He informed President James K. Polk that Morgan had
respectable connections and was worthy of Polk's confidence and patronage.[6]
There were few commissions to be awarded, however, and Morgan experienced two very frustrating years of enforced idleness. It was a dependency
lasting too long, a painful extension of the adolescent search for identity and
honor. In his mind he echoed young Alexander Hamilton, who protested his
poverty and obscurity on St. Croix Island by exclaiming: "I wish there was
a war." Hamilton's desire was realized in the American Revolution; Morgan's
was temporarily fulfilled when the United States went to war against
Mexico.

Morgan and hundreds of young men in the Ohio and Mississippi valleys
eagerly joined the war effort. President Polk's requisitions for volunteers
were quickly filled. In Cincinnati, three regiments were signed up within
three weeks; in Indianapolis, Lew Wallace, a young lawyer, displayed a flag
and a four-sided transparency with the inscription: "For Mexico; fall in," and

his company was complete in three days. In Tennessee, nearly 30,000 men responded to a call for 3,000. In Kentucky, four days after Gov. William Owsley called for 2,400 men—two regiments of infantry and one of cavalry—the quota was complete. Participating in the belligerent fervor, Lexington sponsored a rally attended by 5,000 people. Flags waved, the militia band played "Hail Columbia!" and "Yankee Doodle," and emancipationist Cassius M. Clay upstaged the other speakers by declaring that in spite of his outspoken opposition to the war, "My country calls for help, and, 'right or wrong' I rally to her standard. . . . Now I fall into the ranks as a private, with my blanket and canteen." The crowd roared its approval, and the volunteers elected Clay captain of one of the two cavalry companies organized in Lexington.[7]

John and Cal Morgan enlisted in Company K, commanded by Capt. Oliver Hazard Perry Beard. It was a grand and glorious experience to volunteer in the Mexican War; the city was caught up in the enthusiasm of war fever. "Fayette Volunteers! Remember the history of the past, and be worthy of your immortal ancestry," the newspaper exclaimed. And finally there was the official call to duty: "Fayette Mounted Men, Attention. You are hereby commanded to parade on my grounds on Thursday next at 1½ o'clock, punctually, to take up the line of march to Louisville, in pursuance of the orders of the Executive Department. C.M. Clay, Capt. O.I.C."[8]

With the organization of complete volunteer units occurring in their midst, people had a sense of direct participation in the war. Emotional intensity climaxed on June 4, 1846, the day the cavalry left town. Early in the morning the Clay and Beard companies fell in and marched south to escort a third company from Madison County into Lexington. Relatives, friends, and farm families streamed into the city from all directions to view the scheduled procession. Before reporting to the parade grounds, John, Cal, and the others in Beard's company attended a ceremony at Transylvania University sponsored by the Lexington Female Bible Society. A steady downpour of rain forced the program into the chapel of Morrison College, where each man received a copy of the scriptures. On behalf of the multitude of relatives getting drenched on the lawn outside, Rev. John H. Brown canceled the sermon, offering an eloquent prayer instead.[9]

The rain settled the dust in the streets, and at 3:00 P.M. the sidewalks on Main Street were crowded, the intersections filled with spectators. Bluegrass farmers welcomed the opportunity to escape the solitude of the farm, reconfirm their sense of community, and identify with the historic war movement. The soldiers paraded by on their fine horses; people waved, cheered, and called to their friends and relatives in the ranks.

In recent years their Uncle Alexander had become John and Cal's hunting companion and close friend. After the business failure in Huntsville he had worked as a sutler and postmaster in Leavenworth, Kansas, then settled down on a farm in Fayette County. When Alexander heard the band, saw the flags, and observed the long line of cavalrymen, the primal clannishness of the Morgan family rose in him; mounting his horse, Alexander fell in beside John and Cal. He was offered a commission as aide but turned it down to serve as a private alongside the two boys.[10]

On June 9, 1846, when Company K was mustered in at Louisville, John was elected second lieutenant and immediately promoted to first lieutenant, second in command of seventy-eight men. Cal and Uncle Alexander continued as privates. The company was one of ten in Col. Humphrey Marshall's 1st Regiment of Kentucky Mounted Volunteers, a force of 828 officers and men enlisted for twelve months.[11]

In Louisville on June 30 the regiment paraded through the streets from Camp Owsley at the Oakland Race Course. "The display was a grand and imposing one," said a reporter. "Such a display of horse was never before seen in our city." But underneath the fine appearance, there was a lack of military training and discipline. One officer was fired upon and almost killed by his own men when he attempted to discipline them. Cassius Clay, learning that a few members of his company were at a house of ill-fame, surrounded the establishment with a detachment of guards and retrieved his men, but not before they did considerable damage to the premises. When the soldiers finally departed, Louisville residents sighed: "Our city is now relieved of the presence of volunteers."[12]

Discipline continued to be a problem as they approached the battlefront. Fatigued with drill and camp life and played out with gambling, fishing, and hunting, volunteers found diversion in firing their weapons and fighting each other. Two regiments almost came to blows over possession of a catfish caught in the Rio Grande River. Regular army officers in the high command were frustrated in their attempts to convince volunteers to obey orders. Many volunteer companies violated general orders by bedding down in hostile territory without picket guards. Cassius Clay and his company, while on a scouting expedition, awoke one morning as prisoners of war. Men got tired of the monotonous ration of beans, coffee, pickled pork, crackers, and flour and organized foraging parties to confiscate the chickens and goats of the villagers. Gen. Zachary Taylor, commander in northern Mexico, issued and reissued orders against plundering private property. Exasperated, he complained: "With every exertion it is impossible to control these [volunteer] troops, unaccustomed as they are to the discipline of camps, and losing in bodies the restraining sense of individual responsibility."[13]

From Louisville the Kentucky regiment was directed to travel to Memphis by steamboat and from there overland to San Antonio, where Marshall was to report to Gen. John E. Wool. On July 10, the men disembarked on the west bank of the Mississippi River opposite Memphis, and in the sweltering July weather soon confronted one of the staggering problems of conducting offensive war against Mexico. In *The Mexican War* Otis A. Singletary wrote that "seldom in history have two nations gone to war with such cavalier disregard for realities." Illness struck in the forms of heat exhaustion and dysentery. In the entire army the record of medical care was poor—hospital equipment was almost unknown, and soldiers or walking patients were detailed as nurses—but at least the regular soldiers were seasoned and their officers trained in sanitary procedures. For the volunteers Congress provided one surgeon and one assistant surgeon for each regiment, but the medical officers usually lacked experience in military medicine.[14] In the entire war 1,549 Americans were killed in battle or expired from battle wounds; 361 lost their lives in accidents; and 10,986 died from illness.

Marching horseback across Arkansas and Texas, Marshall's regiment lost twenty-six men to illness, and many others were discharged for medical reasons. As soldiers fell sick, they were left behind in the care of healthy companions, with orders to reunite with the unit in San Antonio. Twenty-eight were left in Memphis, and thirty in Little Rock, including John and Cal Morgan. Uncle Alexander remained by their side as attendant. From Fulton, Arkansas, Adj. Edward M. Vaughn sent word: "There have been almost as many cases of sickness as there are men in the Regiment . . . attributable as much to the imprudence of the men as to the climate. Fruits are found here in abundance, which they eat, whether ripe or not."[15]

The debilitated soldiers, attempting to catch up with the regiment, had an arduous ride. William A. McClintock from Bourbon County, a private in Company D, also fell behind in Arkansas. On September 7, 1846, in northeastern Texas, he and a group of about six men rode forty miles in the rain and spent the night in a farmer's cabin. "I found the driest puncheons I could, wrapped in my wet blankets and lay on the floor, not to sleep, for the wind blew in the rain, every few minutes through the chinked walls in my face. Add to this an old sow and litter of half drowned pigs, were immediately under me and kept up a grunting and squeaking throughout the night."[16]

McClintock, the Morgans, and the others hastened to San Antonio, but when they arrived they learned that Colonel Marshall's orders had been revised: en route, the Kentucky cavalry had been directed to march to Port Lavaca, Texas, on the Gulf of Mexico, where they were to embark on ships for Gen. Zachary Taylor's headquarters in Camargo, Mexico. The stragglers reported to General Wool in San Antonio, recuperated a few weeks, and departed for Camargo in details. Private McClintock reached San Antonio on September 26 and left four weeks later in a small body of men led by John Hunt Morgan. McClintock struggled to keep going, but on October 26 he recorded: "I awoke last night with a violent attack of billious cholic, no one knew what to do for me, no medicine, no physician nearer than Corpus Christi distant 30 miles. For several hours I endured the tormenting pain. I had some opium with me and I took a pill but without effect. I then took an emetic, still it would not do. I thought that something which would nauseate my stomach might afford relief. I accordingly chewed a quantity of tobacco and swallowed the juice. This or something else had the desired effect, and after five or six hours of intense suffering I obtained relief, but was utterly prostrated."[17]

In addition to sickness, Marshall's men were plagued by lack of supplies and equipment. In Louisville there were not enough tents, and rations were irregular. There were sufficient rifles to equip four companies—including Beard's—but six companies were armed only with swords and pistols. The troops were not paid for months, and in September several were "barefooted, and some of them literally without breeches, many without hats and coats." A volunteer wrote home from Camp Calhoun near Port Lavaca that since he did not have a dime of pay, he and his friends had "traded off all of our superfluous clothing long since for whiskey, potatoes and other *necessaries of life.*" The editor of the Lexington *Observer and Reporter* condemned the government for failing to meet the payroll, inadequately providing supplies, and sending Marshall's regiment on a round-about route.[18]

In spite of the problems, the volunteers were on a great adventure. Private McClintock portrayed the Texas sky as "darkly, deeply & beautifully blue, beyond description or comparison. The stars here shine with a lustrous brilliancy which I have seldom or never seen. No climate in the states can equal the pureness and serenity." At the Rio Grande he reflected: "As I stood and surveyed it, my heart swelled with emotions of pride and Joy that I had overcome distance, danger, and disease, and now stood, ready to invade the very homes of our insidious and obstinate foe."[19]

McClintock and the Morgans arrived in Camargo by November 19, fortunate to have avoided the stifling heat and devastating diseases that had struck there during the summer of 1846. Troops who had survived the dying time delighted in showing new arrivals the "Yawning Graveyard," which had claimed the bodies of about 1,500 volunteers. Camargo was on the San Juan River above its confluence with the Rio Grande. It was near sea level, with no tempering provided by altitude, and the camp was surrounded with walls of rock, blocking the cooling effect of winds. The volunteers had pitched their tents near the river, contaminating the water supply; and dysentery, measles, and malignant fevers swept through the encampment. When coffinmakers used up the wood from gunboxes and crackerbarrels, funeral details had to bury men in blankets, and the men said the mockingbirds had heard the band playing the death march so frequently that they included it in their repertoire.[20]

While the Kentuckians were organizing and converging on northern Mexico, Taylor's army had won the battles of Palo Alto, Resaca de la Palma, and Monterrey. But during the winter of 1846-47, four-fifths of the United States forces were diverted from Taylor to Gen. Winfield Scott for a knockout blow on Mexico City via Vera Cruz. Santa Anna, the Mexican commander, learned that Taylor's men were being transferred and determined to attack his weakened army.[21]

In order to counter Santa Anna, Taylor's troops combined in the area of Saltillo. The Kentucky cavalry hastily marched from Camargo to Montemorelos, southeast of Saltillo, arriving in a drizzling rain on the evening of December 22. On the road they met hundreds of the residents of Montemorelos, in carriages, and walking beside donkeys, fleeing into the country in response to a rumor that Santa Anna was about to attack. The rain was the first in three months, and it settled the dust and put the American army in a festive mood. The next day there was time to ride into the little town of 2,000 people, nestled in the hills on three sides, with lofty mountains to the west. The streets and sidewalks were well paved; orange trees heavy with fruit surrounded the small Spanish cathedral; and except for the empty streets and United States flag in the plaza, it was a typical Mexican village.[22]

The citizens of Montemorelos returned, and Marshall's regiment was transferred north to Monterrey, where rumors of imminent battle continued. On January 26, 1847, General Taylor arrived, and Morgan received orders to prepare his detachment to march at an hour's notice. Two days later the cavalry marched southward toward Saltillo, and just after dark on the second day of the trek, Marshall halted the command and sent Morgan out to investigate something that resembled a squadron of cavalry on the horizon. Morgan scouted and reported that it was nothing but a clump of palm trees. While the Kentuckians rode southward to the Saltillo area, the Mexican army of 19,525 soldiers headed northward from San Luis Potosí. With less than 5,000, Taylor pulled back his southernmost troops eleven miles, from Agua Nueva to the mountain pass at Buena Vista, where he prepared to defend the United States.

Marshall's cavalry was part of the rear guard covering the removal of supplies from Agua Nueva on February 21. In the middle of the night, when the picket guards were driven in by advance parties of the Mexican army, the last supply wagons left, and the Americans burned the town to destroy provisions that could not be transported. The experience made a lasting impression on Capt. James H. Carleton: "The noise of the falling timbers, the roar of flames, the huge column of ascending smoke, the appearance of armed and mounted men moving between the spectator and the fire, with the brilliant light flashing here and there on burnished arms and glittering appointments—taken in connection with the scattered shots interchanged [with the enemy], the heavy rumbling of our rapidly retreating train of wagons, intermingled with the distant trumpet-signals now and then faintly heard in the direction of the approaching enemy—all conspired to render that cold, deep midnight, one which could never be forgotten."[23]

By the next morning, February 22, the force from Agua Nueva united with the main army at Buena Vista. The American right was secure behind a network of deep, impassable gullies, and artillery placed between the bluffs and gullies covered the road. The two armies would clash on the American left where a plateau rose gently southeastward for about a mile from the road to the base of the mountains. It was a strong defensive position, and the Mexican army was debilitated by the march across the desert, but its 16,000 soldiers still outnumbered the American force of 4,759 by over three to one. Only about 500 of Taylor's men were regular army and only 700 had come under enemy fire. The American volunteers had overcome disease, distance, and insufficient training; now they would be tested in battle.[24]

Positioned in the pass on the morning of February 22, the Americans had the unusual experience of watching the appearance of the enemy army. The Kentucky cavalry, reduced by death and disability to about 235 men, was stationed on the extreme left, at the edge of the steep bluffs on the base of the mountains. Astride his horse, John Hunt Morgan saw colorful brigade after colorful brigade march up and wheel left and right, spreading across the drab, grayish-brown valley. Infantry, artillery, and cavalry regiments dressed in resplendent uniforms—red, blue, green, and yellow—pivoted with precision and formed in lines along the sierra between the mountains. Soft breezes fluttered through the bright plumes on the high caps and ruffled the brilliant silken banners of the separate companies, and someone pointed out that the color of horses in each cavalry corps was uniform. Suddenly, out of the barren desert had come a large, impressive army.[25]

At about 11:00 A.M. Taylor politely refused Santa Anna's demand that he surrender. At 3:00 P.M. the Mexican artillery opened fire, and an hour later a Mexican detachment of light infantry attempted to flank the American left by climbing the bluffs adjoining the mountains. Marshall was ordered to dismount his riflemen and place them in a commanding position on the edge of the slopes. The Morgans were among the men who scrambled up the steep hills and exchanged fire with the enemy until nightfall, when they were ordered to return to their horses on the plateau. The Mexicans then gained the upper hand by climbing to the summit of the mountain. The advantage was slight, however, given the rough terrain. In his official report, Marshall commended the dismounted cavalry for acting with "promptness and bravery" and fighting with "coolness and skill" in the skirmish.[26]

The next morning, February 23, 1847, after celebration of the Mass and a concert of sacred music, Santa Anna began an offensive against the American left on the plateau. The 2nd Indiana Infantry bore the brunt of the attack for about half an hour. Then, thanks to an incompetent colonel's mistaken command, the Indianans began falling back. The retreat turned into a rout and the 2nd Illinois, next on the right, also fell back. Meanwhile, Marshall's riflemen, reinforced by a body of dismounted Arkansas cavalry, remained on the slopes on the far left. The enemy fire was "hot and incessant," yet the men "stood as firm as the rocks of the mountain." But when the Indiana and Illinois infantry retreated, the troops on the bluffs were isolated from the remainder of the American army. To Marshall it seemed that the progress of the enemy was "unresisted, if not resistless." To avoid being surrounded and captured, he retreated.[27]

As the Americans turned back, the Mexicans advanced. During the action, Uncle Alexander Morgan and five other men in Company K were killed. Captain Beard later described how it happened: "The enemy came rushing down the hill like so many devils, cursing us and crying *no quarter!*" The men of Company K ran for their horses and were crossing a deep ravine on horseback when enemy lancers caught up with them. Alexander and several others turned and "fought with desperation" until "run through with the enemy's lances." The Morgan boys' father told his other brother, Samuel D. Morgan, that Alexander was "lanced to death in ascending a mountain fighting to the last and having his bowels out, faced and fought until litterly [*sic*] cut to pieces."[28]

The Kentucky and Arkansas cavalry retreated to the hacienda three miles north of the pass, where they regrouped. On horseback, about 400 courageously met more than 1,000 Mexican lancers who were attempting to seize the ranch and flank the American army. The opposing horsemen clashed head on and fought hand to hand. When the melee drifted near the hacienda, Americans hidden behind the walls of the courtyards delivered a devastating fire. At that point, the Mexicans panicked and fled, and Marshall's troops saw no more significant fighting during the battle. Meanwhile, at the front the line held until darkness ended the fighting.[29]

The American army had stale crackers and water for supper, and slept in battle lines on their weapons and without fires. In the chill of the next morning, as the brilliant stars faded and daylight approached the valley, a single shout suddenly rang out: "Victory! Victory! Victory!" Almost as one, the entire army jumped to its feet and looked across the network of deep gullies and ravines, littered with the bodies of fallen horses and broken equipment, to the camp of the Mexican army on the plateau. There were no horses, no soldiers, no colorful banners or plumes—nothing but the brown sand and the gray mountains extending southward toward San Luis Potosí. The enemy had retreated during the night. Lt. John Hunt Morgan joined in the cheering: "The enemy is fled. The field is ours. Victory! Victory! Victory!"[30]

The Kentucky volunteers had given an excellent account of themselves. The 2nd Kentucky Infantry had lost its commander, Col. William R. McKee, and their second in command, Henry Clay, Jr., in bitter fighting. Marshall's cavalry had 34 wounded and 27 dead, including Adjutant Vaughn and Private McClintock. In his official report, Taylor praised the regiment: "The Kentucky Cavalry, under Colonel Marshall, rendered good service dismounted, acting as light troops on our left, and afterwards, with a portion of the Arkansas Regiment, in meeting and dispersing the column of cavalry at Buena Vista."[31]

Marshall's regiment served the remainder of the twelve-month enlistment without combat; on June 7, 1847, Company K, which had left Lexington with seventy-eight men, was mustered out in New Orleans with forty-five.

On Saturday, June 19, along with the other cavalry company from Lexington, the veterans arrived home on the morning train. A large crowd met them at the depot, and in the afternoon Judge George R. Trotter spoke at a welcoming ceremony on the courthouse square.[32]

Gradually Lexingtonians came to appreciate the significance of Buena Vista. When the first rumors that Taylor had been defeated were corrected by the official reports, the American people realized that against overwhelming opposition a great victory had occurred. Every man at Buena Vista was crowned with laurel, and General Taylor was thrust into the limelight as the successful candidate for President of the United States in the next election.

In celebration of Buena Vista, the county fathers invited everyone from Fayette and surrounding counties to an enormous Kentucky barbecue. "At an early hour in the morning every avenue leading to the city was crowded with persons in carriages, on horseback and on foot, and by the hour fixed for the procession, the streets of the city were crowded with the dense mass of both sexes who had come . . . to 'do honor to the brave,'" the newspaper related. At 10:00 A.M. the militia band started the parade; fire companies passed in review; and the long line of brave, suntanned volunteers with "firm and measured tread" accepted the gratitude and admiration of the crowd.[33]

The mass of some 10,000 spectators gathered round to hear prominent Lexington attorney George B. Kinkead give the welcoming address. "Gentlemen Volunteers," he began, "I have been deputed as the Organ to give you a public welcome to your homes after the dangers and hardships of a twelve months' military campaign. In the name of this vast assembly, whose presence this day gives assurance of their esteem and gratitude, I bid you welcome to your country and kindred and friends." Of Buena Vista, he said: "On the morning of the battle-day—henceforth to be so renowned in the annals of the Republic—there was but this one feeling pervading your breasts, as you cast your eye on the flag above you, and thought of your country and homes, never perhaps again to be seen by you. Thus it was too, throughout the length and breadth of our far-spread Republic, when the news of that victory flew over it as on the wings of the wind. Millions of hearts beat quicker at the story of the battle and victory, and . . . there was not a bosom that did not swell high with patriotism and pride, for the valor of his countrymen."[34]

After the speech, barbecue was served at tables arranged in a square, 100 yards on each side. The ladies ate first, then the tables were cleared and the first group of gentlemen ate, and the second, until the entire crowd was served: "It was the remark of all that they have never seen a barbecue more handsomely arranged and better provided." When lunch was over, attention turned again to the speaker's stand, where John and Cal Morgan's father was honored as a member of the festival committee, composed of men who had lost close relatives at Buena Vista. Fifteen planned toasts were given, including one to Zachary Taylor, whose "victories . . . attest his military genius;

his retiring modesty and kindly sympathy prove the soundness of his heart—while that of his head has never been questioned; he is none the less dear to Kentucky, because he is a Kentuckian." One of sixteen informal toasts was to "The Heroes of Buena Vista: By their firmness and valor, they have given themselves to history as the Spartans of the Republic." The ceremony ended at four o'clock but Rev. William Pratt, pastor of the First Baptist Church of Lexington, was so pleased with the "sumptuous dinner," "excellent order," and gala atmosphere that he stayed out until 10:00 P.M.[35]

A few weeks later the national government requisitioned Kentucky for two additional regiments of infantry, but few enlisted from the Bluegrass region, and very few from the 1846 group reenlisted in September, 1847. But Morgan, who desperately wanted to get back in the army, formed a volunteer cavalry company and petitioned Washington to muster it into service and annex it to Col. Manlius V. Thompson's 3rd Kentucky Infantry regiment. The second requisition for Kentucky had no quota for cavalry, but Morgan hoped that special authorization would be given. In case the War Department refused to accept his cavalry company, he also applied for a commission in the regular army.[36]

While he waited impatiently for word from Washington, October 5 came, and Thompson's regiment rendezvoused at Louisville. On October 25, Morgan wrote to his connection in the Treasury Department that his company had broken up, and it was doubtful that he could fill another one. However, he still hoped for a commission in the regular army: "I am, at present, engaged in no business; waiting to hear from the seat of Government," he pleaded. "Could you not obtain for me an immediate answer from the president? . . . Are not the letters of recommendation which I've sent sufficient? If they are not I'll send more."[37]

Thompson's and the other infantry regiment of the second requisition left Louisville on the first day of November and reached Mexico after hostilities had ended. Morgan continued to petition for a commission: "I'll raise a Company to serve either as an independent Company or to be attached to some Regiment. I should like very much to get to raise a *Cavalry co.* But General I'll willingly take any situation they would give me. Please write and let me know my fate." A month later, the treaty was signed ending the war.[38]

Morgan had gained self-confidence by overcoming distance, illness, the hardships of camp life, and the danger of battle. He had gone to war with the united blessing of the community and had been welcomed home as a patriotic conqueror. He had acquired one year of military experience, even though discipline was so lax and contempt for authority so prevalent that the instruction was not entirely beneficial. He brought home a captured Mexican sword and decorative carpet, which he gave to Uncle Samuel Morgan in Nashville.[39] The war had enabled him to temporarily establish himself as a Morgan of honor; he was terribly frustrated when it proved impossible to make military service a lasting commitment.

FOUR

Honor Gained

When it finally dawned on John Hunt Morgan that an immediate military career was out of reach, he settled down in Lexington, entering business with his young friend Sanders Bruce. The Bruces, an established manufacturing family, wealthy, successful, and respected, lived in the beautiful Thomas Hart residence on the corner just across Second Street from Hopemont and only a few yards from Henry Clay's law office. Before he died in 1836, John Bruce, Sanders's father, had proudly showed visitors through his hemp factory on Mulberry Street. He was born in Northumberland, learned ropemaking in London, and was equipping ships in Gibraltar when he helped rig the fleet of Admiral Horatio Nelson before the Battle of Trafalgar. In Gibraltar, too, he met and married Margaret Ross Hutton the daughter of a Scottish soldier stationed at the fortress. About 1810 he and Margaret emigrated to America and came to Lexington, where, in partnership with Benjamin Gratz, he earned a fortune that passed to Margaret and their five sons and two daughters when he died. The Bruce children were equally successful: William W. Bruce manufactured hemp; Benjamin Gratz Bruce promoted livestock breeding; Dr. James Morrison Bruce practiced medicine on Mill Street, treating poor people at no charge; and Sanders Bruce, Morgan's partner, retailed china and glassware.[1]

The partnership brought Morgan into contact with Sanders's eighteen-year-old sister Rebecca. Rebecca was intelligent, tender and lovable, with a soft round face and friendly eyes twinkling with gaiety and laughter. John had begun to experience moods of despondency, which Becky's cheerfulness relieved. The firm of Morgan & Bruce purchased a few slaves whom they rented out to haul hemp, corn, lumber, and other items in the local market. They also bred and trained racehorses, eventually achieving some prominence when their horse Dick Doty defeated Flying Flea in an important race in Louisville in 1853. John's calls at the Bruce house became more frequent, and on November 21, 1848—in Christ Church Episcopal, where his parents had married—he and Rebecca said their vows. He was twenty-three and she was still eighteen. John Bruce was dead, and Margaret was pleased to have the couple move into the family mansion with her. Thus, like his father, Morgan depended upon his wife's relatives for housing. His Grandfather Hunt was still alive, and perhaps John saw him early in the mornings, emerging from his business office in the corner of the main floor of Hopemont on his way to inspect his farms.[2]

John and Becky had been married five years in 1853 when she gave birth to a stillborn son. Subsequently, pain and soreness persisted in one of her legs, and physicians recommended exercise and travel. Visiting John's sister Kitty and her husband Calvin M. McClung in St. Louis in 1856, she seemed to improve. "She exercises freely," McClung reported, "and has a fine appetite. So good in fact, that she says, she would be ashamed to eat as much as she wanted, if she were any place else. I have not only strong hopes, but have little doubt her *local* disease is produced by her *general* ill health and debility. If this be so, I think she will return home *well*."[3]

John also took her to Hot Springs, Arkansas, and she remained for extended bathing. After four weeks she said: "I wish I could write you a favorable account of myself, but there is no *perceptible* change in my limb. There is more soreness, which those more experienced than myself pronounced to be a favorable symptom. Nearly all the afflicted ones, have grown worse, before they began to improve." She had enjoyed the time John had spent with her at the springs. "He was with me so much, and was like a different person away from the cares of business. Tell him I would give the state of Arkansas, if it were mine, just to have him with me."[4]

Next, Morgan took her to New Orleans, hoping medical experts there could prescribe a cure. From their hotel room she wrote: "My maid suits me very well. She is aimable [sic] and willing. She and Eliza [probably a personal servant or nurse] have been out sightseeing this evening. They are kept very close, for there are so many thieves about, that we are afraid to leave our rooms, without they are in them. Locks to the doors are no protection." Her bonnet being out of fashion, she purchased a new one: "I *only gave $16.00* for it. It ought not to have been more than $10.00." Apparently Becky had septic thrombophlebitis, the infection of a blood clot in a leg vein, which would cause the arteries supplying blood to that leg to shut down, giving it a pale color. In those days the illness was called white leg or milk leg because of the theory that the new mother's milk had shifted from the breast to the leg. There was no cure for the condition, and in some cases the infection was fatal.[5]

The Morgans and Hunts were sympathetic. John's Aunt Mary Hunt Hanna once said: "I am too glad to hear of Becky's improvement. It is a great thing to be more comfortable, to one who has so long suffered. She is truly lovely." Becky also suffered the pain of not fulfilling her role as wife and mother. Children were symbols of status, and family continuity was such a high priority that one of a wife's most important contributions was having babies. Becky knew John was disappointed, and she realized that society regarded her with pity; her barrenness made her feel incomplete and unfulfilled. She drew near her mother for emotional support and turned to religion for comfort. On Whitsunday, May 23, 1858, after nearly five years as an invalid, she was baptized in Christ Church and was confirmed the next Sunday evening.[6]

John's business career had taken flight after Hunt died and capital became available from his mother. With funds borrowed from Henrietta he bought sixteen slaves to hire out in hemp factories, and in 1853, one year before their father died, he and his brother Cal became partners in hemp manufacturing. Business was good for three years; then surplus stock accumulated, prices fell, and by 1860 most of the small hemp factories in Kentucky had closed. In May, 1857, John said that he regretted having to go into bagging for another year. "It is a poor business & with a very *bad prospect*," he lamented. John and Cal succeeded when others failed partly because they were attentive to business, but the key was their Uncle Thomas H. Hunt, hemp manufacturer and commission merchant in Louisville. As their agent, adviser, and protector, Uncle Tom continually counseled on market conditions, financial problems, and potential investments, as well as selling Morgan hemp and forwarding shipments to Mobile and New Orleans.[7]

Like other Lexington manufacturers the Morgans used slave labor at their factory on West Main Street near the cemetery. They owned thirty slaves and hired additional slaves and free blacks. In April, 1859, John wrote: "I dismissed three of our Free Negroes today. They were constantly drunk & bringing whiskey in bottles to the factory. Their example was only injurious to our own boys." Three days later: "Everything is getting along first rate. The boys are well & doing their work."[8]

In 1859 the Morgan brothers expanded into the wool trade. In the 1840s and 1850s, sheep herding had developed on an extensive scale in the United States, and woolen factories were springing up in many parts of the nation. John and Cal formed a partnership with Frank W. Jones under the name of Calvin C. Morgan & Co. Jones purchased large quantities of wool in the Las Vegas–Sante Fe area of New Mexico Territory and transported it by mule train and steamboat to Uncle Tom in Louisville. The Morgans soon lost confidence in Jones, however, and replaced him with their brother Richard. In 1860 they sold 310,243 pounds of wool in St. Louis, Louisville, Cincinnati, and New York. The Morgans had entered wool and woolens at the right time: when the secession crisis occurred, demand for wool for military uniforms caused rapid expansion, and Uncle Tom pleaded for more raw wool. As their enterprises expanded, each brother's name was attached to at least one company. The hemp business was J.H. & C.C. Morgan & Co.; the commission firm for purchasing raw wool was Calvin C. Morgan & Co.; and when the brothers entered woolen manufacturing themselves, the factory was under the name of the third and newest partner, Richard C. Morgan & Co. John had achieved honor in the community, and he was sensitive to the need of his brothers, too, to establish a reputation. All his life Morgan identified with young men struggling to establish an identity.[9]

In addition to owning factory slaves, the brothers traded in slaves for profit. The Kentucky Non-Importation Act of 1833 prohibited bringing slaves into the state for sale, but slaves already in Kentucky were being sold down the Mississippi River to work on the large cotton and sugar plantations opening up in Louisiana. Lexington was a major market for that trade. Dealers bought large numbers of young men and women and marched them away in long coffles, manacled two abreast and connected with heavy chains that rattled their hopeless tune and echoed in the consciences of sensitive individuals—such as Mary Todd, who eventually married Abraham Lincoln.[10]

Once a month, on court day, slave traders gathered around the auction block in Cheapside, the public area beside the courthouse named for London's famous market square. The streets were lined with buggies and wagons, and saddle horses and mules were tied to the wooden hitching posts around the courthouse yard. The auctioneer sought highest bids for household items, farm implements, cows, horses, mules, and slaves. Country cousins visited with city kin; hucksters and peddlers worked the crowd; and evil and good battled in timeless drama. Here George DuPuy, slave minister of the black Baptist Church, came up for sale as a result of the death of his master; William M. Pratt, pastor of the white Baptist Church, collected money from his deacons, purchased George on the block, and set him free. Here Eliza, a beautiful young woman of tender upbringing, was presented for sale; a French stranger from New Orleans wanted her but was outbid by Calvin Fairbank, a representative of the underground railroad. As Fairbank counted out the $1,485 he had bid, someone in the crowd asked what he planned to do with her. "Free her!" he exclaimed.[11]

The Morgans traded in slaves with Lewis Robards, the most notorious dealer in Lexington. Robards bought slaves from planters and at auctions, collecting them in the slave pen behind his house on North Broadway. Most were locked in tiny brick cells eight feet square, furnished with straw and ventilated with a small iron-grated window high on the heavy wooden door. But Robards's specialty, his choice stock, was young mulatto girls suitable for sale as mistresses or "fancy girls" in New Orleans. They were kept in well-furnished apartments on the second floor of his office on West Short Street. Robards would serve buyers at the bar and take them upstairs, encouraging them to conduct intimate examinations of the women's bodies. The Morgans had Robards's agent, Rodes Woods, represent them in out-of-town ventures, and they once loaned Robards $6,100. When Robards defaulted, John filed an attachment against the slave jail and against one of Robards's slaves, Rebecca, who was eventually sold at sheriff's auction to partly satisfy the debt.[12]

Ownership of slaves offered a distinction far beyond the monetary value of the investment. The slave master was counselor, judge, and jury for his slaves; in providing for their basic needs, he enhanced both his own self-esteem and his status in the community. Nevertheless, in exercising virtually unlimited power over other human beings, the master was himself corrupted, brutalized, and loaded with a heavy burden of guilt.[13]

In 1857 the Morgan brothers began hiring out slaves as laborers on steamboats. The hiring-out system gave the institution of slavery the flexibility required by industrialization and urbanization. By 1850 about one-fifth of industrial slaves were rented, and demand continued strong throughout the next decade. In the 1850s an estimated 10,000 slaves worked as deckhands and cabin servants on Ohio and Mississippi River steamers. Along with other urban slaves, steamboat crews had certain freedoms and amenities not afforded rural slaves, but working conditions were often undesirable. Rolling heavy barrels of flour and whiskey along narrow gangplanks, carrying wood down slippery banks, wrestling the boat off sandbars, and heaving fuel into the blazing furnace, these slaves lived in extreme danger. Defective boiler construction, inadequate safety features, and the carelessness of captains and crew killed and seriously injured hundreds of rented slaves each year.[14]

In the late 1850s the Morgans had two slave crews working the western rivers. Between voyages their overseer employed them scouring decks in Paducah and St. Louis, and rolling cotton on the levee in New Orleans. In January, 1857, twenty-three Morgan slaves were on the steamer *Northerner* when it was frozen in the ice on the Ohio River above Owensboro, Kentucky. The men were taken off the boat and walked south to the boatyard in Memphis. Passing through Crittenden County, they were mistaken for a band of runaways by a Mrs. Lucas, who filed a claim against the Morgans for the supper the crew ate after she abandoned her house in fright. In February, 1857, the *Belfast* had an accident on the Mississippi River below Memphis, and several Morgan slaves became ill from exposure. When the owners of the boat offered, as a favor, to pay for the work days lost from sickness, John directed Cal: "You had better reply to this. They seem to think that we ask the payment as a *favor*. They are *wrong* for we demand it as a *right*."[15]

Morgan instructed his agent in Memphis to look out for the health of the steamboat slaves, and an inspection on the *New Uncle Sam* revealed that "all of them were out of health—all had colds and looked badly. Upon inquiry, I learned from them that they slept in the hold of the vessel, which is always damp and that their bed clothes are always damp. Were they my Negroes I should remove them at once, as I am sure their health is in danger from such a life." John Morgan did have the crew removed, but slave hiring was at best a cold business. The agent reported that Peter Bruce had rheumatism and was no longer able to perform the work: "My advice is to put him on the block and sell him for whatever he will bring without a any [sic] guaranty as to health."[16]

The ownership of slaves and horses strengthened Morgan's reputation and self-esteem, as did success in business and marriage to Becky. He was elected a Mason and Captain of the Union Volunteer Fire Company, and served briefly on the city council and school board.

But there was still the yen for military service. In February, 1852, when he was twenty-six years old, married, and in business with Sanders Bruce, Morgan organized an artillery company attached to the 42nd Regiment of the Kentucky militia and equipped by the state quartermaster general with a new six-pound bronze cannon. John was now "Captain Morgan," a title that not only conferred status (as had Calvin's rank of Colonel) but also identified him with the military tradition of the Morgan family (there was a grain of truth in the hyperbole which made the rounds in Lexington in the twentieth century that every Morgan was at least a major). The attainment of militia rank was an important opportunity for ambitious young men to distinguish themselves. Yet in 1854 the Kentucky legislature decided that with the passing of the frontier, the militia was no longer needed; they canceled regular muster and scheduled drills only once every six years. This killed the militia; all units became inactive, including Morgan's artillery company. He retained the title, but his aspiration for involvement in military affairs was once again frustrated.[17]

Destruction of the Kentucky militia violated the Southern military tradition and ran counter to the spirit of martial ardor stirring in Southern society. For whatever reasons—frontier conditions, slavery, race repression, taste for romantic literature, defense of honor, and finally the secession crisis—Southerners expressed their infatuation with marching soldiers by organizing hundreds of volunteer militia companies. In Kentucky, in 1857 Gov. Charles S. Morehead encouraged the movement by offering weapons from the state arsenal.

As part of this movement, Morgan raised an infantry company of sixty men and commissioned Thomas Lewinski, prominent neo-Gothic architect and Polish soldier of fortune, as drill instructor. The Lexington Rifles were Lexington's only military company, and when they began drilling in Cheapside on court days and marching in holiday parades, their "true military bearing and graceful evolutions" attracted universal admiration. Dressed in stylish green uniforms with gold stripes down the sides and fashionable shako hats—green with a black brim, gold band around the base, gold rope in back, and topped with a bright green plume—they were the pride of the people.[18]

Proprietors of mineral springs invited the Rifles to entertain their guests. In 1858, for instance, they performed at Crab Orchard Springs in Lincoln County. After the parade the men mingled with the crowd of 500 and enjoyed the pleasures offered by that popular resort. The Rifles inspired respect. Local newspapers praised them for their potential value in emergencies and times of disorder, and they enabled Lexington to participate in the romantic cult of militarism. Their caps bore the seal of the state of Kentucky, and the state armed them with new long-range rifles, bayonets attached. John grew a full beard, and in white trousers, green jacket with gold epaulets, and officer's sword, he was a dashing figure—Captain Morgan, a man of honor. His men admired and loved him. At the armory on the northeast corner of Main and Upper Streets they hung a large banner which read: "Our laws the commands of our Captain."[19]

Morgan and the Lexington Rifles entered fully into the romantic and hedonistic social life of antebellum Lexington. The Southern system of honor failed to develop self-discipline in the individual. Beset by the specters of shame and guilt, freed from manual labor by slavery, with time on their hands, upper-class Southern gentlemen escaped into the world of pleasure and like children accepted what pleased them, rejected what did not. They spent money freely, and attempted always to race faster, bet higher, and drink more. Not everyone participated, of course; there was a strong religious, conservative spirit as well, and some men filled their leisure with political action, community service, and church work as Calvin Morgan had escaped into the world of romantic literature. Evangelical Christians condemned gambling and worldly pleasure, but the old system of "virtuous" manhood that permitted swearing, gambling, drinking, and wenching still held sway in aristocratic society.[20]

For John Morgan, pleasure offered relief from moods of depression, when the dark gray fog of negative thoughts crowded in, colors seemed to fade, food lost its taste. In the gloom of such despondency, past enjoyments could not be remembered, and future good times could not be imagined. Rather than submit to such spells of melancholia, Morgan escaped into the world of play, where reality was suspended and sadness dispelled through camaraderie and merrymaking. Later, Basil Duke wrote: "Like the great majority of the men of his class—the gentlemen of the South—he lived freely, and the amusements he permitted himself would, doubtless, have shocked a New Englander almost as much as the money he spent in obtaining them. . . . General Morgan, with the virtues, had some of the faults of his Southern blood and country."[21]

One of the pleasures that Lexington society encouraged was gambling. Betting on horse races was a Bluegrass institution; taverns provided rooms for billiards and card games; and professional gamblers dealt games in which gentlemen ran up as much as a $3,000 debt in one evening. Gaming was so prevalent and so much a part of life that a man could be a compulsive gambler and never attract attention. Widespread betting on elections prompted reformers to caution that gamblers were undermining democracy by bribing voters in order to insure their stakes. In 1854 the General Assembly passed "an Act to prevent the pernicious practice of betting on elections," establishing as the penalty a $100 fine and forfeiture of winnings. When prosecutors neglected to enforce the law, Governor Morehead warned that political wagering was "a great and growing evil." In 1859 Gov. Beriah Magoffin said,

"The bribery and betting and mobs at our elections are alarmingly on the increase."[22]

The orgy of political betting reached a climax in the presidential election of 1860, and John and Cal Morgan entered into it with enthusiasm. Neither Republican Abraham Lincoln nor Northern Democrat Stephen A. Douglas had significant support in Kentucky. The question was whether Kentuckians would vote for native John C. Breckinridge, nominee of the Southern Democrats, or for John Bell, the Tennessean running for the Constitutional Union Party on the platform of preservation of the Union. In August, 1860, during the campaign, an election for clerk of the state court of appeals was a bellwether. Supporters of Bell, Douglas, and Breckinridge each had a candidate. In the taverns many agreed that Unionist candidate Leslie Combs would win; debate centered on the margin of victory. Morgan made the same mistake he would make during the Civil War—he underestimated pro-Union sentiment in Kentucky. He bet $500 that Combs would not carry the election by 5,000 votes. "It is *I think* a certain thing," he said. Kentucky Democrats would never vote Unionist: "The masses of the Democratic party will not be carried over to a party that have been their uttermost enemies." Combs won by nearly 25,000 votes, but Morgan had hedged his bets so completely that he won ten dollars. The game was too satisfying to risk losing altogether and being thrown out of action.[23]

A friend suggested that Morgan run for office himself. "I know of no person opposed to me in politics," he replied, but "I would prefer running my money." In the presidential election itself, Cal wagered $5,000 that Bell would not carry the state by over 10,000 votes. Bell won by about 13,000 votes, and Cal lost but had apparently hedged with other wagers. With his friend Blanton Duncan in Louisville, John ventured $500 that Lincoln would be the next president, $500 that Breckinridge would win more electoral votes than Bell, $500 to $100 that Bell would not be the next president, and the "handsomest double buggie [*sic*] in Louisville to cost not over $300 that Breckinridge gets nine states in the South." John won all of these bets, yet his winnings as well as his losses were diminished by extensive hedging. Duncan, who had neglected to counterbalance his risks, lost $11,900 and went bankrupt. "I positively will have to borrow my market money Every week this winter," he lamented. "There is an old saying about squeezing blood out of a turnip, which just now applies to me. If you would like to buy my dwelling house & give the balance, I can make settlement at once." Morgan gave Duncan time to recover, and they remained close friends.[24]

The Morgan brothers gathered with friends in the taverns and played cards far into the night. They had riotous sojourns in Louisville, where they gambled and drank at the Galt House and visited an expensive bawdy house on Fifth Street. Upperclass Southern society condoned not only gambling but male promiscuity as well. Among themselves the young gentry boasted about their conquests and made sexual experience a point of honor. Women were a favorite topic of conversation, and the Morgans' business correspondence was permeated with sensual references. Maggie Simpkins, one of Cal's friends, made sport of his wide reputation as a ladies' man and teased him about his flirtation on a rail car during a journey to St. Louis. R.T. Morrison of Lexington described his eighteen-year-old girlfriend: she was intelligent, talkative and "unsteady & inconstant as the wind, with a touch of the pirate in her temper, heartless & dashing as a gay 'gambolier,' she's as wicked as the devil's own child, & treads life's desperate dance with the only aim to brush the bloom from Pleasure's life, with quite enough of beauty withal to render all this attractive."[25]

Rodes Woods, the slave gang overseer, wrote the Morgans from New Orleans: "If either of you should come down this winter I can give you a good room and plenty to eat such as it is and you can have the pleasure should it be such of being surrounded by 50 Acres of whores for I am about the centre and some very pretty ones among them." From Memphis, J.C. Hawkins congratulated Cal for falling in love: "I take it for granted she is both pretty & young." J.C. Hensley wrote from Memphis concerning business contacts, taxes, and stock investments—and added: "Plenty of nice women here any size or color. I wish you were here a little while that I might put you to a friend of mine." From Louisville, Blanton Duncan teased John Morgan: "I presume of course that you as well as all of our distinguished merchants are in a state of suspension, as the weather is rather too inclement for you to parade up & down waving your sword & that other favorite instrument, mentioned by Cal, at the head of your fine military company."[26]

Devout Christians were shocked at the open manner in which Morgan enjoyed worldly pleasure; people called him a gambler and libertine. When his young brother Thomas joined the First Baptist Church of Lexington, Pastor Pratt recorded in his diary: "No more members of his family Christian. Quite a proud aristocratic family & I hope his example may be a blessing to them all." Gentlemen never mentioned illicit sexual activity in polite company, and the subject never came up in family conversation. With Becky and his relatives John was a respectable man. Aunt Mary Hunt Hanna said he was "such a good son, devoted husband and kind to the poor." Duke expounded the Southern code of ethics when he pointed out that Morgan never attempted to be secretive or hypocritical about his diversions, and he never did anything "which touched his integrity as a man and his honor as a gentleman."[27]

Morgan admitted his own imperfections and tolerated similar weakness in others. The suffering he had experienced in prolonged adolescence gave him an unusual identification with the distressed and downtrodden. He had great sympathy with helpless and disadvantaged persons and was very sensitive to the feelings of others. Legend said he never turned away a beggar, and his factory was an informal unemployment office for mechanics looking for work. When he recruited the company of volunteers to return to the Mexican

War but failed to enlist them in the army, he reimbursed each man for wages lost in the days of rendezvous. Without fanfare, Morgan went about being generous in his own quiet manner. He was extremely gentle and good-hearted; there is no trace of calumny or malice in his letters. He loved his family, and the women closest to him said he was always polite and compassionate, a gentleman with a "lovely disposition."[28]

By the late 1850s, when Morgan was in his thirties, he had found balance and harmony in the Southern system of honor. His invalid wife was dependent upon him and in no position to question his manhood or challenge his headship of the family. He was man of the house for Becky and Mrs. Bruce, and after Hunt died in 1849 and Calvin, Sr., in 1854, he became the father figure for his younger brothers and sisters: "Brother Johnny and Sister Becky," they addressed him and his wife. Tradition holds that each night before going to bed, he would cross the street and bid his mother goodnight, checking that Hopemont was securely locked when he left. Through personal duels, Mexican War service, and militia duty, he had proved his valor and fulfilled the Morgan tradition. He had established an identity as Captain Morgan, the respected leader of the Lexington Rifles, a Mason, the leading partner in a prosperous business family. When moods of depression threatened, he could escape into the aristocratic amusements readily available. He was justified in his own eyes and those of the world, and these were his happiest adult years. He thoroughly identified with the Southern way of life; his self-esteem, his emotional equilibrium, his very identity depended upon it. When Southern civilization was threatened, Morgan's own adjustment was endangered.

FIVE

The State Guard

It seems paradoxical that Morgan, who had longed for a military career and had always been interested in military activities, delayed entering the Civil War until more than five months after fighting began. Some believed he was waiting for Becky to die. Her condition had gradually worsened until in January, 1861, there was no choice but to amputate her leg. After that, she remained in bed, and on Sunday afternoon, July 21, 1861—the day of the first battle of Bull Run—her long years of suffering ended in death. If John had been delaying because of Becky, he was then free to go; but he did not until September. In Lexington he had achieved honor and self-worth, and with all of his needs being met, he was able to maintain emotional balance and feel secure. He joined the Confederacy only when most Southern sympathizers from Kentucky did, when they felt forced to leave in order to maintain their honor and self-respect.[1]

Slavery and many other economic and cultural ties bound Kentucky to the South. Yet slavery was declining in the state—in 1860 only 19.5 percent of the population was slave and only seventy slaveowners had fifty or more slaves. Furthermore, Kentucky's predominantly agricultural economy was diversified and independent from the system of large plantations that prevailed in the deep South. When Kentuckians debated secession and the nature of the Union, they searched desperately for common ground of agreement. Roger W. Hanson, respected Lexington attorney, declared: "I am one of those who believe that when the time comes for Kentucky to fight, she will be united as one man." He was using his influence, he proclaimed, to avoid the "greatest of all calamities," a war in which Kentucky citizens would fight each other. A Lexington journalist proclaimed that a war between the sections was vicious enough to gratify the most bloodthirsty; "add to this calamity a war in Kentucky, wherein neighbor fights neighbor, brother meets brother in battle, and father and son enter opposing armies and we would think the veriest hater of his race would be content." Gradually it became clear that the people were hopelessly divided, and Kentuckians had heavy hearts. When news of the beginning of the war came, Rev. William Pratt wrote in his diary: "Our hearts are filled with sadness and great gloom in the community." Unable to choose between North and South, the people of Kentucky took the only position they could agree on—peace and neutrality.[2]

West Tennessee was more thoroughly Southern, but the people there were reluctant to leave the Union. Many made up their minds to secede only after the war began and Lincoln called for 75,000 militia to attack the South. One west Tennessean said: "I was for Union as long as there was any hope of remaining in it with peace and honor," but when Lincoln's proclamation was issued, that day had passed. For most pro-Southern Kentuckians the breaking point occurred only after Union troops entered the state, and the Kentucky government abandoned neutrality and embraced the Union cause in September, 1861. It was then that the main character in Sally Rochester Ford's wartime novel, *Raids and Romance of Morgan and His Men*, left his home in Louisville to join the Confederate army. The fictional youth said: "I must go, father, and go now. It will not do for me to delay longer. . . . To remain at home while the Southern cause is calling aloud for aid, would be disgrace, infamy. You yourself, father, could not respect me, if I should hesitate, now that our Kentucky is invaded by the dastard abolition foe."[3]

Morgan aligned with most Southern sympathizers in Kentucky in support of Beriah Magoffin, the pro-Southern, Democratic governor elected in 1859. When Magoffin and the legislature created the State Guard in March, 1860, a pro-Southern state militia organization, the Lexington Rifles were among the first volunteer companies to join. After South Carolina seceded, Magoffin strengthened the State Guard; Morgan's company received thirty-seven new rifles and began intensive drilling. He reported that he now had seventy-five men and ninety-seven guns, and asserted that in the event of a call to active service, every weapon would be manned. The men painted and redecorated the armory and invited the public, especially the women, to an open house and drill exhibition on Tuesday evening, February 5, 1861. In full dress uniform they delighted a large gathering of guests with precise execution of the manual of arms and inspection of arms. The evening closed with an impromptu dance to music by the Young America Concert and Orchestral Band. "A better disciplined corps can not be found in the State Guard," a local newspaper boasted.[4]

In an atmosphere heavy with military enthusiasm, Morgan's brother-in-law Sanders Bruce enrolled a second militia company, the Lexington Chasseurs; on January 18, 1861, in commemoration of the War of 1812's battle of Raisin River, both commands turned out and marched to Odd Fellows Hall, where the ladies of Lexington presented a flag to a third company, the Old Infantry, commanded by S.W. Price. All three were part of the State Guard, but the Chasseurs and the Old Infantry attracted pro-Unionists. Men held rallies, delivered fiery speeches, and chose sides. A smouldering rivalry cast a shadow over the normally sparkling social life and burst into the open on February 22, George Washington's birthday. The three militia companies had scheduled a joint dress parade and shooting contest in the afternoon, but when the streets began filling up with farm families that morning, the North and South confronted each other on Main Street.[5]

A traveling theater troupe had booked a performance of the play *The Woman in White* in the large opera house on the second floor of Odd Fellows Hall. Placards were posted all over town, but to celebrate Washington's birthday and to call greater attention to the drama, William C. Harris, the sponsor, stretched a thirty-foot American flag high over Main Street. It was held in place by ropes attached to the roof of the three-story Odd Fellows Hall and the chimney of Mrs. Elizabeth Webb's millinery shop across the street. By midmorning it was up and waving at Main and Broadway, right in the center of town. Immediately, a large crowd assembled in the intersection below, angrily debating whether it should be removed. Someone fetched Roger Hanson, and in his role as magistrate, he informed Harris that no United States flag had been flown in Lexington since Lincoln's election, and he would have to take it down. Harris, bolstered by the Chasseurs who had just joined the throng, refused.[6]

At that juncture, John Hunt Morgan rode up Main Street on a gray horse, dismounted in front of the hall, shook hands with Sanders Bruce, and said, "We must stop this foolishness." Turning to the crowd, he delivered one of the longest speeches of his life:

Fellow Citizens, it doesn't look to me as if you had any occasion to get excited, that flag still represents the United States, of which Kentucky is one, these people of the theater who have floated it have not done so in any defiance, it does not fly for any partisan purpose, but in honor of the birthday of George Washington, the Virginian. Now go home and take care of your women and children, if war breaks out you are free to go and fight on either side, but don't let us think of battle here in our homes. We'll draw the battle line on the battlefield, and not destroy the shelter of our homes and the hospitality of our town. I am sure these actors did not come here to challenge you to mortal combat, so let each man go about his own affairs, and such of you as are inclined, bring your ladies to the theater tonight, and you will see a good play, you can take my word for it.[7]

The crowd dispersed; a parade and marksmanship tournament were held in the afternoon; and that night the play was presented, with the flag yet flying—as much a symbol of Morgan's peacemaking as of loyalty to the government it represented.

Conciliation became much more difficult after the war began. When the Lexington Rifles and other Southrons learned about Fort Sumter and Lincoln's call for volunteers, they burned with eagerness to sign up immediately with the Southern army. Swept up in the passion of the moment, Morgan telegraphed Jefferson Davis, offering to raise 20,000 men to "defend Southern liberty against Northern conquest." A Confederate official replied that everything was uncertain, and Southern friends should be prepared for a call in the future. Some Kentuckians volunteered in April and May, but most Southern sympathizers remained to defend the home state.[8]

The day he telegraphed Davis, Morgan raised a Confederate flag on the woolen factory in "cordial sympathy with our Southern friends," and announced that the firm would begin specializing in the manufacture of State Guard uniforms. For over a year the woolen factory had produced uniforms for militia organizations springing up in Kentucky and surrounding states. When war came and drilling increased, militia companies changed their dress uniforms for more serviceable and less ostentatious woolens, creating an expanding market. Lexington had six woolen factories, one of which advertised for raw wool under the headline "Wool! Wool!" Morgan jeans were described as "a beautiful cloth . . . both low priced and serviceable." Some of the Morgan uniforms probably outfitted companies that joined the Union army, but after the war began, the company changed to gray and sold only to units with Southern sympathies.[9]

In April and May, 1861, groups of men joined both the Union and Confederate armies, but a majority of Kentuckians were united in favor of neutrality within the Union. On May 20 the state officially declared neutrality in the war. Gradually, however, Union sentiment increased until neutrality was abandoned, and many Southern sympathizers felt they could not remain in the state with honor. Unionists in the legislature created the Home Guards, a Unionist state militia to counter the State Guard. The Home Guards were given equal funding with the State Guard, and volunteer companies with Federal leanings throughout the state were encouraged to enlist. In Lexington the Chasseurs and Old Infantry enrolled in the Home Guards, and in the last days of Becky Morgan's life it became clear that Sanders Bruce, even though he owned slaves, was pro-Union.[10]

The Morgans were united in Southern sympathy. Charlton had graduated from Transylvania University and been appointed United States Consul to Messina, Sicily. In February, 1861, he resigned and came home, declaring that he could no longer hold office under an administration pledged to "the destruction of Southern institutions and the degredation of slaveholding communities." In May, Cal donated the labor of one of the steamboat crews to the construction of fortifications near Memphis. In early July, seventeen-year-old Tom went off to Camp Boone, Tennessee, to enlist in the Confederate infantry. John was designated acting major in the State Guard; Dick was appointed captain and regimental adjutant; and Uncle Tom Hunt became a regimental commander with the rank of colonel.[11]

As long as Kentucky was neutral, it was honorable to stay and defend her borders as a unique state that refused to get involved in the war. At first both the Union and Confederate governments respected Kentucky's position. Then, as pro-Union feeling grew, the Lincoln administration opened recruiting stations in Kentucky and began shipping "Lincoln guns" to arm the recruits. One of the Union posts was Camp Dick Robinson, only thirty miles south of Lexington. Members of the State Guard opposed these violations of Kentucky neutrality, but their leaders lacked a coordinated policy of resistance. Individuals, however, attempted to prevent delivery of the rifles. In

August, a consignment designated for Camp Dick Robinson was shipped from Cincinnati, but a band of Southerners in Cynthiana stopped the train and threatened to seize the shipment unless it was removed. It was returned to Cincinnati, shipped by boat to Louisville, and transported to Lexington by rail. Early on the morning of Wednesday, August 20, the boxes of rifles were unloaded at the depot of the Louisville and Lexington Railroad.[12]

At three o'clock in the afternoon, a detachment of about 200 Union cavalry from Camp Dick Robinson marched into town. If they had taken the guns and left, there would have been no problem, but they checked their horses into livery stables and prepared to spend the night. Was the Union army occupying Lexington? Such a challenge could not go unanswered. Suddenly a bugle sounded from the roof of the Lexington Rifles armory; the courthouse bell rang; and men came running from all quarters of the city. The Rifles rushed to the armory for their guns, and the Home Guard units rallied alongside the Union cavalry posted at the depot, even dragging out and loading an old cannon. The citizens were thrown into the wildest excitement, and a fight seemed certain until two of Lexington's most prominent residents stepped in as mediators. United States Senator John C. Breckinridge, former Vice-President of the United States and leading Southern rights spokesman in Kentucky, and attorney Madison Johnson met with the Union officers and then went to the Rifles armory. They proposed that the Unionists be allowed to leave peacefully with the guns if they would get out of town before nightfall. Morgan accepted these terms, and the crisis ended. Just as he had in the Washington's birthday incident, Morgan displayed restraint and worked to keep the peace.[13]

Meanwhile, it was becoming almost impossible to get uniforms through to the Confederate army. In May the Union navy blockaded the Mississippi River, and in June the army closed shipments south out of Louisville on the railroad. The Morgans attempted to smuggle jeans through the Federal blockade, but wagoners refused to haul into the South for fear of prosecution. In early September John Morgan himself went south with two wagonloads of gray jeans. On the turnpike near Lebanon, Kentucky, he was apprehended by a company of Home Guards and held prisoner in the log building of Pleasant Hill Church for three days.[14]

Kentucky neutrality was rapidly coming to an end. After Confederate troops marched into Columbus and Union soldiers occupied Paducah, the General Assembly demanded that the Confederates withdraw, and on September 18 declared that Kentucky would stand for the Union. Immediately, Unionists in Frankfort took control of all state militia and called in the arms of the State Guard. On Thursday, September 19, a regiment from Camp Dick Robinson marched into Lexington and occupied the city—the very move—this time official—which had produced the crisis in August. They camped at the fairgrounds, and the men were given the liberty of the town. That night news came that former Gov. Charles Morehead and other prominent Southern supporters had been arrested, and the pro-Southern Louis-ville *Courier* had been suppressed. In his suite at the Phoenix Hotel, Breck-inridge learned that he was to be jailed. He summoned help by sending out the coded note: "Hawks are about."[15]

The next evening, Friday, September 20, Morgan gathered his men at the armory and directed his first act of war. After dark the doors were shut and the sounds of the shuffling of marching feet and shouts of command came from the large building. Inside, a small squad was pretending to drill while others loaded the rifles on two hay wagons, filled the empty rifle crates with brick, and marked them "Arms from Captain Morgan, State Armory, Frank-fort." The mock drilling continued while Morgan and the main body slipped out the back door, delivered the boxes to the railroad depot and marched quietly out the Versailles Road with the guns concealed under the hay. In the darkness Morgan had begun his revolt against the United States; like a thief in the night he had stolen the guns issued to his command by the state.

The scheme had the teasing, taunting vitality that would become his trademark. It was as if he resented being denied the symbols of community support that were an integral part of going to war in the mid-nineteenth century. In the Mexican War there had been fanfare, and in the seceded states companies and regiments were sent off with banquets, flag ceremonies, and dress parades. Morgan apparently compensated by hoodwinking the Union-ists. As soon as the guns were safely on their way, he returned to Lexington and secluded himself among friends to enjoy firsthand the reaction to his own departure. The Federals opened the crates, found the brick, and or-dered Morgan's arrest. Large crowds gathered, and ridicule and derision led to violence: groups of Southern and Northern men began shooting at each other. The Union regiment came in from the fairgrounds to restore order. Morgan sent messages to his men to rendezvous at sundown, and they left, soon overtaking the squad that was guarding the guns several miles out of town on the Versailles Road.[16]

Social psychologists theorize that a common characteristic of potential revolutionaries is that each one senses the denial of satisfaction of one or more basic needs. An individual becomes a revolutionary when the gap be-tween what one wants and what one gets widens, when the gap between expectations and gratifications becomes intolerable and frustration is focused on the government. Only after his state joined the North, only after North-ern troops occupied his hometown, and only after he was ordered to disarm did Morgan cross the Rubicon from peaceful businessman to revolutionary. Basil Duke concluded that he had no choice: an officer of the State Guard who disarmed "could look for little backing from his comrades." Creditors soon closed in and attached Morgan's property, leaving him, in the words of the Atlanta *Commonwealth*, propertyless, "houseless, wifeless, with little to live, love, fight or die for, but the new republic."[17]

SIX

Gambler and Guerrilla

From all over Kentucky the majority of State Guard members were volunteering for Confederate service; it was the greatest single wave of Kentucky enlistment in the Southern army. The Lexington Rifles and about 200 additional men rendezvoused at Bloomfield, near Bardstown, and elected Morgan to lead them through the lines. Leaving on Saturday night, September 28, they marched for two days and nights, passing without incident between towns with strong Home Guards. Near Bowling Green, Kentucky, they entered Confederate lines and made camp with many of their State Guard friends.

For the Confederacy it was still the morning of bright hope. There had been only one battle: on the day Becky Morgan died the Confederate army of Gen. Pierre G. T. Beauregard had repelled a Federal invasion of Virginia, sending the Union army racing back to Washington in a rout. Lincoln's new commander of the Army of the Potomac, George B. McClellan, had not resumed the offensive. Defending the Confederacy in the West was Gen. Albert Sidney Johnston, a Kentuckian who had attended Transylvania University and graduated from West Point. Johnston had his army deployed in a long, thin line from Cumberland Gap to Columbus, all the way across southern Kentucky. Greatly outnumbered, he was relying more on bluff than substance to protect Nashville and halt the Federal forces advancing southward toward Bowling Green on the Louisville and Nashville Railroad.

Morgan's year of volunteer cavalry service in the Mexican War, two years as commander of an artillery company of the state militia, and four years as captain of the Lexington Rifles provided significant experience in small unit administration and leadership. The Rifles were well armed and well trained by the standards of the day, and Morgan could have enrolled them in an infantry regiment. On the other hand they had fine horses, and since he had preferred the cavalry branch in the Mexican War, it would have made sense to enlist as cavalry and train the company in cavalry tactics. It also appears that Morgan would have settled easily into camp life, entering with gusto into drill and guard mounting, dress parades, and such leisure activities as playing cards, drinking, and betting with fellow officers. In Mexico and during militia bivouacs in Kentucky, he had thrived on camp routine. But now it was different—there was too much waiting, too much time to think.

Guard duty was dull and monotonous; the hours dragged; inner tensions gained strength; self-esteem deflated; and dark clouds of depression formed. Morgan was like John Mosby of Virginia, who said: "Camp duty was always irksome to me, and I preferred being on the outposts." Duke wrote that routine picket duty "did not accord with his nature, which demanded the stimulus of adventure." While other officers were organizing and training recruits, serving on garrison detail, and politicking at headquarters, for the first twenty-seven days—not even bothering to muster in—Morgan began his own irregular war against the enemy that had driven him from his home.[1]

Totally on his own initiative, he would select ten to twenty volunteers, and at nightfall, on horseback, they would advance into territory occupied by the Union army. Far behind the lines, they would prowl around all night among the Federal outposts, seeking to entrap unwary sentries. They covered almost every foot of ground for miles around, hid in almost every clump of trees, and shot at the enemy from nearly every hill. Deep in the woods, shaded from the moonlight, they held secret conferences with informers who opened and closed each report, "For the love of God never breathe my name." One night Morgan and a companion were reconnoitering on foot when they became separated from the others by a body of Union cavalry. Lying perfectly still in a thicket at the edge of the road, they counted 120 soldiers riding by only a few feet away. When daylight came, they would attack an enemy picket line, listen to the number of "long rolls" beaten to call the troops into battle position, and in that way determine the strength of the Union camp.

Compelled into action by inner conflict, Morgan happened upon the commonsense tactics of one of the oldest forms of fighting known to mankind—guerrilla warfare. The Bible tells how Gideon, Abimelech, David, and other Hebrew warriors used it in Palestine; it was used in warfare in the ancient Greek and Roman worlds, and in Europe in the Middle Ages; in the American Revolution, Francis Marion and other patriot leaders used it against Great Britain. But the guerrilla war par excellence was conducted by the Spanish against the occupation of Spain by Napoleon's army (1809-13). It set the standard for years, and out of it came the name "guerrilla" for petty or little war. Guerrilla warfare involved taking the offensive: hit and run; attack when you have superior numbers and power; withdraw to avoid decisive battle; acquire accurate intelligence reports; use local civilians as informers and guides; stalk the enemy; harass him like a gnat; destroy his communications; force him to disperse his strength; use the cover of night to surprise him; use treachery and deception; break the rules and do anything necessary to win; and—most fundamental of all—always preserve yourself so you can continue destroying the enemy.[2]

During the twenty-seven days before Morgan mustered in, he was beyond the protection of international law. Soldiers practicing guerrilla tactics as partisans were conducting legal warfare and deserved the rights of prisoners of war when captured. Partisans were combatants enrolled in an organized army, sharing continuously in the war, wearing the uniform, and answerable to the laws of war and to the system of military justice, but detached for guerrilla warfare. After swearing in, Morgan and his forces generally came under the legal definition of partisan corps, but in true guerrilla fashion he continued throughout his career to make his own rules.[3]

For one thing, he had begun to pose as the enemy. Uniforms varied in both armies, and six months into the war it was not uncommon to see Confederate troops in blue—but that was a matter of necessity. Because Morgan used the enemy uniform as a disguise, the pretense constituted perfidy and legally suspended his men from the right to be treated as prisoners of war when captured; scouts or soldiers disguised in the uniform of the enemy were subject to hanging as spies. Mosby, who later became Morgan's guerrilla counterpart in the East, also used uniforms for disguise, and there were others who did so infrequently. In December, 1862, a Union cavalry regiment wore Confederate uniforms in a raid near Charlotte, Tennessee, for instance. But no officer in either army used the tactic as frequently or extensively as Morgan. He would assume the identity of a Union cavalry officer stationed opposite him on the front lines, such as Col. John Kennett, commander of the 4th Ohio Cavalry. This practice illustrates how far on the edge of guerrilla warfare he operated, and it serves as one explanation for Union abhorrence of Morgan. When he masqueraded as a Union officer, he threatened civilized, traditional warfare in which combatants could identify one another.[4]

Guerrilla warfare was a high-risk activity and Morgan immediately acquired a taste for it. Raids relieved the pain of boredom and insidious depression, and the excitement provided short-term pleasure. Totally immersed in the activity, he learned that depression was blotted out, and outside reality did not exist. He experienced a sense of power, control, and triumph in the face of despair and helplessness. In a world of his own, he was the master of fate; the sky was the limit; everything was possible. When he had a problem to attend to, Morgan's mind and body were fully stimulated and filled with life, and his movements appeared easy and graceful as he managed the moment. He discovered an identity as a winner: daring, forceful, and self-confident. The state of euphoria produced was as addictive as alcohol or drugs. Like compulsive gambling, it dictated the tendency to return to the activity. Morgan conducted four or five raids every week; as soon as he was rested from one, he began planning and anticipating the next. While his men slept, he would steal out alone and pass himself off as a Union officer to pro-Union farmers in order to gain intelligence.[5]

This explains why Morgan's men noticed such a striking change in his appearance and manner when he was in imminent danger; they asserted that they had never really seen their leader until they saw him in battle. "In an engagement Morgan is perfectly cool," one of the men observed, "and yet his face and action are as if surcharged with electricity. He had the quickness of a tiger, and the strength of two ordinary men." Duke wrote that in perilous situations Morgan's voice would change, and he would take on a more forceful and audacious manner: "His presence of mind and address, in the midst of a great and imminent danger, were literally perfect." He had "a quality even higher than courage—I can describe it only as the faculty of subjecting every one to his will, whom he tried to influence; it was almost mesmeric."[6]

Guerrilla warfare proved ideal for Morgan. Constant danger and excitement provided pleasure, and in the earliest days furnished so much stimulation for the men that they "evinced little desire for intoxicants."[7] The aggressive, independent nature of guerrilla war allowed Morgan to be forceful, powerful, and in control of the situation. The continuing nature of irregular warfare allowed him to return again and again to the game. Like a neurotic gambler, Morgan attempted to stay in the action as long as possible; he had to force himself to leave the scene of great danger. The psychological effect and Morgan's revolutionary zeal made him one of the greatest guerrilla warriors in history. Total involvement made him totally fearless—free to act, feel, and think with great abandon and creativity.

The object of the pathological gambler is to assure a continuation of the activity; money is only a means to enter and stay in the game. In guerrilla warfare the most basic principle is to continue the action; troops are used to enter and stay in the fighting. Morgan's command was the money, to be risked, to be entered in the action, but not to be lost—the men had to be preserved at all cost. This is why Morgan was reluctant to meet the enemy on equal terms. He had no appetite at all for an equal fight: if he were defeated it would mean the end of the game, the termination of the pleasure. Totally committed to guerrilla warfare, he was extremely reluctant to participate in conventional warfare because it did not put him in control, did not produce the shift in conscious mood to which he was addicted. To comprehend Morgan's private inner world is to understand the forces that shaped his exceptional career.

As one of his officers said: "He went into the Rebellion *con amore*, and pursues it with high enjoyment." But for Morgan the war was more than a thrilling game; it was revolution, and one measure of the intensity of his commitment was the viciousness of his warfare. During one foray, pushing up a road early in the morning in advance of a party of about fifty men, Morgan's videttes caught a glimpse of sunlight glistening on the bayonets of a Union infantry force just over a rise. Unaware that they were observed, the Federals marched on in Morgan's direction. He dismounted his men, posted them in thickets on each side of the road, and sent eight or ten to the rear to hold the horses while he went forward alone on foot to a house whose windows commanded a view of the oncoming force. He saw sixty or seventy soldiers but was unable to determine whether they were part of a larger command. He withdrew and concealed himself in the undergrowth with his men, listening as the chatter of conversation and tramp of the column grew louder. About forty yards ahead, they halted, suspecting the presence of the enemy. Immediately, Morgan stepped into the road and shot the officer riding at the head of the column. A brief, confusing skirmish ensued, but after a few minutes both commands retreated in haste, assuming they were about to be outflanked.[8]

Between expeditions, on October 27, 1861, Morgan was sworn into the Confederate army and elected captain of a cavalry company. His able brother-in-law Basil Duke was first lieutenant. (Duke had grown up on a farm in Scott County and had practiced law in St. Louis; he was married to John's sister Tommy.) Morgan purchased horses, clothing, and equipment under government authority, but in guerrilla fashion he stole much of his accoutrement from the enemy. On November 6, a superior officer ordered him to return two slaves he had taken from a Union farmer. He was allowed, on the other hand, to keep "one brown mare, white face and feet; 1 iron-gray mare, flea-bitten on head and neck; 1 riding saddle, 2 bridles, 1 pair saddlebags, 2 flannel shirts, 1 bedcover, blanket and quilt." Once he came in with forty head of fat cattle, fresh beef for several regiments.[9]

A principle of guerrilla war is to harass and exhaust the enemy and cause him to disperse his strength by attacking his communications. In the Civil War, for the first time in the history of warfare, railroads were used extensively to transport men and supplies; the long miles of track, wooden trestles, and lumber-supported tunnels of the vital Louisville and Nashville Railroad were inviting targets for guerrilla sorties. When Southern forces withdrew from the region north of Green River, they burned the small bridge over Bacon Creek, on the main track about fifty miles north of Bowling Green. Through his network of informers, Morgan learned that a construction crew had finished the woodwork and was preparing to lay rails on the restored trestle. Deciding to attack, he left camp at nightfall on December 4 with 105 men and rode all night under a clear sky in unseasonably warm weather. At dawn, in a stretch of woodland between the two armies, they dismounted and made camp, resting and waiting for darkness.[10]

A few miles to the north workers laid one rail on the bridge and positioned the other. Then, late in the afternoon, along with their guards from the 1st Wisconsin and 19th Pennsylvania Infantry regiments, they boarded the construction train and departed, leaving the site unguarded. At 9:00 P.M. Morgan's raiders arrived and heaped stubble and wood on the bridge. At his signal they applied torches, and the flames leaped high into the air, beams cracked, one end fell, then the other. Of the five uprights, four were destroyed, and the fifth was left smouldering in the middle of the creek. This was a very minor accomplishment—within a few days the trestle was restored—but General Johnston mentioned it in his regular report to the War Department.[11]

A few nights later they burned a ferry boat on Green River at Munfordville, and on another night Morgan and five men fell upon the little Wood-sonville railroad depot, within 200 yards of Union picket lines. They captured five or six very surprised Union stragglers playing cards in the building and burned the station, lighting up the sky and inspiring the Union officers in Woodsonville to form battle lines. Combining his teasing, taunting humor with psychological warfare, Morgan sent one of the stragglers to warn that he would burn the entire village when he returned. The event was insignificant, but George W. Johnson, governor of the rump Confederate government of Kentucky in Bowling Green, was quite proud that his son had participated. "Morgan is an excellent officer," the governor wrote his wife, "much talked of here; intelligent, active, daring and prudent also. He thinks a great deal of Matty and is very kind to him. The character of his service is very dangerous, but I trust God will preserve our son."[12]

The Civil War was also the first in which the telegraph was employed extensively in strategy and logistics. Lines were strung up quickly between key points, and in both armies civilian operators transmitted messages by battery-powered field equipment to coordinate the movement of trains and armies in the field. Morgan took great delight in becoming the chief antagonist of the Union military telegraph system in the West.[13]

On January 19, 1862, the long, thin Confederate line collapsed on the right when Union Gen. George H. Thomas won the battle of Mill Springs in south central Kentucky. Following through on the victory, Thomas directed W.G. Fuller, telegraph superintendent, to proceed from Somerset to Lebanon with utmost haste and string telegraph lines south into the newly won territory. Fuller organized a thirty-man gang and established base camp on the highway south of Lebanon in a log church—the same building where Morgan had been imprisoned four months earlier. On Friday morning, January 31, a detail of line stringers was setting poles and hanging wire several miles south of camp. Superintendent Fuller had gone to Lebanon to get the payroll, and a four-man mess crew was washing dishes. It seemed safe to assume that the nearest rebels were thirty-five miles away.[14]

But Morgan had been longing to return to the log church, and when the grapevine brought intelligence that Home Guard Lieutenant Short—the man who had arrested him—was still there, he determined to capture his former warden. (Throughout the war Morgan fought in a very personal manner, molding his participation to meet his own needs.) With nine men and a local guide, he set out on Tuesday night, January 28, in a driving rainstorm. It rained all night, and while they slept in the home of a Southerner the next day, the storm continued. By evening the creeks had risen so high that one man almost drowned crossing a stream. They found shelter again and waited until Thursday night to resume the march. For sixty miles they went through the darkness, the horses wading in mud and swimming cold, swollen streams. In the area behind enemy lines, the men relied on friendly guides to steer them around Union encampments. Once Morgan pretended to be a special courier for Union Gen. Don Carlos Buell in order to obtain assistance from a Union farmer.

Reaching the log church on Friday morning, Morgan was surprised to find three Union supply wagons drawn up next to the building. His men captured the mess crew and inventoried the supplies stored inside. There were telegraph instruments, Union army overcoats, pork, beans, hardtack, coffee, and other stores. That night they burned church, wagons, and supplies and then departed, taking an overcoat for each man, a large United States flag, and ten prisoners—including Short, whom they captured at his home. Traveling through Union lines, they wore the blue overcoats and passed as a squad of Union cavalry.[15]

It was getting dark when they came to a crossing on Green River. The river was flooded out of its banks, muddy and swirling, and Montgomery the ferryman, a Lincoln supporter, was reluctant to operate. Morgan convinced him that they were on an important mission for the United States, and the crossing began. It took several trips, and midway on the second passage, Montgomery recognized a friend among the captured Union soldiers. Realizing that he had been deceived, he turned the ferry downstream, heading it under low hanging willow trees in an attempt to rake the horses into the water. One horse was drowned, but then the boat went out of control and ran aground. The ferryman and his slave crew jumped overboard and clambered up the bank. "The night being so very dark, it was impossible to shoot them" Morgan reported. The next day, approaching Southern-held Glasgow, Morgan formed in column and paraded in, twenty horsemen in blue overcoats, with the large United States flag flying in front. The citizens were startled, but not nearly as much as were several Confederate stragglers hanging out in the small town.[16]

Back in Lebanon, Superintendent Fuller met the exasperating consequences of a guerrilla raid. Construction was delayed for days, and even when the wires finally reached Columbia he had to tell the local commander, Gen. Jeremiah T. Boyle, that no communication was possible because Morgan had destroyed all the instruments. Volatile to begin with, Boyle was beside himself with vexation—here was an operational telegraph line connecting his headquarters to the entire communication system of the nation, and because of Morgan he could not use it. Crimson with rage, he threatened to shoot Fuller. If there was ever a time for ingenuity this was it, and Fuller produced. Using the wire ends as a key to send and his tongue as a sounder to receive, Fuller invented a unique method of operation. Boyle slapped him on the back and declared: "You are too useful to be shot yet."[17]

Boyle and other Union officers agreed with Northern war correspondents that Morgan's guerrilla tactics were beyond the pale of civilized warfare. Even though he was a regularly commissioned officer, to the enemy he was a thief, murderer, and outlaw. Reacting to the burning of the Bacon Creek bridge, a reporter for the Cincinnati *Gazette* called him "one of the greatest scoundrels that ever went unhung." The Cincinnati *Times* protested that he seemed to be commissioned as a land pirate at the head of a band of thieves. Morgan became "the renowned guerrilla," head of a "desperate band" whose "chief employment, besides attacking pickets in a stealthy, cowardly way, is to ride about the country in all kinds of plundering expeditions, stealing horses, clothing, and whatever their hands may find." Boyle complained: "Morgan or some other rebel is ravaging the county of Metcalfe and toting off the stock of all kinds."[18]

Morgan's raiding along Green River ended when Johnston's defensive line in Kentucky collapsed completely and fell back into Alabama. Regretfully abandoning Nashville, the great manufacturing center and supply depot of the western Confederacy, Johnston left Gen. John B. Floyd in charge of covering the army's retreat and saving as many stores as possible. Cavalrymen commanded by Morgan and others loaded munitions on wagons and buggies, but large crowds of panic-stricken citizens turned into rioting mobs, carrying away bacon from the wharf on the Cumberland River, barrels of beef from the railroad depot, and bales of clothing thrown by accomplices from the fourth and fifth stories of warehouses on the public square. All the soldiers could do was quell the worst disorders.[19]

Morgan became part of the thin screen thrown out to protect Johnston's army from Union divisions under General Buell in Nashville. For most cavalry officers it was routine duty, but for Morgan this was a time of continual harassment of Federal pickets and raids behind the lines. His daring coolness and absence of fear captured the admiration of both armies, and five weeks later, when the Southern army advanced to Corinth, Mississippi, he had become a legend.

Morgan had a fundamental appreciation of the harassing nature of guerrilla operations. He considered surprising and killing picket guards part of the effort to discourage, annoy, and goad the enemy to desperation. With this practice Morgan was two years ahead of his time but in violation of international law. Pickets, sentinels, or outposts were not to be fired upon except to drive them in or when a positive order had been issued authorizing an attack. In late September, 1861, when picket fighting broke out near Washington, D.C., McClellan issued a general order prohibiting the shooting of pickets, denouncing it as repugnant to civilized warfare. Over the years, however, medieval etiquette gave way to modern, total war; by the summer of 1864 both armies had sharpshooters killing sentinels careless enough to expose a portion of their bodies above head logs on the parapets.[20]

Riding through remote fields and swamps in the dark of night, jumping rail fences, and scrambling up rocky creek banks, Morgan would become familiar with almost every trace and bridle path. Carrying unconventional shotguns and crawling through the brush at midnight, his men would creep to within a few yards of a Union outpost—close enough to hear the pickets talking and laughing. When the moon went down or behind a cloud, Morgan would signal, and the men would rise to their knees and fire, aiming their shotguns low for maximum effect. Pickets surprised by Morgan never forgot the sudden flash and roar of shotguns, the curses and commands, the moans of the wounded. "Every flash was followed by a groan," Duke said, "and, by the quick vivid light, we could see the men we hit writhing on the ground." Within a few seconds it would be over as Morgan's men ran to their horses and galloped away; they hit and ran.[21]

Union guards attempted to protect themselves by withdrawing from advance positions at sundown. In response, Morgan once demonstrated all day against a post manned by a Union cavalry company, and that evening, when the Union men pulled back, waited in ambush at the house where they camped each night. He and four other guerrillas, armed with shotguns loaded with buckshot, were concealed in the grass behind a low fence in the yard in front of the house. When the command of twenty-five horsemen approached, the officer in charge called a halt thirty feet from the house and directed a couple of men to reconnoiter on foot. Lying on the cold ground, gripping his shotgun, Morgan heard the horses breathing and the footsteps of the men checking each side of the road. They found nothing, but the officer ordered the entire company to dismount and form a skirmish line in the yard. When the first men stepped near the fence, Morgan yelled "Now!" and he and his men jumped to their feet, firing point-blank across the fence into the faces of the Union men. The officer and several others crumpled to the ground; the remainder mounted and raced northward toward the main army encampment. But as they fled, every few yards out of the dark woods came the roar of shotguns, fired by Morgan's men stationed on a chain picket designed to accomplish what it did—send the panic-stricken survivors fleeing to sound the alarm at headquarters.[22]

All along the front, Union pickets began imagining that Morgan was lurking in every grove of cedar trees. They thought they saw him riding through the mist along a rise in the distance, and the hooting of owls and movement of stray livestock in the underbrush caused them to report seeing him in several locations at once. A rumor circulated that Morgan was the phantom-like horseman who had been killing pickets in Pilot Knob, Missouri, where green recruits told of seeing a mysterious night rider, a tall, heavy man with flowing beard, mounted on an immense black stallion, fleet as the wind. Shot after shot was fired at him, but he seemed to bear a charmed life.[23]

Among Union pickets, Morgan was not only feared but hated as a cold-blooded murderer, and some Northern war correspondents demanded his execution. One wrote: "It occurs to me that skulking freebooters who thus come within our lines, committing robbery and murder, and making observation of our position, are spies, and should, when taken, be promptly put to death."[24]

Generally, though, Northern reporters admired him for his daring, exaggerated his significance, and padded their dispatches with rumors and stories that contributed to the popular myth of his ubiquity. For example, Morgan supposedly entered Nashville one Sunday evening disguised as a Connecticut candy manufacturer, had four drinks at the St. Cloud Hotel, lost $1,100 at faro, and attended the theater. On another day he was said to have entered the lines as a driver of a wood wagon and then as a miller delivering a load of meal. The miller tale described how Morgan visited Gen. Alexander McDowell McCook and, pretending to be an informer, set an entrapment by telling where Morgan could be captured. The story, which has never been confirmed, related that McCook sent 150 men into the ambush, where they were all captured. Morgan reportedly called upon newspaper editors in Nashville, dined with Union officers and pumped them for intelligence, and visited the office of Military Governor of Tennessee Andrew Johnson, becoming indignant when a secretary became suspicious.[25]

Making light of all these tales, a correspondent from Philadelphia declared:

If a queer looking person walks along the street, with a white hat, cocked on the left side, and, in a cogitating mood, enters a house, that man is John Morgan; if a queer looking individual walks along the street with a felt hat cocked on the right side, and in a cogitating mood does not enter a house, that man is John Morgan; if a man of elegant attire rushes wildly into a hotel, especially if it is raining, it is Morgan; if a gentleman dressed in drab leans against a lamp post, it is Morgan; if a person demurely enters a hotel, and immediately repairs to a private room, and rings the bell furiously for a bottle of brandy, it is Morgan; should a person demurely enter a hotel, and immediately repair to a private room, and not ring the bell furiously for a bottle of brandy, it is Morgan.—Why, if we can place any credit upon information of a 'contraband' or 'reliable gentleman' nature, the inscrutable guerrilla has been in the city some half a dozen times in the past ten days.[26]

The story circulated that one morning in Nashville there was great excitement over news that Morgan was at a well-known boardinghouse where he had boldly spent the night. According to the anecdote, the Federal provost marshal ordered out a large force, surrounded the house, and demanded that Morgan come out quietly to avoid bloodshed. Great was his chagrin when he was informed that "John H. Morgan" was but six hours old, having arrived in the night—the newborn son of a patriotic Southern woman.[27]

Morgan was pronounced killed several times and assumed captured on innumerable occasions. One Sunday evening at the ferry landing in Covington, Kentucky, a mob apprehended an Indiana farmer attempting to cross the Ohio River. Several people swore he was Morgan, wearing spectacles as a disguise. Cries of "Hang him! Shoot him! Drown him!" rent the air, and in piteous tones the frightened civilian begged for his life. They conveyed him to a hotel for questioning, and on the way the crowd chanted "John Morgan's caught." At the hotel he was identified as William Herndon, a former tavernkeeper in Boone County, Kentucky.[28]

It was testimony to Morgan's success as a guerrilla that he had created the illusion of ubiquity. The ultimate acclaim occurred in Nashville on Christmas Day, 1862, when a Union commission investigating the conduct of the war in middle Tennessee earlier that year, asked Major W.H. Sidell whether he had heard frequent reports of Morgan being in two places at once. "I have no doubt that rumors of his presence often were erroneous," Sidell answered, "but, strictly speaking, I cannot recall any instance in which I heard of his being in two places at the same time." [29]

One incursion which reinforced the impression that Morgan was everywhere at once was his raid on the waterfront in Nashville, almost in the shadow of headquarters of Buell's 65,000-man Army of the Cumberland. With twelve men dressed in blue overcoats, he masqueraded as a Union officer and entered enemy lines on the Lebanon Pike on Wednesday afternoon, February 26, 1862. Proceeding to the Cumberland River landing in town, he determined to attack the Federal boats in the river. Three men volunteered to row a skiff out to the steamboat *Minnetonka*, tied to trees in the backwater 500 yards upstream from a fleet of gunboats, troop transports, and supply vessels supporting Buell's army. Morgan watched from the shore as the boarding party set fire to the *Minnetonka*. The plan was to cut her adrift and send her blazing and smoking into the fleet downstream, but the vessel was secured with chain cables and so burned at her mooring. A crowd of about 2,000 people gathered, and someone warned Morgan that a large party of cavalry had just passed; he should escape immediately. He was only a few hundred yards from the Yankee artillery batteries around the state capitol, and he could see the United States flag waving above its spire. Yet instead of rushing away, he remained for thirty minutes, ecstatic with pleasure, to mix with the spectators and watch the burning boat and the sailors scurrying about on the vessels down river.

On the way out, when he reached a tollgate on the edge of the city, he concealed the horses and men in a clump of cedar trees and spent over an hour posing as a Union officer inspecting passes of citizens who came along. Darkness came, and he was still reluctant to leave. He was hiding in the woods with his men when a company of Federal cavalry paused on the road, separated from Morgan by a rail fence. "I dismounted and took a shot-gun and started for the fence," John reported, "where I could easily have killed two or three of them. Just as I was rising to put my gun through the fence they called to each other to fire, which they did and then ran for the city." Morgan's soldiers returned the fire and then marched to camp, carrying one comrade severely wounded. [30]

On February 27, Morgan moved his headquarters southward a few miles to Murfreesboro, a beautiful little village in the fertile Tennessee Bluegrass, one of the most productive agricultural regions in the Confederacy. For Confederate soldiers located there, one of the great anticipations of life was parading down East Main Street past the mansion house of Col. Charles Ready near the public square. After the war a veteran recalled that every man would "primp for the march by this house, and how proudly he stepped and with what perfect mien he marched . . . all to have the privilege of 'showing off,' and having the opportunity for a sly glance at the beautiful Queen sisters standing on the upper veranda." The sisters, daughters of the colonel, were so devoted to the Confederacy and so friendly to regiments marching by their house that they apparently became special mascot "queens" of the men.[31]

The Ready home was a large, two-story brick house, with upper and lower verandas. On the side along Church Street there was a formal flower garden landscaped with magnolias, fragrant jessamines, lilacs, and roses crossbred in the government greenhouse in Washington, D.C.[32]

Charles Ready, one of middle Tennessee's most prominent lawyers and planters, had been a United States congressman from 1853 to 1859. He was a diligent, hardworking attorney who argued cases before the state Supreme Court and served in the ranks of the Whig Party. He attended church regularly; he owned slaves; and he and his wife Martha reared a son and four daughters.[33]

Like many young women, the Ready girls were caught up in the spirit of romance that set the tone of upper-class Southern society in the 1850s. On lavender stationery imported from London, the young ladies of Murfreesboro invited friends to tea—"You must come in party dress," one read. Promenading on Main Street in bonnet and shawl, they talked of romantic love, and in solitude they opened their diaries and confided their dreams of attracting one true love. They visited a fortuneteller and tried their fortune with coffee grounds and with a mirror reflecting in the well. They said that if you had to snuff the candle twice before going to bed, you would not marry for two years, and the number of seeds in an orange predicted the number of your children.[34]

Wealthy, influential beaux presented their cards to the servant girl who answered the Ready door, and Mary, the eldest daughter, married William A. Cheatham, prominent Nashville physician and brother of the mayor of Nashville, Richard Cheatham. Martha, the second daughter, was the elegant "Mattie," a model of the trim-figured Southern belle with dark brown hair, fair complexion, rosy cheeks, and gray eyes sparkling with intelligence and strength. She was perfect in deportment in school and always "up to snuff" with her homework, had perfect posture, was amiable and pleasant, and in the eyes of her little sister Alice, was "the best Sister in the world." A trendsetter in fashion, in Washington Mattie was said to be the first young lady to wear a curl on her forehead, a coquettish coiffure that others copied immediately. Shopping for her mother, she teased: "I am almost inclined Mama to keep your bonnet and wear it. It is so pretty and becoming to me."[35]

In Washington during her seventeenth year, Mattie had many suitors, but the most persistent was Illinois Representative Samuel Scott Marshall. Marshall was thirty-six years old, a lawyer and former circuit court judge. He was considered a good catch in the marriage market, offering security, national prominence, and social position; but when he proposed marriage, Mattie replied with a gentle "not now." She did not want to turn him down, because becoming an old maid was always a haunting fear, and Marshall was a good man; she simply did not love him. "And you say you don't love Marshall a *bit*, Mattie?" asked sister Mary. "Now I do not *believe* that. I am actually in love with him myself." Marshall left the offer open, with the understanding that Mattie could see other men.[36]

Returning to Murfreesboro after Colonel Ready's term in Congress ended, Mattie was courted by a local gentleman named Bonhoare, a man of wealth. He was interested in matrimony as well, but again, for Mattie, romantic love was missing. Finally, after about four years, she was relieved of her indecision about Judge Marshall: he remained loyal to the Union; while the Ready family, including Mattie's brother Horace, became ardent Confederates. It was a good thing she had not married him, Mattie sighed, "for it would have been more than I could stand—with him on one side and brother Horace on the other."[37]

When a regiment of local volunteers marched off to Virginia, Mattie presented them a banner inscribed "Victory or Death." After Fort Henry fell, Mattie and Alice wept, and their mother packed the silver for a swift retreat. When General Johnston abandoned the Kentucky line and withdrew to a defensive position running through Murfreesboro, Colonel Ready became friends with Gen. William J. Hardee, who visited in the Ready home and appointed Horace Ready as an aide on his staff. One day the colonel was strolling through the army camp when he met Morgan and invited him to dinner. He sent a slave home with word that "the famous Captain Morgan" was coming: "Tell Mattie that Captain Morgan is a widower and a little sad. I want her to sing for him."[38]

Morgan felt at home with the Ready family and found excuses to return—to bring captured newspapers or to pick up mail for delivery to a nearby town. In her diary on March 3, 1862, Alice referred to "the already celebrated Capt. John H. Morgan," and told how he had come to the Ready house direct from a raid. A large crowd gathered outside to catch a glimpse of him, and for a few people the attraction of fame overcame propriety: they edged into the great hall of the mansion and stood at the parlor door to gaze at the cavalry officer. Other visits followed, and one night after dinner, as the servants poured refreshments from the colonel's fine wine cellar, Morgan overcame his shyness and began recounting his exploits—how he had burned bridges, captured stragglers, and destroyed telegraph equipment. "He would become excited, his eyes flash, and cheeks flush," Alice noted.[39]

Romance blossomed—storybook love like that in romantic fiction and poetry; and the gallant horseman set his heart upon winning new laurels for the princess. On Friday, March 7, 1862, Morgan halted a command of twenty-six men, including a few Texas Rangers, before the Ready house, dismounted, and asked for Mattie and Alice. He informed them that in their honor he was on his way to Nashville to capture a Union general to exchange for Gen. Simon Bolivar Buckner, taken prisoner at Fort Donelson. After promising to deliver the prisoner to their door upon his return, Morgan mounted and rode away at the head of his men.[40]

Dressed in Union overcoats the party proceeded through farms and on backroads to the Lunatic Asylum, six miles southeast of Nashville. Hiding in a clump of woods, they pounced on passers-by on the pike. When a wagon train came along, it was suddenly surrounded by six mounted men. The unsuspecting wagoners halted, assuming they were Union soldiers checking passes.

"Cut your traces," Morgan directed.

"This is going too far, sir," the head driver said. "What do you mean?"

"Obey me instantly or it shall go further," Morgan thundered. "I'll show you what it means." He and his men drew their revolvers and leveled them at the wagoners. Realizing they had been captured by the enemy, they surrendered, carrying out Morgan's further instructions with haste.[41]

Soon Morgan had over eighty prisoners, but no general. He sent off his men and prisoners in three detachments in different directions, but as Duke said, "this sort of service always gave him great pleasure, and he was loth to give it up"; therefore, Morgan rode on alone. He soon discovered a Federal cavalry detachment stopped at a house beside the road. There was another small dwelling nearby, and he approached and asked the man of the house for a drink. The citizen fetched a bucket of water, and taking a mouthful from the gourd dipper, John spit it out on the ground. "It tastes bad," he swore. Then looking the man sternly in the eye and raising his voice he demanded, "Tell me instantly the name of one of those men yonder in picket." The man replied that one was Lieutenant Burns. "Well," said Morgan, "they are not doing their duty there." Checking that his blue coat was buttoned, he rode up to the Federal officer.

"How are matters, Lieutenant Burns?" he asked.

"All right, Colonel."

"Where are your men?"

"In the house there."

"Nice way of attending to your duty, sir. Consider yourself under arrest and hand me your sword and pistol."

Burns obeyed and, following Morgan's instructions, ordered his five men out one at a time. Morgan took their weapons and ordered them to mount and march. They assumed they were being taken to headquarters.

"We are going in the wrong direction, Colonel," Burns said.

"No, it's all right. I am Captain Morgan." Only then did Burns and his squad realize they were prisoners of war.[42]

In camp a few days later, a stout-looking young man from this detail said:

"Morgan, I have often heard of your feats and never believed them, nor did I believe any one man could take me prisoner, much less one man take six. I shall be ashamed to go home again or acknowledge I was in the war, for I profess to be a fighting man." Then, his temper rising, he got to the point: "I can whip you sure." John smiled and said pleasantly: "Oh, never mind, we will take good care of you; your pay will go on, and you will run no risk of being killed."[43]

While Morgan was capturing Burns, however, the main body of his command had been overtaken by the 4th Ohio Cavalry. In a running fight, they were scattered; some were taken captive themselves; and most of the Union prisoners escaped. It took until Sunday morning to round the raiders up, but they still had thirty-eight prisoners in all.

By Saturday night, when Morgan had not returned, the Readys grew worried. On Sunday morning Alice and Mattie were in church when they received a note from Morgan saying that he was on his way with prisoners. Unable to sit through the sermon, the girls left and spread the word that Morgan was coming. A large crowd had gathered in front of the Ready home when the heroes rode into town. "The first signal of their approach was a number of Texan Rangers galloping by here on horseback to the first street crossing the one below," Alice recorded. "In a much shorter time than I can write it, the grand Cavalcade appeared from that street. There was I suppose 60 or 70 horsemen including prisoners and with Morgan and [Lt. Col. Robert] Wood at the head. As soon as they came in sight it seemed impossible for any one to sustain their enthusiasm. There were heartfelt cheers and waving of handkerchiefs."[44]

Halting the center of the column at the Ready door, Morgan raised his hat and said to the sisters: "Ladies, I present you with your prisoners. What disposal shall be made of them?" Mattie replied: "You have performed your part so well, we are willing to entrust it all to you." With their prisoners, the heroes remained fifteen or twenty minutes, savoring the moment of glory.[45]

In addition to taking prisoners and harassing the Union army, the asylum raid produced useful military intelligence. Interrogation of the captives revealed that Buell had about 65,000 men in Nashville and that no preparations were underway for an advance. The information was forwarded immediately to General Johnston. Morgan's official report told how he had posed as a Union officer, and General Hardee approved. Endorsing the report as an account of "another gallant act performed by this valuable officer," he recommended Morgan's promotion to colonel.[46]

Soon after that expedition, a rumor came that General Buell was about to hang four of Morgan's men captured on the raid. They were to be executed as outlaws, in violation of the rules of war, the report held. Rather than going through channels, Morgan set out under flag of truce to see Buell—a captain proposing to negotiate with a general. But on the road to Nashville the truce party met head on with a cavalry force under Gen. Ormsby M. Mitchel, coming out to seek and destroy Morgan. Mitchel, a graduate of West Point and an astronomy professor at Cincinnati College before the war, was exasperated that his expedition ended with a truce, and even though he furnished safe escort to headquarters, he spread the word that Morgan had abused the white flag, using it to thwart his mission. This was the first of many times Morgan would be accused of violating the flag of truce.[47]

Buell was astounded when Morgan arrived at headquarters. How could an enemy captain, in command of less than 100 men, request a personal interview with a general in charge of 65,000? But thanks to widespread informality in both armies plus Morgan's audacity and willingness, in guerrilla fashion, to make his own rules, the meeting did take place.

Buell asked to what circumstances he was indebted for the honor of the visit. Morgan replied that he was on a Christian errand: he had heard of Buell's threat to hang four of his men, and he wanted to inform the general that he had thirty-six Federal prisoners and would hang nine Federals for every one of his men. Buell disclaimed the rumor and declared that he would never violate the rules of civilized warfare. Morgan then proposed to exchange the thirty-six prisoners for his four men, saying that the disparity in numbers was a fair valuation of his own brave soldiers. Buell replied that he was compelled to decline, as he could not negotiate with an officer inferior in rank. "That is unfortunate, sir," Morgan said, "as the objection could not hold good in any other sense," and the interview ended. Buell's restraint was wise; Morgan's threat of retaliation represented the danger of a breakdown of international law and an escalation of violence.[48]

Morgan's next raid occurred when he learned from informers that Gallatin, Tennessee, on the main L&N line north of Nashville, was ungarrisoned. Keeping the destination secret, he organized a command of forty men and sent them out of Murfreesboro in separate squads on Saturday, March 15, at 4:00 P.M. To Colonel Ready, who accompanied him to the outskirts of town, he said, "Tell the young ladies I will bring them a trophy on my return." Dressed in blue overcoats, the men marched all night through Union territory, reaching the loosely guarded area behind the lines before daybreak. On the road he was kept informed of enemy movements by a system of runners established by a trusted citizen of Murfreesboro, probably Ready. As he had in the Green River area, John was taking advantage of the friendly local population.[49]

Disguised as Federals, Morgan and his aide, Lt. Col. Robert Wood, a grandson of President Zachary Taylor, trotted into Gallatin at 4:00 P.M. on Sunday afternoon and went to the telegraph office at the railroad depot.

"Good day, sir. What news have you?" Morgan asked the operator.

"Nothing sir, except it is reported that damned rebel, Capt. John Morgan, is this side of the Cumberland with some of his cavalry." Then drawing his navy revolver and flourishing it as if to demonstrate how desperately he would use it, he continued, "I wish I could get sight of the damned rascal. I'd make a hole through him larger than he would find pleasant."

"Do you know who I am?" Morgan asked quietly.

"I have not that pleasure."

"Well, I am Captain Morgan."

The operator dropped his gun, turned pale, and kept quiet while Morgan and Wood gathered up his code books and secret dispatches, which, along with other intelligence acquired on the raid, enabled Morgan to report to Johnston with perfect accuracy that Buell's army in Nashville had begun to move—with the intention, as it turned out, to unite with Gen. Ulysses S. Grant in southwest Tennessee, where Johnston would fight them in the battle of Shiloh.[50]

By now Morgan's roleplaying had become a ritual, and he sought opportunities to experience the euphoria of posing as a Union officer. He played each role for all it was worth, extended the mood as long as possible, and became convinced that he was clairvoyant, able to sense imminent attacks from the enemy.[51]

Morgan derived further personal pleasure by conducting good-humored, sardonic repartee with George Prentice, editor of the Louisville *Journal*, a Yankee paper. A man of medium stature with stout, sloping shoulders, Prentice suffered from *chorea scriptorum*, or scriveners cramp; he could not write except for a few scribbles with a pen enlarged with silk wrapping. Nevertheless, he became one of the most colorful editors in the war, dictating copy for twelve hours each day, pausing to retrieve hasty notes on scraps of paper thrust in his hat and pockets. His wife was Southern, and his two sons fought with Morgan; one was killed in action. Yet Prentice appreciated the guerrilla nature of Morgan's tactics, and he comprehended that his readers, both Northern and Southern, were greatly fascinated with everything Morgan did.[52]

When Morgan read an article in the *Journal* that described him as "a thieving, pillaging marauder for whom hanging was none too good," he had the telegraph operator reply that if Prentice would visit the war zone, Morgan would capture him. Several days later Prentice printed Morgan's telegram and continued the dialogue by styling Morgan and Wood a "precious pair of bandits" and wandering robbers. "They may congratulate themselves that they have no consciences, but, unfortunately for them, they have necks, and we nooses. We have no doubt that they feel shockingly nervous and catch their breath at the sight of a rope-walk, and shudder at the apparition of everything bearing the slightest resemblance to two up-rights and a cross-piece."[53]

Gallatin was renowned for its zeal in the Southern cause, and when Morgan announced that they would spend the night, the entire population—men, women, and children—rallied to meet their needs. The women swooped around his horse, Black Bess, clipping locks of hair from her mane and tail, until she was taken to the livery for protection. When an engine and tender came through with a construction gang, Morgan's guards captured it, and the next morning the citizens assisted in destroying the railroad water tank and burning nine boxcars. Then they filled the boiler of the locomotive with turpentine, and shutting all the valves of the engine, gave it a full head of steam and started it on the road toward Nashville. Eight hundred yards down the track it exploded. When Morgan's command left town, a large group of women followed for several miles.[54]

Morgan had acquired useful intelligence and had cut the L&N Railroad for a few days. Wanting to tell Mattie about it on his way south to link up with the withdrawing Confederate Army, he sent her a note asking whether Murfreesboro was clear of Federals. She hurriedly penned a reply: "They are eight miles from here. Come in haste," and handed it to the courier. A few hours later, in the early morning, Morgan appeared with five prisoners. He and Mattie talked until daylight, and family tradition holds that they became engaged on that March nineteenth. At dawn he bade her farewell by forming the soldiers on the square and leading in the singing of "Cheer, Boys, Cheer" in the "sweetest tones." Tom Morgan, who had transferred to John's company, sang the solo part, and "all seemed to mellow and soften their voices to suit the time and occasion."[55]

In five and a half months of guerrilla warfare, Morgan had done nothing of great military significance, but for a captain in command of a single company it was an outstanding record—enough to gain him promotion to colonel, effective April 4. He had killed a few Union soldiers, captured over twice his own number, and brought terror to the hearts of many pickets. He had demolished a small railroad trestle and a few train stations, destroyed a locomotive and nine cars, delayed a new telegraph line for a few days, and burned a ferryboat and steamboat. Probably of greatest immediate military significance, he had obtained accurate and valuable intelligence. His superiors assured him that he would be allowed to continue guerrilla fighting, and he looked forward to new adventures with compelling anticipation. He had no way of knowing that his career already had national significance or that his name was a household word throughout the Confederacy.

SEVEN

"O! For a Dozen Morgans"

News of Morgan's exploits in the vicinity of Nashville rang through the South. In late March, Gen. Mansfield Lovell in New Orleans named fortifications on the Mississippi River above Baton Rouge "Fort John Morgan" in honor of "the gallant Kentucky Ranger, whose daring and dazzling exploits have recently won the admiration of his countrymen." A war correspondent reported: "He is incessantly on the move, appearing suddenly and unexpectedly at some other place more than a hundred miles distant." Another proclaimed: "He has a way of finding out things which no one but himself, or one equally fertile in resources and schemes, could invent. He knows all the movements of the Yankee Generals—where they sleep at night, and where they intend to go next day. We doubt if the world contains his superior on this line. He is certainly the Marion of this war." Marching south to Huntsville, he was greeted for the first time by large crowds everywhere along the route, giving him a continual ovation.[1]

The unofficial sobriquet "the Marion of the War" was one of the highest awards the people had to give—Morgan was the only Confederate leader continually associated with a hero of the American Revolution. Gen. Francis Marion was the most successful guerrilla leader in the Revolutionary War. With his backcountry militia he struck at British outposts and communication lines in the South Carolina swamps, effectively supporting the main army with the tactics of attrition. He fought with hit-and-run raids, ambush, surprise and night marches, and night attacks. He used horses for mobility and frequently dismounted to fight. Making his own rules, he set aside international law to violate flags of truce and shoot picket guards. Mason L. Weems, the mythmaker who initiated the apotheosis of George Washington, also glorified Marion, coauthoring with Peter Horry a book that transported Marion into folklore as the Swamp Fox and the Robin Hood of the Revolution. Then, in 1844, popular Southern writer William Gilmore Simms published a biography of Marion, presenting him as a pure and noble spirit, a true model for sons of the South.[2]

In March, 1862, Southerners styled Morgan the second Marion. Charlestonian Paul H. Hayne, poet laureate of the Confederacy, wrote and published "The Kentucky Partisan," a poem connecting Morgan to Marion and his fellow guerrilla Thomas Sumter, the Gamecock:

Hath the wily Swamp Fox
 Come again to earth?
Hath the soul of Sumter
 Owned a second birth?
From the Western hill-slopes
 Starts a hero-form,
Stalwart, like the oak tree,
 Tameless, like the storm!
His an eye of lightning!
 His a heart of steel!
Flashing deadly vengeance,
 Thrilled with fiery zeal!
Hound him down, ye minions!
 Seize him—if ye can;
But woe worth the hireling knave
 Who meets him, man to man![3]

Naming Morgan the "Marion of the West," Hayne exulted: "God! Who would not gladly die, / Beside that glorious man?"[4]

It was significant that Marion was a *Southern* hero of the Revolution. His reincarnation in the person of Morgan was part of the Confederate identification with the high ideals and success of the American Revolution, as well as with a hero of Southern history.

As a folk hero Morgan also mirrored Southern society's affinity for the chivalric theme. The romance was a new literary genre that involved the expression of unrepressed feelings and free exercise of the imagination, rather than strict fidelity to reality. History was retold; the past was fictionalized and present institutions mythified; the never-never became a mode for the here-and-now. Southerners cast themselves in roles that preserved their honor; they embraced the romantic cult of chivalry to justify slavery, the hierarchical system, and the aristocratic way of life. European romanticism entered the culture through Southern periodicals such as the *Southern Literary Messenger, Southern Quarterly Review,* and *DeBow's Review,* but the chief vehicle was historical novels.[5]

The historical romances of Sir Walter Scott, the Scottish author, were America's first best-sellers; they were read throughout the nation but especially in the South. Mark Twain wrote in the 1880s that the South had "Sir Walter disease," an illness that "sets the world in love with dreams and phantoms." Scott's books strengthened the chivalric ideal and the code of the country gentleman who was characterized by hospitality, courtesy, deference to women, and defense of honor. Another theme in Scott's novels was the practice of glamorized guerrilla warfare. The novel *Rob Roy* was based on the life of Rob Roy MacGregor Campbell, leader of an uprising in Scotland in 1715. Scott romanticized Roy Roy as a sort of Robin Hood of Scotland, an outlaw whose band of clansmen raided the duke's cattle herds and castle and stole rent money from the duke's tenants. Ever elusive, Rob Roy fought with hit-and-run tactics, and his career was marked by adventurous deeds and hairbreadth escapes.

Following Scott, Southern writers reinforced the myth of chivalry, using it to demonstrate that the South was unique and its social patterns ordained. They wrote of sentimentality, patriotism, rousing adventure and glory. In 1836, Beverley Tucker of Virginia published *The Partisan Leader,* a novel that warned against the election of Martin Van Buren as president and predicted secession and Civil War in 1849 over the tariff issue. Tucker glorified and recommended partisan war as the best strategy to fight the North.[6]

William Gilmore Simms agreed with Tucker. Author of more than eighty books and the most important Southern writer in the 1830s and 1840s, he saw evidence of Southern superiority in the victory of Francis Marion and other Southern guerrillas of the American Revolution.[7]

In a series of seven novels, beginning with *The Partisan* in 1835, Simms heralded the guerrillas of the Revolution as forerunners and models for the secession movement. Captain Porgy, a fictional guerrilla chief of aristocratic breeding, fought alongside Francis Marion in what in the pen of Simms became an epic movement that not only drove out the British invaders but united the region in triumph, hope, and jubilation. His vision was of the South defending its unique way of life through the chivalric code—like medieval knights, high-bred planters trained in arms and horsemanship would use partisan tactics to repel invasion, inspire and unify the Southern people.[8]

The association of partisan tactics with chivalry partly explains why Morgan became the representative of the chivalric code to many Southerners.[9] The Richmond *Whig* declared: "The exploits of Captain Morgan are more like the romantic and daring feats of the days of knighthood and chivalry than anything else we can compare them to." When the 2nd Georgia Battalion of Mounted Partisan Rangers voted unanimously to transfer to Morgan's command, their leader affirmed: "The record of your chivalry and daring has fired their enthusiasm and awakened a most anxious desire to share the perils and glory of 'Morgan's men.'" Kate Cumming, a nurse and hospital administrator from Mobile, considered Morgan "brave, chivalrous and patriotic." To some he was the "prince of chivalry." His second in command, brother-in-law Basil Duke, said he was a practical man but "irresistibly reminded one of the heroes of romance."[10]

A journalist in Mobile declared that Morgan's "gallant and knightly valor and chivalry" brought him nearer to the hearts of his countrymen than any other leader. "The sentiment which the people feel for Morgan is the personal affection conciliated by admiration for the man, and his fame will be as enduring as that of the more prominent leaders of our armies, whose high position charges them with the chief responsibility of our country's fortunes. Their glory will be deservedly proportionate; but the name of Morgan will live in history side by side with theirs, as Marion's does with Washington."

The mayor of Danville, Virginia, proclaimed Morgan "the recognized representative of chivalry, patriotism and daring and indomitable courage." One analyst stated: "His knightly and heroic deeds will live freshly in the memories of his admiring country men, and glow brightly on the historic page."[11]

Morgan had not only become the second Marion, he inspired a grassroots movement for the adoption of guerrilla warfare as a national strategy to complement the regular Confederate army. The myth of Southern superiority had fueled widespread frustration with Jefferson Davis's defensive strategy. The Richmond *Whig* declared that in boyhood, Southerners acquired familiarity with arms and horses: "Their highest ambition is to meet the enemy. Action—action—action is that for which they pant—and is that alone which can satisfy the cravings of their impetuous hearts."[12]

The Confederates won at First Bull Run, but from the West came news of the catastrophic surrender of about 12,000 men at Fort Donelson on the Cumberland River. The Tennessee and Cumberland Rivers and the strategic supply center of Nashville were lost; Union soldiers invaded western Tennessee. The *Whig* protested: "This sort of war is unworthy of the Southern Confederacy. We must change it in *toto*"; the editor went on to propose an invasion of Pennsylvania. Then General McClellan's 100,000-man Army of the Potomac—the most formidable military force the American people had yet seen—invaded Virginia and began moving up the peninsula toward Richmond.[13]

President Davis called Lee to Richmond as his adviser, and Lee decided it was time to change to an offensive-defensive strategy. He recommended that Richmond be defended by a concentrated offensive in the Shenandoah Valley which would draw Federal strength from the peninsula and force the enemy to disperse. Out of his urgings came Stonewall Jackson's brilliant campaign in April and May, 1862.[14]

The people approved of the shift in policy, but they had an addendum of their own: like Spain against Napoleon, the Confederacy should adopt the guerrilla strategy, writers proclaimed.[15]

This was not the first time demand for partisans had been made. At the beginning of the war, the Virginia legislature had authorized ten companies of partisan rangers to secure western Virginia. And there had been frenzied appeals to the Confederate government for authority to organize guerrilla units. On June 18, 1861, Assistant Adj. Gen. N.H. Chilton ordered that irregular organizations were to be enrolled and used by generals in the field. President Davis and his advisers in the War Department believed in conventional tactics, however; on March 19, 1862, Acting Secretary of War Judah P. Benjamin reversed Chilton. "Guerrilla companies are not recognized as part of the military organization of the Confederate States, and cannot be authorized by this Department," he declared.[16]

The government notwithstanding, many people regarded Morgan's success as confirmation of the potential of guerrilla war. With Turner Ashby of

Virginia, Sterling Price of Missouri, and others, the movement would probably have occurred without Morgan, but he was recognized as the model guerrilla. In Murfreesboro, Alice Ready defended his killing of pickets: "I think he is right and only wish we had more such men," she sighed. "O! for a dozen Morgans." The Richmond *Examiner* declared: "The recent astonishing feats of Jack Morgan in Kentucky and Tennessee afford examples of what enterprise may do." The Atlanta *Confederacy* affirmed that Morgan's company had given the Yankees more trouble then any other. The Huntsville *Democrat* advocated organization of guerrilla companies everywhere: "We believe that the Guerilla service affords the most favorable opening for effective warfare of all the modes of service in the Confederate Army. Small bodies of men, under cool, bold, daring leaders, who count not the cost, provided they can serve their country efficiently, such as Capt. John H. Morgan has proved himself to be, would be of vast service."[17]

On April 2, the Richmond *Whig* reproached the Confederate government for not encouraging men who wanted to enlist as guerrillas. "Many truehearted and daring sons of the South have asked leave to raise small parties of men to fight the enemy in their own way wherever they might be able to find him, whether inside or outside of his lines." If the Yankees in Nashville were terrified of Morgan, the editorial continued "what would they say and do if there was a guerilla party, headed by a Jack Morgan at every available point of their advance into the South?"[18]

Other Southern newspapers concurred. The New Orleans *Crescent* pronounced: "We see the heroic Morgan, with only one hundred men at his back, keeping the invaders in constant terror, killing and capturing the enemy's pickets, destroying their means of transportation, and harassing them in every conceivable way." The Vicksburg *Whig* urged: "Let us have such a war as Capt. John Morgan is now waging in the vicinity of Nashville." An editorial printed in Knoxville and Atlanta recommended: "We should have a Morgan with his band, to cut off and destroy supplies, burn bridges, tear up roads, and harass, annoy and cripple the vile Hessian invaders, on every mile of road between the Confederate lines and the Ohio River." The Lynchburg *Virginian* exhorted: "Bands of determined men led by dashing officers like Ashby and Morgan, hanging upon the rear of the enemy in every part of the country, would soon convince them that they were dealing with a people 'terribly in earnest.'"[19]

The graduating class at Virginia Medical College heard a commencement address on guerrilla warfare by Virginia Congressman Charles W. Russell. If Richmond and all Southern cities were lost, he said, and the regular armies defeated, guerrilla bands would continue the fight. "At last, the enemy, exhausted even to despair by a vain pursuit of impracticable conquest, would have to abandon the country to independence." The *Southern Literary Messenger* agreed: if all the cities and armies fell, the spirit of the people would live, and "we must trust solely to guerillas."[20]

DeBow's Review declared: "We must prepare ourselves for a guerilla war. The enemy must be conquered; and any method by which we can honorably do it must be resorted to." A nation with the geographical size and population of the Confederacy could never be defeated as long as the people were united and determined. "A People in Arms" would be invincible and would melt away the Union armies like an iceberg floating into a tropical sea. If perchance the men in occupied territory should fail to fight in the resistance movement, "it may well be doubted whether the citizens of Virginia are made of such stuff as fits them to preserve freedom, or entitles them to it," the Richmond *Enquirer* emphasized.[21]

A company of volunteers began organizing in Richmond and another in Atlanta. While their recruiting was going forward, a bill was introduced in the Confederate House of Representatives on April 8, the day after Shiloh, authorizing the President to commission units of partisan rangers for detached guerrilla war. It passed in the House with no problem, but the Senate military committee recommended against it because it would weaken the Conscription Act passed on April 16. The first surge of volunteering had subsided, and able-bodied men between eighteen and thirty-five were required in the ranks of the regular army. The Richmond *Enquirer* assured senators that guerrillas were unfit for regular duty anyway. They would be "genuine 'bloods,' reckless of danger and dissatisfied with an unproductive security. Such men have no more business in the ranks of a massive army than strong men, in this hour of our country's need, have at home. Their impetuosity is not adaptable to the rules and tactics of pitched battles and organized warfare, but is peculiarly fitted" to guerrilla war.[22]

When the bill came up for final debate in the Senate on April 21, Senator Henry C. Burnett of Kentucky spoke in its defense. Playing upon the underlying Southern prejudice against West Point, Burnett claimed that irregular fighting was superior to the conventional tactics taught at West Point. There were 304 West Point graduates in the Confederate army, and most of the accomplished officers were among them, but many Southerners discounted military training, insisting that the intuitive Southern spirit was more essential. The law was necessary to give the President authority to issue commissions in spite of West Point generals. The brilliant achievements of Morgan and others, as one editor proclaimed, had "thrown a shade over the most polished graduates of that far-famed institution."[23]

When Senator Burnett finished speaking, a loud burst of applause came from a group of soldiers in the gallery. It was the first such disruption in the Senate, and the somber solons were open-mouthed with shock. Senator Louis T. Wigfall of Texas said the outburst befitted the mob in Washington but not Southern gentlemen and demanded that the gallery be cleared of spectators. Calmer heads prevailed, however, and the soldiers were allowed to observe the enactment of the bill.[24]

Entered as "An Act to organize bands of Partisan Rangers," it gave the

President authority to commission rangers in companies, battalions, or regiments. They were to be received in the regular army; they would have the same pay, rations, and quarters and be subject to the same regulations as regular troops. However, following the precedent of Sumter in the Revolution, the government was to pay them in cash for captured munitions of war—this was to give them incentive to be aggressive. Like Morgan, the rangers were in the army; like him, they were to conduct guerrilla warfare behind the lines of the invading armies.[25]

The response was enthusiastic. Recruits could remain close to home, avoid the tedium of camp life and the drudgery and discipline of regular service, and have adventure, fame, and glory at the same time. From remote byways, wooded mountains and dark valleys, swamps and marshes, from every corner they came—foxhunters, mountaineers, and woodsmen, carrying their trusty rifles. A correspondent in Florida reported: "Our guerrilla parties occupy nearly every hammock and cross-road in the east, and have already struck terror to the enemy by their bold attacks upon their pickets." And from Mobile: "One of the most cheering signs of the times is the rapid increase of our partisan forces, and the daring and vigorous operations by which they render the invaded sections so hot for the enemy."[26]

An aura of romance surrounded the movement; an Atlanta editor avowed: "To the young and daring it has the charm as well as the romance of the Knight arrantry in the days when a 'Richard of the Lion Heart' dared Saladin and his Moslem hosts in the 'Holy Land.' To indulge in the same spirit of chivalry that animated the Christian Knights in that older time, is now the privilege of our gallant youth."[27]

A poem entitled "Guerrillas" encouraged partisans to creep up on the enemy and slay him at his campfires in the night. "The Guerrilla's Song" urged them to grant no quarter—that is, take no prisoners. And a melodrama, *The Guerrillas*, played at the Richmond Varieties Theater during the Christmas holidays in 1862. One performance was attended by several veterans of the battle of Fredericksburg, a great recent victory for the Confederate army. During the scene when the guerrilla chief returned home to find his farm in ruins and his parents murdered, a stillness fell over the audience, and there was perfect silence in the theater. But as the chief began his oath of vengeance on the vile Yankees, a soldier in the back on the main floor sprang to his feet, waved his hat, and exclaimed: "That's like Fredericksburg; we paid the Yankees there!"[28]

There was danger that Union generals would treat the partisan rangers as outlaws and execute them when captured. General Sherman accused them of committing illegal acts and protested: "If we allow the passions of our men to get full command then indeed will this war become a reproach to the names of liberty and civilization." When a Federal commander on the northern border of Virginia threatened to burn and lay waste private property in retaliation for partisan raids, the Virginia legislature passed a resolution,

May 17, 1862, defending the warfare as "perfectly legitimate," and encouraged its vigorous prosecution. In western Virginia a Union commander had two Virginia state partisans court-martialed, and they were sentenced to be hanged. The Richmond *Whig* threatened retaliation on prisoners of corresponding rank: "Let the enemy hang the Rangers, and the war will be in earnest." In the end, the Union officials exercised restraint as Buell did in his Nashville encounter with Morgan. The Virginia partisans were not executed.[29]

General-in-Chief of the Union Armies Henry W. Halleck did not know how to deal with the partisans. In 1861 he had written a book on international law in which he made no distinction between outlaw "free-booters" and partisans. To him, all irregulars were illegal, and men captured while engaged in any kind of guerrilla warfare were not guaranteed the rights of prisoners of war. As a departmental commander in the West in March, 1862—before the partisan act passed—he had said guerrillas should be hanged as robbers and murderers.[30]

At least Halleck was responsible enough to admit his confusion, and when he became general-in-chief, he sought the opinion of a scholarly expert, Dr. Francis Lieber, a professor at Columbia College in New York. On August 6, 1862, Halleck requested a definition of guerrilla warfare. Lieber responded with an essay entitled "Guerrilla Parties Considered with Reference to the Laws and Usages of War." He defined *guerrillas* as unauthorized outlaw bands carrying out robbery and depredation outside the authority of the army or government. He agreed with Halleck that such men were criminals and did not have the rights of prisoners of war. *Partisan* troops, on the other hand, were detached bodies of the regular army, a definition that fit the rangers organized under the partisan act, as well as Morgan and several other irregulars.[31]

The partisan leader commands a corps whose object is to injure the enemy by action separate from that of his own main army; the partisan acts chiefly upon the enemy's lines of connection and communications, and outside of or beyond the lines of operation of his own army, in the rear and on the flanks of the enemy. Rapid and varying movements and surprises are the chief means of his success; but he is part and parcel of the army, and, as such, considered entitled to the privileges of the law of war, so long as he does not transgress it.[32]

By sanctioning the type of warfare practiced by Confederate partisans, Lieber contributed to the prevention of an inhumane policy of retaliation. Halleck and the Lincoln administration accepted his definition and issued orders on November 20, 1862, that partisan rangers were to be exchanged when captured.[33] Another result of his essay was to strengthen the popular definition of "guerrillas" as "outlaws"—such as William C. Quantrill, who committed crimes totally without authority of any government. There were many such criminals, both pro-Confederate and pro-Union, but they answered only to themselves. Units conducting authorized irregular warfare usually referred to themselves as partisans, to be distinguished from the criminal gangs. For students of the war, the confusion continues. One reason more attention has not been given to the practice of classic guerrilla warfare by Morgan and others is that "guerrilla" has meant "outlaw" to the Civil War scholar.

Lieber's definition was reemphasized in General Orders no. 100, issued by the Union War Department on April 24, 1863. By and large, Union commanders followed the official policy and treated partisans as prisoners of war, but individuals sometimes followed their own feelings. Grant ordered on August 16, 1864: "Where any of Mosby's men are caught hang them without trial."[34]

Lincoln, who hoped to avoid bloody retaliation, was more inclined toward leniency than his generals. In the spring of 1863, when guerrilla raids by Morgan, Forrest, and others had tied down thousands of Union soldiers on garrison duty, he predicted that as the rebellion grew weaker and Union forces stronger, the Confederacy would turn increasingly to guerrilla warfare. His solution was to recruit freedmen for garrison service, freeing white soldiers for the front lines. He refrained from harsh and vindictive policies, hoping the South would not be driven to "a violent and remorseless revolutionary struggle." Lincoln's overall strategy included basic aspects of counter insurgency in that it cut off outside assistance to the rebels and aimed to break the will of the people to resist.[35]

A few partisan units operated behind enemy lines and complemented the efforts of the main armies, as they were meant to do. In August, 1862, Capt. R.G. Earl led a company armed with shotguns in a raid on a Union supply center in northern Alabama, killing twenty-eight enemy troops and burning 500 bales of Yankee cotton. In the Shenandoah Valley partisans conducted reconnaissance and raided enemy communications in exemplary fashion. John D. Imboden's 1st Virginia Partisan Rangers supported Stonewall Jackson's Valley campaign and in May, 1864, assisted General Breckinridge in one of the war's most effective uses of partisans in close cooperation with a large army. Breckinridge had Imboden's cavalry and partisans under John H. McNeill, Harry W. Gilmor, and John S. Mosby harass the flanks and rear of Union Gen. Franz Sigel's army, marching southward in the Valley. Striking the Baltimore and Ohio Railroad at Piedmont, Virginia, the intrepid Mc-Neill and his fellow partisans slowed the Union advance to a crawl, giving Breckinridge time to prepare for victory over Sigel at the battle of New Market.[36]

By far the most successful command organized under the partisan act was that of John S. Mosby. With a tiny physical frame and a slight stoop in the shoulders, he made up for his size by wearing a scarlet cape, gray felt hat with ostrich plume, and two Colt revolvers with brass studs. By constantly threatening Union columns in northern Virginia, he earned the respect of Stuart, Lee, and Secretary of War James A. Seddon. Lee once exclaimed: "Hurrah for Mosby. I wish I had a hundred like him."[37]

Mosby was like Morgan in preferring the active, dangerous life: "Nothing can reverse my own decision to stay in the foremost ranks, 'where life is lost and freedom won,'" he wrote his wife. Like Morgan, he had had a troubled youth, being expelled from the University of Virginia for shooting a medical student in a hallway. He was pardoned, and went on to become a lawyer. Like Morgan, he occasionally disguised himself and his men as Federals, and he was continually on the move, seldom resting for more than a day. Because he too seemed ubiquitous, he was called the "Gray Ghost."[38]

Unlike Morgan, Mosby favored small raiding parties throughout the war. The largest number of men he led was 350, and he preferred bands of twelve to eighty, who had greater mobility and were easier to conceal. Unlike Morgan, too, he sometimes dispersed his men among the civilian population for concealment, and this practice made him the truest Civil War guerrilla in the classic sense. Morgan became a brigadier general; Mosby rose only to colonel, promoted to that rank on December 7, 1864, late in the war.[39]

Mao Tse-tung said that guerrillas are invincible when they have highly motivated officers, but without dedicated leaders they can do nothing. As long as a guerrilla unit had a Morgan, Mosby, or McNeill as leader, it was successful. The strongest partisan organization in Mississippi was the 1st Mississippi Partisan Rangers, a regiment recruited by Col. William C. Falkner, great-grandfather of William Faulkner. Before the war Colonel Falkner had frequently fought in street affrays in Ripley, Mississippi; he was shot in the left foot in one free-for-all and lost the ends of three fingers of his left hand in another. He shot and killed two men on separate occasions, was tried for murder and acquitted both times. Perhaps his men were afraid not to obey him. In any event, the regiment performed effective service while Falkner was commander. Under less able leaders, however, the same organization became disorganized and undependable.[40]

Reimbursement for Union munitions captured under the partisan act was never a major item in the Confederate budget. In fact, it was not until about a year after the law was enacted that the War Department issued regulations on how payment was to be made. Perhaps it was just as well; in August, 1863, when Mosby asked $30,000 for weapons he had confiscated, Secretary of War Seddon launched an investigation and censured Mosby for too much attention to sutler's wagons and not enough attacks on enemy troop columns.[41]

Worse yet, Richmond was flooded with complaints of villainies suffered at the hands of partisans. In east Tennessee they tore up fences for firewood, stole food, saddles, bridles and horses, allowed their horses to wander into truck gardens and grain fields, insulted citizens, and taunted old Union men by riding them on rails. In the North Carolina mountains they broke open corncribs, fed their horses, and rode away, leaving corn scattered on the ground. They got drunk and terrorized the residents. Gov. Zebulon B. Vance said they were "a grievance, intolerable, damnable, and not to be borne!"[42]

Departmental commanders complained that the indulgent life of the mounted rangers demoralized infantrymen and destroyed discipline: men in the infantry were tempted to desert to join the free-booting partisans. In January, 1864, Gen. Thomas L. Rosser in Virginia wrote to Lee: "Without discipline, order, or organization, they roam broadcast over the country, a band of thieves, stealing, pillaging, plundering, and doing every manner of mischief and crime. They never fight; can't be made to fight."[43]

Within three months of enactment of the law, the War Department began the first of several steps to curb the partisan movement. Responding to reports that volunteering for ranger units was impeding enlistment for regiments of the line, the administration ordered that approval of the general in command of the local department was necessary before a partisan unit could begin recruiting. A few weeks later, on July 31, 1862, General Orders no. 53 removed the exemption of partisans from the conscription law and specified that volunteers enrolled as partisans had to be over thirty-five years old.[44]

In January, 1863, Secretary Seddon reported that the rangers had done more damage to the Southern people than to the enemy, and recommended their transfer to the regular cavalry. During the same month, Stuart and Lee joined the chorus of generals demanding repeal of the partisan act. They agreed that except for Mosby, the partisans were detrimental: "The evils resulting from this organization more than counterbalance the good they accomplish," said Lee. On February 17, 1864, Congress repealed the law, bringing all ranger bands into the regular army except for commands exempted under the discretionary authority of the secretary of war. Seddon made two exemptions—Mosby's and McNeill's men were retained as partisans.[45] The Union policy of leniency had proved in retrospect to be very wise. It avoided escalation of bloodshed and gave time for the partisans to fail and resentment against them to build in the Confederacy.

In the American Revolution, George Washington had adopted the strategy of attrition, with the goal of exhaustion of the enemy. It was a defensive strategy arising out of American weakness, putting the burden on Britain to suppress the rebellion. Washington realized that the Continental army could win independence by retaining an army in the field; the patriots could ultimately win by not losing. The object was to maintain resistance until political opposition in the British government forced the nation to abandon the war.[46]

In order to maintain the support of the people, state governments, and Congress, Washington satisfied the patriot movement's aggressive impulses by hit-and-run attacks on the periphery of the British army, raids such as the surprise attack on Trenton. It was Washington's patient strategy that provided the basis for the guerrilla rising in South Carolina; also, the military situation in the Southern theater presented an opportunity for guerrilla activity. The absence of a regular United States army in the South had allowed the British to disperse in small posts, a strategy designed to intimidate rebels and encourage pockets of loyal residents.[47] The warfare conducted by Marion, Sumter, and others on British outposts would have been ineffective on its own, however, for effective guerrilla warfare requires a regular army to force the enemy to remain concentrated. Without such support the guerrillas would have been hunted down and destroyed one by one. Washington therefore ordered Gen. Nathanael Greene to South Carolina as department commander, and he coordinated the guerrilla raids with operations of his field army, in what historian Russell F. Weigley considers the most impressive campaign in the Revolutionary War.[48]

In the Civil War, the enemy of the South was located much closer, had no ocean to cross, and was more determined to win because defeat would mean disruption of the Union and the existence of another nation on the continent, with a lengthy contiguous border. The Union armies invading the South remained concentrated, not dispersed in posts. New transportation and communication enabled them to move faster, with greater coordination. On the other hand, increased accuracy of weapons had given preponderant power to the defense, making obsolete the Napoleonic strategy of annihilation through frontal assaults. The Southern army and nation were stronger and had greater resources than the patriots.[49]

In both situations the enemy had naval superiority, although the Union had more complete control of the seas than had the British. In both, it was up to the enemy to reassert authority over a large area and reestablish political allegiance, and in both, the enemy thought at first in terms of annihilation through conventional warfare by a regular army. But the North's invasion of Confederate territory provided an opportunity for guerrilla operations, which had popular local support, and it is extremely difficult to defeat a guerrilla uprising in such a situation. Much of the South was rough country, with rugged hills, mountains, heavy forests, rivers, and swamps— ideal terrain for guerrillas who were familiar with it and acclimated to it, and who had a sense of fighting for the home hearth. And the lengthy supply and communication lines of the Union were vulnerable to sabotage. As Che Guevara acknowledged: "It is practically impossible to guard every inch of a highway or railroad."[50]

When the partisan act enrolled and uniformed the rangers, it prevented them from fading into the surrounding civilian population between operations and was thus an exception to classic guerrilla warfare. On the other hand, it made them legal soldiers, protected by the laws of war when captured. The law provided a decentralized system of authority, allowing the local guerrilla leader to take advantage of such field conditions as weather, terrain, and situation of the enemy. At the same time, the law provided opportunity for operation in concert with regular armies in the field.

Like Washington, Jefferson Davis began with a defensive strategy, one which took advantage of the fact that all the Confederacy had to do was survive, while the North had the more difficult task of conquest. If he had remained on the defensive, using the strong regular armies to compel the North to concentrate, and having departmental commanders coordinate with guerrilla units, Davis might have stalled the Union juggernaut. The partisan law envisioned a special branch of service complementing the main thrust of the regular armies, a formidable strategic instrument opening a hundred second fronts in the enemy rear, frustrating and wearing down the invaders, nullifying the advantages of superior manpower and resources in the North, and striking at the mind and will of Northern voters. Guerrillas could have paralyzed Union logistics, and many local successes could have changed the relative strength of the opposing forces.

A lengthy guerrilla war might have worn down the resolve of the Northerners. They might have asked, is it worth the bloodshed and political division at home? The revolution might have survived if the Confederacy had established a seemingly hopeless military stalemate, a deadlock. If the South could have demonstrated that the cost of winning the war would be many years of terrible conflict; if the South could have achieved a paralysis of will in the North, encouraging the Peace Democrats to throw Lincoln out in 1864 and elect a candidate who would grant the Confederacy independence and bring the boys home—the war would have been won. General Sherman, who understood the political nature of the war as well as any general, said Morgan and other leaders of raids were the "most dangerous set of men which this war has turned loose upon the world," and he declared that they would have to be killed or captured before peace could be established.[51]

As will be shown later, Bragg used guerrilla strategy effectively in the western theater in 1862, keeping Buell's army tied down while Forrest and Morgan destroyed his supply lines. The trouble was that once Bragg had the initiative, he went on the offensive into Kentucky instead of remaining on the defensive, conserving his strength, attacking outposts, and eroding Buell's army. Later that year, after retreating from Kentucky, Bragg had the unusual distinction of using a significant portion of his regular army to support a guerrilla raid by Morgan's men on Hartsville, Tennessee.

The defensive strategy was used in 1864 by Gen. Joseph E. Johnston north of Atlanta. Outnumbered 100,000 to 62,000, his Army of Tennessee held frontal assaults to a minimum and conserved its strength. Weigley maintains this was "the first western campaign of the Confederacy to be marked throughout by a coherent strategy appropriate to the Confederacy's resources." Arthur Manigault, commander of a South Carolina infantry regiment in Johnston's army, speculated that if Johnston had remained in command, Atlanta would not have fallen. "We always fought to great advantage behind breastworks" under Johnston, he wrote.[52]

After the war, Grant concluded that Johnston's strategy would have been appropriate for the South in general. The North's resources were not limitless, nor were the people united in support of the war. Members of the Democratic Party worried about Lincoln's violation of civil liberties and feared that Republicans were building a one-party system. The abolition of slavery stirred the sensitive issue of race relations. Northern sentiment in favor of the war was somewhat fragile; many wanted the South to go in peace. Furthermore, in modern nationalistic wars, the side with the greatest material strength and population does not always win. Morale plays a vital role, and the stronger power may despair of victory, as did France in Algeria and the United States in Vietnam.[53]

But President Davis was unable to withstand the pressure to take the offensive. Because George Washington's army was admittedly weaker than the British, and the patriot movement was obviously far below Great Britain in strength, the strategy of attrition had seemed reasonable. The Confederates, however, refused to view themselves as underdogs; years of romantic mythmaking had convinced them that they were superior, "invincible and indestructible." Davis came to be regarded as something of a traitor for restraining the great Southern armies from rolling over the inferior Yankees in a quick war of independence.

Lee, trained at West Point like Davis, advocated taking the initiative and defending the South by determining where crucial battles would occur. He adopted the strategy of annihilating the enemy army with decisive Napoleonic battles and, after Antietam, advanced the goal of a victory on Northern soil to force the North to the negotiating table. Grady McWhiney and Perry D. Jamieson have posited that Lee's strategy of the tactical offensive led him to bleed the Southern army to death in hopeless frontal assaults.[54] His offensives, along with thrusts in the West, did give the South an outlet for aggressive impulses. What the Confederacy should have done, however, was to imitate George Washington and satisfy the need for trophies with hit-and-run attacks, operations that would have defended Southern honor and conserved Southern strength at the same time.

As it was, the Confederate strategy left guerrillas out in the cold. The object was not to wear down the enemy gradually but to knock him out with one fatal blow. All resources were to be marshalled for that one climactic battle, when the nation would strike with all its might. Guerrillas seemed to detract from that effort, to take away manpower needed on the big day. They were mavericks who broke the established rules; they were unprofessional and erratic; and they could not be combined in the framework of disciplined armies.

Therefore, few department commanders coordinated with the partisan rangers, and the War Department only tolerated them. President Davis comprehended the value of irregulars as a complementary arm of the regular forces; he realized that they raised public morale, and that most leaders like Morgan and Mosby would be of little use in any other way. Nevertheless, it was his firm conception that the war should be fought with a uniformed, organized army using conventional tactics. Only after his regular forces had surrendered did Davis embrace guerrilla warfare for exhaustion of the enemy. He and his advisers had little appreciation of its potential for long-term attrition; they saw irregulars as regular cavalry operating behind the lines, in close concert with the regular army. The investigation of Mosby illustrates this attitude—Mosby was being warned to behave more like a regular cavalryman and less like a guerrilla.

And yet Mosby and other partisan leaders succeeded without much encouragement and proved their strategic value. If more leaders had done so, perhaps the reservations of the regular commanders could have been overcome. The failure of the partisan rangers in the summer of 1862 reveals that many Southerners lacked the patient dedication necessary to support a successful revolution. Many causes have been suggested for the collapse of the Confederacy, and none seems as fundamental as the disruption of Southern morale. In the end the South's spirit was broken, and its will to fight dissipated.

All the romantic expectations notwithstanding, successful guerrilla warfare was hard and unglamorous, and required a very high degree of allegiance to the cause. It demanded complete renunciation of self and continuing devoted loyalty. Southerners lacked that level of commitment. Looking back, Edward Pollard decided the South did not have a "resolute spirit." There was, he concluded, "a thorough demoralization of the armies and people of the Confederacy; there must have been a general decay of public spirit."[55] The breakdown in Southern morale was presaged by the failure of the partisan act.

Historian Charles Royster proposed that the American Revolution meant the sacrifice of present convenience for a better future. Participants envisioned that the war would redeem the world from the forces of tyranny and guarantee later generations prosperity, harmony, and greatness. The true spirit of 1776 was one of anticipation; hope in the future gave the patriots enthusiasm to defy reasonable calculations of success. Conversely, the Southern revolution meant the defense of present convenience in order to perpetuate the enslavement of black people. In their imaginations, the patriots of 1776 created millions of supporters around the world, people cheering them on in their struggle for liberty.[56] Confederates realized they were isolated, the last society on earth clinging to slavery.

The failure of the partisan act was also a result of the fact that historically, Americans have avoided terrorism, and many Southerners had no taste for guerrilla warfare when it came right down to it. And the failure may indicate that Southerners were more of one mind with their Northern sisters and brothers than they realized. Few Southerners had the dedication to the ideals of the Confederacy necessary for violent guerrilla warfare. In the end, the side that adopted total war was the North. Lincoln, in a hurry to end the conflict, urged his generals to take the offensive and win before political opposition developed at home and before bitterness in the South made restoration of the Union even more difficult. Early in the war, as a commander in the West, Grant had little appreciation for cavalry raids behind enemy lines; on October 30, 1862, he telegraphed that Morgan was not likely to be found at a certain location: "If Morgan is there he will likely run; it is not his policy to fight, but to plunder and interrupt our lines of communication as much as possible." Later, when he became overall commander, he adopted the strategy of attrition, with the main army holding the Confederate army constantly at bay while destructive Union cavalry and infantry raids made war on the economic resources of the South and the morale of the people. He instructed one of his commanders: "This expedition goes to destroy and not to fight battles." And thus it was that during the course of the war the South moved away from total war and the North moved toward it.[57]

Some of the same Southern newspapers that advocated guerrilla war in 1862 condemned it when Union cavalry regiments began raiding deep into the Confederacy in the summer of 1863. They called the Northern raiders "mounted bandits" violating humanity and honorable warfare. It was robbery, arson, murder, "a mode of warfare recognized by no code nor creed of civilization." A Knoxville paper called a Yankee raid a "mongrel monster alive and hideous"; it was "neither Christian, heathen nor human; but fiendish, satanic and devilish, and upon the whole profitless. . . . Such an incursion weighs nothing and determines nothing as to the great final result of the war."[58]

John Hunt Morgan was the primary model for the popular movement for guerrilla warfare resulting in the partisan act. Few partisan commands had leaders as able as Morgan, however, and most did more harm than good. The failure of the law and its repeal indicated the level of commitment of the Southern people as revolutionaries.

EIGHT

From Shiloh to Cave City

In Huntsville, Alabama, during the brief lull in military activity after his raid on Gallatin on March 16, 1862, John Hunt Morgan soon tired of innocent diversions and longed for more tantalizing entertainment. The people of Huntsville, proud of him as a native son, welcomed him royally. His host, John T. Fackler, held a party in Morgan's honor, and Fackler's young daughter Gypsy sang for the guests. Morgan made her honorary adjutant of the squadron, and Duke wrote out the commission in verse. After a few days, though, John felt the sadness coming on. He had not had a furlough since he joined the army, which was not unusual, but he knew himself well enough to realize that his personal morale was essential.[1]

It was common knowledge that the most lively center of night life in the upper Confederacy was the capital city of Richmond. There beautiful young prostitutes worked in brothels such as Eliza Herbard's on Cary Street, and they plied their trade on the sidewalks and in hacks and carriages on the streets. Every night on the upper stories of business houses on Main Street, gambling tables were spread; dealers dealt the cards; and gentlemen smoked cigars, sipped whiskey and water, and wagered thousands of dollars. Morgan's friend from Louisville, Blanton Duncan, was there, working for the Confederate government, and they could party all night. Richmond was almost 600 miles away, but riding the trains would relieve the boredom. Leaving Duke in charge of the men, therefore, he headed for Richmond—absent without leave.[2]

He had expected to travel anonymously but found that he was recognized everywhere. In Lynchburg the local paper noted his visit, heralding him as "the Marion of the War, whose deeds of chivalric daring in the West have made his name a familiar household word in every family in the South, and spread terror throughout the ranks of the enemy in Tennessee." Arriving in Richmond the following evening and checking into Spotswood Hotel, he found the town "all agog to see him." Obviously, his plans for a quiet visit were disrupted; his trip was in the newspapers. More troubling, reporters wanted to know if he had any information on the rumor of a great impending battle in the West. It would not have mattered greatly for a colonel to miss a major battle, but for one who had become famous to be absent without leave would be disastrous.[3]

After Morgan left Huntsville, Duke received orders to march to Corinth, Mississippi, and unite with Gen. John C. Breckinridge's division. They reached there on April 3, the day Morgan arrived in Richmond, and Albert Sidney Johnston's entire army was astir with preparations for attacking the Union army of General Grant at Pittsburg Landing on the Tennessee River. Duke more than likely telegraphed Morgan in Richmond, warning that he was needed at the front; in any event, sometime in the evening of Thursday, April 3, having just arrived, John took a hack to the depot, boarded the first westbound train for one of the most frantic rides of his career. Over 700 miles, from Richmond back through Lynchburg, to Knoxville, Chattanooga, Huntsville, and Corinth—two days and two nights he rode the rails, each time taking the first train headed west, whether mail, freight, or passenger, riding sometimes in the engine and sometimes in the mail car. It was a miserable journey—his rest and relaxation had been cut short before it started, and for all he knew the predicted battle might be underway as he traveled. The demoralization he had hoped to relieve settled and took hold of him.

If Johnston's surprise attack on Grant had occurred on schedule on Friday, April 4, Morgan would have missed it. Fortunately for him, heavy spring rains changed the forest roads to rivers of mud, and separate corps of Johnston's 40,000-man army jammed the intersections and became entangled, delaying the attack until Sunday, April 6, and giving Morgan time to return. He was seen within three miles of the battlefield on Saturday night at midnight.[4]

On Sunday morning Johnston opened the assault on Grant's Army of the Tennessee, which numbered about 42,000 and would be reinforced by the second day with about 20,000 of Buell's men. Morgan still had not resumed his duty; Duke led the squadron, which was kept in reserve all morning in Breckinridge's division on the right. Waiting, they held their horses and listened to the sounds of battle. On the left and center, toward Shiloh Church, "the uneasy, broken rattle of the skirmishers gave way to the sustained volleys of the lines, and the artillery joined in the clamor, while away on the right, the voice of the strife swelled hoarser and angrier, like the growl of some wounded monster—furious and at bay."[5]

At noon Johnston ordered Breckinridge's division into action; they were to attempt to push through on the right, where the Confederate effort was stalled. Movement eased the tension, and Morgan's men sang "Cheer Boys Cheer," the Kentucky marching song. At the line of battle Gen. William J. Hardee, one of the corps commanders, directed Duke to prepare to assault a strong artillery position across a ravine and on an eminence covered with underbrush. The gun emplacement had several pieces of artillery, belching fire and smoke, and the blueclads were moving around the guns with precision. The position looked invincible to Duke, who had never seen a major battle before and had certainly never charged an artillery battery. Turning to a young fellow from a disabled Confederate artillery company, he asked,

"What's the best way to charge a battery?" The man looked Duke squarely in the eye for a few seconds and answered: "Lieutenant, to tell you the God's truth, thar' ain't no *good way* to charge a battery." Luckily, Hardee managed without Morgan's men, and the final order to attack never came.[6]

According to Duke, Morgan was with the squadron by about 1:00 P.M., when they were ordered to press forward on the left of Breckinridge's advancing infantry and attack the first enemy they observed. Galloping forward on horseback, they came upon a regiment in blue uniforms, its commander waving a saber and giving orders in French. Morgan dismounted a platoon of Company A and sent them to reconnoiter. They soon reported that it was all right; the blue uniforms were worn by the 18th Louisiana Infantry under Col. Alexander Mouton.[7]

The advance resumed, and they came to a wide field where a portion of the Kentucky brigade was exchanging musket fire with Federal troops in the woods beyond. Suddenly the Kentucky foot soldiers ran forward, and the Union line gave way. Morgan had the bugler sound the charge, and across the field he led his cavalry at full gallop, with sabers drawn. They were accustomed to fighting dismounted, and the attack resembled a wild horse race more than a military movement. In the confusion all line was lost; it was a crowded mass that converged on the Federals, who fired one volley and retreated. Some of Morgan's men attempted to use the saber and failed ridiculously. His command would never use it again.[8]

The enemy fled, and Morgan regrouped. Four of his men had been killed and several wounded, including Duke. The Kentucky infantry continued pushing ahead, whereas in Morgan's squadron, as Duke described the situation, "it was impossible to conjecture how strong the enemy was just here, but Colonel Morgan, fearing that he might come in force sufficient to endanger this flank, disposed his command on foot, to make all possible resistance in such an event. Our skirmishers, thrown forward, could not find him, and the receding din of the battle seemed to promise perfect safety against all such dangers."[9]

That single cavalry charge was the contribution of Morgan's command to the battle of Shiloh. All afternoon the fighting raged; at the Hornets' Nest, the Bloody Pond, and the Peach Orchard men fought bravely while Morgan's men remained in their safe rear position. Shortly after 2:00 P.M. General Johnston was killed, and there was a brief lull; then the Confederates surged forward, driving the Federals back toward Pittsburg Landing. If Morgan had been a traditional cavalryman, he would have supported Breckinridge's Kentucky infantry in this, their baptism of fire. Breckinridge's infantry fought in the thick of battle all afternoon, taking 1,393 small arms, eleven swords, four cannon, and several flags.[10]

But as a guerrilla, Morgan was true to form. In a regular battle the true partisan will be reluctant to expose his men to danger; he will seek cover and attempt to avoid a decisive confrontation. And as a gambler, Morgan could not bring himself to play his cards in this game—the odds of losing his men were too great. There was no way he could be in control in this situation, and he was already in a state of depression; the euphoria and self-confidence would not come—he was paralyzed. He was a great guerrilla chief in the wrong place at the wrong time, and in those long afternoon hours, with the roar of battle in the distance, he determined to operate as independently as possible in the future. Never again would he participate in a major battle.

It is instructive to compare Morgan's participation at Shiloh with that of Nathan Bedford Forrest, who was also a colonel in command of a cavalry unit. Before the battle Forrest was detached from Breckinridge's division to guard the extreme Confederate right at Lick Creek, which flowed into the Tennessee River. No enemy advanced in that sector of the front, and by 11:00 A.M. of the first day of battle, he could not stand still any longer. "Boys, do you hear that musketry and that artillery?" he yelled. "It means that our friends are falling by the hundreds at the hands of the enemy, and we are here guarding a damned creek. Let's go and help them. What do you say?" Moving toward the action, they found Gen. Benjamin F. Cheatham and asked for authority to charge. Cheatham hedged, and Forrest replied: "Then I'll charge under my own orders." And that he did for the remainder of the battle. Wherever there was fighting, there was Forrest—slashing, cutting, and bleeding with the worst.[11]

Forrest was one of the South's greatest semiregular cavalry leaders. He could lead guerrilla raids behind enemy lines and harass the enemy with great success. But when there was a fight, he was never content to hold his ground, and he could not flee to avoid being whipped. Not only did he attempt to get there first with the most men, as he told Morgan; he fought until they won or died trying. At Chickamauga he proved again his ability in a major conflict. But Forrest's inclination to battle tenaciously was not in the guerrilla tradition. When Grant said Forrest was one of the ablest cavalry generals in the Confederacy, he was thinking of Forrest's traditional side. When Sherman said Forrest was a devil who would have to be subdued, he was worrying about Forrest's unpredictable shifts to guerrilla tactics.[12]

In the midafternoon of April 7, Gen. Pierre G. T. Beauregard, Johnston's successor, broke off the battle and began an orderly retreat toward Corinth. As part of the rear guard, Morgan was back in his element. According to newspaper reports, on Tuesday morning he surprised an enemy camp, killed a large number of Federal troops, and burned a supply of tents left behind by the Confederate army. That same morning Forrest was severely wounded in a skirmish—yet Morgan took the headlines. According to newspapers in Georgia and Virginia, nearly the whole quantity of ammunition and stores of Beauregard's army were "saved by our gallant and indefatigable Morgan, whose very name is a terror to the enemy of the Southwest."[13]

Morgan was not the kind of man who stirred up enmity in his own army, or he would have been condemned for having gone to Richmond. His friends were loyal, and the press valued him too highly as a hero of the cause to expose him. In his official report, Hardee commended Morgan for the single cavalry charge. And Col. Robert P. Trabue, commander of the 4th Kentucky Infantry, mentioned that while Morgan had filed no report, "his conduct is represented to have been such as all expected of so gallant a commander"— a cryptic commendation if there ever was one.[14]

After Shiloh, Beauregard stationed his army in Corinth, opposing Gen. Henry W. Halleck, whose command inched its way southward for nearly two months. Beauregard encouraged Morgan's guerrilla career by adding a fourth company to his squadron, bringing it to 325 men; by directing the quartermaster to turn over $15,000 for equipment; and by authorizing raids on enemy communications. Even without the valuable services of Duke, who was convalescing, Morgan planned to penetrate deep into Kentucky as far as Lexington and possibly into northern Kentucky. He set out with extra ammunition and supplies on pack mules.[15]

Passing through Union lines in Tennessee and camping in loyal neighborhoods, Morgan had the men "play Union." (In one village an elderly pro-Southerner said: "You need not tell that tale to me; I've seen you before; you're Morgan's men.") He attacked only when he had superior numbers and firepower. On May 1, informers in Pulaski told him there was a large party of convalescing Union troops a few miles to the north, constructing a telegraph line toward Huntsville, which had been taken by the Federals. Morgan ordered a mounted frontal assault and captured 268 prisoners.[16] They were rounding up the captives when a company of Union cavalry approached from the north on the Columbia Road. Morgan threw out skirmishers, who determined there were only about fifty, and then he scattered them with a mounted charge. The Richmond *Enquirer* proclaimed: "Our guerrillas are operating throughout middle Tennessee in an eminently successful manner." That night they stayed in Pulaski, to the delight of the young women, who fed Black Bess candy and sweet cakes and clipped her hair. The next morning, when pickets on the Huntsville Road announced the approach of a regiment of Federal cavalry, Morgan quietly marched away toward Murfreesboro.[17]

On the perimeter of Murfreesboro they drove in the Yankee pickets, and Morgan made his first attempt to confuse and disrupt enemy communications by tapping their telegraph lines. Among his men was a telegraph operator with a pocket instrument, and this man, pretending to be the Murfreesboro operator, sent a dispatch to Nashville reporting that Morgan had captured Shelbyville and was about to take Murfreesboro. The ruse accomplished nothing—the Federals were not tricked—but it gave Morgan a great deal of pleasure.[18]

At dark on May 5 the column reached Lebanon, Tennessee. This was Morgan's first independent raid since his promotion to colonel, and already he had contracted the disease of "headquarterism"—the practice of establishing headquarters in a large house or hotel in town while the men camped on porches and in bivouac on the outskirts. A guerrilla fighter should share the hardships of his men in the field; it is essential for effective leadership. But in the Civil War many officers of both armies were afflicted.

In Lebanon, Morgan set up headquarters in a hotel and positioned his men throughout the town, with pickets on the roads. He issued orders to saddle up at 4:00 A.M., but the dispatches never reached the company commanders. This was one of the problems with headquarterism: it cut off the commander from his subordinates, forcing him to communicate through couriers, who were not always efficient. Rain fell all night, and just before day the videttes on the Murfreesboro Road left their post and went into a house to dry out. This was another problem: discipline tended to be lax. The leader was warm and dry—why not the men? Vigilance was lost: before the guards on the Murfreesboro Road realized what was happening, Col. Frank Wolford's 1st Kentucky Union Cavalry swept past, the advance of a force of 600 cavalry under Gen. Ebenezer Dumont. One of Morgan's videttes, Pleasant Whitlow, jumped on his horse and raced in front of Wolford's men, screaming the alarm. In doing so, he gave the men at the hotel time to resist and enable Morgan to escape, but Whitlow was killed. Dumont's cavalry followed in hot pursuit, all the way to the Cumberland River thirty miles away. The "Lebanon Races" ended with Morgan's men scattered and Black Bess standing on the riverbank. There was no time to save her, and Morgan would never see her again.

That night in Carthage, Morgan wept. Six men had been killed, over 100 captured, and all but twenty of the rest scattered all over the countryside. Despite all that, he accepted no fault; he blamed the defeat on officers who had come with the added companies and had not been handpicked by him. Duke usually handled discipline; if he had been present, there probably would have been greater vigilance, but it is doubtful that even his influence could have kept the pickets out in the rain. Credit should be given to Dumont for using the bad weather and darkness to achieve total surprise.[19]

After three days, about fifty men had straggled in, and Morgan decided to take them to the scene of his first scouts near Bowling Green, Kentucky. There they would be familiar with the terrain, and the citizens were friendly. Morgan desperately needed a victory to restore his self-confidence and that of his men. And it was only a slim chance, but if luck smiled, they might seize a northbound L&N train carrying his captured men to prison camp in the North. Along the way he picked up the notorious outlaw Champ Ferguson and four of his men to act as guides, and Morgan asked two local militia companies to join him, bringing his total force to 150 men.

Marching at night on little-used bridle paths, they approached Bowling Green. A scout reported that it was guarded by 500 Union troops, so Morgan went on northward to Cave City, a station on the L&N in the Mammoth Cave region. Nearing there on May 11, he was still feeling low. He said later:

I was very far from well. My hands were swollen and sore—and my feet so swollen I could scarce get more than my toe in the stirrup. I had on a jeans suit, a citizen weighing some 200 lbs. had exchanged with me. I was effectually disguised and looked like a little boy going to meeting in his father's clothes. I rode up alone to the station, got off my horse and sat down on the rails to rest my feet. The conductor came up and taking me for some old farmer who was waiting for the train, inquired the news.

"Oh! nothing much" I replied, "only they tell me that John Morgan's captured."

Whereupon he fell to cursing Morgan—vowing that he never was so glad of anything in his life—that Morgan ought to have been hung long ago—he hoped the guerilla scoundrel would get his deserts now, etc. etc. I told him I agreed with him. Just then a party of my men rode up and as soon as they saw me exclaimed:

"Well Capt. Morgan what are we to do?"

Imagine the face of that conductor.[20]

Morgan and the advance guard seized the station and captured the next train that pulled in. The entire command soon arrived, and together they destroyed the train: four passenger cars, a locomotive, and forty-five freight cars. Morgan remembered how they filled the firebox with wood, set it on fire, fired each car, and sent it racing down the track toward Nashville. "It was a grand sight that burning train going at headlong speed to destruction," he said. For weeks passengers going through Cave City were awed by the scene where the locomotive had exploded. For 100 yards on both sides of the track the underbrush and grass were burned, saplings and trees torn out by the roots, and small metal fragments scattered on the ground.[21]

At noon, guards north of the station heard a passenger train approaching, bound for Nashville from Louisville. The men erected a barrier by placing upright beams in a cow gap, and a squad hid in the trees up the track, ready to throw logs on the rails behind the train once it stopped. A great many women were among the passengers, and Morgan enjoyed telling Virginia French of McMinnville what happened when he entered their car.

I was amused at the Yankee ladies. Poor things, they were going down to Nashville to see their friends. They crowded round me crying: 'Oh, Capt. Morgan what are you going to do with our trunks? What are you going to do with us?' I give you my word Mrs. French—the trunks came first. They doubtless had in them some of those three story Yankee Bonnets to astonish Nashville with.[22]

One pretty girl—she had been only lately married—her husband was with her—a Federal officer in poor health—this pretty girl grasped my hand in both her's [sic] sobbing, 'Oh, Capt. Morgan what will you do with my husband?' I could not resist such a sweet face. I said, 'Madame, I do not know whether I am doing you a kindness or not—but if you desire it—your husband shall accompany you home.' She kissed my hand and thanked me a thousand times—my hand Mrs. French, that had not been washed for two days—and was as black as it could be besides with firing that train![23]

Morgan confiscated $6,000 in cash from the express agent, took two officers and a few enlisted men as prisoners, and allowed the train to return safely to Louisville, with the ladies and their baggage. Then he marched back to Confederate lines in Tennessee.[24]

The Federal authorities were enraged. "John Morgan, the pimp of Southern chivalry . . . has collected a few followers and captured an unarmed train, in Kentucky, robbing the passengers and the express company," a correspondent wrote. "Pity some of the aristocracy of Murfreesboro could not lionize him, pet him, kiss him, for his daring bravery in such honorable warfare." Union Gen. George Morgan deployed infantry to guard trains and stations in central Kentucky and demanded cavalry to guard wagon trains supplying his campaign at Cumberland Gap. James Guthrie, president of the L&N Railroad, complained to the postmaster general that Morgan's raids had cost the company more than it had made in four years of carrying the mail.[25]

Andrew Johnson, military governor of Tennessee, recognized the raid as a serious threat to his efforts to strengthen public sentiment for the Union. It occurred on the day before what Johnson had hoped would be the largest Union rally ever held in Nashville. The effect of the meeting was dampened by the fact that the favorite topic of conversation among the crowd was Cave City. Johnson sensed the tremendous appeal Morgan had with the people, and he viewed guerrilla raids as a menace to his authority. He complained to Washington that incursions such as this undermined Union successes in larger engagements and inspired secessionists to greater resistance.[26]

Meanwhile, Morgan left his men in Chattanooga and traveled to Confederate headquarters in Corinth, Mississippi, to obtain permission to organize a regiment. All along the circuitous route through Atlanta, Montgomery, and Mobile, crowds acclaimed him as a hero. In Atlanta the women's hospital association presented him an inscribed gold-headed cane for his "deeds of daring in defence of our oppressed country." An Atlanta editor cheered: "Hurrah for Morgan! . . . Our people had rather get a sight of him than Queen Victoria. Again we say, Hurrah for Morgan." In Mobile, Hinson and Holt's store collected arms for Morgan's men.[27] From Charleston, Morgan received the gift of a pair of pistols that had belonged to Gen. Bernard E. Bee, who was mortally wounded at First Bull Run; his widow had been waiting for a man worthy to have them, and she had selected Morgan.[28]

Southern journalists emphasized the successes at Pulaski and Cave City, and paid little attention to the rout at Lebanon. Stories of the Cave City raid were exaggerated until the $6,000 in confiscated cash became $350,000 by the time news reached Richmond. But what attracted the most attention was Morgan's treatment of the women on the captured train and his conversation with the wife of the Union officer. More than any other event, it was viewed as confirmation that Morgan was a true Southern gentleman in his deference to women. The chivalric code dictated that the cavalier should always protect women. In Virginia, for example, a group of Union women taken captive by Turner Ashby offered their bags to be searched for contraband, and he replied: "I have no right to look into ladies' baggage, or to examine their trunks. Southern gentlemen do no such thing."[29]

The Cave City story took on the dimensions of a romantic saga of chivalry. One of the favorite scenes was when the wife kissed Morgan's hands in gratitude for the release of her husband. As the Richmond *Enquirer* embellished it: "She frantically seized his hands, and with a joy that was uncontrollable, bedewed them with her tears, while she imprinted on them a warm kiss of gratitude for this assurance that her husband would neither be killed nor taken from her." Morgan's reputation as a protector of women, a "Christian, Southern gentleman, and a humane warrior," was firmly established.[30]

Newspapers were sprinkled with Morgan anecdotes. One told how, when Morgan's train stopped at Opelika, Alabama, a small boy came down the aisle selling cigars. Morgan took one and reached for his purse.

"I don't charge you anything for cigars," the boy said.

"Why?"

"Oh, you are Colonel Morgan who has been fighting for us, and you are welcome to anything I have got."

Grinning, Morgan gave him five dollars and told him to keep it as a memento.[31]

The version published in Atlanta made the boy a newsboy, and when Morgan came back through Atlanta, conspicuous among the large crowd that gathered to see him were many newsboys. They besieged the doors of every car and anxiously scanned the face of every man who emerged. When the hero stepped out, the nearest newsboy ran up to him and asked if Morgan was in this car.

"Yes, I am Colonel Morgan," he replied.

"Here's the evening paper, Colonel; I don't charge you anything."

Morgan thanked him and walked on. The spell was broken, and eventually word got around that he did not give five dollar notes to every cigar or newsboy.[32]

Another story described an encounter in Mobile. Making purchases in a store, Morgan handed the clerk a Federal note. The clerk, assuming he was a Yankee, declared:

"We don't take that kind of money here, sir."

"You don't? Why, hasn't our fleet got in yet?"

"No, and it isn't going to."

"Well," Morgan said confidently, "it will be here shortly, and then I guess you'll take the money."[33]

Among the crowd that met his train at Okolona, Mississippi, was Kate Cumming, the hospital administrator. "The weather is oppressively warm," she noted, "and I do not feel well, but learning that John Morgan was to pass through I could not resist the temptation of seeing so great a lion; for he is one of the greatest of the age." When she was introduced to him, she paid him several compliments, and he "blushed like a school boy." She told him she hoped to hear much of his achievements for the Confederacy in the future, and he answered that he only wanted to hear of himself twenty years from now. The people cheered when the train started off, and she noticed that, "much as he was used to homage, he looked abashed and blushed again."[34]

Morgan had been granted authority to organize the 2nd Kentucky Cavalry regiment, and he soon had almost 400 men, including two companies of Texas Rangers. Duke, recovered from his wound at Shiloh, had the reorganization well underway when one day a Union force of infantry and artillery under Gen. Ormsby M. Mitchel appeared on the other side of the Tennessee River at Chattanooga and began exchanging shells with Confederate batteries. When the Federal infantry started to withdraw, Morgan grabbed a canoe and insisted on crossing the river to reconnoiter. Shells were still flying in both directions, and occasionally one would splash in the river. Duke attempted to persuade him that it was too dangerous and, failing that, joined him in the boat. There was Morgan, a full colonel in command of a cavalry regiment, crossing the Tennessee River in a canoe under fire. They disembarked on the opposite shore where enemy infantry had stood only moments before. This was the kind of danger Morgan craved, but to Duke it was irrational and foolhardy.[35]

According to a correspondent of the Mobile *Register*, on a separate occasion Morgan conducted a similar reconnaissance seven miles up the river. Accompanying him were two of the many colorful characters who had recently joined the command. John's cousin "Wash" Morgan had signed on as an aide with the rank of major. Wash was the son of Gideon Morgan (commander of the Cherokee regiment in the War of 1812) and Margaret Sevier (who was part Cherokee); he dressed as an Indian and identified with his Indian heritage. After a shoot-out on the streets of Knoxville, he had recruited a company of his Cherokee relatives for the Confederate army. And Col. George St. Leger Grenfell, an English soldier of fortune who had fought for and then against the French in Algeria and had battled pirates on the coast of Africa, had become assistant adjutant of the regiment. There they were in a canoe—a guerrilla chief, a Cherokee Indian, and an English mercenary; it was more like a romantic poem than reality. They disembarked on the northern bank and proceeded inland, soon happening upon a man and a boy. Morgan asked the man if he knew anything about the "Secesh" fellows on the other side of the river.

"No," he responded, "but I've heard that that rascal Morgan was over thar yesterday, but the derned fellow flies about so thar's no tellin' whar he is now."

Morgan and Grenfell put several questions to him, and Morgan asked if he was a good Union man. He swore that he was.

"Well," said Morgan, "can't you paddle us over the river? We would like to see if anyone is over there."

"I will," the man replied, "if you will first let me run to the house a minute to change my breeches."

"Oh, these will do now," said Morgan, "as we are in a hurry."

They all four boarded the canoe, and the man began paddling. In the middle of the river Morgan shifted his weight, and Wash cried out, "Colonel Morgan, if you don't keep still you will upset us."

"Are you Colonel Morgan, sir?" the man cried in terror. "For God's sake don't hang me!"

"Well, hurry over and I'll see about it," Morgan smiled.

Once the duped boatman had performed his duty, they set him free.[36]

These adventures enabled Morgan to bear the days in camp, and gradually the reverses he had suffered in April and May faded away. War correspondents had ignored his failure to act at Shiloh and gave little notice to the disaster at Lebanon, instead praising his rear-guard skirmish after Shiloh and his capture of the construction crew, and casting the Cave City raid in legendary proportions. Morgan the hero had been rewarded with adulation and the authority to organize a regiment for continual guerrilla warfare.

NINE

The First Kentucky Raid

By the summer of 1862 the Morgan legend had become an important factor in Morgan's career. The new 2nd Kentucky Cavalry regiment, authorized by Beauregard, included 370 Kentuckians from every part of the state, and the reputation of Morgan's men attracted a regiment of Georgia partisan rangers, a squadron of Texas Rangers, and a company of Tennessee partisans, bringing the number of men to about 900. This was below brigade level, but Morgan declared it a brigade nevertheless and adopted the informal authority of brigadier general. During what became known as the First Kentucky Raid, he signed official documents "Acting Brigadier General John H. Morgan," although he would not be promoted to brigadier general until December.[1]

In early June, the command was transferred to Knoxville and assigned to Gen. Edmund Kirby Smith, who was in charge of defending eastern Tennessee. In Virginia the Peninsula campaign of McClellan was well under way, and in the western theater the Federal invasion of the Confederacy crept forward. On June 18, Kirby Smith withdrew from Cumberland Gap. Beauregard retreated from Corinth to Tupelo, Mississippi; Halleck, his Union counterpart, occupied Corinth, sent Grant to Memphis to campaign down the Mississippi Valley, and directed Buell's Army of the Ohio to march across northern Alabama toward Chattanooga, threatening the Atlanta corridor. In the East, invasion would soon stall and be withdrawn; in the West, Union armies were moving forward, albeit with agonizing slowness.

In Knoxville, Morgan drilled his brigade in the tactics that he had adopted instinctively and spontaneously. His psychological compulsion to stay in the fulfilling game of fighting while preserving his force for future participation had stimulated him to adapt traditional tactics to irregular warfare. Intuitively, he realized it was hazardous to attack with the conventional mounted cavalry charge. Instead, horses could be used, as they had in his career thus far, to provide mobility and enable him to select when and where to fight. Where the enemy was weak, he could end an engagement quickly with a mounted assault; but if the opponent had significant strength or was entrenched, he could dismount his troops, giving them the discipline and fire power of infantry. The men were able to go into action relatively fresh, and while they fought, the horses rested—held by men detailed to the job—and were readily available for pursuit or retreat. Fighting as mounted infantry got the men into the action and brought success without great expenditure of manpower. Duke wrote that they "could maneuver with more certainty, and sustain less and inflict more loss." Morgan adopted the system to preserve his command: he did not want to use all his chips in one game; he wanted to save his men in order to remain constantly in action. He was probably not conscious of it, but in retrospect his tactics were an effective response to the increased power of the defense.[2]

Morgan was totally unburdened with education from the military schools, and he did not study the army training manuals, but he was more experienced in traditional drill than many officers. He had served in the cavalry in the Mexican War, with the artillery in the Kentucky militia, and as an infantry officer in the Lexington Rifles. His men were as well trained as most Civil War commands, where training was generally below par by European standards. There was no minimum standard of efficiency, and no training cycle; and many units had never even had target practice.[3]

The brigade had two mountain howitzers furnished by the War Department, the only wheels in the command. These "bull-pups," as the men called them, were light and maneuverable—horses could pull them in close proximity to the enemy without attracting attention. After Shiloh, the men abandoned the saber, pronouncing it as useless as a fence rail. The increased accuracy of rifles had outdated it, and the cavalry of both armies eventually adopted the rifle. Morgan's men carried various infantry rifles, but they preferred the Enfield, considering it convenient and accurate. Men who could get them also carried two Colt revolvers.[4]

Although some of Morgan's admirers claimed that he invented the tactic of fighting cavalry dismounted, there was actually a strong tradition of using horsemen on foot in the United States army. Francis Marion did it, and mounted infantry was used in the War of 1812, the Indian wars of the nineteenth century, and the Mexican War (Morgan fought dismounted at Buena Vista). In the Civil War, John Bell Hood used part of his command as infantry when he was attacking an ambush in July, 1861, and Forrest fought dismounted as early as December 28, 1861.

Nor did Morgan create the strategy of the raid, as others proposed. It was an accepted principle that cavalry detachments could create diversions and disrupt communications, and the concept of partisan warfare involved detachment of light cavalry for raids. Forrest, Stuart, and many others in both armies conducted raids, and it would be an exaggeration to assert that they copied Morgan.[5]

Duke contended that Morgan practiced new and unprecedented tactics not in the textbooks, fighting in a "thoroughly irregular and revolutionary manner." Thomas Henry Hines, another of Morgan's officers, claimed that Morgan created "peculiar tactics, whose chief object was to harass and confuse the enemy, rather than to fight and kill."[6] What Duke and Hines had in mind was Morgan's adaptation of traditional infantry and cavalry tactics to guerrilla warfare in a conflict that made use of such technological advances as the steam railroad and the electric telegraph. Combining light mounted infantry raids with the hit-and-run tactics of guerrilla war, Morgan practiced the strategy of attrition. His total dedication to such fighting and his continual use of it set him apart. His supporters viewed his methods as innovative and ingenious; his critics considered them disjointed and counterproductive.

Duke was correct in charging that Morgan's promotion to brigadier general was delayed for several months because of prejudice against his irregular tactics. An anonymous poem, "The Schoolmaster," published in the *Southern Literary Messenger* certainly agreed:

> John Morgan's credentials—
> The very essentials
> To honor and glory, you know,
> Were not signed at West P—
> So consequently
> His promotion has been rather slow.
>
> "Why, d—n it," says Pat,
> As he stamps on his hat,
> "Does shape-skins make soldiers—indade!
> On the temple of Fame
> They'd ne'er scratched a P—'s name,
> Till Morgan first taught 'em to raid."[7]

Morgan's First Kentucky Raid is an example of his guerrilla tactics writ large in the form of a strategic raid. The brigade of 867 men left Knoxville, Tennessee on July 4, 1862, and advanced through Tompkinsville, Glasgow, Lebanon, Harrodsburg, Midway, and Georgetown. In Cynthiana, after the most significant skirmish of the expedition, they turned south and returned through Paris, Winchester, Richmond, and Somerset into Tennessee, a march of over 1,000 miles in twenty-four days. The sheer audacity of the campaign, the irregularity of it, created a victorious situation from the beginning. Morgan's command was operating so far behind the lines that there were no forces equal to them, and he returned like lightning, before the adversary had time to concentrate. He used mobility and rapid movement, sometimes pressing on under cover of darkness.

Guerrilla operations depend on intelligence, and Morgan's team kept him well-informed. He threw out scouting parties in front, on the flanks, and to the rear. On the move he used a system of "rolling" videttes in which his elite, handpicked advance guard reconnoitered and protected every crossroad until the head of the column arrived, and then leapfrogged to the front again. Morgan gave special attention to the advance guard, and he was never surprised by a significant hostile force when his command was moving. Once, however, he was riding with the advance in the darkness of early evening when the column reached a small covered bridge on Rolling Fork

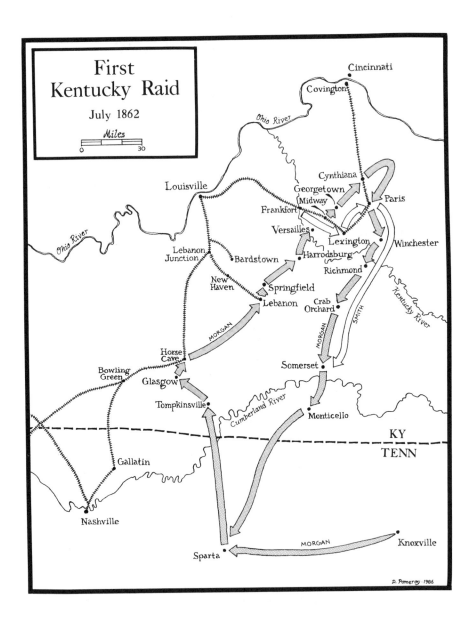

First
Kentucky Raid

July 1862

Miles

0   30

Cincinnati

Covington

Ohio River

Louisville

Cynthiana

Georgetown
Midway
Frankfort
Versailles
Lexington
Harrodsburg

Paris

Winchester

Lebanon
Junction
Bardstown

New
Haven
Springfield
Lebanon

Richmond

Crab
Orchard

Kentucky River

MORGAN

SMITH

Horse
Cave

Bowling
Green
Glasgow

Tompkinsville

Somerset

MORGAN

Cumberland River

Monticello

KY

TENN

Gallatin

Nashville

MORGAN

Knoxville

Sparta

D. Pomeroy · 1986

River, six miles from Lebanon, Kentucky. He was leading the way into the pitch darkness of the bridge when shots rang out, and a rifle ball knocked his hat off. A small party of enemy troops had ripped up the flooring of the bridge and were firing from the other side. Morgan brought up the bull-pups and cleared them out, and no one was injured. It was foolhardy for the commander to ride the advance, but the danger excited him, and he often did it throughout his career.[8]

Accurate reports of enemy strength enabled Morgan to attack when he had overpowering numbers and to avoid the relatively strong garrisons at Frankfort and Lexington. When stationary, the men were vigilant, and scouts were dispatched regularly in all directions. For example, in George-town the men were positioned in line of battle, on the alert, and parties were sent out constantly to reconnoiter the roads and attack any pickets they contacted. Intelligence assured Morgan that the forces in Frankfort and Lexington were not concentrating, so he broke off detachments to harass the enemy and confuse them as to strength and position. Feints were conducted against Lexington, Frankfort, and other towns. The pickets were driven in, and in Lexington martial law was declared. Other companies broke off to burn the railroad trestles of the Kentucky Central Railroad from Cincinnati and the Louisville and Lexington Railroad from Louisville.[9]

Morgan used the telegraph, too, to confuse the enemy and keep them off balance. He had recruited George A. Ellsworth, a Canadian telegraph operator who had previously worked in Houston, Texas. Ellsworth would "milk the wires" of intelligence and use a ground wire to cut towns from the circuit, then answer for them when other operators called. He disrupted communication and sowed confusion in all directions. Near Horse Cave, Kentucky, early in the raid, he tapped the line on the L&N Railroad during a thunderstorm. Sitting on the end of a crosstie, water up to the knees of his cavalry boots, he continued to operate while the thunder rolled and the lightning flashed, thus earning the name "Lightning Ellsworth."[10]

When the advance guard entered Lebanon early one morning, the telegraph operator fled from his office and hid in the willows of the railroad embankment. Ellsworth took the chair and began answering to the letter "B", the call letter for Lebanon. Operator "Z" reported that a troop train with 500 Indiana infantry had passed his station going south toward Lebanon. The first problem was to learn where "Z" was located, so Ellsworth initiated the following interchange.

To Z: A gentleman here in the office bets me ten cigars you cannot spell the name of your station correctly.

To B: Take the bet. L-E-B-A-N-O-N J-U-N-C-T-I-O-N. How did you think I would spell it?

To Z: He gives it up. He thought you would put two B's in Lebanon.

To B: Ha, ha. He's a green one.

To Z: Yes that's so. What time did the train with soldiers pass?
To B: 8:30 last night.

Lebanon Junction was about thirty miles north, where the Lebanon Railroad connected with the main L&N line. Further conversation with "Z" revealed that at 11:00 P.M. the train had met one of Morgan's advance companies a few miles north of Lebanon, had exchanged rifle fire for twenty minutes, and had withdrawn to New Haven, midway between Lebanon and Lebanon Junction. Then "Z" told Ellsworth that the train had just returned to Lebanon Junction, where it was awaiting orders. Ellsworth had obtained the useful intelligence that the advance had turned back the troop train and that presently it was not a threat.[11]

When Morgan reached Midway, there was danger that forces from Frankfort to the west and Lexington to the east might use the Frankfort and Lexington Railroad to converge on him and attack from both directions. Since telegraph operators often recognized one another's touch on the key, Ellsworth forced J.W. Woolums, the Midway operator, to send, so that he could learn to imitate his style. Then, posing as Woolums, Ellsworth milked the intelligence that Gen. William Thomas Ward in Lexington had ordered a force in Frankfort to attack Morgan. Under instructions from Morgan himself, Ellsworth told Ward that the Confederate raiders had left Midway, advancing on Frankfort. Ward, assuming the fake dispatch to be genuine, ordered the offensive withdrawn to Frankfort to defend the state capital. After this successful ruse, operators became more wary; they warned each other to watch for Ellsworth on the line, and began sending military messages in code.[12]

When the expedition reached Georgetown at sundown, Ellsworth found the telegraph office locked and the operator gone. He broke in, intercepted several messages, and wired Lexington:

"Keep mum. I am in the office, reading by the sound of my magnet in the dark. I crawled in when no one saw me. Morgan's men are here, camped at Dr. Gano's place."

Lexington replied: "Keep cool. Don't be discovered. About how many rebels are there?"

Ellsworth answered that he did not know but would stay up all night to keep Lexington informed. At this point the Cincinnati operator became suspicious.

"How can you be in the office, and not be arrested?"

"Oh, I am in the dark, and am reading by the magnet."

"Where is your assistant?"

"Don't know."

"Have you seen him today?" Lexington inquired.

"No," Ellsworth said, and the wires went silent—the Georgetown operator had no assistant.[13]

Ellsworth's work enabled Morgan to trick and tease, and provided another way to pose as the enemy. It gave him great pleasure. Over the wires, Morgan taunted George Prentice, the Louisville *Journal* editor, and as he was leaving Kentucky he reminded Supt. W.G. Fuller of the raid on the log church in January: Morgan told Fuller that he was making good use of his pistols and fieldglasses and promised to return them at the end of the war. And to Gen. Jeremiah Boyle, now in command in Louisville, he wired: "Good morning, Jerry. This telegraph is a great institution. You should destroy it as it keeps me posted too well. My friend Ellsworth has all your dispatches since July 10 on file. Do you want copies?"[14]

The London *Times* declared Ellsworth's intelligence-gathering the first and most striking innovation in the war. In the long term it might have been more effective to milk the wires without making his presence known: although Ellsworth remained with Morgan through the Great Raid in July, 1863, and continued sending messages, the other operators recognized him after Midway and Georgetown on the First Kentucky Raid. Secret interception of communications would not have been as entertaining, however, and Ellsworth was one of the coterie of clowns that Morgan had attracted. He was muscular and boasted constantly of his fleet sprinting. One day Jeff Sterritt, the Sir John Falstaff of Morgan's elves, arranged a race between Ellsworth and another man, conspiring with others to insist that each racer carry a "jockey" on his back. Jeff himself jumped on Ellsworth and began pricking him in the hips with a set of giant Texas spurs. At first Ellsworth balked; then he took off and won the race. Another day, he was seized with the urge to chase after a bushwhacker in the Crab Orchard vicinity. Without asking, he and a companion took Grenfell's horse and rode away. The bushwhacker's shotgun got the best of them, severely wounding Ellsworth's partner. Ellsworth escaped with his life and bleeding friend but lost the horse, the saddle, and Grenfell's coat, which contained all of his money. The men had to hide Ellsworth for three days while Grenfell's wrath cooled.[15]

At Tompkinsville and again at Lebanon, Morgan dismounted his men and sent them forward in a frontal assault. The Federals gave way on the first volley and surrendered. Only once—at Cynthiana—was Morgan surprised by the strength of resistance. Scouts had reported that the town was guarded by 450 undisciplined Home Guardsmen, and he expected to rout them easily. Actually there were only 350 Federals: 15 of the 18th Kentucky Infantry; 75 recruits of the 7th Kentucky Cavalry; Home Guards from Newport, Bracken County, and Cynthiana; and 16 Cincinnati firemen commanded by Capt. William H. Glass and manning a twelve-pound brass cannon pulled by four fire-engine horses. Morgan came in on the Georgetown Pike, dismounted all except one company, and positioned the men in battle lines on the bank of the Licking River. On the opposite bank the Union force occupied a strong defensive position in houses, their rifles thrust out of every window with a view of the river and the covered bridge. Others were stationed between the houses and in the yards, their rifles bristling above the lawn fences.[16]

Morgan ordered a frontal assault on foot, sending Company A through the narrow bridge, supported by three other companies. The two howitzers, placed near the road 350 yards from the bridge, opened fire on the houses, and the fight began. When the first men of Company A emerged on the far side of the bridge, they were met not only with deadly rifle fire but also with grape and canister from Capt. Billy Glass's cannon. They charged three times and were repelled, suffering several casualties each time. Finally Duke led Company A across the river at the ford near the bridge. Holding their rifles above their heads, they splashed through the waist-deep water and established a line behind a warehouse and a few yards beyond the bridge. Morgan sent the bull-pups across the bridge, and they attempted to deploy on the road near Duke, only forty yards from the enemy sharpshooters—so close that rifle fire drove the gunners from their post and one of the teams fled into the enemy line, dragging its caisson. Finally, Morgan ordered the mounted company in reserve to cross the bridge on horseback and create a diversion so that Company A could advance. The mounted men flanked the Federals; Duke moved forward, and the enemy retreated and surrendered. Morgan had about forty casualties and the Union men about ninety, according to Duke. Morgan captured several prisoners, who were paroled; that is, they were released after promising not to participate in the war until officially exchanged for a Confederate soldier captured by the Union army.[17]

As he did all along his route, Morgan mounted his men on good horses and armed them with captured weapons. What supplies he could not use or carry, he destroyed. In Harrodsburg and other Bluegrass towns he pressed some of the best horseflesh in Kentucky into Confederate service; at the end of the raid every man was splendidly mounted and well armed, and there were extra horses and saddles for the men who had been left behind in Tennessee. At Tompkinsville they destroyed a cache of munitions and stores; at Lebanon they dumped a store of gunpowder in the creek and seized two large warehouses, distributing meat, flour, sugar, and coffee to the citizens. Then they burned the warehouses, along with a new hospital and fifty-two ambulances. At Somerset on the way out they loaded captured army blankets, shoes, saddles, and other stores on wagons and hauled them away.[18]

For Kentuckians in the invasion force, the raid took on the political objective of the liberation of their home state. They were united with other members of the Kentucky bloc in the Confederacy in demanding as a secondary aim of the war that Kentucky be freed from Union rule. They had fled as fugitives, and their homes were occupied; they were refugees unable to go home with honor, even if the Confederacy won its independence without including Kentucky. This was why the first Kentucky infantry brigade was named the "Orphan Brigade." The great dream of the Kentucky bloc was that the Confederate army would occupy the state for an extended period of time, allowing Southern feeling to develop and expel the Yankees. It was unrealistic, but they pursued the dream relentlessly through 1864.[19]

Around the campfire at night and riding along the trail, Morgan's men raised their voices in songs protesting their exile. The plaintive lyrics of "Answer to the Kentucky Exile" told how they had been driven out and were determined to plant the Confederate flag on Kentucky soil and rescue their homes from the tyrant. In Knoxville on July 4, the day the raid began, Duke had written "Morgan's War Song" to the inspiring rhythm of a revised version of "La Marseillaise":

> Kentucky! Kentucky! Can you suffer the sight
> Of your Sisters insulted, your friends in the fight?
> Awake! Be free again![20]

And in a lighter vein they sang a popular marching ditty:

> Georgia girls are handsome,
> And Tennessee girls are sweet;
> But a girl in old Kentucky,
> Is the one I want to meet.[21]

General Johnston, General Breckinridge, and others had issued proclamations challenging Kentuckians to rise en masse to aid the Confederacy; one of these had been written by President Davis. Morgan joined the chorus during this raid. He published announcements to the people of Kentucky denying that he meant to destroy private property or interfere with the rights of citizens. He promised to repay anyone who suffered property damage at the hands of his men. And calling for recruits, he exhorted: "Strike for your altars and fires! God and your native land!" Duke wrote later that what was needed was "revolutionary fermentation" resulting in "revolutionary fever."[22]

In Harrodsburg, Morgan was so greatly impressed with his enthusiastic reception that before he realized what he was doing, he made a public speech. One of the women said it gave her pleasure to see him in Harrodsburg, and he replied: "Madam, when I entered Harrodsburg and found that here in the very center of Kentucky the ladies had assembled to welcome me, it was the proudest and happiest moment of my life. Oh! if the men of Kentucky had but the spirit of the women she would long since have been free." A hush spread over the crowd, and he turned to them:

You have complained that you had not the opportunity to join the Southern army. We have come to give it to you. We are Kentuckians like yourselves. At the very beginning of the war we gave up our families, and homes, and friends, and property—everything we had to go and fight for the South and we are willing, if it were possible, to do all this again. We have returned, through hostile forces, to the very heart of your state to see if you will join us. How can you stand tamely by seeing your friends engaged in a deadly strife—your women insulted and dragged to prison? It seems to be enough for any man of . . .

Suddenly he became aware of the terrifying fact that he was making a public address; he stammered, grasped his horse's mane, and abruptly ended his statement.[23]

On a practical day-to-day level, Morgan, as a guerrilla, paid more attention to local opinion than most officers. Relying upon the people for information and support, he studied the sympathies of a community, noting whether they were "Union strong" or Southern. Therefore, he was especially sensitive to Federal attempts to enforce loyalty in Kentucky. His reference to arrests related to the campaign of pacification initiated by the Federal military authorities in Kentucky under General Boyle. Provost marshals had been appointed in each county and authorized to arrest anyone suspected of offering assistance to the Confederacy. Any individual under suspicion had to take an oath of allegiance and give bond for future loyal conduct or be arrested and imprisoned. Some provost marshals abused the system, making arrests without giving reasons and carrying out vendettas against personal enemies.[24]

Morgan proclaimed that he would protect all Southern sympathizers, "and if any are disturbed in any way whatever, I shall visit the perpetrators with a severe and speedy retaliation." He put priority on capturing the provost marshal in each county. "He would be kept, sometimes a day or two, and thoroughly frightened," Duke wrote. "Colonel Morgan, who derived infinite amusement from such scenes, would gravely assure each one, when brought into his presence, that one of the chief objects of his raid was to catch him. It was a curious sight to see the mixed terror and vanity this declaration would generally excite—even in the agonies of anticipated death, the prisoner would be sensibly touched by the compliment." After terrorizing the captive into agreeing to protect Southern people in the future, Morgan would release him. "It was thought better to turn all the captured provost marshals loose and let them resume their functions, than to carry them off, and let new men be appointed, with whom no understanding could be had," Duke explained. Morgan had thus begun a campaign of terrorism against Federal officials in order to protect Southern sympathizers in Kentucky and encourage other citizens to join the Confederacy.[25]

The raid caused great excitement in Kentucky. In every community along the route, people swarmed to town to see Morgan's men and be identified for a brief moment with a phenomenon larger than life, with timeless adventure and revolutionary fervor. They found a rough, wild, and picturesque body of men—sun-browned, hardened, swarthy veterans of the revolution. Every one dressed according to his own peculiar taste, the prevailing fashion being a jacket, pants thrust in high cavalry boots, colored shirt, huge clanking spurs, broad-brimmed hat, and a pair of revolvers buckled around the waist. The Texas Rangers wore Mexican blankets and huge black sombreros, and carried double-barreled shotguns and bowie knives. Wash Morgan's Indian leather complemented the facial features and complexion of his strong Cherokee heritage.

Besides John Morgan himself, already a world-famous legend, there was Basil Duke, great nephew of Chief Justice John Marshall and one of the most handsome men in either army. Duke seemed to glide back and forth, giving orders with an air of effortless authority and self-confidence. He was tall, dark, and splendidly adorned in an immaculate regulation gray cavalry uniform. Grenfell wore a bright red skullcap and carried a saber. Pat Thorpe had on his Zouave jacket, the sleeves studded with red coral buttons. And there was Jacob T. Cassell, the scout who on a moonless night could tell whether artillery had passed by feeling the tracks on the trail.

Young men in the crowd never forgot Morgan's corps of orderlies. They were youths as young as thirteen, and some of them, such as Jack Brown from Gallatin, Tennessee, had run away from home to join Morgan. The lad's mother was in such distress that Morgan wrote: "Jack arrived last Saturday. Is well, in fact looks better than I ever saw him has grown a great deal. He is not willing to leave here."[26]

Champ Ferguson and his outlaw band—notorious for never taking prisoners—were present, too. Champ was over six feet tall, had coal black, curly hair and a red face with a ferocious expression. To him the war was a personal vendetta: his aim was to kill Tinker Dave Beatty and his men, who fought with the Union army. Beatty and his friends had visited Ferguson's cabin in Clinton County, Kentucky, and had humiliated and whipped his wife and daughter. He vowed to kill every one of Beatty's men, and riding with Morgan provided the opportunity of searching for them and stealing horses and slaves in the meantime.[27]

Early in the raid Duke cautioned Ferguson not to kill Morgan's prisoners of war. "Why, Colonel Duke," the burly outlaw replied, "I've got sense. I know it ain't looked on as right to treat regular soldiers tuk in battle in that way. Besides I don't want to do it. I haven't got no feeling agin these Yankee soldiers, except that they are wrong, and oughtn't to come down here and fight our people. I won't tech them; but when I catches any of them hounds I've got good cause to kill, I'm goin' to kill em."[28]

The raid was as colorful as a crusade, and the circuslike display attracted pro-Union and pro-Confederate spectators alike. Almost the entire able-bodied population gathered and gazed in wide-eyed wonder. Southern women waved handkerchiefs, threw flowers, and wept. Then they went home and cooked, and sent servants with baskets of food. Overwhelmed, in Georgetown on July 16, Morgan telegraphed Kirby Smith: "I am here with a force sufficient to hold all the country outside of Lexington and Frankfort.

These places are garrisoned chiefly with Home Guards. The bridges between Cincinnati and Lexington have been destroyed. The whole country can be secured, and 25,000 or 30,000 men will join you at once."[29]

It was true that resentment against Federal authorities was increasing. People were alarmed by the arrests made by Boyle's provost marshals; the handling of runaway slaves had been inconsistent. "All concur in their statements in regard to the great change that has taken place in the State; they report but few Union men now in Kentucky," Morgan wrote to a friend. Men had joined his ranks who six months before had been bitterly anti-Confederate, and if Kentucky could be held sixty days, he said, 25,000 men would be added to the army.[30]

But Morgan was confusing curiosity about him and resentment against Federal authority with support for the Confederacy. Actually, there were few signs of active support during the raid. Even the extremely pro-Southern men who aided Morgan did so with fear and trembling. Those who voluntarily opened their meathouses and haylofts insured themselves against the Federal provost marshal by insisting that Morgan's officers declare that they had forced their "hosts" to render assistance. Moreover, Morgan accepted all recruits who came in, and the total was less than 300 men.[31]

In Richmond, Kentucky, Dr. William Jennings did recruit a company that joined up when the command came through near the end of the raid. Before leaving, Jennings brought Morgan and his staff home to meet his wife, Lucy, and have lunch. Lucy recalled how immodestly the officers laughed at the suggestion of being caught and hanged as guerrillas, and how Morgan praised her for having the courage to entertain the "robber chief," and the "marauder & his band." Then he asked Lucy if she had heard how his mother had been persecuted by the Yankees in Lexington.[32]

Henrietta Morgan was fifty-six years old, had been a widow eight years, and had stiffened her back and set her face against many challenges. But when Lexington was occupied by Federal troops and John left, she had to call on all the reserve strength of character she possessed. All five of her older sons had joined the Confederate army, and her two daughters were married to Confederate officers. Only the youngest son, sixteen-year-old Key was still at home. Hopemont was surrounded by Union soldiers. In the early morning calm, smoke from their campfires drifted around the cornices of the house, and when the windows were open Henrietta could hear them laughing and chattering. They were bivouacked in tents on the university lawn, between the sycamore tree and locust grove directly in front of Hopemont. All day blue uniforms passed back and forth on the sidewalk, for Union officers had occupied the Benjamin Gratz house next door, and across the lawn was the home of Dr. Robert Peter, the prominent chemist and physician whom the soldiers depended upon for medical care. In front of Morrison Hall stood a guardhouse and a stable for the horses of the guard, and directly opposite Hopemont the Federals made their headquarters in the Thomas

Bodley house. There stood Hopemont, a monument of gray in a sea of blue and the focus of much of the bitter wartime hatred in the town, for this was the home of the mother of John Hunt Morgan, the Marion of the War and hero of the Confederacy. Hostile eyes watched the house constantly and noted who came and went.[33]

Late in the evening of February 18, 1862, while the Union guards fired a salute and the flag was being lowered on the lawn, Key Morgan and two or three fellow Transylvania students went to the janitor and asked for the key to the door leading to the roof of Morrison Hall, explaining that their ball had lodged there. Having gained the roof, they hoisted a Confederate flag and left. The janitor cut it down and placed it in the cellar; Key retrieved it and took it home. Within a few minutes Union soldiers appeared at the front door of Hopemont and sent a squad into the house to search for the flag. They found it, tore it up, and divided the fragments among themselves.[34]

When Morgan's men came to Versailles, twelve miles west of Lexington, excitement became intense. Unionist rabble-rousers threatened to level Henrietta's house, along with that of her sister Eleanor Curd. Realizing that he would be unable to protect the two women, Provost Marshal F.G. Bracht ordered them out of town for their own safety until after the raid. For Henrietta, the Civil War had come to mean being besieged in her own home. Former friends and neighbors who had gone Union were no longer friendly. She had Aunt Betty and other servants do her shopping, and she seldom ventured outside the house. She prayed for peace and every day, on a regular schedule, she wrote to one of her children.[35]

Morgan said to Lucy Jennings:

Madam, I understand at Lexington they threaten my Mother's & Sister's, Mrs. Duke's life & to burn their property. Burn it if they dare, let them but touch the hairs of their heads. My name they say is used by these Lincolnites to terrify these women & children of theirs. I have never as yet disturbed one of them, but so help me God if they trouble those helpless women and children whom I love so fondly I will make the name of John Morgan more terrible than in their wildest imagination [they] ever conceived that it could be. Their women & children shall then drink the cup of woe that others, dare to offer mine.[36]

John was in dead earnest. He believed in retaliation and had already practiced it in terrorizing provost marshals for intimidating Southern sympathizers. Later, retaliation carried out on his authority would lead to some of the worst depredations of his command. This early statement illustrates the danger that guerrilla warfare can escalate into anarchy and barbarism.

When news of Morgan's raid was confirmed at the headquarters for Union troops in Kentucky, General Boyle was frantic. In a constant barrage of messages to Secretary of War Edwin M. Stanton, he increased his estimation of Morgan's strength to 3,000 men. Lincoln told Halleck: "They are having a stampede in Kentucky. Please look to it!" Halleck wired Buell: "Do all in your power to put down the Morgan raid even if the Chattanooga expedition should be delayed." Buell dispatched two cavalry regiments combined with Home Guards; a force of about 3,000 was pursuing the rebels when the raid ended. Their commander, Gen. G. Clay Smith, marched them day and night from Paris to Somerset, but they never closed within firing range. As usual, Morgan had created waves of frustration for the Union war effort. The destruction of telegraph materials caused cancellation of a proposed telegraph line from Glasgow to Tompkinsville, and Union General Morgan at Cumberland Gap had his supplies cut off for eight to ten days.[37]

The impact of the raid was increased by two other expeditions that occurred simultaneously: Forrest destroyed Federal supplies in Murfreesboro and burned bridges on the Nashville and Chattanooga Railroad; Col. Frank Armstrong cut the Memphis and Charleston Railroad in Alabama. Obviously, Buell had to take action to prevent such incursions. The result was his triad system of defense of his supply line. First, he immediately deployed two infantry divisions in upper middle Tennessee to guard the gateway to Kentucky. Second, he ordered construction of a stockade to defend every railroad trestle that would require more than a few hours to rebuild, each such fortress to be manned by at least half a company of men. He theorized correctly that once the forts were completed, they would be adequate unless assaulted with artillery. The work began, but the construction details were so small and the labor so menial that progress was slow.[38]

The third and ultimately most meaningful response of the triad system was Buell's strengthening of the cavalry branch of the army in the West. In the beginning, Union army officials had underestimated the role of cavalry in the war, and that arm of the Union forces was weak, outnumbered, and inferior to the Confederate cavalry. Forrest, Morgan, and others were teaching the Federals their mistake, and one of Buell's division commanders pleaded for more cavalry: "To chase Morgan and Forrest, they mounted on race horses, with infantry in this hot weather is a hopeless task." Buell obtained authority to organize eight new regiments and soon 7,000 Kentuckians and hundreds of men from Indiana and Ohio had been recruited. In Tennessee, Gov. Andrew Johnson was given authority to raise a regiment.[39]

Politically, Morgan's raid had stung the North like a hornet. Union troops occupying Kentucky were attempting to protect the loyal border state from the enemy. Morgan's men spread terror, disrupted lives, and made a mockery of Federal security. "Morgan, Morgan, Morgan" was the topic of every conversation. The stages stopped running, and traffic shut down on the turnpikes. A wagon master inquired, "Is it safe to take my train up to Lawrenceburg or is Morgan still there?" The Union army had failed to provide safety for the citizens in the state. A man in Cynthiana said it was a burning shame that Morgan came into Kentucky and left victorious. Halleck was called to

Washington as general-in-chief during the raid, and it was humiliating to be asked about it. He scolded Buell: "The stampede among our troops was utterly disgraceful"; Lincoln's administration was greatly dissatisfied with Buell's advance on Chattanooga, he said, and "especially with the inefficiency of some of your forces at the time of Morgan's raid." Halleck warned that he had been asked to replace Buell. In turn, Buell ordered an investigation of the defeat at Tompkinsville and blamed garrison commanders for allowing the incursion to occur with impunity.[40]

"Glorious Col. Morgan has dashed into Kentucky, whipped everything before him, and got off unharmed," Jones the War Department clerk gloated. "Three Cheers for Morgan!" a Richmond headline read. A journalist in Richmond designated Morgan a trump, the "watchword to the South" and terror of the North. This was the kind of offensive warfare the Southern people longed for; the raid had demonstrated that the North was vulnerable and Southern forces could win. To a Richmond analyst, it was "one of the most daring and successful raids into the heart of the enemy's country recorded in the annals of war." A quartermaster officer in Knoxville estimated that the expedition had destroyed eight to ten million dollars worth of Federal property.[41]

Morgan presented a flag captured at Cynthiana to Mrs. Eli M. Bruce, wife of the popular Kentucky congressman. She responded that all Kentucky refugees hailed the success as a harbinger of an early return from exile: "You have shaken the gauntlet of the South in the face of the enemy, almost at his own doors; and, as I trust our conquering flag will soon cross the border, yours will be the gallant band to lead the way."[42]

Southerners exulted that stockholders and moneychangers on Wall Street were trembling in their shoes, and the knees of Yankee politicians were smiting together like Belshazzar's at the handwriting on the wall. It was satisfying to learn that Northern towns such as Cincinnati, known as "hogtown" because of its pork industry, had prepared for defense: "Swinopolis has turned out in large numbers and her mayor has threatened himself to enter the field! A desperation like this is without precedent! He should be called Gen. Pork. His fat followers will be good game for Morgan's men, who would gladly 'give [lard] to grease their shining blades.'"[43]

To Morgan himself the raid was a triumph for his personal revolution; it restored his self-esteem and redeemed his honor. The excitement and intense pleasure of it blotted out depression and gave him a sense of power and control. As a revolutionary guerrilla, he had made what he hoped would be the first strike in the liberation of Kentucky from the "crop eared Puritans" and the restoration of Southern civilization in Lexington, enabling him to go home with honor.[44] With a brigade of over 850 soldiers, he had used the same guerrilla tactics as with squads of ten or twenty men. Completely without authority other than that of his own revolution, he had retaliated against provost marshals in Kentucky by apprehending and terrorizing them—independent action that illustrates one of the dangers of guerrilla warfare, when the guerrilla leader makes his own rules. His exaggeration of Southern support in Kentucky turned out to be detrimental to the Confederacy, as did the raid's most significant result: Buell's strengthening of Union cavalry in the West. By mid-1863, Confederate raiders would operate with less impunity.

TEN

The Gallatin Raid

Returning to Tennessee at the close of the First Kentucky Raid, Morgan broke off and accompanied the howitzers to Knoxville for repairs, thereby avoiding the tedium of camp life. The command proceeded to Sparta, where Duke and Grenfell attempted to turn it into a disciplined fighting machine, able to perform the manual of arms with precision and march from column into skirmish line with model symmetry. Dress parades were scheduled and daily drill initiated by company and regiment, on foot and horseback. The morning they first attempted to mount guard according to regulation, all was going well; but just when Duke began to think it would be easy, Sgt. Gano Hill's deep voice thundered over the parade field: "You men of Company I on the left there, scrouge up and quit your crowding!" The ranks exploded with laughter and all semblance of order disappeared.[1]

If the men were to be taught, they had to be in camp. Some of them did not like that life any better than Morgan did; from the beginning they were incorrigible in running away and straggling through the country during periods of inactivity. Most would be gone only a night or two, but some left for months and went home on unauthorized furloughs. The practice was very common in the Confederate army, especially in the detached cavalry where men had their own transportation. In Sparta, Duke posted regular camp guards, but running the guard developed into such a popular game that nearly half the regiment had to be put on duty to guard the rest.[2]

Grenfell and Duke were attempting to impose traditional military discipline, and it might have worked under some commanders. Southern soldiers were generally effective when their officers were brave and efficient and inspired respect. When an officer exercised firm authority, however, he had to take into consideration the individual pride of his men. Individualism was very strong. Forrest was successful with the discipline of compulsion and fear—he was so strict that his men said they feared him more than the enemy—as was Morgan's friend Col. Roger Hanson, commander of the 2nd Kentucky Infantry regiment. Hanson was of medium height, with huge slumping shoulders, a stern expression, and twitching eyes and mouth. He had been wounded in a duel and one leg was shortened, giving him a unique roll-and-jerk gait. His men called him "Bench Leg" and "Old Flintlock," but they respected him and obeyed his stringent regulations.[3]

Forrest's and Hanson's methods notwithstanding, the efforts of Grenfell and Duke failed because they departed from Morgan's practice of discipline, which was consistent with his personality. As a gambler and hedonist who refused to discipline himself, Morgan would have been a hypocrite to expect his men to deny themselves pleasure between raids. And since he gloried in disrespect for authority and independence, rigid discipline would have been difficult to enforce. Instead, he used what social psychologists today call democratic leadership. He permitted the men to retain their independence in matters that did not concern their official duties, and if a man disappeared from base camp for a couple of days between raids, he asked no questions. "I prefer fifty men who gladly obey me, to a division I have to watch and punish," he said. On duty, he gave them freedom to make full use of their individual talents to further the success of the command. This positive approach contributed to his effectiveness as a guerrilla leader. Operating behind enemy lines, throwing out detachments in every direction, he needed self-motivation, unity of purpose and loyalty. He inspired self-imposed discipline by concentrating on the improvement of cooperation and morale. He knew his men and took interest in their welfare; he celebrated and publicized their achievements, using promotions to encourage bravery under fire. Morgan gave the men a conviction that they were successful and thereby contributed to an esprit de corps that was very high early in the war.[4]

Gen. Braxton Bragg's inspectors general condemned Morgan's brand of discipline, asserting that the men considered themselves members of a gentleman's club in which everyone was responsible only to himself. Duke phrased it differently; he said each man "was zealous, attentive, and obedient, not so much from fear of authority and punishment, as from feelings of pride and patriotism: more from a sense of what was due to himself than of what was due to any superior." What happened was that Morgan's leadership style inspired tremendous enthusiasm in his men. This kind of authority demanded that the leader set the example in daring; as Grenfell observed, in Morgan's regiment "every atom of authority had to be purchased by a drop of blood." In this respect, Morgan's unflagging disregard for danger, his energy, and his dedication served him well.[5]

Morgan was courteous and gracious with his men, always concerned about their comfort and desires, and they loved him for it. Duke said his kind dispositon was his greatest fault. He was more attentive to subordinates than to superiors, and he fraternized with the enlisted men frequently. One morning he fed, curried, and saddled the horse of a private who had been ordered to care for his horse the night before. He selected officers he could work with and developed a team spirit by fostering cooperation among them. "I am convinced that nothing so much contributes to success as an entire harmony between a Genl. and his subalterns," he remarked.[6]

Regardless of regulations, he threw out seniority and promoted for merit: "Seniority means deeds," he would say, and he issued promotions on the battlefield for valor, thus encouraging daring. When he was informed that Lt. Leland Hathaway, an adjutant, was the first rider over a log breastwork in Indiana on the Great Raid in 1863, he lifted his broad felt hat and, with a smooth sweep of his lithe body and a wide smile, declared: "Well done Mr. Adjutant, I salute you as '*Captain* Hathaway!'" Years later Hathaway remembered: "He left me thrilled through and through. I could not tell by which most, his matchless smile and bow or his gracious and welcome words." Tom Quirk, a young Irish immigrant who had worked in a Lexington bakery before the war, was promoted to captain and placed in command of Morgan's scouts in the middle of a skirmish. It is also important in guerrilla warfare, which is frequently behind the lines, never to abandon wounded comrades, and Morgan made it a point to carry off every wounded man who could be safely moved, thus preventing capture by the enemy.[7]

If Morgan's men were inferior in drill and unaccustomed to military restraint, in the presence of the enemy they were obedient, loyal, and zealous. They were willing to attempt any feat and challenge any danger, and like Pleasant Whitlow at Lebanon, there were others later who risked their lives to save the beloved chief. And to be wounded was an honor. In a skirmish near Murfreesboro in March, 1863, a young man from Bardstown was working in the artillery battery, exchanging fire with Yankee cannon 300 yards up the road, when his gun discharged prematurely, blowing away his hand. Morgan told how he visited the soldier in the field hospital: "He was perfectly cheerful & seemed so happy to see me. Raised up in his bed & said 'Gen. I did my duty yesterday & never left my piece altho all had been killed or had left but two others & myself' & that he was going to his gun again as soon as possible."[8]

In the midst of a skirmish in Liberty, Tennessee, in the spring of 1863, a private had his leg torn off by a shell; it was left dangling by a few shreds. As he was borne to the rear, the litter passed Morgan. The soldier put his hand into his cartridge box and pulling out a few packages of cartridges said: "Here, General, are some good Enfields. Give them to the boys who need them." In March, 1864, remnants of Morgan's scattered command pleaded for transfer to their beloved chieftain. "Shall we, can we be expected to remain contented in any other command than that of our own Morgan, whom we have tried & found true, whom we have trusted and found worthy?"[9]

Lenient discipline enabled Morgan's corps of jesters to feel comfortable at headquarters, where they were given an easy berth and special status as his "chartered libertines." Jeff Sterritt, Jack Trigg, and Tom Ballard—three of his favorites—were continually getting into scrapes that would have been trouble for other men. In the third year of the war, after Morgan was promoted to brigadier general, an enterprising faro dealer opened a gambling casino near headquarters in McMinnville, Tennessee. Responding to complaints of regimental commanders about frequent absences of the men, Morgan threatened the dealer; when that failed, he ordered the provost guard to arrest the dealer and every man found in the place. Among the prisoners were Sterritt, Trigg, and Ballard. Morgan arranged a drumhead court-martial and in a moment of gleeful comedy had them brought before him. He upbraided them for their reprehensible conduct, for taking advantage of their privileged position at headquarters, and promised to make them an example long to be remembered.

"Trigg," he asked finally, "what were you doing there?"

"General, I went there to find Ballard."

"Well, Ballard," the general said, "what were you doing there?"

"I went there," said Ballard, "to find Sterritt."

Placed in this difficult spot, Sterritt—asked the same question—proved himself as usual the chief of jesters, the Falstaff of the command.

"Do you mean, general, what I was doing when I was arrested?"

"Yes, what were you doing then?"

"Well sir, to the best of my recollection, I was betting against the ace."

There was a pause while Morgan fought the urge to laugh. "You incorrigible wretch," he said, "what ought I to do with you?"

"If you have any doubt about the matter, general, you might give me a thirty days' furlough."[10]

In middle Tennessee during the second winter of the war, Tom Murphy, an Irish immigrant, was assigned to the group of elves. He had been posted as an advance picket in the early part of the night, which was cold and dark. Shortly before midnight, when he was anticipating the arrival of his relief, he heard a tremendous uproar on the road in front, the clatter of many hoofs approaching at a mad gallop. Assuming that the entire Yankee cavalry was coming at him in the darkness, he blazed away with his rifle and pistols, then turned and rode full speed for his picket base.

"What's the matter?" the commander of the guards queried.

"The whole damned Yankee army is a'top of us, but I fixed one of 'em, I know!"

The entire command was called to arms, but when it was discovered that a large herd of cattle had stampeded, broken through a fence, and rattled down the road and that Tom had initiated a false alarm, Morgan ordered Tom to appear before him. The questioning was under way when the report came that Tom's bullets had killed the bull of the herd.

"Why Tom," said Morgan in great amusement, "I'm surprised at you; to shoot an unoffending beast just as you would a Yankee! The bull wouldn't have hurt you. I'll guarantee that you don't even know whether or not he had horns."

Tom discerned John's change of mood and took advantage of it. A "horn" was an object on the head of a bovine, but more important to the Civil War soldier, it was a drink of liquor.

"No, begorra!" Tom replied, "the night was so dark, and I was after leaving in such a hurry that I couldn't see, sir, if he had horns or didn't. But, general, owning to the cold and the scare, I'd like mighty well to have a horn meself." Morgan gave him a drink and transferred him to headquarters immediately.[11]

When Morgan returned from Knoxville, he led a raid behind enemy lines against the main artery of supply for Buell's army. Shipments were coming from Louisville on the L&N to the huge supply depot in Nashville, and he struck at Gallatin, north of Nashville, in the most strategically significant action of his career. The expedition involved civilians in a direct manner, setting in motion a chain of events that marked a basic turning point in Morgan's revolutionary strategy: temporarily, the violence of his warfare was escalated; permanently, he began a policy of retaliation on the private property of Union civilians. The robbing of citizens and banking institutions later in his career had its origins in Gallatin in August, 1862.

Civilian informers told Morgan that the twin tunnels on the L&N about seven miles north of Gallatin were guarded by Col. William P. Boone, with only about 200 Kentucky infantry (actually Boone had 375 men, 125 in town and the others at the tunnels and on detached duty in Sumner County). The tunnels, which are still used today, were dug through porous slate under an outcropping of the Cumberland Plateau and shored up with heavy timbers. Heading south, trains first pass through "Little South," which is about 600 feet long, then "Big South," nearly 1,000 feet in length. If Morgan could wreck these structures, the L&N would be closed for months.[12]

In advance of his column, Morgan sent teenage couriers along the seventy-mile passage to alert friendly civilians to prepare forage and food. The night they neared Gallatin, local guides brought the information that Boone was sleeping with his wife in the hotel. At daybreak on August 12, Morgan detached a party of fourteen men, who moved quietly through the streets and captured Boone in his room. Varying accounts of Boone's surrender circulated, but Morgan's favorite held that when the men knocked, Colonel Boone asked, "Who's there?" and heard the answer: "John Morgan." Whereupon Mrs. Boone said, "I surrender and so does the Colonel!"[13]

All of Boone's pickets were asleep and surrendered without firing a shot; 124 Federal rifles were stacked on the courthouse lawn, and Boone and his men were paroled and sent walking north toward Bowling Green. Within eighteen hours the guards at the twin tunnels also surrendered with no resistance and were paroled. Through accurate intelligence provided by civilians and by marching under cover of darkness, Morgan had surprised the enemy and won the objective with no bloodshed.[14]

Soon after the town was secure, a southbound subsistence train with twenty-nine cars of forage, rations, and seventy cavalry horses rolled into the station and was easily captured. In the telegraph office, Ellsworth had relieved operator J.N. Brooks and was attempting to imitate Brooks's sending. The Nashville operator inquired whether it was safe to send a passenger train from Nashville through Gallatin, then became suspicious and asked if the sender was Brooks.

"Yes," replied Ellsworth.

"What news have you?"

"Everything O.K."

"How is the down freight?" Nashville asked, referring to the train that had just been seized.

"Here all right," Ellsworth assured him.

"Guess no, that isn't Brooks' writing; who is it?" There was silence, and then Nashville signaled: "If its Ellsworth at key, I would like you to protect Brooks." Ellsworth identified himself and promised that Brooks would be paroled, which he was, along with all the other captives.[15]

With the assistance of many of the men of Gallatin, the raiders loaded wood on several flatcars, coupled them to the locomotive, and headed northward toward the tunnels. There, after accepting the surrender of Boone's guards, they stacked old crossties and chunks of wood on the track in Big South Tunnel. Then they set fire to the wood on the flatcars and sent the locomotive, with a full head of steam, speeding into the tunnel, where its boiler exploded when it struck the barrier. The fire ignited the roof supports, the slate rock collapsed, and the conflagration spread to a vein of coal in the mountain, which burned for several days. Morgan's men had shut down Buell's supply line—it would take ninety-eight days to rebuild the tunnel. They also wrecked 600 feet of track and burned a bridge a mile south of Big South Tunnel and another trestle two and a half miles south of Gallatin. In the railroad yards, the citizens of Gallatin helped burn the watering station and the remainder of the freight cars and supplies. The raid was a success, but in the end Morgan made a mistake. Instead of remaining true to the hit-and-run principle and departing with his entire force, he left behind a small rear guard under Lieutenant Manly with instructions to wait until daylight to burn the amphitheater at the fairgrounds where Boone's regiment had been quartered.[16]

The three simultaneous raids in July had caused brief delays in communication for Buell's Army of the Ohio, but the Gallatin raid delivered the *coup de grâce* to Buell's main artery of supply and caused him to suspend his advance on Chattanooga. Buell, forty-four years old, reserved and stern, with flecks of gray in his dark beard, was like his friend George McClellan in his emphasis on logistics. Buell had assisted McClellan in organizing and training the Army of the Potomac and, like him, was reluctant to advance unless everything in his army was up to textbook standard. (Eventually, Buell was relieved of command and investigated for having the condition common among Northern generals—what Lincoln called the "slows.") Throughout the summer he had urged the quartermaster department in Louisville to rush supplies to Nashville on the L&N and by boat via the Cumberland River. The magnitude of the flow on the railroad is demonstrated by the fact that between June 14 and August 11, the L&N transported to Nashville 3,900,000 coffee rations, 3,800,000 sugar, 3,800,000 salt meat, and 3,400,000 hardtack. Falling water had caused suspension of river shipments on July 23, and now there was no alternate route; Buell's army was cut off from its supplies.[17]

Buell ordered the arrest of Boone and his men upon their return to Union lines and hoped to avert further similar fiascoes by commanding that posts hold out "to the last extremity." He attempted to rebuild the tunnel, but fifteen days after the raid repair work still had not begun because workers refused to start without adequate protection. Strengthening his triad system of defense, he diverted two regiments of infantry for guard duty and speeded up construction of the trestle stockades—which, as far as the tunnel was concerned, was closing the barn door too late. Morgan had left the two howitzers in the machine shop in Knoxville and had come on the raid without artillery. If the tunnel had been guarded by a stockade, it would have been very difficult to capture it, as subsequent events proved. Buell also pleaded for more cavalry: "We are occupying lines of great depth," he told Halleck. "They are swarming with the enemy's cavalry and can only be protected with cavalry. It is impossible to overrate the importance of this matter."[18] And most directly, Buell responded by concentrating his entire cavalry force under Gen. Richard W. Johnson, a West Point officer, and ordering them to seek and destroy Morgan. Johnson set out with about 700 horsemen, boasting that they would catch Morgan and bring him back in a bandbox.[19]

Bragg, meanwhile, had been making secret preparations for a major invasion of Kentucky, and with Buell halted, he hailed the Gallatin raid as the first blow in the campaign. "Our cavalry is paving the way for me in Middle Tennessee," he wrote Beauregard. The guerrilla raids of Forrest, Armstrong, and Morgan had given the initiative to the Confederacy in the West: they had stalled the Federal invasion of Tennessee and set the stage for a major Confederate incursion into Kentucky.[20]

From Gallatin, Morgan's main body of troops marched eastward fifteen miles to Hartsville and made camp. The next morning, August 13, Union Col. John F. Miller came up from Nashville in a troop train with a brigade of infantry composed of men from Indiana, Ohio, and Michigan, along with an Indiana artillery battery. On a bridge on the Nashville Pike at the edge of Gallatin, they skirmished with Lieutenant Manly's force, killing him, another officer, and one enlisted man. According to James W. King, a Michigan infantryman, the Federal advance happened upon Manly's force unexpectedly. "Our boys fired, killing three of them. Two of which were Captains [Lt. Manly and the unidentified officer]. One of the rebels had his horse shot under him whom we captured. The rest of the Rebels put spurs to their horses and were soon out of sight." Miller learned that the civilians of Gallatin had assisted in the capture of Boone, and he became convinced that most of the burning had been done by civilians. He issued orders to arrest every adult male and search every house. Several guns were found and confiscated. The Federals also plundered a number of retail stores. In the afternoon, Miller warned the Gallatin men never again to provide aid and comfort to the enemy, then released them and returned to Nashville.[21]

News reached Morgan in Hartsville that the bluecoats had yelled "No quarter for Morgan's men!" and had murdered Manly and the other officer after they surrendered. Other reports indicated that the Yankees had robbed and pillaged the homes and businesses of Morgan's friends. Hearing of a Union soldier who stole four silk dresses from one house, and another who had been collecting women's petticoats, Virginia French in McMinnville said the Federals were fighting a silk dress war: "The war has now come down to ladies underclothing," she declared.[22]

In Hartsville, one of Morgan's officers, Capt. Gordon E. Niles, who was an experienced editor from Lockport, New York, used the abandoned office and equipment of the Hartsville *Plaindealer* to establish the *Vidette*, a regimental newspaper. Morgan had read papers like this in the Mexican War; Sterling Price had one in Missouri; and Lee's army had newspapers for brief periods. In one of the first issues of the *Vidette*, Morgan published his policy of retaliation, the most important proclamation of his career. Reports had come in that his pacification of Federal provost marshals during the First Kentucky Raid had failed; they were still taunting, arresting, and threatening the property of Southern sympathizers. In particular, he was incensed by an article in a Cincinnati paper announcing that supporters of Morgan would be forced to pay for the acts of "their favorite chieftain."[23] He had come to this point gradually, taking personally the treatment of his mother, the killing of Lieutenant Manly, the pillage of Gallatin and brief arrest of his friends there. These threats to him and his revolutionary movement demanded a response. In part, his proclamation read:

> I, in my justifiable attacks on Federal troops and Federal property, have always respected private property and persons of Union men. I do hereby declare that, to protect Southern citizens and their rights, I will henceforth put the law of retaliation into full force, and act upon it with vigor. For every dollar exacted from my fellow-citizens, I will have two from all men of known Union sentiments, and will make their persons and property responsible for its payment. God knows it was my earnest wish to have conducted this war according to the dictates of my heart, and consonant to those feelings which actuate every honorable mind, but forced by the vindictive and iniquitous proceedings of our Northern foes to follow their example in order to induce them to return to humane conduct, I will for the future imitate them in their exactions, retaliate upon them and theirs the cruelties and oppressions with which my friends are visited, and continue this course until our enemies consent to make war according to the law of nations.[24]

Under international law, the right of retaliation gave a commanding general authority to respond to violation of the rules of civilized warfare by the enemy with retaliatory measures in the form of similar acts. Morgan was still a colonel, but in his thinking he was far more independent than most generals. In his own personal revolution he had taken it upon himself to protect his civilian supporters; therefore, under no authority other than his own, he would retaliate by making war on Northern civilians.[25]

On August 19, the day the proclamation was published, a Federal infantry force of about 300 men came to Gallatin from Nashville. They went from house to house, commanding all males of twelve years and older to "fall in." They told the boys and men that they were to be taken to Nashville and hanged as spies for aiding Morgan. Ethelbert Campbell, who had come to town on his little sorrel mare to sell chickens and eggs, hesitated. "What for do you say to me to fall in there? I ain't no soldier. I ain't no soldier—never had a fight in my life. Don't want to be killed, or to kill anybody either, tain't my religion. I am a member of the Old Shiloh Camp Ground Presbyterian Church." The Federal officer was unmoved. "Fall in, you blabbed mouthed rebel," he shouted, and Campbell obeyed. About sixty were arrested, including several elderly men, and they left at 9:00 P.M., walking down the railroad track toward Nashville.[26]

That night at midnight in camp at Hartsville, Basil Duke was lying awake under a great oak tree, gazing at the misty shapes gliding in the shadows on the other side of a creek that gleamed in the light of a full moon, when a faint sound fell on his ear. Listening, he distinguished it as the quick hoofbeats of a fleet horse approaching at rapid gallop. The sound ceased when the rider was challenged by pickets, then resumed, clanging fiercely on the gravel pike as it drew nearer. With splintering bang and clash the horse bounded full stride across the bridge over the creek and into the midst of Morgan's men. A boy of about twelve was hanging on the horse, gasping for breath and scarcely able to stay in the saddle. When he could speak, he told what had happened to the males of Gallatin and said that he had come for help. Within five minutes the bugle rang out, and soon the men were in the saddle, moving swiftly to the rescue.[27]

Morgan told Virginia French what happened in Gallatin: "It was a grey morning when we reached the place—instantly we were surrounded by the whole lady population—crying, sobbing entreating us to save their friends—beautiful girls with dishevelled hair—in their nightrobes, with bare feet upon the damp streets—just as they rushed from their homes—wives weeping, mothers beseeching us to save their boys—oh! Madame it was heartbreaking. I do not believe there was a dry eye in my whole command." The women recounted how their homes had been searched, rings torn from their fingers, earrings from their ears and breast pins from their bosoms. One woman described how after killing the three men on August 13, the Federals had kicked and cuffed one of the bodies.[28]

Leading the advance toward Nashville, Morgan came to the bridge where Manly had been killed. Seeing dark stains on the flooring of the small structure, he pointed and screamed that it was Manly's blood. The cry "No quarter today, boys" resounded and echoed up and down the column: "No quarter today." About halfway to Nashville they overtook the Federals. Morgan recounted: "The first Yankee I came up to had an old man nearly exhausted, driving him forward at the point of the bayonet—he was perhaps 80 years of age—I think that was the only time in my life that I felt all humanity leave my heart." With his horse he forced the soldier down the railroad embankment, where the man dropped his rifle and pleaded desperately for his life, but Morgan slid the horse down the precipice and shot him.

There is no Union report of this event, and there is no telling how many prisoners were killed after they surrendered that day. Morgan said: "There were so many of them that when they threw down their arms we couldn't shoot them all." This was the first of two occasions when he departed from his policy of respecting the rights of prisoners of war. (The other was also a time of intense personal emotion, after the death of his brother Tom in a skirmish in Lebanon, Kentucky.)[29]

The running pursuit continued to Edgefield Junction, where the fleeing Federals took refuge in one of Buell's stockades. Like all those structures, it was made of heavy logs set upright, ten or twelve feet high, with loophole openings for rifle fire, and was surrounded with ditches. Morgan plunged at it again and again with repeated frontal assaults. Captain Niles was killed, only four days after creating the *Vidette*. Finally, Duke persuaded Morgan that it was hopeless; artillery would be required to capture stockades, and they had none with them. Returning to Gallatin with the liberated boys and men, Morgan's troopers were welcomed as saviors. The women hugged and kissed them; persuading the rescue party to spend the night, they prepared a feast.[30]

The next morning, August 21, Buell's search-and-destroy mission under General Johnson caught up with its objective. Morgan was asleep in a large house on East Main Street when a courier brought word that farmers near Hartsville had seen a large force of Federal cavalry headed to Gallatin. In great haste the men moved north on the Scottsville, Kentucky, turnpike, hoping to escape. But as they were galloping through the intersection with the Hartsville Pike, the advance of Johnson's force appeared. Morgan first told Duke they must flee, particularly since they lacked accurate information on enemy strength; he said that he could "get fights enough, but could not easily get such a command again, if he lost this one." But the opposing forces were closing, and Morgan smiled and said: "We will have to whip those fellows, sure enough. Form your men, and, as soon as you check them, attack." It was the first time he had skirmished with an evenly matched cavalry force.[31]

A mounted charge by the Texas Rangers checked the advancing blueclads, giving the others time to dismount and form a skirmish line, kneeling behind low fences along the Scottsville road. To the right, south of the Hartsville

Above, John Wesley Hunt, grandfather and namesake of John Hunt Morgan. Bluegrass Trust for Historic Preservation. *Right*, John Hunt Morgan and his mother. Courtesy of Mary B. Mathews.

Above, Calvin Morgan, father of
John Hunt Morgan; *right*, John Hunt
Morgan as a lieutenant in the Ken-
tucky Mounted Volunteers, 1846-47.
University of Kentucky Library.

Above, Morgan as a young businessman, about 1850. Bluegrass Trust for Historic Preservation. *Left*, Rebecca Bruce Morgan, Morgan's bride in 1848, died in 1861 after a long illness. University of Kentucky Library.

Wearing boots, spurs, and civilian clothing, Morgan was prepared at
any moment to masquerade as a Union officer or a traveling
businessman. Library of Congress.

Morgan's raiders were a picturesque body of men, each dressed according to his own taste. *Harper's New Monthly Magazine* (August 1865). Courtesy of Burton Milward.

The raiders bivouacked around the courthouse in Paris, Kentucky, July 1862. *Leslie's Illustrated Newspaper* (August 16, 1862). Courtesy of Burton Milward.

Wooden trestles of the L&N Railroad, the major supply artery of the Union army in the West, were inviting targets; Morgan's raiders burned the Bacon Creek bridge December 5, 1861. Seaboard System Railroad.

The fight at the Licking River bridge, Cynthiana, Kentucky, July 18, 1862. *Leslie's Illustrated Newspaper* (August 16, 1862). Cincinnati Historical Society.

An equipment and baggage train of the L&N Railroad overtakes a regiment of General Buell's army in Kentucky, January 1862. *Leslie's Illustrated Newspaper* (January 18, 1862). Seaboard System Railroad.

A wood-burning locomotive of the L&N Railroad in an early post-Civil War photograph. Seaboard System Railroad.

News that Morgan had taken Cynthiana raised apprehensions in Covington, Kentucky, in July 1862. *Leslie's Illustrated Newspaper* (August 9, 1862). Cincinnati Historical Society.

At Salem, Indiana, in July 1863, raiders burned the railroad depot and bridges and looted the retail stores. *Leslie's Illustrated Newspaper* (August 8, 1863). Cincinnati Historical Society.

Civilians fled in terror when Morgan's raiders charged into Washington, Ohio, in July 1863. *Harper's Weekly* (August 15, 1863). University of Kentucky Library.

A group of Morgan's officers, imprisoned in the state penitentiary in Pittsburgh, clowned for the camera. University of Kentucky Library.

At night in the Ohio State Penitentiary, Morgan and his officers were locked in single cells three and a half feet wide, seven feet long, and seven feet high. Ohio Historical Society/Columbus *Dispatch*. Under a cellblock like the one below, the prisoners dug their escape tunnel. Ohio Historical Society.

John Hunt Morgan and Mattie, shortly after their wedding.
University of Kentucky Library.

A highly romanticized portrayal of Morgan and his staff. Library of Congress.

A late portrait of Morgan reflects the stress and fatigue of war. Library of Congress. *Below*, Pvt. Andrew J. Campbell, who shot Morgan at Greeneville on September 4, 1864. Photograph presented to the author by Frank G. Rankin.

Above, Basil W. Duke, Morgan's brother-in-law and second in command. When Morgan died, Duke lamented that the glory and the chivalry were gone from the war. University of Kentucky Library. *Left*, Johnnie Hunt Morgan Caldwell, Morgan's daughter, who died childless at the age of twenty-three. Bluegrass Trust for Historic Preservation.

A crowd of ten thousand gathered around the Lexington courthouse for the dedication of an equestrian statue of Morgan in 1911. Courtesy of Burton Milward.

road, two companies occupied the edge of a cornfield; to the left, other men were in line at the edge of a woodland facing a large bluegrass meadow. Johnson's men took down the eastern fence of the pasture, and 300 of them came charging forth with sabers drawn. It was a mounted frontal assault against infantry in a makeshift defensive position. Morgan's men held their fire until the horses were within thirty yards. "Then was seen the effect of a volley from that long thin line, which looked so easy to break, and, yet, whose fire was so deadly," Duke wrote. "Every man had elbow-room and took dead aim at an individual foe, and, as the blaze left the guns, two thirds of the riders and horses seemed to go down." The attack was broken; the Federals came again and were repulsed. Then Confederates in the cornfield on the right pressed forward; the gray advance became general, and the Union men retreated to the protection of a heavily timbered hill half a mile in their rear.[32]

The rebel horse-holders brought the mounts, and as Morgan's men stormed the hill in earnest, giving the Rebel yell at the top of their voices, the Federals went into a state of confusion. Company and regimental organizations were lost; men panicked, throwing away their rifles and discharging their revolvers in the air. Like a drove of cattle they scurried, officers and men vying for position in headlong scamper. For three miles along the Hartsville Pike they left evidence of their disgrace: Enfield rifles, pistols, sabers, saddlebags, canteens, currycombs, brushes, and hats all cast aside helter-skelter. Johnson, after attempting to reform his troops, determined that the safest course was to sound the retreat. He was racing back toward Hartsville with his staff when Duke's men overtook and captured them. The man who had boasted he would bring Morgan back in a bandbox was Morgan's prisoner. The Union losses were 21 dead, 47 wounded, and 176 missing to Morgan's 5 killed, 18 wounded, and 2 missing.[33]

The skirmish demonstrated the superiority of the tactic of fighting dismounted. Morgan gained the advantage through the superior firepower of infantry in defensive position, then followed through with mounted pursuit to achieve the victory. In a head-to-head fight he had routed Buell's cavalry. The next day in Hartsville he proclaimed: "Officers and men, your conduct makes me proud to command you. Fight always as you fought yesterday and you are invincible."[34]

After an abortive attempt by subordinates to replace his democratic leadership with conventional military discipline, Morgan had conducted the most strategic raid of his career. He had closed the L&N Railroad for ninety-eight days, brought Buell's advance on Chattanooga to a halt, and handed Bragg the initiative. With his offensive closed down, Buell had concentrated upon reopening and protecting his supply line. He renewed his pleas for more cavalry, deployed additional men to defend railroad bridges behind the lines, hastened the construction of stockades, and flung his available cavalry at Morgan—only to have them defeated and captured by the prey.

On the Gallatin expedition Morgan took advantage of Southern feeling in middle Tennessee by exercising the guerrilla principle of involving civilians in military activity. Civilians informed him that the tunnels at Gallatin were weakly guarded; civilians served as couriers and guides; sympathizers along the route provided food and forage; citizens near Gallatin advised where the enemy commander was sleeping; and the men and boys of Gallatin participated in the destruction of Federal property. It was in response to this escalation of civilian involvement that Union soldiers searched residences, plundered businesses, and arrested the male citizens of Gallatin. Returning blow for blow, Morgan killed Union prisoners after they had surrendered.

Of greatest significance, Federal treatment of his friends in Gallatin contributed to the proclamation of his independent policy of retaliation on the North. For the remainder of his life, Morgan made war on the property of Northern civilians.

ELEVEN

Bragg's Kentucky Invasion

The First Kentucky Raid and the Gallatin expedition, along with strikes by Forrest and other cavalry commanders, had brought Buell's army to a halt. Morgan's reports from Kentucky were a catalyst for the greatest offensive of the Confederacy in the West during the entire war—Bragg's invasion of Kentucky. By late summer of 1862 the Confederacy had cast aside the defensive strategy and seized the momentum, taking the war to the enemy. It was the high-water mark for the strategy of annihilation. Lee's victories in the Seven Days campaign and Second Bull Run (Manassas) had given him the initiative, and in early September he invaded Maryland.

Morgan's report to Kirby Smith from Georgetown on July 16, 1862, that 25,000 to 30,000 Kentuckians were anxious to join the Confederate army, was rushed to Richmond the same day. It seemed to confirm the belief of the Kentucky bloc and Southerners in general that most Kentuckians were Southern sympathizers, that all that was needed was a continuing Confederate presence in the state to cause an uprising which would bring Kentucky into the Confederacy. Southerners had been greatly disappointed when Kentucky, a slave state, refused to secede; and when Kentucky declared for the Union, a natural defensive line along the Ohio River had been lost. Davis and many others believed that the hearts of the people were Southern and that they would revolt if given an opportunity. To Virginia, the state was a lost daughter. "We can but feel the most intense interest in the fate of Kentucky," a citizen of the Old Dominion wrote. "We were once one people, one State." Commentators determined that the people were lost sheep, stolen out of the fold by Puritan abolitionists, Yankee capitalists, and demagogic politicians. Then, standing the metaphor on its head in a manner which revealed the lack of reality in this reasoning, one analyst declared that if only given a chance, the sheep would fight with the fury of tigers. Appealing to Kentucky's sense of honor, William Gilmore Simms wrote: "Alas, for Kentucky! she has been slow—too slow—and must pay the penalty for protracted slumbers. But if not too late to save from suffering, it is yet in her power to keep from shame!" The Richmond *Examiner* pointed out that the only factor which saved Kentucky from total disgrace was participation by Kentuckians in the Confederate war effort.[1]

Morgan's statement and his subsequent official report of the First Kentucky Raid offered hope. "A great reaction is going on in Kentucky which is thought will revolutionize the State," an editor in Savannah wrote. The Atlanta *Southern Confederacy* predicted that current ferment would result in a Kentucky "redeemed, regenerated and disenthralled." The Confederate high command embraced the premise that Kentucky would revolt, and the assumption became the main pillar in Bragg's plans for an offensive. On August 1, he wrote: "The feeling in Middle Tennessee and Kentucky is represented by Forrest and Morgan to have become intensely hostile to the enemy, and nothing is wanted but arms and support to bring the people into our ranks, for they have found that neutrality has afforded them no protection."[2]

For Bragg's campaign, Davis furnished sample proclamations to the people of Kentucky pleading for their support. He directed that Bragg take along Provisional Kentucky Governor Richard Hawes and, when the army reached the state capital of Frankfort, install him as head of the new Confederate government of the commonwealth. The ordnance department provided a long train of wagons containing 20,000 extra rifles to arm Kentuckians ready to cast off the vile yoke. The Confederate administration followed the advice of the Kentucky delegation in Congress to send as many Kentucky officers as possible on the incursion; they would encourage recruitment. The overall purpose of the offensive was never clearly established, but it was assumed that Bragg's army would have the hearty support of the people and be reinforced with enlistments. And it was assumed that the Confederates were going into Kentucky to stay. Bragg wrote: "My army has promised to make me military governor of Ohio in ninety days." In Bragg's mind, the destruction of Buell's army had become secondary; the liberation of Kentucky was the foundation stone of the campaign.[3]

The invasion opened successfully when Kirby Smith defeated a Federal column at Richmond and occupied Lexington. Bragg's army advanced into south central Kentucky, headed in the direction of Louisville, and Morgan's brigade of 1,100 men marched toward a conjunction with Smith in Lexington. Leaving Hartsville on August 29, they moved slowly, allowing time for a detachment to close up with the two howitzers, which were again operational. At last, they were going home with a large army to free the state and stay there. In jubilant spirits they cheered and sang the songs of the Kentucky movement. "Answer to the Kentucky Exile" was particularly appropriate to the occasion:

> Let others bow submissively beneath a tyrants will,
> We will give ourselves to freedom and will fight for freedom still,
> And will plant our glorious standard on Kentucky's verdant shore,
> And rescue from the tyrant our homes forevermore.
>
> > Yes, we'll march, march, march,
> > To the music of the drum,
> > We were driven forth in exile,
> > From our old Kentucky homes.[4]

Once they reached the Kentucky border, the men began handing out Morgan's proclamation to the people, a printed broadside declaring that Morgan had returned with a powerful army, determined to occupy the state permanently: "AROUSE, KENTUCKIANS! Let the old men of Kentucky, and our noble-hearted women, arm their sons and their lovers for the fight! Better death in our sacred cause than a life of slavery!"[5]

In Glasgow, Southern friends told Morgan that indictments for treason had been filed in Barren County Court against him and other Confederates. In Morgan's view, there was no place for such legal proceedings in liberated Kentucky—he had his men enter the county court clerk's office and destroy all the court records. This violated international law, for as Halleck wrote: "None but a barbarous and uncivilized enemy would think of destroying or withholding" public documents.[6]

Morgan easily could have made Lexington by nightfall on September 3, but he paused in Nicholasville for the night, sending scouts on ahead to inform his friends that he would make a triumphal parade into his hometown at 10:00 A.M. the next day. It seemed a lifetime, but he had been gone only eleven and a half months. He had left like a thief in the night and was determined to return with honor. He was not disappointed; it was a grand welcome, one of the proudest days of his life. The streets were crowded with men, women, and children, many of them waving Confederate flags and the women wearing red and white streamers on their bonnets. In a column of fours the command rode down Limestone Street to Main, past the former armory of the Lexington Rifles to Cheapside, where they dismounted and mingled with the friendly throng.[7]

Morgan used the office of the *Observer and Reporter* for his headquarters and camped his men in the courthouse yard, with their horses fastened in the university lot in front of Hopemont (the first night, residents complained that the whooping of Wash Morgan's Indian friends kept them awake). But within a few days they were gone, and Morgan's mother lamented: "I had not five minutes private conversation with John while he was here. There was a crowd around him, or someone in pursuit for pressing business."[8]

Kirby Smith divided Morgan's brigade, sending Duke to northern Kentucky in a feint on Cincinnati and Morgan himself to southeastern Kentucky, where he was to delay Federal Gen. George Morgan in his retreat from Cumberland Gap toward the Ohio River. John Morgan was to retard the Federal Morgan long enough for Confederate Humphrey Marshall to come out of southwest Virginia and attack his rear. Entering the mountains of eastern Kentucky, Morgan was well aware of the threat of bushwhackers. He had narrowly missed being shot himself in Casey County, on the way into Kentucky, when unseen bushwhackers firing from the hills had shot and wounded a teenage slave orderly riding alongside him. As a precaution, he issued a proclamation cautioning that he would shoot bushwhackers and lay waste the entire surrounding area.[9]

They made contact with the enemy column at West Liberty, in the mountains in the rain on Friday afternoon, September 26. Morgan sent two companies to attack the flank of one of the advance brigades and force the Federals to close up and delay. He and his staff, wearing oilcloths to keep dry, were breathing their horses and discussing the need for intelligence when a group of mountaineers with guns approached.

"I'll pass for Colonel DeCourcy," Morgan whispered, referring to Federal Col. John F. DeCourcy, 16th Ohio Infantry, who was commanding a brigade in the enemy force. The local civilians approached and inquired who they were.

"That's Colonel DeCourcy," said Morgan's adjutant, Robert A. Alston.

"Why, the boys told us DeCourcy's brigade was behind, and we're mighty glad to see you."

Looking them in the eye, Morgan said: "Wouldn't you like to join us?"

"Oh, no," the spokesman answered, "we can do more good at home, killing the damned Secesh."

"Oh, have you killed many Secesh?"

"I reckon we have. You'd have laughed if you'd seen us make Bill kill his brother."

"What did you do that for?"

"Why, you see, Bill went South, and we burned his house, and he deserted; we arrested him, and said we were going to hang him as a spy; he said he'd do anything if we let him off, that his family would starve if we hung him. Last Wednesday we took him and made him kill his brother Jack. He didn't want to do it, but we told him we'd kill them both if he didn't, and we made him do it."

With a straight face Morgan interrogated them on the strength of the Federal column marching through, the politics of citizens in the area, and the location of roads and pathways. When he had all the information they could provide, he declared: "I am John Morgan, and I'm going to have you hung."

The bushwhackers fell to their knees, some of them begging for their lives, others praying, one moaning over and over, "What will Susy do without me?"

They were conducted to camp, tried by drumhead court-martial, sentenced to be shot, and escorted to an open field. The execution squad was drawn up, and the lieutenant of the guard commanded:

"Ready! Present arms!"

And in that instant which seemed like an eternity, just before the order to fire, Morgan suspended the sentence and sent the mountaineers on their way, warning them to sin no more.[10]

For the next several days, in classic guerrilla style, Morgan's men pestered the Federal column of infantry and cavalry like a swarm of gnats. Crossing swift mountain streams they jumped from rock ledges, plunging into deep water, riding like madmen to turn the advance of the enemy. "We fought them in front," a man wrote, "barricaded the Mountain passes by felling timber, then while they were removing it, we would dash around in the rear and attack them. We captured a large drove of cattle which they were driving with them for the purpose of eating. We relieved them of their wagons. We captured their men. . . . We prepared ambuscades and they marched in and found themselves suddenly fired on in the darkness of the night." The Federal Morgan was seriously annoyed, particularly at the loss of subsistence and lack of fresh water—his troops drank from stagnant pools for three days. Marshall's army never came, however, and Morgan was too far outnumbered to achieve any more than delay. The Federals escaped, and Morgan returned to the Bluegrass area.[11]

Meanwhile, Bragg's army had advanced slowly into south central Kentucky and in Glasgow he issued the opening salvo of his pacification effort:

> Kentuckians, I have entered your State with the Confederate Army of the West, and offer you an opportunity to free yourselves. . . . Believing that the heart of Kentucky is with us in our great struggle for constitutional freedom, we have transferred from our soil to yours not a band of marauders, but a powerful and well-disciplined army. . . . Kentuckians, we come with joyous hopes. Let us not depart in sorrow, as we shall if we find you wedded in your choice to present your lot. If you prefer Federal rule, show it by your frowns and we shall return whence we came. If you choose rather to come within the folds of the brotherhood, then cheer us with the smiles of your women and lend your willing hands to secure you in your heritage of liberty.

But there were few smiles or recruits in the southern counties. Of their reception in Tompkinsville, a brigade commander said: "It was evident that we had no friends there."[12]

Bragg proceeded to Bardstown and went on the defensive, clearing the way for Buell to occupy Louisville. In Bardstown there was the first warm reception but not the expected rush of enlistments. In the entire campaign, 1,500 joined Kirby Smith and 2,500 enrolled under Bragg—only about one-tenth of the projected numbers. Soon Bragg began warning Kirby Smith that unless volunteering quickened, they would have to abandon Kentucky. He was coming to the conclusion that Southern supporters in the state lacked commitment. Later, he wrote his wife that Kentuckians had said: "We are with you; only whip these fellows out of our country, and let us see you can protect us, and we will join you." Kirby Smith told Bragg: "Their hearts were evidently with us, but their blue-grass and fat-grass [cattle] are against us."[13]

As planned, Bragg installed Hawes as governor, but Hawes occupied the executive mansion in Frankfort only a few hours before an advancing Union army forced him into exile, which is where the provisional government remained. The offensive had been weakened by inadequate planning and lack of coordination between Bragg and Kirby Smith, and it was weighted down by logistic problems; but the crucial factor was that Bragg lost his courage. When the Kentucky revolution failed to materialize, he became moody, vacillating, and lacking in self-confidence. He lost the daring and decisiveness required to defeat Buell.[14]

Morgan reunited with Duke's force in central Kentucky and was screening Kirby Smith's army in the Lexington area when Bragg fought the battle of Perryville on October 8. It was not a clear victory for Buell, but Bragg retreated, convinced that he could not hold Kentucky without an uprising of the populace. Morgan hated to cover the regular army, and south of Richmond, guarding the retreat of Kirby Smith's infantry, he requested permission to double back through Lexington and strike the L&N in southwestern Kentucky, cutting Buell's supply line as Buell fell back into Tennessee. There would be more forage and rations there, and Morgan could enjoy being independent and in control. In the track of a large army there were few opportunities to pose as an enemy officer or to strike individual blows for the revolution by terrorizing provost marshals.[15]

Kirby Smith approved, and at 1:00 P.M. on October 17, Morgan broke off from the main army and struck north for Lexington. Near Clay's Ferry he stopped at a Union man's house and, identifying himself as Union Col. Frank Wolford, secured the man's aid as guide. For hours they rode side by side, with Morgan playing the role of Wolford.

In the early morning of October 18, Morgan's command conducted a comedy of errors, the most confused surprise attack of their war service. The plan was to surprise the 4th Ohio Cavalry camp on the grounds of Ashland (the Henry Clay estate in Lexington) at daybreak: Duke's regiment was to advance dismounted from the west; W.C.P. Breckinridge's battalion was to approach on foot from the east and soften them up with the two howitzers; and Richard Gano's Texas Rangers, in reserve behind Breckinridge, were to charge in on horseback to complete the rout.

When the firing began, rifle balls from Breckinridge's force flew over the heads of the surprised Ohioans, into the ranks of Duke's men on a knoll on the opposite side of the camp. Duke wheeled and fell back; Breckinridge advanced and was overrunning the enemy position when his howitzers opened fire, scattering their own men. The firing ceased, and the Confederates were rounding up prisoners on the pike in front of Ashland when from the east, out of the rising sun, the Texans came galloping forward, blazing away at both captives and captors with rifles, shotguns, and pistols. Totally exasperated, Morgan rode between the prisoners and the advancing Texans, screaming, "Cease fire! Cease fire!" Several balls pierced his coat and one prisoner was hit. In the skirmish itself, Wash Morgan was mortally wounded. Taken to Hopemont, he called for a black cigar and said, "I want to show you how a Morgan can die."[16]

Later that day a courier from Kirby Smith came to Lexington with orders countermanding permission to leave Kentucky via the western route. Smith regretfully reported that Bragg was ordering Morgan to proceed to south-west Virginia to guard the salt works and lead mines there. Southwest Virginia was considered one of the worst assignments in the entire Confederacy, a veritable graveyard for commanders. Bragg meant to bury Morgan far away, where he could not mislead the high command again concerning Southern sentiment in Kentucky. Most of those 20,000 rifles were still in the crates, and the creaking of the wagons bearing them along with his retreating army was resounding in Bragg's ears. Duke read the message and simply stuffed it in his pocket. After the war he admitted it was a "breach of discipline," but at the time he rationalized that Marshall's command was sufficient to guard the salt works—which it was—and Morgan's continued on their way.

On the Louisville Road near Bardstown, Morgan dodged a Federal force and captured and burned a supply train of 150 wagons. On the night of October 21, he camped at Leitchfield, where the men captured a company of Home Guards and imprisoned them in the courthouse. William A. Milton was in charge of the prisoners, and at bedtime Morgan came for an interview with their captain. As he left, he said to Milton: "Mr. Milton, as this officer is to be shot tomorrow morning, I want you to know that you will be held personally responsible for his appearance, and also for the appearance of several others of his company. They have been persecuting our friends and especially the families of some of our men. I intend to make an example that will be remembered." It was obvious from their worried expressions that the prisoners believed him. They began murmuring among themselves, and Morgan took Milton aside and said, "Of course, you perceive this as all *by play*. I want to impress these people with a wholesome fear as far as possible, to put a stop to their persecuting their neighbors, but you keep up the scare and be as hard as you know how to be. I'll see you in the morning."

All night long the prisoners wept, prayed, and pleaded with Milton to use his influence with Colonel Morgan; several wrote letters and messages of farewell to their families. When the command was ready to leave the next morning, Morgan called out the captain and said that after talking it over with his officers, he had decided to set them free if they would swear not to molest their neighbors or take up arms against the Confederacy during the war. The terms were accepted, and all the prisoners were sworn. Some were so relieved they kissed Morgan's feet.[17]

On the night of October 24, Morgan's force encamped in a level field near Greenville, the men sleeping on the ground under blankets and oilcloths. A heavy snow in the night gave the camp the appearance of an enshrouded graveyard; Duke recalled that when the field came alive with motion in the morning, a man rising out of each mound, it made him think of the resurrection. In Hopkinsville they received a warm welcome, with many women preparing a sumptuous feast and the unmarried women vying for attention. There Morgan detached raiding parties to burn bridges and wreck the L&N

track in several locations, harassing the Union army in its trek out of Kentucky. Morgan's Southern friends identified several local Union men who had been persecuting them, and he arrested them and intimidated each one into promising right behavior in the future.[18]

From the point of view of the strategy of annihilation and as far as the liberation of Kentucky was concerned, the campaign had failed; but amid their condemnation of Bragg, Southern journalists heaped laurels on Morgan. The Richmond *Dispatch* affirmed that Morgan's arc rivaled Jeb Stuart's second ride around McClellan's army in October, and the Charleston *Courier* exulted: "For greatness of conception, daring and rapidity of execution, this expedition of Morgan's has not been surpassed since the commencement of the war."[19]

But in reality Morgan had done the Confederate war effort a disservice. By contributing to the assumption that Kentucky would revolt, he had a part in giving the offensive a basic weakness to begin with; it was an unrealistic dream, launched under a false premise. The initiative that Morgan had done so much to create for the Confederacy in the West was lost. It would have been an ideal time for Bragg to remain on the defensive and shift to the strategy of attrition; even under the strategy of annihilation, if the Kentucky dream had not been foremost in Bragg's mind, he would have been able to think more clearly. Perhaps he would have attacked Buell in Alabama or seized Nashville and fought defensively to hold it. Even if he had still chosen to invade Kentucky, he would have done so on a more realistic basis and possibly with greater self-confidence. As it turned out, the Kentucky campaign did accomplish something: when the two armies repositioned themselves, the Federals, now under William S. Rosecrans, were in Nashville and the Confederates in Murfreesboro; the Union drive on Chattanooga had been reversed, and Bragg was back in middle Tennessee. The Kentucky exiles were bitterly disappointed; they laid all the blame on Bragg, and the resentment was mutual.

Before the return of the main armies, Gen. John C. Breckinridge, now commander of the Army of Middle Tennessee, determined to demonstrate the Confederate presence in the region. A small rear guard had been left in Nashville by the Union army, and intelligence indicated that 300 empty freight cars were clogging the railroad yards, having delivered supplies before Morgan destroyed the tunnel in August. Breckinridge's plan was for Morgan's force to burn the cars, which were north of the Cumberland River and within range of the artillery batteries on Capitol Hill. Forrest's command was to create a diversion on the south side of the river, pretending to threaten the city itself. On November 5, the day after Morgan's men arrived in Gallatin again, the raid began. Both columns marched all night, and at daybreak Forrest's feint made a great noise and alarmed the residents while Morgan's raiders slipped through the woods and into the yards. What scouts had not reported was that Union infantry were camped there between the tracks and among the cars. Lieutenant Quirk's videttes burned a few boxcars, but the shooting was so heavy that Morgan had to withdraw without achieving major destruction. The objective of establishing Confederate presence had been achieved, but the raid demonstrated the necessity of accurate intelligence for successful guerrilla operations.[20]

Two nights later Morgan marched out of Gallatin with 200 men to ambush Rosecrans's Army of the Cumberland coming south to Nashville on the Louisville and Nashville pike. When the sun came up the next morning, November 8, the guerrillas were in position several miles north of Nashville, dismounted and concealed in dense woods behind a hill about seventy-five yards from the road. Morgan stationed them where they could fire a volley or two into the vastly superior army and make a fast withdrawal on horseback. Two sutler's wagons passed, and an advance guard of cavalry. Then came the Union infantry, well fed and splendidly equipped, bayonets glistening in the sun, the men in the ranks singing, joking, and laughing. "We could hear them as they marched," one of Morgan's men recalled, "but as lightning without warning, two hundred guns cracked and . . . lo! the scene was changed to screams and oaths." The column recoiled, formed in line and charged the hill, killing one of the raiders before they could mount and retreat.[21]

Circling through woods and fields, Morgan struck the road again in the rear of the Federal column. He posted the men in a thicket while he, with Quirk and three men, galloped down the road toward the Union army to overtake and capture stragglers. He had taken about forty, had sent them under guard to the main force, and was bringing in another ten when Union Col. William B. Stoke's 5th Tennessee Cavalry came up the pike, backtracking. Taken by surprise, Morgan's men scattered, and he and his party of four were surrounded. Playing the role of a Federal colonel, Morgan thanked them for coming to his relief. He explained that he and his squad had been arresting Union stragglers when the Rebels came out of the thicket and attempted to capture them. They could see that he had no insignia of rank or identifying symbol of either army, and an officer asked about his butternut trousers. Morgan seemed suddenly to lose his temper, shouting that he would bring his entire regiment and that would convince them. Then, leaping his horse over a fence, he escaped through the woods, followed by Quirk and the other three men.[22]

The next afternoon, November 9, John left his command and went to Murfreesboro to renew the courtship with Mattie. They agreed to be married on Sunday, December 14. At the same time he sent Grenfell to Bragg to request permission to conduct independent guerrilla operations. Bragg not only approved and relieved Morgan of routine screening duty; he recommended him for promotion to brigadier general, saying that he already considered him a general, and authorized the quartermaster department to supply funds as needed for Morgan's command. His wrath from the Kentucky invasion had cooled, and he remembered that guerrilla cavalry raids had given him the momentum before. Bragg's action showed perception and magnanimity. He accepted Morgan's faults and put his greatness to use, interpreting his insubordination on the swingback as part of Morgan's nature and learning from it that Morgan was of no use in routine cavalry duty.[23]

Bragg informed Richmond: "Col. John H. Morgan is peculiarly suited for the special service in which I propose to employ him—partisan war on the enemy's lines in Kentucky. He has raised his own command, and nearly armed and equipped it from the enemy's stores." The Confederate nation needed victories, and even though Morgan had weaknesses, popular small successes covered a multitude of sins. Bragg expected a great deal of Morgan and Forrest, and President Davis approved. The L&N was still closed, and Bragg hoped his cavalry raiders would keep it shut down.[24]

Bragg had tasted the fruits of victory from guerrilla warfare before the Kentucky invasion, and with Forrest and Morgan as his teachers, he had come to embrace it as an adjunct to major operations. On December 1 he issued orders giving Morgan carte blanche to conduct guerrilla raids on Federal communications north of Nashville. "You will assail [the enemy's] guards where your relative force will justify it; capture and destroy his trains; burn his bridges, depots, trestle-work, &c. In fine, harass him in every conceivable way in your power. . . . You are not limited in the extent of your operations, every confidence being reposed in your zeal, discretion, and judgment."[25]

When Morgan reported that an enemy force at Hartsville was thrown out from the Nashville front in an isolated position, Bragg himself organized a raid, using part of his army to create diversions in support. The plan was based on reports of Morgan's new company of elite scouts led by Tom Quirk, recently promoted to captain. Answering directly to Morgan, these would earn the reputation of never allowing Morgan to be surprised when they were in the advance. On this occasion their intelligence was valuable but inaccurate on the side of underestimating the size of the enemy force, but the expedition was a classic case of a guerrilla chief turning obstacles into opportunities. In terribly inclement weather, Morgan used the cover of darkness to conceal the march of about thirty miles through middle Tennessee. He overcame the natural obstacles of the icy Cumberland River and rough winter roads that had lulled the enemy into a false sense of security. Other factors were Morgan's familiarity with the terrain—he had camped in Hartsville and knew every byway—and Bragg's diversions, which effectively prevented interference from Nashville. Also, most of the Federal troops at Hartsville were green recruits who had never been under fire.[26]

Bragg detached from Roger Hanson's 1st Kentucky Infantry brigade (the Orphan Brigade) two regiments of infantry, the 2nd and 9th Kentucky, and a battery of Kentucky artillery. They were assigned to Morgan for the raid and placed under the command of his uncle, Col. Thomas H. Hunt—(Hunt had recruited and led the 9th Kentucky since October, 1861. He knew every man in the regiment by name, and they were proud of his tall, erect appearance and magnificent military mien. They respected him and obeyed his discipline. On a march through the mud in the first winter he had become concerned for his men, and alighting from his horse, Old Pomp, he threw his bridle over his shoulder and marched on foot through the swollen streams and slushy roads the remainder of the day.) Bragg deployed the remainder of the Orphan Brigade and two brigades of Benjamin Franklin Cheatham's division, with part of Joseph Wheeler's cavalry, in two separate diversionary attacks along the Nashville front.[27]

Morgan's 1,400 men plus Hunt's 740 infantry made up a force of 2,140. Quirk's scouts estimated the enemy at 1,300, enabling Morgan to expect to outnumber them better than 1.5 to 1. On Saturday morning, December 6, Morgan left Murfreesboro and met Hunt's command in Bairds Mills, a few miles south of Lebanon, at 11:00 A.M. It was about thirty miles from the objective, and the weather was cold and snow was falling—four inches would accumulate by early evening. Many of the infantry had only old rags on their feet to protect them from the wet snow and freezing cold, and several were armed with shotguns. There were not enough horses to mount the infantry; they had to walk, and Morgan had never conducted a raid in which infantry were part of the strike force. In an effort to relieve the infantry— who were, after all, fellow Kentuckians—he conducted an experiment: the cavalry surrendered their mounts for a few miles to give the "webfeet" a rest. But the wet feet of the infantry soon began to freeze, and they clamored to dismount. In the meantime, the cavalrymen's boots had become saturated, and they, too, froze once their wearers were back in the saddle. Kentucky brotherhood notwithstanding, the "webfeet" and "buttermilk rangers" condemned each other with all the richness of a soldier's vocabulary.[28]

The infantry began crossing the icy Cumberland River at ten o'clock that night, using two small flat-bottomed ferryboats at Purier's Ferry. The boats leaked, and when Johnny Green crossed with some of the artillery horses, the animals became restless and kicked a plank loose from the bottom of the vessel—the men had to bail water for life or death. North of the river the roads were almost impassable. "One long hill was up rocks like stair steps, each step being about two feet rise. The infantry had to take hold of each wheel of the artillery & almost lift it up that hill," Green recalled.[29]

When the cavalry reached the ford that had been selected, Duke found that rising water made it too deep, and he located another crossing down the river. It was scarcely an improvement—there was a narrow bridle path to the riverbank only wide enough for passage single file. At the river each man had to gather his horse, take a deep breath and plunge over a four-foot bluff into the water, submerging horse and rider in an extremely cold bath. The opposite bank became cut up and muddy and more difficult to negotiate as the crossing continued. The first men over made fires and attempted to dry out, but Duke realized that the night was far spent and moved on with 700, half of the force. "The weather was extremely cold and after the plunge in the river, our clothes froze on us," one of them recalled.[30]

The infantry and half of the cavalry reunited, and Morgan sent one regiment of cavalry to the rear of the enemy camp to prevent a retreat. This depleted the attacking strength to about 1,200 men—700 infantry and 500 cavalry—but according to reconnaissance reports, this was still an approximately even number, and the attackers would have the advantage of surprise. The crucial matter was to conquer the Hartsville garrison and escape before the 5,000-man Federal force at Castalian Springs, nine miles to the west, discovered their presence.

Day was breaking when Morgan's advance scouts, dressed in blue overcoats, surprised and shot the Federal pickets before they could return fire. A black servant of one of the officers went running into camp shouting at the top of his voice, "The Rebels are coming! The Rebels are coming!" When Morgan came up, the cavalry wheeling by fours into line, across a ravine ten feet deep and beyond a snow-covered meadow he distinctly heard the Yankee officers yelling, "Company, fall in!" and saw the men scrambling around their bivouac fires and tents, forming a long blue battleline on the edge of a dense grove of beechwood trees. The camp covered a sizable portion of ground, and it was obvious there were more men than Quirk had reported. The 39th Brigade, commanded by Col. Absalom B. Moore, had three infantry regiments (two from Ohio and one from Illinois), an Indiana cavalry regiment, a Kentucky cavalry company, and a battery of Indiana artillery— about 2,100 strong. On the field Morgan was outnumbered nearly two to one. Sensing his concern, Duke said, "You have more work cut out for you than you bargained for." Morgan answered, "Yes, you gentlemen must whip and catch those fellows, and cross the river in two hours and a half, or we'll have six thousand more on our backs."[31]

Morgan dismounted the cavalry and positioned them under Duke on the left; the artillery was in the center; and Hunt formed the infantry on the right. The Confederates' Rebel yell was answered by relatively mild cheers from the Federal line. Abruptly, Duke's men advanced at double-quick, exchanging brisk fire for twenty minutes and gradually driving the Union right wing back upon the center. Then Hunt's infantry dashed over the ravine and closed with the enemy on the Confederate right. "Boys," Hunt called, "kill a man with every shot." The blue line wavered; Hunt commanded: "Charge bayonets! Forward march!" At that instant about seventy-five cavalry (those who had been delayed crossing the river) came up, dismounted, and yelling and gliding over the ground like panthers, pushed through the center—contributing to confusion and retreat all along the Union line. The Union troops had been in the service only three months, and this, their baptism of fire, was too much to endure—some continued shooting from behind rocks and trees, but many ran and hid in their tents.[32]

A white flag was hoisted, and after the Federals were relieved of their weapons, the Rebels rummaged through the tents and supply wagons. The Kentucky infantry had been through Shiloh, Vicksburg, and Baton Rouge, and they needed shoes and clothing. Johnny Green rushed into the tent of Colonel Moore, put on his beautiful overcoat, and was helping himself to the fine flannel shirts in Moore's valise when Moore appeared, exclaiming:

"My good fellow, don't take my clothes."

"Here," said Green, handing him the shirts.

"Oh! Do give me my overcoat."

"No," Green replied, "You won't need it; you will be kept warm in prison & I'll need it."³³

Henry Lane Stone, of Morgan's cavalry, wrote home the next day: "I captured a splendid overcoat, lined through and through, a fine black cloth coat, a pair of new woolen socks, a horse muzzle to feed in, an Enfield rifle, a lot of pewter plates, knives and forks, a good supply of smoking tobacco, an extra good cavalry saddle, a halter, and a pair of buckskin gloves, lined with lamb's wool—all of which things I needed."³⁴

Supplies that could not be carried were burned, and while the cavalry piggybacked the last prisoners over the waist-deep Cumberland River ford, Morgan settled back to share the exhilaration of victory with Mattie. Throwing his leg over the saddle and tearing a leaf from a notebook, he wrote her a quick note and sent it off in haste by courier. He said later: "I had just got my men, prisoners, and the beautiful Parrott guns we had taken over the river and sitting there on my horse with my staff around me, when a shell cut the limb of a tree just above me. The enemy were on our track and we had just escaped him." The encampment at Castalian Springs had heard the artillery fire, seen the smoke, and marched to the rescue—too late.³⁵

The Union had 58 killed, 204 wounded, and 1,834 taken prisoner—total casualties, 2,096. Morgan's task force lost 21 dead, 104 wounded, and 14 missing—139 casualties. When the column marched into the camp of Bragg's army in Murfreesboro late Monday afternoon, December 8, there were almost as many prisoners as guards, and overhead fluttered three Union regimental standards and five cavalry guidons. Many in the Army of Tennessee cheered until they were hoarse, and George Winchester, a quartermaster, wrote in his diary: "This is a joyous night in camp. Every mouth is full of Hosannas to the heroic Morgan!"³⁶

That night at their campfires, Morgan's men cooked bread and meat and had sugar in their boiled coffee—all compliments of the United States Army. Meanwhile, in Nashville, General Rosecrans telegraphed Gen. George H. Thomas in Gallatin: "Do I understand that they have captured an entire brigade of our troops without our knowing it, or a good fight?" Thomas replied that Moore's entire force was taken. Shuddering at the chill this would bring from Washington, Rosecrans pleaded: "It seems to me impossible that the entire brigade could have surrendered. Are there none left?"

When President Lincoln was informed, he demanded to know why an iso-lated brigade had been stationed at Hartsville and who was to blame for the debacle. The answer was slow in coming, and on Tuesday afternoon his chief of staff wired: "President demands explanation of Hartsville affair." The next day General-in-Chief Halleck demanded that the President be furnished the name or names of the individuals responsible. Finally, the commanding gen-erals blamed Colonel Moore for ignorance and negligence, and Halleck rec-ommended he be dismissed; however, he was reassigned to administrative duty in the rear, and in September, 1863, he resigned on account of dis-ability.[37]

On the Southern side, Gen. Joseph E. Johnston, recently appointed com-mander of the western department, wired Richmond: "Morgan, the partisan, performed a brilliant feat yesterday, taking 1,800 prisoners—more than his own number. I recommend that he be appointed brigadier-general immedi-ately. He is indispensable." Bragg issued General Orders no. 155 congratu-lating Morgan and Hunt, assuring them of the admiration of the entire army, and hailing the raid as "the precursor of still greater victories." Confederate morale had declined after the failure of three coordinated offensives in Sep-tember and October: Lee had retreated from Maryland after Antietam, Bragg from Kentucky after Perryville, and Earl Van Dorn and Sterling Price from northern Mississippi after Corinth. Never again would the Confeder-acy launch such an offensive. On September 22, Lincoln had issued the Emancipation Proclamation, which ended the chance of European interven-tion but made the South even more determined. News of Morgan's victory, coming after general reverses and in a period of depressed morale, was par-ticularly welcome. The Charleston *Courier* reprinted a dispatch from Mobile under the headline: "Brilliant Exploit of Gen. John H. Morgan—Fourteen Hundred Prisoners, Six Pieces of Artillery, Etc. Captured." War clerk Jones shared the national jubilation: "Our Morgan has been in Kentucky again, and captured 1200 men. Glorious Morgan!"[38]

The invasion of Kentucky would likely have occurred without Morgan's exaggerated reports that the people were anxious to revolt; it was the late summer of Confederate offensives, and invasion was in the air. Also, the Kentucky dream was larger than Morgan and the Kentucky exiles; it encom-passed the Confederate high command and was a secondary objective of the nation. Where Morgan's faulty optimism had its most detrimental impact was in the mind of his commander, Braxton Bragg. He accepted Morgan's word at face value and based the offensive on the liberation of Kentucky; when the uprising failed to occur, the disappointment contributed to his vacillation and lack of self-confidence.

Accompanying the invasion, Morgan resumed his independent efforts to liberate the state, recruiting residents and harassing the enemy. After the Kentucky incursion, Bragg approved and supported the Hartsville foray and was proud of what historian Kenneth P. Williams regarded as "one of the boldest and most successfully executed minor operations in the war."[39]

But as subsequent events revealed, it was in the wrong place. Twelve days before, Big South tunnel had been restored, and supplies were streaming down the track to Nashville, fueling Rosecrans's army for a future attack on Bragg.

TWELVE

Wedding Bells
and the Christmas Raid

Word spread through the Army of Tennessee in Murfreesboro that Morgan had given the Federal prisoners captured at Hartsville to his bride for a wedding present. On Friday, December 12, the Ready family servants were decorating the parlor with holly, cedar, and mistletoe and preparing turkey, ham, and other delicacies. Jefferson Davis arrived to quiet the complaints against Bragg and restore harmony to his command; on Saturday the President reviewed the troops and signed promotions, including Morgan's to brigadier general. A rumor went through the Union army that Davis attended the wedding Sunday evening, but actually, he left town during the day and was not present.[1]

The wedding was a scene from the romance novels come to life; Mattie had held out for romantic love, and in an atmosphere of military success, fame, and glory, her dreams were consummated. She was a beautiful Southern belle in her elegant lace gown and bridal veil; John stood handsome and proud in his new general's uniform. She was twenty-one, and he was thirty-seven. The groomsmen were her brother Horace (an officer on Gen. William J. Hardee's staff) and Colonel Grenfell. Gen. Leonidas Polk, looking tall and impressive in his Episcopal bishop's robe, performed the ceremony; looking on were Generals Bragg, Hardee, Cheatham, Breckinridge, and the headquarters staff. During an elaborate dinner, two regimental bands played outside, and one came in to play for dancing. On Main Street in front of the house, Morgan's men built bonfires and cheered. A friend congratulated Mattie: "It is certainly the match of the Times—'The Belle of Tennessee' & the dashing leader whose name rings throughout the civilized world."[2]

After dinner a group of officers were having wine in the library when someone suggested that Dr. David Yandell, a surgeon, perform his popular impersonations of senior officers. He did Polk and was finishing Hardee when Bragg was called from the room. The performance so far had been good, but it was widely known that his star piece was a caricature of Bragg as a grim old aristocrat. "Do Bragg," they pleaded, and he began, striding to and fro, scowling, waving his arms, and rasping out jerky sentences on two of Bragg's favorite themes: lack of discipline and use of whiskey in the army.

Suddenly Bragg walked back in—Yandell stopped, his face turning pale. "Go on, doctor," said Bragg, "don't let me interrupt you. It is certainly entertaining and doubtless quite accurate." The recently published memoirs of Gen. Arthur M. Manigault, one of Bragg's brigade commanders, indicate that Bragg was more human and better loved by his men than is generally believed.[3]

Meanwhile, the chill of December night fell on the men quartered in the farm fields and pastures north of town, and they moved closer to their campfires. On the right, in the 2nd Arkansas Infantry, Sgt. Andrew J. Campbell dutifully carried out his assignments, but his heart was not in it. He was nearly six feet in height, with burly frame, thick shoulders, large hands, and nondescript facial features except for a thick mustache. Campbell had migrated from Ireland shortly before the war started and was living in Helena, Arkansas, when conscripted into the Confederate army. Deep down he was more sympathetic to the Union, and within the next fourteen months—as morale declined and the pay came irregularly—he would desert and enlist in the Union cavalry. He had never met Morgan, and the dancing and cheering at the Ready mansion were not a part of his world. But less than two years later, in an ironic twist of fate, he would confront Morgan from the Union side and experience an important turning point in his own life.[4]

On Monday evening Morgan's staff gave him and Mattie a dance at the courthouse, and around the punchbowl they talked about their next raid into Kentucky and preparations for moving to the staging site in Alexandria, Tennessee. Mattie accompanied John to Alexandria and stood beside him on the reviewing stand when he conducted his first complete regimental review on Sunday, December 21. "Company after company moved forward into line with horses prancing, bugles blowing, and flags waving," wrote one of the men. "It was a grand and imposing scene."[5]

The next morning, December 22, the command left and the newlyweds were separated, eight days after they were married. Bragg was continuing the policy of using Morgan and Forrest in raids on enemy communications. On December 11 he had sent Forrest into western Tennessee to attack the Mobile and Ohio Railroad, the supply line of Grant, who was advancing through northern Mississippi toward Vicksburg. Forrest's expedition, together with a raid by Van Dorn, forced Grant to cancel his offensive and return to Tennessee.

The assaults on Grant were well-timed; those on Rosecrans's army were not. The L&N should have been wrecked as soon as it reopened on November 26; by the time Bragg supported the Hartsville raid and attended the wedding, vast amounts of stores and munitions had been stockpiled in Nashville. Bragg did not realize until December 20 that the rail line was operating, and by then it was too late. He hoped Morgan's raid would have the same effect as the destruction of the tunnel in August and possibly restore momentum to the Confederacy; and it might have if it had occurred in late

November or early December. In retrospect, it is clear that the Hartsville raid should have been directed at the L&N. Bragg was guilty of being too friendly with Morgan, approving the Hartsville expedition and celebrating the nuptials when Morgan's men should have been out burning railroad trestles.[6]

When Rosecrans took command of the Army of the Cumberland, he adopted Buell's triad defense of the 180-mile Union supply line. "Old Rosy" was forty-three years old, intelligent and able. An Ohio farm boy, he had graduated from West Point, served in the Engineering Corps for ten years and fought under McClellan, Halleck, and Grant. His first priority was to restore the Big South tunnel and to protect it and other important points from attack. He deployed two brigades of infantry to guard the tunnel and a regiment to protect telegraph line stringers. He canceled all other railroad repair projects and combined all available construction workers into a force of 500 laborers to rebuild the tunnel. To provide subsistence in the meantime, he directed that supplies be brought by rail to just north of the tunnels and stockpiled at Mitchellsville, Tennessee; from there they were hauled on wagons to Nashville. This makeshift system was so inadequate that reserve stores in Nashville were exhausted, and it was impossible to gain more than 20 percent on consumption. Lincoln and Halleck became very impatient with Rosecrans's long stay in Nashville, but he replied that many of his men were barefoot, without blankets, tents, and effective weapons. He absolutely refused to advance until the L&N was open and his supplies replenished.[7]

With restoration of the tunnel in progress, Rosecrans continued to erect a stockade at every significant railroad bridge. On November 21, 1862, he told Halleck: "We are using every tool to get out stockade timber, to secure our railroad in the rear." Rosecrans delivered the logs, but infantrymen constructing the forts hated the work, and up the track in Kentucky it went forward at a snail's pace. By early December he had deployed over 10,000 men to defend the L&N Railroad, 6,921 in Tennessee and about 3,500 in Kentucky.[8]

But the third point in Buell's triad system still represented the greatest danger to Confederate guerrilla operations in the West. Rosecrans continued Buell's attempt to strengthen the Union cavalry, which was yet so weak that Federal cavalry regiments usually remained within the protection of infantry lines, surrendering control of the country around Nashville to the Confederate cavalry. (This disparity is further condemnation of Bragg and his cavalry for not learning about the reopening of the L&N until twenty-odd days later.) Rosecrans went to the top, to Secretary of War Stanton, informing him that his cavalry were "half armed and two-thirds demoralized" and urgently requesting 4,000 sets of horse equipment 3,600 carbines, and 3,600 Colt revolvers. After the order was delivered and he requested more, the War Department asked why he was requisitioning a larger proportion of cavalry arms than any other commander. He answered that 2,883 recruits were on the way, and with present arms 1,321 of his 7,417 cavalrymen would still be unarmed. By the day the railroad opened, Rosecrans had transferred an infantry regiment from Bowling Green to Mitchellsville to load the mountain of supplies there for immediate shipment. He very effectively provided logistics for his army and paved the way for effective protection of communication lines in the future.[9]

For the time being, however, the L&N was still vulnerable, and Morgan's Christmas Raid took advantage of it. The objective was to burn the two great wooden trestles, both 80 feet high and 500 feet long, through rugged Muldraugh's Hill five miles north of Elizabethtown. They were the largest bridges between Louisville and Nashville and—next to the twin tunnels— the most strategic target. Intelligence reports indicated that they were protected by heavily garrisoned stockades, and this time there was no surprise. Kirby Smith was greatly concerned that the plan had been openly canvassed in the Union army. Correct estimates of Morgan's strength and destination were published in the Nashville newspapers, along with reports of Union preparations for defense. Hardee told Morgan that it would be impossible to burn the bridges.[10]

Dire warnings notwithstanding, Morgan's men marched 500 miles in fourteen days, striking along the main L&N line through Elizabethtown to the bridges, then returning via Bardstown, Lebanon, Campbellsville and Columbia. They captured and paroled over 1,800 prisoners, inflicted 150 casualties, burned a total of 2,290 feet of railroad bridgework, wrecked thirty-five miles of track and telegraph line, and destroyed three depots, three water stations, several culverts and cattle guards, and large quantities of Federal stores. Morgan had 26 casualties: 2 dead and 24 wounded. Beginning with the burning of Bacon Creek Bridge—a replacement of the structure Morgan had burned in his first attack on the L&N—the railroad was closed from December 26 until February 1, five weeks. If the expedition had occurred in late November or early December, the offensive by Rosecrans resulting in the battle of Stones River would have been delayed by at least one month.[11]

The raid was a classic Morgan operation. Quirk's company took the advance and reported directly to the general, enabling him to avoid strong Federal forces at Lebanon and Glasgow on the way back. Using hit-and-run tactics and conducting forced night marches in extreme weather, the command struck the railroad and weakly guarded towns, and avoided head-on contact with the Union pursuit force under Col. John Marshall Harlan. Expressing the universal frustration of conventional commanders fighting guerrillas, Harlan said that Morgan displayed "an entire unwillingness" to meet him upon "any fair terms."[12]

Traveling light, the raiders seemed to move with lightning speed. The only wheels were the artillery pieces. When the raid began, each man had ammunition, weapons, two horseshoes, twelve nails, a blanket, oilcloth, and an overcoat. Sending out feints, they confused the enemy and caused them

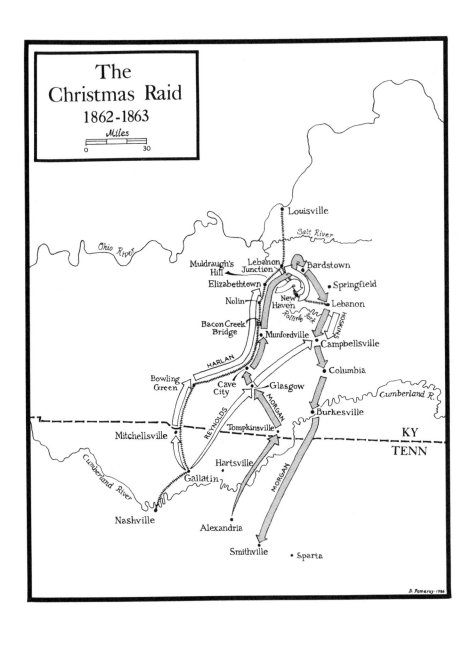

The
Christmas Raid
1862-1863

Miles
0   30

Louisville
Salt River
Ohio River
Muldraugh's Hill
Lebanon Junction
Bardstown
Elizabethtown
Springfield
Nolin
New Haven
Lebanon
Bacon Creek Bridge
Rolling Fork
HOSKINS
Munfordville
Campbellsville
HARLAN
Columbia
Bowling Green
Cave City
Glasgow
MORGAN
Cumberland R.
Burkesville
REYNOLDS
Mitchellsville
Tompkinsville
KY
TENN
Cumberland River
Hartsville
Gallatin
MORGAN
Nashville
Alexandria
Smithville
Sparta

D. Pomeroy 1986

to exaggerate Morgan's strength. He had a division of 3,900 men, but the best scouting reports Col. William A. Hoskins had in Lebanon estimated that the raiders numbered between 7,000 and 11,000. Hoskins told reporters later: "I labored under great disadvantage from the fact that I could get no definite information of Morgan's force."[13]

The division of two brigades led by Colonels Duke and W.C.P. Breckinridge was the largest force that Morgan ever commanded, before or after. He had learned at Gallatin that artillery was required to attack stockades, and he had brought seven pieces, four with one brigade and three with the other. In Kentucky only two of the Buell-Rosecrans forts were finished: the one at Bacon Creek, in which ninety-three men held out for five hours of artillery shelling before surrendering; and the one at New Haven on the trunk line toward Lebanon, which resisted ninety minutes of shelling by one mountain howitzer and still refused to raise the white flag. Most of the stockades, however, were like the one at Nolin Creek manned by seventy-six men: as soon as Duke gave them a look down the barrel of his artillery, they surrendered. A follow-up report by the Union army after the raid concluded that these stockades fell not from the privation of a lengthy siege or loss of life but from the moral effect of Morgan's artillery. The recommendation was that the stockades be completed and manned with well-seasoned soldiers who would not be intimidated by shelling. To Morgan's credit, rather than using dismounted frontal assaults against the stockades on this raid, he relied on artillery and on the fear that his reputation stimulated. The tactics were effective and did not waste his men in vain attacks on strong defensive positions.[14]

Morgan's leadership produced the esprit de corps necessary in guerrilla warfare and gave the campaign its soul. The march began in the sunshine that Monday morning, and two hours later "a cheer began in the extreme rear and rapidly came forward, increasing in volume and enthusiasm, and soon General Morgan dashed by, with his hat in his hand, bowing and smiling his thanks for these flattering cheers, followed by a large and well mounted staff." Merriment reached a peak Christmas morning on Green River when advance guards captured a large sutler's wagon of candy and cakes and women's shoes. The men ate the sweets and distributed the shoes to women along the route.[15]

On December 26, after burning the Bacon Creek and Nolin Creek bridges, they headed up the L&N track, burning crossties and telegraph poles, heating and twisting rails, and winding telegraph wire around trees and sinking it in the streams. The next day the artillery vigorously shelled the warehouses and railroad depot in Elizabethtown, where 652 men of the 91st Illinois Infantry were stationed. The Federals answered with several volleys of rifle fire, but after gaping holes were made in the brick buildings they occupied, they surrendered. This was Morgan's first independent raid into Kentucky after his proclamation of retaliation, and as soon as the Illinois men laid down their arms, Morgan's men took their overcoats and boots.

Then the invaders went shopping in the retail stores, paying Confederate currency for extra trousers, boots, and leather to make boots. There were no wagons or pack animals, so some men put on several shirts and trousers, giving them the comical appearance of overstuffed pillows. Morgan purchased $1,200 worth of silks and other items and paid the same way. Since Confederate money was next to worthless in Kentucky, these purchases were tantamount to looting, and seizing the clothing of the Union prisoners violated international law.[16].

With his purchases completed, in the afternoon Morgan strolled through the streets of Elizabethtown with Miss Belle McDowell, a well-known Confederate sympathizer from Louisville. He was dressed in a butternut shirt and butternut jeans pants, with long black cavalry boots and blue overcoat. He told Belle that Mattie was the prettiest lady in the South and it was hard to leave her so soon after the wedding, but that Mattie was very patriotic and wanted him to perform his duty.

"You should not have married," Belle replied, "for there are a thousand hearts that beat at the sound of your name."

"I wish that I had a thousand hearts, and I would give them all to my wife," John said. Belle jestingly asked him not to destroy the Muldraugh trestle; if it were burned, she could not get home to Louisville. In a serious tone, John responded, "If you knew how the enemy destroys our immense structures your heart would be hardened."[17]

The next morning, December 28, the command moved northward, wrecking the track for five miles from Elizabethtown to the trestles. The southern bridge was defended by 500 men and the northern by 200, both in unfinished stockades. Morgan conducted simultaneous sieges, shelling them with artillery, and after about an hour they surrendered. Federal officers on the scene blamed the superintendent in charge of construction for delays in finishing the stockades, and he was dismissed. With the bridges burning and his staff writing paroles for the 700 prisoners, Morgan had Ellsworth tap the telegraph line north of the bridges. The 71st Indiana Infantry had been captured once before, and he wired Gov. Oliver P. Morton thanking him for the regiment and suggesting that next time he send the oilcloths and overcoats without the men. (On this raid Ellsworth contributed to morale but made no significant tactical contribution.) That night Morgan's force encamped a few miles east of Muldraugh's Hill, along the western bank of Rolling Fork River at the Bardstown Road ford. He had broken camp and was crossing the river on his way to Bardstown the next morning when Rosecrans's pursuit task force attacked.[18]

Rosecrans had welcomed the raid as an opportunity to capture Morgan, and with high hopes he had personally organized to that end. Ever since the L&N had reopened on November 26, he had expected an attack, and when Forrest struck in west Tennessee on December 11, he assumed that the rumors and newspaper reports of an imminent Morgan foray were correct. On

December 14, the day of the wedding, he alerted all troops in the stockades on the railroad from Nashville to Louisville to be on the lookout. Four days later he ordered them to procure stores of wood and fresh water. "We will close the gates against raids into Kentucky," he declared. On December 19, three days before the raid began, he sent a division of infantry on a reconnaissance in force on his left to determine whether Kirby Smith was preparing to march with Morgan. When by Christmas Eve his men had not made contact with any Confederate troops, he assumed Morgan had gone to Kentucky. "Pay any money to ascertain Morgan's exact strength and position," he telegraphed to Gallatin and Bowling Green. By nightfall he learned that Morgan was indeed advancing into Kentucky, and he wired his commanders an accurate estimate of Morgan's strength. "We will catch and kill those rascals yet," he promised.[19]

On Christmas Day, Rosecrans took time out from organizing his offensive on Bragg at Murfreesboro to put together a hammer-and-anvil operation to capture Morgan. For the hammer he selected Colonel Harlan, commander of the second brigade, first division of Gen. George H. Thomas's command. Harlan was a strong-willed lawyer from Louisville, a graduate of Centre College and Transylvania University law school (after the war he became a member of the United States Supreme Court). Rosecrans had picked him to occupy Hartsville after the disaster there, and now he was ordered to bring his 2,300 infantry and battery of artillery to Gallatin and pursue Morgan by train. He was to turn Morgan away from the L&N line and drive him back upon the Union forces converging in southern Kentucky to close off the Rebel retreat.[20]

The anvil in southern Kentucky was composed of two separate commands. When the raid began, Col. William A. Hoskins was on garrison duty in Lebanon, and he was reinforced with troops from Danville and Columbia, bringing his strength to 3,300 men, which included an artillery battery and a small contingent of cavalry. The other command was stationed southwest of Lebanon in Glasgow, the county seat of Barren County and a hub of county roads in the region, the gateway from Kentucky to middle Tennessee. For Glasgow, Rosecrans chose Gen. Joseph J. Reynolds, commander of a division of Thomas's corps. With his 5,000-man division, which included twelve pieces of artillery in two batteries and 600 cavalry, Reynolds was to march from Gallatin to Glasgow and take his stand.[21]

Rosecrans was confident that Harlan, the hammer, would force Morgan back upon the anvil, Hoskins and Reynolds. "Lay your wires to kill him," he ordered. "Don't credit the big stories he sends abroad, but tell your men to fight them." Not everyone shared Rosecrans's optimism. A division commander in Gallatin, Gen. Speed S. Fry, spotted a basic flaw in the plan. He asked if it would not be wise to send cavalry after Morgan. The answer came back from headquarters that Rosecrans preferred to use infantry. Then, as Rosecrans contemplated the fifty-five-mile march of Reynolds's infantry from Gallatin to Glasgow, he suggested that the men take packhorses and take turns riding bareback. Reynolds ignored the idea.[22]

The day after Christmas, Harlan crowded his men into three troop trains and departed from Gallatin. For six miles they made good time; then, a mile below Big South tunnel, the rear train suffered an engine breakdown and was switched onto a siding to await a replacement from Nashville. There it was sitting when a passenger train from Nashville steamed along and stopped. The Union officer in charge of the disabled train asked for that engine, pointing out that the brief delay for the passengers would be insignificant compared to what would happen if Morgan destroyed vital bridges. Nevertheless, the conductor refused and left with his passengers. The replacement from Nashville finally arrived, but the crippled troop train did not reach Bowling Green until ten o'clock that night. By then Morgan's men had burned the bridges over Bacon and Nolin Creeks, north of Munfordville.[23]

On December 27, Harlan learned that the track was clear to Munfordville, and his force boarded the three trains, each man with an extra day's rations. Ten miles away the third train quit again, and another locomotive had to be brought from Bowling Green. Harlan was waiting for them in Munfordville when they came in at 10:00 P.M. By then Morgan had taken Elizabethtown. In Munfordville, Col. Edward H. Hobson joined Harlan with 600 men, half of them cavalry, giving him a total of 2,900. They set out on foot from Munfordville at 3:00 A.M. on December 28 and were on the march of about twenty-eight miles to Elizabethtown when Morgan's men burned the Muldraugh trestles. They marched all day and all night, and on the morning of the 29th they attacked Morgan's rear guard. After a brief skirmish, Morgan's men left, and Harlan marched about five miles south to relieve the stockade at New Haven. He drove off the Morgan detachment and saved the stockade and railroad bridge. Then he went on the defensive in Lebanon Junction north of Muldraugh's Hill for the remainder of the raid, leaving it up to Hoskins and Reynolds to block Morgan's escape.[24]

In the rear-guard skirmish on Rolling Fork River, Duke was leading the retreat, his horse splashing through the water in the ford, when artillery shrapnel from Harlan's battery struck him in the head and knocked him unconscious from his horse. Quirk jumped down and gathered his limp form, throwing him across the neck of his own powerful bay and saving him from drowning. At the nearest farm he impressed a carriage and filled it with soft bedding, providing the beloved colonel a conveyance for the remainder of the raid.[25]

Duke was considered by many to be the conscience of Morgan's command, and it may have been more than coincidence that discipline broke down that night in Bardstown, as he lay wounded in bed. Some of the men opened the county jail and freed several prisoners who claimed to be Southern sympathizers accused of stealing horses. Others burglarized the post office, taking $325 in government funds and scattering private letters in the street. When the owner of one of the largest stores, refusing to accept Confederate currency, locked up and left town, a mob of Morgan's troops battered down the doors and surged in, cleaning the shelves; as one group left, another entered, crowding the doorway. John Allan Wyeth, one of Quirk's scouts, described the scene: "I was amused at one trooper, who induced others to let him out by holding an ax in front of him, cutting edge forward, one arm clasping a bundle of at least a dozen pairs of shoes and other plunder, while on his head was a pyramid of eight or ten soft hats, one on top of the other, just as they had come out of the packing box." What had begun as shopping with Confederate money had turned into the first plunder of a private business by Morgan's men. There is no evidence that Morgan approved; nor is there any that he attempted to stop it or punish anyone for it. He let it fall under the policy of retaliation on the private property of Union civilians.[26]

But the looting was minor compared to the extramilitary activities of Champ Ferguson and his gang. Near the end of the expedition, on New Year's night, they split off from the main force to conduct one of Ferguson's personal battles. After it was over, he came to Duke's carriage to relate what had happened. He and his band of three men approached the house of Elam Huddleton, one of their enemies in Adair County. The men opened fire on the windows of the garret of the house, and Ferguson lunged against the front door, breaking it down and grabbing Huddleton as he rose from a pallet by the fire and stabbing him to death with a long knife. Ferguson concluded the account by showing Duke the weapon, still covered with the clotted blood of the victim. The wounded Duke said that his stomach, already weak, became extremely nauseated at the sight.[27]

On the morning of December 30, Morgan headed south out of Bardstown; the raid had been a great success, and all that remained was to return safely through Union lines, avoiding contact with Rosecrans's anvil at Lebanon and Glasgow. He sent two companies down the Springfield Road on a feint against Lebanon. They drove in the pickets north of town and built dozens of fires from fence rails, creating the impression that the entire command was there, camped for the night. The main body marched on in darkness, bypassing Lebanon on little-used side roads west of town, pointed out by a local civilian guide. In the afternoon a chilling rain set in and temperature dropped, turning the rain to sleet that pelted men and horses and froze on their backs. After dark they looked like an army of ghosts, with ice covering their coats and oilcloths and horses. The artillery had to be pulled through quagmires, and the rain and sleet froze on the road, making it too hazardous to ride. They dismounted and trudged through the slush, holding to the stirrup leather, depending upon their horses for balance. They evaded detection and escaped, but they made only eight miles that whole night, and never again would Morgan attempt a long raid in winter.[28]

In Lebanon, Colonel Hoskins had attempted to catch Morgan by going on the defensive, and when his pickets reported that Morgan's entire force was camped north of town for the night, he assumed that he had succeeded. His infantry and cavalry were deployed on a bluff where the Springfield Road crossed Cartwright's Creek, just north of town. Commanding a view of the road for a mile and a half ahead, they were in a very strong defensive position. But the next morning, December 31, when Morgan did not attack and Hoskins sent his cavalry on a reconnaissance, they found nothing but ashes in the Morgan camp. By 5:00 P.M. Hoskins learned definitely that Morgan had slipped away, and an hour later he started in pursuit. His cavalry was worn down from looking for the elusive Rebels, and many were poorly armed—the 6th Kentucky had only sabers and pistols. Hoskins ordered them to march in close where they could be supported by infantry, and if they happened to discover Morgan, they were not to fight until the infantry could sustain them. By New Year's morning they had reached Green River, and Hoskins directed the cavalry to take the advance, but six miles along the infantry overtook them. Hoskins asked why they had stopped and they explained that their horses were tired and they had heard rumors that Morgan had already escaped. Hoskins moved his infantry and artillery forward and let the exhausted cavalry cover the rear.[29]

The rumors were correct: while Hoskins waited on the defensive, Morgan had gained over twelve hours; and by the time Hoskins left Lebanon, Morgan was arriving in Campbellsville, twenty miles south. There the raiders seized a supply of Union commissary stores, ate their fill, and piled the remainder in a heap. They set it on fire and whooped with delight each time a man kicked another box of hardtack or threw another carton of medicine on the blazing mound of hams and shoulders. Nothing of value was left: "Twas with tired limbs but exultant joy that we baffled the enemy and destroyed their New Years' Dinner," an officer said.[30]

On New Year's Day, Reynolds advanced to Campbellsville, but Morgan had left early in the morning, escaping east of Reynolds with a fifty-mile, twenty-four-hour march to Burkesville on the Cumberland River. All day the advance guard would stop on hilltops and listen, and in the stillness ahead of the clattering column they heard a deep roaring sound, riding on the south winds, which seasoned veterans said was the booming of artillery from a major battle in the distance. The following day they reentered Confederate lines and learned that while they were away, Rosecrans had advanced on Bragg and defeated him in the battle of Stones River. On January 1 it had indeed been heavy artillery firing that some of the men had heard.[31]

Historians have assumed that Bragg was placed at a disadvantage by the absence of Forrest and Morgan from the battle. It is true that Rosecrans was heartened by it: "The detachment of Forrest to West Tennessee, and of Morgan, will materially aid us in our movement," he told Halleck on Christmas

Eve. But viewed from a broader perspective, Forrest and Morgan had accomplished far more as guerrillas than they could have in the battle proper. They had performed a strategic role by drawing off Union forces far in excess of their own numbers. In the western district of Kentucky and along the L&N to Nashville, the Union army had 20,357 men guarding communication lines and supply depots. Gen. Horatio G. Wright was commander of the Department of the Ohio, which encompassed the western half of Kentucky. During the raid, when it became obvious that Morgan would succeed, Rosecrans said: "If General Wright, with 20,000 men, cannot take care of Morgan, I shall not send any more troops up."[32]

Furthermore, Morgan's raid alone was directly responsible for the detachment of an additional 7,300 infantry, cavalry, and artillery from Rosecrans's army: the division under Reynolds and the brigade under Harlan, taken from Thomas's center wing. They would have been in the thick of battle if Morgan's raid had not occurred, and even if Morgan had been adept at conventional cavalry service, it is doubtful that he could have neutralized nearly twice his number. The pursuit force increased the number of Union troops deployed in the rear to 27,657, four times the extent of Morgan and Forrest. By forcing the enemy to disperse, they had produced damage far out of proportion to their own strength. At the end of the raid John wrote Mattie: "Our success far exceeded my expectations & if our Generals will or *have* done their part of the work, then our common foe will be driven out of *our* state (Tenn.)." He had no regrets; he had done his part in his own way.[33]

The raid demonstrated that the Federal cavalry was still relatively weak in December, 1862. At the same time, it taught Rosecrans the futility of chasing Morgan with infantry. His 7,300-man pursuit force had not saved the long trestles and had not captured any of Morgan's men; they had fought only one small skirmish at Rolling Fork River. Therefore, he wired to General Wright: "I wish you would get ready a large lot of saddles and horses, and mount your infantry, to pursue him the next time he makes a raid." He also ordered his own field commanders to organize mounted infantry. He was now on the right course, fighting fire with fire, answering the mobility and power of Morgan's mounted infantry tactics with infantry on horseback. This strategy, which complemented the strengthening of Union cavalry in progress, was a major cause in the decline of Morgan's career in 1863, just as the weakness of the blue cavalry and the lack of mounted Union infantry had made possible his success before 1863.[34]

In his report of the battle of Stones River, Bragg congratulated Forrest and Morgan for their complete victories and commended them to the gratitude of the country. During the following weeks, when people read detailed accounts of Stones River listing over 12,000 Confederate casualties and telling how Bragg had withdrawn thirty-five miles to Duck River, the success of Morgan's raid stood out in contrast. Eager for positive news, the papers ran headlines such as "Morgan Again Victorious" and "Brilliant Success."

The Richmond *Dispatch* reported: "Morgan is sweeping Kentucky, destroying the railroads and telegraphs, taking trains, destroying provisions, and paroling prisoners." The major battle was lost, but around the fireplaces in general stores and in the hallways of courthouses, the Morgan legend grew. On May 1 the Confederate Congress enacted a joint resolution of gratitude to Morgan and his men for Hartsville and the Christmas Raid, "services which have conferred upon their authors fame as enduring as the records of the struggle which they have so brilliantly illustrated."[35]

John and Mattie hoped the raid had proved that his career still came first. Colonel Grenfell had participated in the wedding but said later that he had attempted to prevent it, warning that marriage would cause John to become cautious and less enterprising. And Mattie's relatives had admonished her, "You must remember your promises, not to restrain the General in his career of glory, but encourage him to go forward."[36] She promised, but she did not know what a profound influence she would have on his life and career.

John loved Mattie and, renouncing his old ways, entered fully into the relationship. The tragedy was that, given his inner tensions, he became desperately dependent upon her. As long as he was with her, he had reassurance and support, and the clouds of depression stayed away. But when they were apart, the old tensions came forth, making him feel insecure. Love can liberate, can let go and allow the partner to develop and be himself. But in Morgan's case it drained the wellspring of his initiative as a revolutionary guerrilla, and when his status as a national hero declined, it threatened his self-esteem. He was in a peculiar dilemma: if he could not conduct raids, how could he confirm his position as Marion of the War? How could he preserve his self-image as Mattie's hero?

Morgan made a valiant effort to adjust, but on December 23, 1862, the second day of the raid, he wrote Mattie that he hoped it would be finished within six days "& then my *precious one* I shall try & get back to you as fast as possible & then my pretty one nothing shall induce me to again leave you this winter. How anxiously I am looking forward to the moment when I shall again clasp you to a heart that beats for you alone. *Do not forget me* my *own Darling & you may rest* assured that my whole thoughts are of you. Farewell my pretty wife, my command is leaving I must be off." Writing her after the incursion, he asserted: "The greatest pleasure my expedition has afforded is the knowledge that our great success will gratify and delight you."[37]

Morgan was so completely governed by moods and passions that when the affection he had for his command transferred to Mattie, it had a profound effect on his practice of guerrilla warfare. No longer was there a need to stay in the action for emotional fulfillment; instead, he needed to be with Mattie. This meant that he lost his dedication to the basic hit-and-run principle of guerrilla warfare. As would be evident in the coming months, he came to place less priority on fleeing from forces of equal or greater strength to preserve his own men; rather, he became inclined to throw them headlong against the enemy in order to win a quick victory and return to Mattie. In a sense he became an even greater high-risk taker now that his gambling was no longer tempered by the requirement of staying in the game. Moreover, the marriage lessened his determination to liberate Kentucky. He now had a new home with Mattie, and as he told her, Tennessee was their state.[38]

Mattie stayed in Murfreesboro during the raid, but when Bragg's army began withdrawing after Stones River, she and Alice joined the train of refugees leaving Murfreesboro. Their parents remained, but many families stacked household goods and baggage in carriages and wagons and perched the women and children atop the load, with slaves herding the sheep, cows, and hogs along behind. The two sisters were lodged at Hardee's headquarters in Winchester, and soon Mattie learned that John had returned safely. "Come to me my own Darling quickly. I was wretched but now I am *almost* happy and will be quite, when my precious husband is again with me. I can bear anything Darling when you are with me, and as long as I have your love. But when separated from you, and I know that you are surrounded by so many dangers, and hardships, as you have been on your last expedition I become a weak, nervous Child. Have I not lived a great deal Love, in the last two weeks? When I look back now at the time, it seems two years, but in each scene I have passed through there has always been one dear face ever before me, and can you doubt whose face that was?"[39]

Concerning the battle at Murfreesboro, she told him: "I had some dark days dearest, and when the battle was raging around me in such fury, and everybody from the commander-in-chief to the privates were praying for 'Morgan to come,' I thanked God in the anguish of my heart that it was not for me to say where you should be. There was one continual inquiry at the front door—'When will General Morgan be here?'" She said that Hardee's staff was very hospitable, but "Darling I feared you would forget me. You left me so soon. . . . Good night *my Hero*. My dreams are all of you. Your Affectionate Mattie."[40]

The Christmas Raid achieved the objective of destroying the Muldraugh trestles, and the L&N was closed for five weeks. However, it came after Rosecrans had stored vast quantities of supplies in Nashville and therefore did not have the strategic impact it would have had a month before. Be that as it may, the expedition paid for itself by drawing off 7,300 soldiers from Rosecrans's advancing army.

Morgan's second marriage was a major passage in his life. Consciously, he put gambling and high risks behind him and depended on Mattie for security and comfort from depression. Consequently, the source of his creativity and motivation as a guerrilla warrior was lost. The close of 1862 marked the beginning of Morgan's deterioration as a leader; he would serve another twenty months and have many adventures, but never again would he achieve this level of success.

THIRTEEN

The Winter of Romance

One of Morgan's first priorities was to bring Mattie to his new headquarters in McMinnville. Bragg's army was positioned in the Duck River Valley with Morgan on the right, guarding a line of over 100 miles, from Woodbury, Tennessee, to Monticello, Kentucky. "Am determined to have you near me," he pledged. "Cannot bear the thought of your being away from home & my not being with you." Once she came, Mattie declared: "My life is all a joyous dream now, from which I fear to awaken, and awake I must when my Hero is called to leave me again. My husband wants me to remain with him, and of course I much prefer it. They say we are a love sick couple."[1]

It was not unusual for an officer to have his wife and children nearby. Both of Morgan's sisters went south to be near their husbands, and they were not a hindrance. But John's mental conflict gave Mattie unusual sway in their marriage, and she wielded powerful influence on his military leadership. After marching for several days and nights, until the hardiest men were exhausted, he would ride fifty miles more to see her. When the command moved, she had the responsibility of selecting the house for headquarters. Once he sent an important military dispatch to her for forwarding to Basil Duke in the rear. She was quartered so near the front lines that she had to keep her bags packed for instantaneous retreat; the headquarters staff had an ambulance and wagon standing by, and Morgan constantly sent updates on escape routes. Mattie diverted his attention, and he lost his single-minded devotion to the revolution. One night at the front he wrote to her: "Altho I fully expected to be attacked today, still my thoughts were of you & not of war."[2]

For the first time, Morgan became interested in religion. He began reading the Bible and kneeling in prayer each night, and every Sunday morning he would gather his aides and take them to church, seating them in the pew beside him and Mattie. Like many husbands in nineteenth-century America, he conceded that his wife was morally superior. In camp late one night he wrote: "The dear prayer book that you gave me 'my dear precious One' is before me & I shall read Evening Prayer, 21st day. So my Angel you see what a good influence you exert upon me and I am so much happier." He proudly informed his mother that because of Mattie's example and advice he had become a "much better man." He made it clear that his faith sprang from his love for Mattie and was subordinate to that love: "I shall read your letter again before I close my eyes. What great pleasure it affords me to read your dear sweet words of Love. I know every word you utter comes from your dear good Heart. Have more confidence in that than I have in the *Book* now before me."[3]

Mattie and John lived in a comfortable house and seemed oblivious to the weather, which was unusually cold in middle Tennessee from January to March. Ice formed on the rivers and streams, and snow and rain frequently turned to sleet and freezing rain. Bragg's infantry huddled in their tents and cabins, and Morgan's men shivered in lean-tos made of fence rails and oil-cloths, open to the fire in front. They went for days without taking off their boots, and gusts of wind drove the rain in their faces as they slept; when they rolled over the ice on their blankets would rattle in their beds. Often they were aroused by the bugle call "boots and saddles," and they would stumble out in the bleak winter chill. Hungry and faint, they would untie their horses from the side of the lean-to and ride for miles to check a Federal scouting party. They held their own against forces of equal strength, but then a large command of infantry, artillery, and cavalry would advance and force them to retire. Foraging parties from both armies stripped the country of grain, hay, meat, and everything edible. The regiment at Woodbury ran out of oats and fodder, and on the ration of three ears of corn per day, their horses lost their energy and shrank to skin and bones; and a fourth of them died, forcing the men to stand guard on foot.[4]

Twenty-five miles from the hardships at the front, John and Mattie extended their honeymoon into the spring. Nearly every afternoon they made an elegant appearance, riding horseback into the country—she in a beautiful black riding habit, hat, and veil; he in a blue roundabout jacket with brass buttons, blue pants tucked into shiny cavalry boots with spurs, and black felt hat fastened up at the side. A correspondent for the Richmond *Enquirer* observed that Mattie's "full-blown" figure was certainly "apropos to the sterling manhood of Morgan. She loves him very ardently, and I doubt not that the affair was entirely one of the affections. They take long strolls every afternoon, and the evidences of attachment . . . are delicate and dignified upon both sides."[5]

There was a continual round of teas and dinner parties, and on Friday, February 13, the headquarters staff gave a dance in honor of John and Mattie. Two bands were invited from Tullahoma, and arrangements were made for a bounteous banquet, but wartime reality intruded in Camelot. Local resentment was high against Morgan's men for stealing fence rails and other property, and the people were offended that he was enjoying the gaiety of society while his men suffered in camp. Opposition to the dance became so intense in McMinnville that the committee of ladies issuing the invitations refused to sign their names, and all but a few shunned the event, leaving the women who came outnumbered by men eight to one. Lincoln's naval blockade, which had forced the South into an economy of substitutes, compelled alternatives in the menu. There was chicken salad without celery, brown sugar cake without icing, beets and cabbage instead of pickles, and molasses candy in lieu of French confections. The ham was good, but the outstanding delicacy was a commodity quite rare in the Confederacy—coffee, which Morgan had captured on the Christmas Raid.[6]

Morgan and his officers dressed in civilian clothing on this occasion, and Mattie wore a new dress that John had selected especially for her during the raid in Kentucky. It was of magnificent red silk with black lace sleeves, vest, and trim, and she had a full set of pearl jewelry, including a fashionable comb in her elaborate coiffure. "I think the General would try to preserve the wonderful dress in alcohol, if he thought the color could be retained," Mattie said. "I had a splendid time, and of course, was something of a belle—as the ball was in honor of the bandit and his bride." It is a measure of his men's devotion for him that they accepted without complaining his refusal to share their hardships.[7]

About once a month Morgan would wrench himself away to spend a day or two in camp. He masqueraded as Union Captain Johnson of the 5th Kentucky Cavalry, and in his pocket he had a fraudulent written order assigning Johnson to duty as provost guard and directing him to proceed toward Nashville and arrest stragglers. Advancing to the ferry landing on Stones River, he came upon a Michigan cavalry company drawn up on the opposite bank. Morgan tipped his hat and called: "Captain, what is the news in Nashville?"

"Who are you?"

"Captain Johnson, 5th Kentucky Cavalry, just from Murfreesboro, via Lebanon, going to Nashville by General Rosecrans's order. What is your regiment?"

The Union captain identified himself, and Morgan asked, "Are you going further?"

"No. Have you any news of Morgan?"

"His cavalry are at Liberty—none closer." As the Michigan captain started to move away, Morgan suggested they ride to Nashville together. He consented, and Morgan said to Captain Quirk: "Sergeant, carry as many men over at a load as possible, and we will swim the horses. It is too late to attempt to ferry them over." The Federals got down and walked and jumped about, trying to get warm. Quirk crossed with the first group of twelve and when they climbed the bank their blue overcoats fell open, revealing their gray trousers. "Rebels!" the genuine Union men screamed, and they began firing. A brief skirmish ensued, resulting in the capture of the Michigan captain and fifteen men. But a few of the Federals escaped, and since they had probably spread the alarm in Nashville, Morgan terminated the mission. He was still a guerrilla at heart; it was highly irregular for a general in command of several thousand men to pose as an enemy captain and lead a raiding party of fifty men dressed in uniforms of the adversary.[8]

His men practiced guerrilla warfare continually. Rosecrans complained to Bragg that they were lurking about Federal lines wearing Union uniforms and bearing Union colors, and he accused them of violating flags of truce to spy on his fortifications. On February 4, Morgan sent Col. Leroy S. Cluke's regiment into "dead horse camp" in central Kentucky, where forage and food were plentiful, and horses and men could convalesce. Using the tactics of deception, ambush, and hit-and-run, Cluke drove in the pickets in Lexington and occupied Mount Sterling three times, being driven out each time by superior Federal forces. The second occupation was accomplished without firing a shot. A squad dressed in blue uniforms went into town and stole a stack of printed blank forms for official orders. Cluke drafted a fake order commanding the Union regiment in Mount Sterling to march immediately to the relief of Paris, which was reported under attack; they were not to gather their belongings but leave instantly. Cluke gave the missive to Clark Lyle, his best scout, and Lyle in a blue uniform raced full speed into town by the Paris pike. He pulled up at headquarters and went in, all out of breath, his horse winded and reeking with sweat. The Union force obeyed and left without asking any questions. Cluke remained on convalescent duty for six weeks, capturing 200 supply wagons and furnishing his regiment with badly needed provisions. After one of the raids on Mount Sterling, William A. Milton, a soldier in Cluke's regiment, saw a friend with about thirty pairs of blue pants piled before him on his horse. "I needed breeches very bad, so called him to throw me a pair, which he did and which fitted fine," Milton said.[9]

In middle Tennessee, supplies became even more scarce; morale and discipline declined; and the effective strength of each regiment was weakened as the men roved about in search of food. The 2nd Kentucky, Morgan's original regiment and his favorite—"my Regulars," he called them—rebelled against conditions by refusing to carry their weapons. They remained in camp and answered bugle calls but simply fell in sans rifles. Various threats were made to no avail, but finally, when each man lacking a weapon was ordered to drill with a heavy fence rail on his shoulder, they "found" their rifles in nearby farmhouses.[10]

The glory was fading from Morgan's command, and the superiority of Confederate cavalry in the West was passing. Morgan's men faithfully carried out routine screening of Bragg's right flank, but the nation had come to expect great feats from them. Bragg said: "I fear Morgan is overcome by too large a command; with a regiment or small brigade he did more and better service than with a division." And Mattie's brother Horace noticed that John was evaluated by a special measure: "The country and people expect so much from him now that he has a separate & independent command. I think often the people expect too much from our Generals. They have to fight to keep their reputation."[11]

On the evening of March 19, Morgan was on the front lines at Liberty when he thought he recognized an opportunity to redeem himself. A Federal force from Murfreesboro had advanced on the Milton Road and was only a few miles away. Morgan determined to attack them as they marched back toward Murfreesboro. The next morning, without the assistance of Duke, who was still convalescing, he moved forward with 1,000 effectives and two artillery pieces. Scouts said the Union camp had 2,000 to 4,000 infantry, 200 cavalry, and a battery of artillery, but Morgan hoped to surprise them while they were moving and vulnerable. An hour before noon, Quirk challenged their rear guard a mile west of Milton, and they halted and formed battle lines on a steep, cedar-covered hill naturally terraced with large boulders three and four feet in height. Col. Albert S. Hall had deployed his 1,300 men—Illinois, Indiana, and Ohio infantry and a company of cavalry—and two cannon in a very strong defensive position.[12]

Morgan dispatched detachments to the right and left to flank them and prevent their escape. Then he brought up his artillery, and on the first volley he ordered a frontal assault on the hill. Men charged up the rough and broken ground on foot and were cut to pieces by grape and canister from the Union artillery. A remnant reached within thirty yards of the Yankee line, but withering rifle fire from infantry crouched behind the large rocks drove them back. After about an hour, Morgan's men ran out of rifle cartridges, and he called off the attack. The artillery continued to duel until 4:30 P.M., and then Morgan withdrew to avoid a large force of cavalry that Quirk reported approaching from Murfreesboro.[13]

The skirmish was the hardest Morgan had seen. He lost 15 percent of his force: 150 men, 30 of whom were killed. The loss in officers was very heavy: 4 captains were dead and 2 colonels, 2 captains, and 5 lieutenants wounded, for a total of 13. In one company every man was either wounded or had his clothing riddled with bullets. Hall had 7 killed and 31 wounded, including a captain.[14]

This fight was the first manifestation of Morgan's decreased commitment to the hit-and-run principle following his marriage. He had abandoned guerrilla tactics and assaulted a superior force occupying a strong defensive position. His men proved they would obey to the point of suicide, but he had wasted their strength. If he had a conscious appreciation for the superiority of the defense, he failed to apply it in this situation. Duke might have sensed the impossibility of the attack, and one thing he surely would have seen to was logistic administration. Morgan had not brought sufficient ammunition to the field; as he was falling back, he met his ordnance train coming from headquarters with a large quantity of munitions and four cannon. As it happened, however, he was fortunate that the short supply of cartridges forced him to retire—it saved him from being riddled even worse.

Rosecrans rejoiced that Hall "whipped and drove" Morgan from the field, and in the Confederate capital the loss of officers was regretted. In defeat,

Morgan sought strength from his love for Mattie. The second night after the skirmish he wrote:

All day yesterday my darling while in the hottest of the engagement was I thinking of my dear beautifull [*sic*] "Mattie" & precious one. I am satisfied your prayers must have saved me. My coat sleeve was nearly torn off by a ball, but my arm escaped unhurt. It even tore through the lining of "*Your* green jacket." When I again get back to you "pretty one," shall give it up & let you keep it. Darling, I am so anxious to see your sweet dear face & to hear you tell me, that you love me, so much & in knowing that I am perfectly happy, indeed I am the happiest soldier, in the Confederacy, or in the World.

[John was reluctant to close the letter.] Good bye my own & God's blessing. I shall come to you as soon as possible. Am so very anxious my Darling to get to you, & just as soon as I can possibly get off, from this hatefull [*sic*] place, shall fly to your arms & "will you not be so happy to receive me?" Do not forget me Love, & rest assured that my whole thoughts are of you, *alone* & my heart beats but for you. Ten thousand blessings & kisses I send with this, to my Loved & beautifull [*sic*] "Mattie." Your devoted Husband, Jno H.

[Finally he ended with a postscript:] Goodbye my Angel, what would I not give to be with you today.[15]

Later the same evening he wrote a second letter in which he declared: "I am the happiest fellow upon Earth. Darling I love you more than life. My whole existence is perfectly wrapt up in you. & I am perfectly miserable when absent. Days are so long, they seem interminable & when with my pretty Mattie they pass so rapidly. I am so happy when with you Love & absent how sad."[16]

News of Morgan's defeat at Milton circulated in both armies, and it was common knowledge that his command had declined in combat readiness. Therefore, Rosecrans sent a detachment of 1,500 infantry and cavalry under Gen. David S. Stanley on a scouting expedition in Morgan's sector. Morgan was in McMinnville, but Col. Richard M. Gano, the senior officer in the Liberty area, learned of Stanley's approach and stationed his men at Snow's Hill, which he and his fellow officers agreed was the best defensive position available. Morgan's brigade commanders had had little experience in defensive tactics, and that fact was never more obvious. Snow's Hill was a series of level-topped ridges and deep ravines sloping westward from a plateau into the valley where Liberty was located. Gano deployed his two brigades on foot in defensive line midway down the ridges, where they had a clear field of fire against the enemy who would be advancing from the valley. But the slope was not steep enough to impede the attackers, and there was no cross ditch or bluff or natural cover of any kind for Gano's men, they were perched midway up Snow's Hill like pigeons on a fence, and the smooth ridges were like highways thrusting into the center of their line.

At daylight on April 3, Stanley elevated his artillery and began raking Gano's line with telling effect. Then his infantry charged the separate natural ramps and pushed steadily upward like the fingers of a giant monster. A regiment of cavalry advanced on horseback up a dry creek bed on Gano's left and quickly gained Gano's rear. Outflanked, the Confederates retreated in a rout. Basil Duke, reporting for duty for the first time since his wound, heard the cannonading and to his surprise met a group of Gano's men heading toward the rear. There was no panic or fear, no jostling; they were walking their horses and talking rationally. Duke halted them and several others who came along until the road was jammed. They were submissive and serene, but Duke was unable to force them to regroup. Instead, with timid expressions on their faces, they rode off, swam unfordable streams, and stayed away for days. That night Morgan was heading toward the front when he intercepted a private and asked him why he was absent from his regiment. "Well, General, I'm scattered," he said.[17]

The next day Morgan met with his officers and the small number of men still in ranks, and they agreed that their section of the front was totally vulnerable to enemy attack. He wrote Mattie that he hoped to return to her by nightfall, but if not she was to pack her possessions and be prepared to escape in the ambulance in a moment's notice. "Here I am my precious Angel still thinking of my own Dear Mattie, & cursing the fates that separate us," he said. A day later they were reunited, but it took two weeks to gather and reorganize the men, and even then their efficiency was severely impaired. All that was needed to deliver a grinding blow was another cavalry offensive, and that was what Rosecrans had in mind. He wired Halleck: "I trust our cavalry will soon begin to show its virtue in a way the rebels will not relish."[18]

After Snow's Hill, Morgan's decline was becoming a matter of concern for his family and friends. Uncle Samuel Morgan blamed Mattie: "Now, you must not get angry with me, for saying to you," he wrote to her, "that I fear you are sticking *too close* to your husband. Not that I am in favor of wives seeking their ease and comfort away from their husbands, whilst they are enduring privations & hardships." That would be selfish, he continued, but when the wife follows too closely, she "might possibly encumber her husband too much with care and anxiety, so much so as to prove injurious to him, especially to one who has necessarily on his mind such a load of care and responsibility." The Nashville *Daily Union*, a Union paper, had the gall to bring the issue into the open. "Morgan seems to have been losing his character for enterprise and daring; many of his rivals, ladies particularly, are unkind enough to attribute his present inefficiency to the fact that he is married. The fair Delilah, they assume, has shorn him of his locks. Maybe so."[19]

John's love for Mattie had impeded him, and by mid-April Rosecrans's cavalry and mounted infantry had increased in strength and efficiency to the point where they were ready to conduct the kind of raids that had been almost the exclusive prerogative of the Confederate cavalry. Rosecrans planned to raid Morgan's headquarters at McMinnville, capture or kill Morgan, burn the cotton factory, destroy the railroad depot and trains in the yards, and set fire to the trestles leading to McMinnville, thus cutting communications with Bragg's headquarters at Tullahoma. As leader of the incursion he picked Gen. Joseph J. Reynolds, the man who had a personal grudge against Morgan for escaping his lower half of the pincers on the Christmas Raid. Rosecrans assigned him a force of 6,600 men, of whom 2,600 were mounted—1,500 as cavalry and 1,100 as mounted infantry.[20]

Reynolds penetrated Morgan's lines early on the morning of April 19 and masked his objective by detaching a feint on Morgan's outpost at Woodbury, twelve miles toward the front from McMinnville. The main body proceeded toward McMinnville without being noticed. At 8:00 A.M., Morgan received a dispatch from Maj. William Bullit in command at Woodbury that the enemy was advancing in force with infantry, cavalry, and artillery. He hastily sent Mattie away in the ambulance with an escort and dispatched scouts to Woodbury, leaving him with a headquarters guard of about forty men. No other reports of sighting the enemy came in, and at 1:00 P.M., when Bullit indicated that the Federals had withdrawn, Morgan was on the verge of sending a courier to return Mattie when Reynolds's cavalry dashed into town eight abreast, filling the street with a surging mass of brown horses and blue uniforms.[21]

Morgan was sitting astride his horse at the door of a house near the square when they appeared. "Run for it," shouted Col. Robert M. Martin from Muhlenberg County, Kentucky, and instead of saving himself, Martin spurred his horse directly toward the charging enemy, his bridle rein held between his teeth and both pistols blasting. Dumfounded at such audacity, the Union men separated and let him through. He took a ball in the right lung but clung to his horse and galloped away to safety.[22]

During that melee, Morgan and his escort emptied their revolvers and retreated at full speed, all except Maj. Dick McCann, who stayed behind to create a second diversion. McCann was one of Morgan's hardiest and most accomplished scouts. When he took a ball in the belt buckle in an earlier skirmish, Dr. Robert Williams, regimental surgeon, had said, "Dick, are you hurt?"

"Yes," he had moaned, "killed deader than a corpse, shot right through the bowels. Quick Bob, pass me the bottle before I die."[23]

This day he sat his horse in front of the courthouse, and when the Federals charged up, he screamed, "Halt!" The column stopped and an officer inquired, "Who the devil are you?"

"I'm the great chief," Dick said.

"Morgan, Morgan, we've got 'im! We've got 'im!" the cry sounded along the line. Surrounding him, they demanded his surrender.

"I'll be damned if I do. Come on!" he said, attempting to push through. A Union soldier struck him on the head with a saber, laying open his scalp and knocking him to the ground.

Reynolds's official report stated that Morgan got away because he had a fleet horse and the men in the advance guard were personally unacquainted with him, but it was Martin's and McCann's diversions that enabled him to escape.[24]

When McCann's captors realized he was not Morgan, they imprisoned him in an old stable at the home of Virginia French, one of Morgan's best friends in McMinnville. That night during a thunderstorm he pushed out a stone in the foundation and fled. The next morning his keepers were incensed that the surrogate Morgan had vanished, and suspecting the French family, they demanded to search the house. "Very well," Colonel French consented quietly. "Proceed with your examination. Your prisoner is not here and I beg you will satisfy yourselves." Mrs. French stood behind him, her jewelry, money, and other valuables in large pockets under her hoopskirt. "I really felt weighted down," she said later. Two by two the Federals examined the smokehouse and kitchen, tore up the floor of the front porch, ripped loose the underpinning around the house, and looked in all the cabinets. When two men began shuffling through the laundry hamper, Puss, a house servant, protested: "Mighty small man to hide in that basket!" They climbed up the posts of Mrs. French's bed to check the top of the canopy, and finally set fire to the stable and stood around it with rifles ready, apparently hoping McCann would jump out from under a cornshuck. Besides the French stable, the Union raiders burned the cotton factory, the railroad depot, a locomotive, three cars, two railroad trestles, and 30,000 pounds of bacon.[25]

"Who is to blame for this ugly business?" asked the Chattanooga *Rebel*. "Here is a cavalry dash upon one of our chief frontier towns . . . and yet not a shot is fired, and the vandals escape with glory, trophies and all! Who is to blame for it? It certainly is one among the least commendable circumstances which have occurred in Middle Tennessee." On May 8, Morgan's friend Hardee wrote to Gen. Joseph E. Johnston recommending that as commander of the western theater he should meet with Morgan. Hardee stated that Morgan's command was in bad condition and getting worse, that the people's estimation of Morgan was declining and his reputation was being sullied. He said he had heard that Morgan was chafing at having to report to Bragg's chief of cavalry, Joseph Wheeler; this was the explanation that went through the network of Morgan's friends and supporters. In truth, Morgan had no complaint: Wheeler had not restricted him; he had restrained himself.[26]

Unknown to Hardee, Wheeler had already relieved Morgan of screening the right flank and had sent his entire brigade into dead horse camp in Kentucky. The Federals who raided McMinnville pointed out that there was no forage in the Confederate section of middle Tennessee and very little subsistence of any kind. In Kentucky, Morgan could feed his horses, secure mounts for men who had none, and try to restore morale. The men never forgot their deprivation that winter, but going to Kentucky raised their spirits. On the march Pvt. Theodore Bybee's horse fell dead under him, and he walked the last eight or ten miles grasping the stirrup of a comrade.[27]

Except for Cluke's activity in Kentucky, Morgan had not had a significant victory since the Christmas Raid. West of Monticello on May 10, he went on the offensive against a small Union force occupying Horseshoe Bottom on Greasy Creek. The Yankees were deployed in the edge of dense woods, and when Morgan's men charged on foot across a fifteen-acre field and orchard, two artillery pieces swept their ranks. They persisted nonetheless and scattered the enemy in the forest—but at the cost of 32 casualties. Confederate journalists hailed the skirmish at Greasy Creek as the first fruit of Morgan's liberation from routine duty and the restrictive hand of Wheeler. The government has "at last done justice to this gallant soldier," said the Richmond *Dispatch*. "Morgan Again at Work" the headlines cheered, and from Kentucky he was quoted: "I am on the field burying dead Yankees." In Charleston, Emma Holmes observed, "Morgan is himself again."[28]

After a few days John returned to Mattie, but the command stayed in Kentucky until May 26, enjoying the bountiful food in Wayne County and fattening their horses on the rich grass. The ranks filled up, and when they rendezvoused at Liberty, Tennessee, they numbered 2,800 men. Duke established inspections, drills, and dress parades and posted strict guards, supposedly to keep out spies but actually to keep the men in camp. And much to everyone's surprise, the Confederate government furnished all the men with new uniforms. From Monticello, Morgan had brought a fine Kentucky mare as a gift to Bragg's wife. Bragg thanked him warmly and named the horse "Alice" in honor of Mattie's sister.[29]

John had kept his promise to Mattie that after the Christmas Raid he would not leave her again that winter. Except for the aborted sortie in January and Cluke's foray in Kentucky, his men performed regular cavalry service, leaving him and Mattie to resume their honeymoon at headquarters. But severe weather, deprivation of basic supplies, the absence of Duke, and defeats at the hand of the strengthening Union cavalry sent morale and efficiency into a downward spiral. By springtime the command had collapsed to the point that it had to be relieved and sent away to convalesce. Morgan realized that he needed Bragg's permission to conduct a spectacular guerrilla raid, one that would restore his self-esteem, silence the gossip that marriage had ruined him, and reconfirm his status as the Marion of the revolution.

FOURTEEN

The Great Raid: Through Kentucky

The sun came out, blackberries and honeysuckles bloomed alongside the roads, and with their new uniforms and reinvigorated horses Morgan's men seemed to have regained their old fighting spirit. But by June, 1863, Lincoln's war of conquest was hurting the Confederacy. Grant was closing in on Vicksburg, the last bastion on the Mississippi River; Rosecrans was poised to drive Bragg from Tennessee; the blockade was slowly starving the Southern economy; and the Union cavalry in the West was stronger than its Confederate counterpart. On June 3, Lee began his invasion of Pennsylvania, hoping to regain the initiative for the South.

Morgan selected this juncture for launching his longtime dream—a raid north of the Ohio River. It was such a hazardous, high-risk undertaking, a strike of such magnitude, that people reacted with disbelief. Union Gen. Ambrose E. Burnside in Cincinnati said, "I can scarcely believe that Morgan has crossed the river with his whole force." It was so risky that Morgan carefully concealed his real intention from all his superiors including Bragg, his own commander. Historians have called the raid a "wild-eyed scheme," a harebrained, self-destructive enterprise, "a ride of utter rashness." It has defied reason ever since it occurred. Biographer Howard Swiggett concluded that either Morgan was insane or he was involved in a Confederate conspiracy to stimulate an uprising of Southern sympathizers in Indiana and Ohio. Lowell Harrison, an authority on the war in Kentucky, suggested that much of the answer on why Morgan declined after his marriage to Mattie "lies in the personality and character of Morgan himself." Harrison was correct, and his opinion is especially pertinent in regard to the Great Raid.[1]

It is enlightening to view the raid from Morgan's perspective as a guerrilla and high-risk taker. After his defeat at Lebanon, Morgan had recovered with a guerrilla attack on Cave City. Now once again it was time to return to his specialty, to strike deep behind enemy lines and inflict disproportionate damage. Duke contended that strategically the whole idea was the logical outcome of Morgan's theory on the proper way to make war. The raid would restore Morgan's honor in the eyes of his wife, family, and the Southern people. Everyone expected miracles from him; therefore, he would give them one more and be back at Mattie's side, he told himself, within five weeks.

When Morgan suggested the plan to Duke and his other brigade commanders, they were filled with grave apprehension, and when he talked about linking up with Lee in Pennsylvania or staying in Illinois for two months, they realized he was overconfident. "He did not disguise from himself the great dangers he encountered, but was sanguine of success," Duke recorded.[2]

Even today, standing at the Ohio River crossing, one realizes what a gamble Morgan was taking. The wide expanse of the Ohio seems formidable and much deeper and wider than the Stones River, Cumberland River, Green River, and other streams Morgan had forded. To ferry 2,400 men and more than 2,400 horses across the Ohio into enemy country on two small steamboats was a daring enterprise indeed.

Morgan returned to guerrilla war, but he was not the same military leader he had been before his marriage. In the period when he depended upon staying in the action for emotional stability, he carefully preserved his men and avoided placing them in unduly hazardous situations. His need to stay in the game restrained his tendency to challenge the odds. But in planning the Great Raid, his need for action was overshadowed by the necessity of being with Mattie; therefore, his nature as a gambler dominated, and he placed his command in a hazard that reasonable people recognized as extreme.

In spite of his other boastful suggestions, Morgan's plan from the beginning was to march through Indiana, traverse Ohio, and come out in West Virginia. In mid-May he sent scouts to reconnoiter fords on the upper Ohio. He believed that as long as he kept moving, the Union cavalry could not overtake him and the state militia could not concentrate fast enough to present a threat—and even if they did, his veterans could disperse or outmaneuver them. In his mind this was no suicide mission but an undertaking that promised adventure and success, and he welcomed the participation of four of his five brothers, each of whom had by now transferred to his command.[3]

Before he could leave, however, he needed to make arrangements for Mattie, who was pregnant. Having lost Becky and his firstborn child to the complications of childbirth, Morgan took his wife's condition more seriously than most husbands. On June 2, two weeks after dispatching scouts to the Ohio fords, he requested leave to take Mattie to Augusta, Georgia, where she and Alice could sojourn with their aunt, Mrs. C.S.W. Fleming. Bragg's headquarters denied the request, and he reapplied through the staff of his immediate superior, Wheeler. They forwarded the application, and it was rejected twice. Then Wheeler himself intervened, but still Bragg refused; intelligence reports indicated that an advance by Rosecrans was imminent, and Morgan was too valuable to be spared.[4]

John then asked his brother Charlton to escort Mattie, and at the Mc-

Minnville railroad depot he kissed her goodbye. Every few hours he sent her telegrams in care of telegraph operators along the line, then wrote her a letter: "Today you reached Knoxville and I hope you were not much fatigued. It was a long ride for you My Darling. How much I regretted not being able to accompany you—I should have anticipated all your wants. . . .Enclosed find a sprig of geranium which I send emblematically." The evening of the next day he wrote: "I must close tonight. . . .It is getting late and my candle is quite low. Shall read two chapters in my Prayer Book you gave me . . . and in bidding you goodnight send you a heart full of love. . . .You will present me with a beautiful present this winter and how acceptable it will be."[5]

With Mattie provided for, Morgan turned to the work of getting approval for a raid. He asked Wheeler for permission to attack Louisville. There sits the river city, he said, prospering on government contracts, warehouses bulging with military stores for shipment on the L&N, and it has never been attacked (in fact, would not be in the war), and it is a ripe plum, protected by only 300 troops. On June 14, Wheeler went to headquarters and recommended the idea to Bragg in person. With Rosecrans still ready to attack, Bragg could not afford the detachment of Morgan's entire division, but he did approve a force of 1,500 men. He directed that they be Kentuckians who would recruit for the Confederate army, and he ordered that if Morgan should hear that the enemy was advancing, he was to turn rapidly and fall upon their rear.[6]

Wheeler gave the word to Morgan, and he requested 2,000 men. "To make the attempt with less, might prove disastrous, as large details will be required at Louisville to destroy the transportation, shipping, and Government property. Can I go? The result is certain." What Morgan was thinking was that the smaller force was adequate to take Louisville but not to cross the Ohio River. Bragg acceded, but he never forgave Morgan for the deception and never trusted him again. Morgan was guilty of outright lying to his superior officers—not one word was said to Wheeler or Bragg about crossing the river. Bragg had regarded Morgan as a valuable guerrilla, but soon he saw that the man's independence made him dangerous.[7]

Morgan set out immmediately with his entire division: ten regiments in two brigades—2,500 men, or 500 more than authorized. He had two three-inch Parrott guns and two twelve-pound howitzers. They crossed the Cumberland River on June 20 and camped for the night, preparing to assail Carthage, Tennessee, in the morning. A detachment brought in a captured postal wagon train, and in a room crowded with officers reading the Yankee mail, John scribbled a letter to Mattie on a scrap of paper. He informed her that the raid was temporarily suspended, that a courier had just brought orders to fall back and intercept a Federal force threatening Knoxville. "Is it not hard, my Sweet one to be so sadly disappointed?" he lamented. In closing he wrote: "I am so very anxious to see you my 'pretty one' the time drags

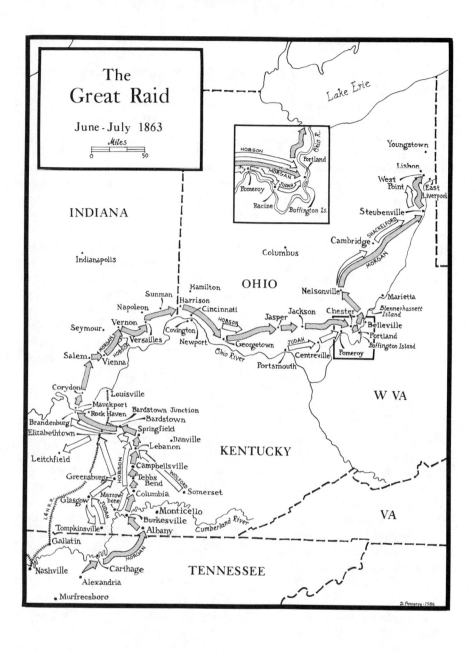

INDIANA

Indianapolis

Lake Erie

Ohio R.

HOBSON

MORGAN   Portland

JUDAH

Pomeroy

Racine   Buffington Is.

Youngstown

Lisbon

West
Point   East
Liverpool

Steubenville

SHACKELFORD

Cambridge

MORGAN

Columbus

OHIO

Hamilton

Sunman   Harrison

Napoleon   Cincinnati

Seymour.   Vernon

Covington

Versailles   Newport

MORGAN   Vienna

HOBSON

Salem.

Corydon.

Louisville

Mauckport

Rock Haven   Bardstown Junction

Brandenburg   Bardstown

Elizabethtown   Springfield

Danville

Leitchfield   Lebanon

KENTUCKY

Campbellsville

Greensburg   Tebbs
Bend

HOBSON   WOLFORD

Glasgow   Marrow-
bone   Columbia   Somerset

L&NRR.   JUDAH

Tompkinsville   Monticello

Burkesville

Gallatin   Albany

MORGAN

Nashville   Carthage   Cumberland River

Alexandria

Murfreesboro   TENNESSEE

Nelsonville

Marietta

Jasper   Jackson   Chester   Blennerhassett
Island

HOBSON   Belleville

Georgetown   Portland

JUDAH   Buffington Island

Centreville   Pomeroy

Portsmouth

W VA

VA

Ohio River

D. Pomeroy · 1986

heavier each day & although passing through exciting scenes still my thoughts are of you My Dearest Wife. The candle is so low that I can scarcely see, but could not resist the pleasure of writing. Sent you some late papers captured. Love to Sister Alice. How is our little recruit? God bless you my own Darling Wife."[8]

Morgan came back across the Cumberland and sent his men toward Monticello, Kentucky, while he went to McMinnville to hurry forward a half-dozen munition wagons. For over a week his soldiers sloshed along roads knee-deep in mud and in total futility; they never caught sight of the enemy they were trying to intercept. Union Col. William P. Sanders, with 1,500 cavalry, came out of Kentucky like lightning. In ten days he drove in the pickets in Knoxville, wrecked several depots and trestles of vital railroads east and west of town, and escaped with only 19 casualties. Sanders was detached from the new Army of the Ohio that Burnside was organizing in Kentucky for a general invasion of east Tennessee. Along with his military governor Andrew Johnson, Lincoln cherished the goal of liberating east Tennessee, and after Burnside was defeated at Fredericksburg in December, he was reassigned to Cincinnati to prepare the advance. The presence of Burnside's army in Kentucky, with headquarters in Cincinnati, brought about an unusual shift of strength in the area behind the lines. Earlier only a skeleton force had opposed the raiders, but now—in addition to the thousands of men guarding the railroad—there was a developing army. Burnside, a man of striking appearance with a bald head and bushy sideburns sweeping magnificently from his upper lip to his ears, was a West Point graduate; he had worked for the Illinois Central Railroad under his friend George B. McClellan and now was an experienced, able commander. And to his good fortune, his headquarters turned out to be ideally located for coordination of the pursuit of Morgan.[9]

Burnside had plenty of advance warning. When Morgan crossed the Cumberland the first time, Rosecrans informed him of Morgan's strength and location, and Burnside alerted his commanders in Kentucky to be prepared to move at a moment's notice. Guarding the gate into Kentucky this time was Gen. Henry M. Judah, commander of the 3rd Division, 23rd Army Corps, stationed in Glasgow. Judah, a native of Snow Hill, Maryland, and son of an Episcopal minister with a New England background, had graduated from West Point and was now a forty-two-year-old career man. He had defended Washington, D.C., early in the war and had taken the field on Grant's staff at Shiloh. But it was a fearful thing to fight the legendary Morgan, and Judah took no chances. While Morgan's men were chasing toward Monticello, he moved southeastward to Tompkinsville, and in order to protect his left flank, he called in his second brigade under Gen. Edward H. Hobson from Columbia to Marrowbone; then he claimed that his 7,000 men were covering all the approaches to Kentucky. Incredibly, by withdrawing Hobson from Columbia he opened the door—the pathway from Burkesville through Columbia to Lebanon was unguarded. Furthermore, he went on the defensive; for example, he told a scouting party, "Under no circumstances approach the Cumberland so near as to compromise a perfectly safe retreat." A week before it happened, Hobson predicted that Morgan would pass east of the Union position. Judah would recover some of his reputation at the close of the raid in Ohio, but he would be relieved of command anyway and assigned to routine administrative duties for the balance of the war.[10]

On July 1, when Morgan approached the Cumberland River the second time and prepared to cross at Burkesville, thirty-five miles upriver from Tompkinsville, Judah reported it and urgently requested a gunboat to prevent the crossing. Burnside issued a second general alert and ordered Judah to attack with his cavalry as soon as Morgan came over. The next day between 2:00 and 3:00 P.M., General Hobson and about 300 cavalrymen skirmished with Quirk's scouts and retreated to Marrowbone, twelve miles west of Burkesville. That brief skirmish was the only challenge by Judah's division, but it may have been more significant than it seemed because Quirk was severely wounded in the arm, and Morgan continued the raid without his best scout. On July 3, Judah told Burnside that the route to Kentucky through Columbia was clear, that Morgan could reach Columbia without encountering a single scout. Nevertheless, he said that he dared not move from his defensive position until Morgan's plans were known.[11]

During the night of July 3, Morgan's advance guard reached the southern bank of Green River and heard the ringing of axes and the crash of falling timber. On the opposite bank, Col. Orlando H. Moore, with 200 men of the 25th Michigan Infantry, had abandoned his stockade overlooking the bridge and was erecting a temporary fortress of timber and earth on a sharp knoll in Tebbs Bend of the river. By morning the makeshift parapet was finished, and it was almost impregnable. Protected on three sides by precipitous river banks and thick woods, it was so well situated that artillery could not shell it effectively; the only alternative was a frontal assault. Once Morgan had reconnoitered, he should have marched on; there was no danger in leaving a small band of infantry in his rear. But it was his policy to attack and roll up victories on the way into a raid; it gave the men confidence and achieved trophies in prisoners of war and towns or forts conquered. The practice had previously been effective but should have been suspended on this occasion.

Nevertheless, he halted the division, wheeled into line at the edge of the field before the little stronghold, and demanded a surrender. But this was July 4, and Moore answered: "It is a bad day for surrender, and I would rather not." Then Morgan dismounted his men and ordered the charge. Screaming the Rebel yell, wave after wave ran forward, only to become entangled in the newly cut tree laps in front of the fort and to be cut down by sparse, deadly accurate rifle fire from Moore's men. After thirty minutes Morgan called off the siege. He lost 35 killed—including a colonel, a major, a captain and 3 lieutenants—and 40 wounded. Moore lost 6 killed and 23 wounded. This was another instance when Morgan failed to appreciate the strength of a defensive position, but to his credit he called off the attack and was delayed only a few hours.[12]

From Tebbs Bend, Morgan moved northward, past the site of the log church that he had burned eighteen months before, to the outskirts of Lebanon. There, at 7:00 A.M. on July 5, he halted before a skirmish line hastily thrown up behind fences and overturned wagons by 380 men of the 20th Kentucky Infantry under Lt. Col. Charles S. Hanson. Threatening to bombard the town, Morgan demanded surrender. Hanson refused, and the four small cannon boomed. Then Morgan ordered a series of dismounted frontal assaults, gradually driving Hanson's skirmishers back to their headquarters in the railroad depot and adjacent brick buildings. At noon Morgan demanded that Hanson surrender or he would burn the town. Hanson refused to acknowledge the message because, he reported, when the flag of truce appeared and firing ceased, some of Morgan's men violated it by moving their artillery batteries and skirmish lines closer to the depot. The fighting resumed at a furious level.

Morgan's artillery was within 300 yards of the depot, but the building was on lower ground and the shells burst through the roof and into the upper floor, leaving the ground level undamaged. At 1:00 P.M., Morgan gave the order to burn the business buildings near the Federal position, and with the conflagration spreading, commanded the 2nd Kentucky to rush the depot. They advanced at double-quick on Main Street and fired point-blank into the windows of the Union headquarters. By then the depot itself was burning, and Hanson ran out the white flag, six hours and twenty minutes after the fight began.

In the final charge, nineteen-year-old Tom Morgan, at the head of the column, was shot through the heart and died in the arms of brother Cal. All morning he had repeatedly exposed himself to enemy fire, and once John had ordered him to the rear. He was the youngest brother on the raid and, second to John, the most popular Morgan in the command. A Christian and member of the Baptist Church, he was highly intelligent, sensitive, handsome, and a talented singer, often leading the men in their marching songs. He had joined the Confederacy in July 1861, even before John did, and had been with Morgan's men longer than any of the brothers. The other Morgans took his death personally, and for the second time John allowed emotions to run amok in his command. His men went into a terrible frenzy, and he permanently escalated the violence under his policy of retaliation.[13]

When the Union captains, Cornelius McLeod and Henry S. Parrish, emerged from the burning depot in surrender, Charlton Morgan threatened to shoot them in retaliation for Tom's death. Colonel Hanson intervened, and with tears streaming down his face, Charlton grabbed him by the beard, shook his fist in Hanson's face, and screamed: "I will blow your brains out, you damned rascal." Fellow officers pulled Charlton away, and he apologized. The next day he poured out his grief in a letter: "My dear Ma, in the death of Tom I feel as my future happiness was forever blighted. I loved him more than any of my Brothers." Word of Tom's death stirred up hate and revenge in the men, and they took retribution by burning much of Lebanon. About twenty buildings were destroyed, including the depot, several businesses and private homes, several law offices, and the courthouse. Irreplaceable deeds and wills, records of the history of Marion County, went up in smoke, and the men moved on down the street to break into and plunder the retail stores.[14]

With the single exception of the rescue of the civilians of Gallatin, Morgan had previously bent over backward to respect the rights of prisoners of war. Just the day before, he had arrested one of his own officers for stealing a watch from a captured citizen. And the same day, when some of the men began looting businesses in Columbia, he had arrested them, compelled them to return the goods, and punished them immediately. But after Tom's death he took no action against the plunderers. He would continue giving lip service to regulations against pillage, but the men knew he approved—the absence of punishment proved it.

Also, during previous raids, he had usually paroled prisoners immediately, but the men who had killed Tom were force-marched nine miles on foot at double-quick, prodded along by Morgan's men on horseback. The march began in midafternoon, and rain showers relieved the heat, but the prisoners suffered from thirst and fatigue. Sgt. Joseph Slaughter of Company B gave out and asked to be transported, as he was unable to continue. He was ordered to go forward or be killed. Taking a few more steps, he collapsed and died. Pvt. Samuel Ferguson fell in the road and was mortally injured when an artillery caisson rolled over him; he died a few hours later. Pvt. Martin W. Cure was seriously injured by artillery wheels passing over his head, but he survived. George Prentice wrote that this incident proved Morgan was no gentleman: "We hope to hear no more of this inhuman wretch's chivalry."[15]

Dropping the prisoners in Springfield, the division veered westward and marched all night, entering Bardstown at 4:00 A.M. on July 6. An advance company of the command had penned up Lt. Thomas W. Sullivan and twenty-five cavalrymen in a brick livery stable. Sullivan had declined one request that he surrender, and now Morgan gave him a second opportunity, with the warning that otherwise he would be blown to hell by artillery. Sullivan refused again, and a brisk exchange of rifle fire ensued. Then Sullivan's sentinel on the roof of the stable said it looked hopeless—four artillery pieces were moving into place 100 yards away, and every street was jammed with Rebel cavalry. Capitulating at last, Sullivan walked out of the stable waving a white flag. "What do you want?" yelled Dick Morgan.

"I accept your terms of surrender."

"Go back! You have refused these terms twice; you have no right to demand them now." Turning to his men, Dick ordered them to shoot Sullivan as he ran back into the stable, but John overruled Dick and accepted the surrender. As they rounded up the prisoners, Morgan's men took their hats and boots, and an officer robbed Sullivan of his belt. "Here is civilized warfare for you!" wrote Prentice. "Here is rebel chivalry! The usages observed by Morgan and his men are the usages not of war but of thieving and pillage."[16]

At ten o'clock in the morning they left Bardstown and marched west all day, intersecting the main L&N line twenty-five miles south of Louisville at Rolling Fork River at dusk. There they seized the stockade and burned the trestle. At Bardstown Junction a few miles north, Ellsworth entered the telegraph office and, holding his pistol to the head of operator James Forker, said: "Hello, sonny. Move one inch except as I direct, and you are a dead man." Listening to incoming messages, Ellsworth learned about a passenger train coming north from Nashville. When the railroad superintendent in Louisville asked "Has the train passed north yet?" Ellsworth told Forker, "Tell him yes." Forker did so, and a few minutes later the train was surrounded by Morgan's men south of the burning trestle. Bullets whistled around the cars, and the passengers leaped under the seats and fell to the floor in the aisles, terrified by the wild yelling of the Rebels.[17]

The engineer braked to a stop, and the grayclads methodically robbed the train. One squad took the money from the express company safe; another seized the United States mail. The passengers were lined up beside the track and relieved of hats, boots, money, and jewelry. A correspondent of the New York *Herald* lost his gold watch to a lieutenant and his pocketknife to a private; he had secreted his purse in his boots, and luckily no one demanded them. The raiders distributed the mail among them and stood around in small groups opening it and burning it in little fires. Morgan, dressed in a roundabout jacket, gray trousers, and cavalry boots, with no insignia of rank, chatted with the women passengers. They persuaded him to allow the train to return to Elizabethtown.[18]

After the train left, Morgan's men marched all night and all the next day and night, July 7, pausing only for a few hours to feed and water the horses. Ellsworth's wiretapping confused the Federals, and Burnside was hindered by the destruction of telegraph wires, but the delays were not vital. Morgan slipped through by rapid marching and by keeping his pursuers guessing. They had no idea that he was making for Brandenburg, Kentucky, to cross the Ohio River, and his advance through central Kentucky and loop westward south of Louisville puzzled them. He kept his options open—as far as Burnside knew, he might turn and go in any direction at any moment. As in earlier incursions, he sent out detachments of one or two companies right and left all along the route, including one against Louisville. Between nine and ten o'clock in the morning of July 8, he arrived at Brandenburg.[19]

Guards at Muldraugh's Hill and other stockades on the L&N were mystified that Morgan did not wreak more destruction on the main line. "Much excitement exists along the whole line of Railroad for his intention is no doubt to try and destroy portions of it," observed an officer in Bowling Green. Burnside did recognize the feints for what they were; sifting through intelligence reports, he drew accurate conclusions about Morgan's strength and location. His field commanders were much less adept. The company Morgan detached to Danville created such confusion for the 8th and 9th Michigan Cavalry that they marched back and forth from Danville to Lebanon, wearing out their horses and taking themselves out of action. Their commander said, "I am astonished and disgusted with the conduct of the Michigan regiments."[20]

Burnside did have a few commanders more able than Judah. On July 5, Judah had dispatched two brigades of cavalry under Hobson to follow Morgan, while he led the remainder of his cavalry from Glasgow to Elizabethtown, taking thirty-six hours to ferry over the flood-swollen Green River, and falling behind Morgan more than forty-eight hours. When Morgan was striking into Indiana, Judah was in Leitchfield waiting to intercept him on his return to Tennessee. He had been no more effective in chasing Morgan than in preventing the Cumberland crossing.[21]

Burnside placed his hope on the cavalry force that concentrated in Lebanon on the afternoon of July 6, less than twenty-four hours after Morgan left. They were led by two amateur Kentucky soldiers, one a lawyer and the other a banker; both were infantry veterans of the Mexican War. From Somerset a force of Cavalry and mounted infantry under Col. Frank Wolford reported to General Hobson of Judah's division, producing a combined strength of 2,500 mounted men. Wolford was an outstanding criminal lawyer from Liberty, a man whose sharp gray eyes, huge nose, and thick black hair gave him the striking appearance of a rugged black hawk. He was a diamond in the rough, an individual of plain strength whose favorite meal was boiled hen and dumplings and whose men called him "Old Meat Axe." He had been seriously wounded in the "Lebanon Races" and welcomed an opportunity to resume his chase of Morgan.[22]

Hobson was the son of a steamboat captain and had been president of the Greensburg branch of the Bank of Kentucky when the war began. Much later he would have the peculiar honor of dying at a Union army reunion in Cleveland, September 14, 1901. Burnside ordered Hobson to move quickly, pushing men and horses to the utmost extremity, impressing new horses when necessary, and living off the country. An officer under Hobson wrote his daughters before departing Lebanon: "Farewell, I know not how this pursuit will end—but I'll be killed or kill some one if we come up with Morgan."[23]

Hobson cut loose from his supply wagons and made good time, closing the gap between his troops and Morgan to twelve hours. On July 8 scouts and informers told him that Morgan was headed for Brandenburg to pass over the river. He requested a gunboat and pressed forward until 7:00 P.M. Then, twelve miles from Brandenburg, he halted and went into Rock Haven, hoping to arrange for a coordinated attack with a gunboat reported to be docked in the little village. But the vessel was gone, and Hobson decided not to proceed. "The night was very dark and my troops very much fatigued," he reported. "I did not deem it prudent to attack the enemy with my force alone, as this point [Brandenburg] is capable of defense by a small force against vastly superior numbers." If he had continued, he easily could have captured the last remnant of Morgan's men who crossed near midnight, but Hobson was paralyzed by the same malady that struck Judah and many others: the Morgan jitters. Burnside was bitterly disappointed; there had been no reason not to fall upon Morgan during the vulnerable time when his force was on both banks of the river. When Hobson arrived at Brandenburg at seven o'clock the next morning, Morgan's men had disappeared into Indiana.[24] The only traces to be seen in Brandenburg were the steamboat *John T. McCombs* and the smoking hull of the *Alice Dean* drifting near the Indiana shoreline.

A couple of days in advance Morgan had forwarded a detachment of more than 100 men to Brandenburg for the purpose of seizing steamboats. On July 7 they rode in, stabled their horses, and concealed themselves in small groups under trees by the wharf and between stores on each side of the level street to the landing. At 2:00 P.M. the *John T. McCombs* threw out her stages onto the wharfboat, preparing to take on passangers bound for Louisvile and other ports upriver. Suddenly, Morgan's men swarmed to the wharf and rushed on deck, capturing the vessel. They removed the passengers, robbed them of their money and what clothing they wanted, and put the boat out along the bank, where it appeared to be aground. Soon the *Alice Dean* came along, and they sent out distress signals, luring her into ambush. They robbed her passengers also and were waiting when Morgan arrived with the main force the next day, between 9:00 and 10:00 A.M.[25]

From midmorning until after midnight on July 8 the ferrying of men, horses, and artillery went on. A small contingent of Indiana militia interrupted the operation briefly by firing a single cannon they had transported to the opposite shore on a wagon. And at noon the Union gunboat *Springfield* caused a delay of about an hour, but after her ammunition ran out, she steamed back up the river. Morgan's men on the bluffs overlooking the landing had time to relax and think as they waited their turn. "We are in line of battle," J.D. Sprakes wrote in his journal. "As here I sit the sun is sinking in the Western horizon reflecting his rays in the beautiful Ohio. What a scene for contemplation. Bygone days, hopes long buried, aspirations unattained crowd upon my brain."[26]

When the last man and last horse were over, they burned the *Alice Dean*, purchased only a few months before by the Dean Company of Cincinnati for $42,000. But the captain of the *McCombs* was a friend of Duke, so they spared it. When Hobson arrived, he dispatched the *McCombs* to Louisville for transports.

To this point the raid had been a successful guerrilla operation. With rapid movement, night marches, disruption of communications, and flying detachments, Morgan had slipped through Burnside's army in Kentucky. Small Union garrisons at Tebbs Bend, Lebanon, and Bardstown refused to be intimidated by Morgan's reputation or his superior strength and fought vigorously from defensive positions, but going on the offensive against him was another question. Judah hesitated to attack on the Cumberland River and Hobson on the Ohio. They felt humiliated and frustrated, and they were eager to compensate for their reluctance and reclaim their reputations during the pursuit through Indiana and Ohio.

FIFTEEN

The Great Raid:
Indiana and Ohio

Day and night from July 9 to 18, Morgan's raiders rode eastward through Indiana and Ohio, burning bridges, canal boats, and depots, ripping up railroad tracks, seizing government funds, extorting money from millers and manufacturers, looting private retail stores, and helping themselves to food in private dwellings.

The destruction was minor compared to that recently inflicted upon Southerners by Grant's army in the Vicksburg campaign. Grant had ordered his men to seize horses, destroy farm implements, and burn all the crops in their track. And the damage was nothing like the sixty-mile swath laid waste by Sherman in Georgia in 1864. Grant and Sherman advanced in force with infantry, and they had time to dismantle and demolish. Morgan moved rapidly; the devastation had to be done quickly and was aimed at Union military and economic resources—except for the seizure of food and horses, residences were exempt. It would have taken only moments to set fire to the homes they entered for food, but Morgan's men burned only the few houses that belonged to the bushwhackers who fired on them. A few grain fields were damaged when riders spilled over into them, but there was no attempt to damage farms or farm property.[1]

Morgan's provost guards were directed to prevent looting, but the men knew that their commander approved, and within bounds they determined to "pay off" the North for scores the Union army had made in Confederate territory. At Brandenburg, Henry L. Stone, a sergeant in the advance guard and native of Indiana, swore: "We intend to live off the Yanks hereafter, and let them feel (like the South has felt) some of the horrors of war. Horses we expect to take whenever needed, food and provisions also . . . I just imagine how the women will cry their eyes out at seeing a Rebel army." A farmer whose pantry was cleaned out said: "They eat as if the sole purpose of their visit to Indiana was to get fat upon Hoosier bread and meat, and make up for the privations they have endured down in Dixie."[2]

Early in the morning of the first day, vidette William A. Milton tied his horse to the hitching rail at the tollgate north of Mauckport. Dressed in blue, he told the woman gatekeeper that he was a Union soldier pursuing Morgan and needed breakfast. "God bless you honey!" she exclaimed, "You shall have whatever you want." Milton ate a sumptuous meal of ham and eggs, bread, and coffee, and as other members of the advance came up, she cooked for them as well. "All I have my dear Union boys can have," she said, "for I know they will catch that old guerrilla Morgan, and I hope when they get him they will hang him." Gulping the last of his coffee and pushing back his chair, Milton announced that they were Morgan's men, but she refused to believe it. "Oh, no, you can't fool me, for you are all too nice looking." She probably had the last laugh, because more than likely she knew the truth all the time.[3]

The wildest rumors flew through the country, and many people were not as calm as the toll collector. It was said that the guerrillas would kill all the men, lay the villages in ashes, and carry off all the women and children. Citizens buried their money in tin buckets, and concealed their horses in back hollows and remote forests. One man tied his horses to small saplings in a sinkhole in the woods and hid his cash in the knothole of an apple tree. Another put his small son, Isaac, in a dry goods box. The women and children of Vernon were evacuated to farmhouses and crowded together in rooms with no standing room left. When a sentry accidentally fired his rifle, they began weeping and wailing and spent the remainder of the night in great suspense. In Decatur County "the women & children went about screaming and hollowing fit to kill themselves & when the news came that they were fighting at Sunman & Napoleon and that there was more of their men than there was of ours some of the women like to have went crazy."[4]

At Vienna, scout Curtis R. Burke dismounted at a house to get something to eat, knocked at the door, and found the mother and children crying. They told him they were afraid the Rebels would burn their house. Burke assured them the house was safe and that the husband and father, who had been captured, would be paroled immediately. His quiet reassurance and gentlemanly manner allayed their fears, and as he rode away after a hearty supper, he looked back to see them standing in the door, waving goodbye.[5]

The target of looting was not homes but retail stores. Like boys robbing an orchard, the men impressed buggies, carts, market wagons, and vehicles of every description and filled them with groceries, books, stationery, cutlery, calico, silks and satins, hoops, hats, and other female garments. One man had a chafing dish on the pommel of his saddle; another carried a birdcage and three canaries for two days; and even though it was midsummer, another had seven pairs of iceskates around his neck. The division was burdened with a two-mile caravan of the spoils of war. In one instance Morgan intervened: a few men broke into the Masonic Lodge in Jackson, Ohio, and when they emerged in the regalia of the order, he reprimanded them and ordered them to return the garments. In Seymour some of the men went into Henderson's Apothecary and after drinking all the whiskey in the cellar, poured the vinegar, kerosene, and other bulky liquids on the basement floor and began rummaging through the drugs on the shelves. Coming to an astringent medicine the doctor had mixed for diarrhea, one fellow swallowed a full quart and shouted: "That hain't brandy!" The proprietor told him what it was, and he remarked, "Well, I guess 'twont hurt us," and left with what must have been the worst case of constipation in the command.[6]

The pillage was beyond the pale of civilized warfare, as was the robbery of prisoners of war and civilians. Many of the state militia captured in Indiana and Ohio were relieved of their boots, clothing, and money, and cash was taken from many civilians. When the raiders were searched later, their pockets were stuffed with United States money. One man had $1,100 in his canteen, and another had a $20 greenback in the bowl of his pipe.

On the other hand, it was legal under international law to confiscate the financial resources of an enemy government, and Morgan's officers left no stone unturned searching for Union funds. In Indiana they took about $690 from the Harrison County Treasurer and $5,000 from the Ripley County Treasury. They apprehended bank cashiers in Corydon, Indiana, and Georgetown, Ohio, forcing them to open their account books so that Morgan's auditors could determine whether government deposits were present. Both banks had taken their money out of town under guard, however, and there was nothing to confiscate. With all the attention to finance, Morgan was operating on the brink of serious criminal activity—armed robbery of private funds from banks—and on his next raid it would get out of control. Construing the operation of gristmills and textile mills as part of the war effort, Morgan demanded about $1,000 ransom from each owner, who usually paid.[7]

Morgan was more amused than annoyed at the plundering; his greatest shock was the strength of the popular resistance. When captured, he said that he could have whipped the state militia, but that since crossing the Ohio he had found "every man, woman, and child his enemy . . . every hill-top was a telegraph and every bush an ambush." He had never raided in entirely enemy territory before. In Kentucky and Tennessee many people were Southern sympathizers and many others neutral, but in Indiana and Ohio it seemed that everyone was hostile. Gov. Oliver P. Morton of Indiana mustered all able-bodied white males into the militia and dispatched runners to every township to ring the bells and arouse the squirrel hunters and farmers. Within forty-eight hours, 65,000 men were under arms, many of them bushwhacking, cutting down trees in the road, and using every means possible to delay Morgan so the Union cavalry could catch him before he left the state.[8]

The state militia annoyed the raiders and caused brief delays, such as a short skirmish in Corydon, and another serious problem was the acquisition of local guides. Morgan always counted upon captured civilians to point out the most direct route, but the men impressed in Indiana and Ohio deceived Morgan's advance guard, and some—even under threats against their lives—

refused to cooperate at all. On the last day in Ohio, ninety critical minutes of daylight were lost searching for a guide.[9]

Morgan made no attempt to recruit Southern sympathizers as guides or to coordinate with them in any manner, even though the raid passed through the heart of Copperhead country, and in attempting to explain the raid, some writers have connected it to that movement. The Copperheads, or butternuts, were Northern residents who supported the South by forming secret societies such as the Knights of the Golden Circle to press for peace. They were usually adherents of the Democratic Party. In Ohio one of their leading spokesmen, Clement L. Vallandigham, ran for the Democratic nomination for governor advocating total repudiation of Lincoln, Lincoln's war, and his Emancipation Proclamation. In 1862, Democrats won the state legislatures of Indiana and Illinois, and both lower houses adopted resolutions for an armistice and peace conference. In Indiana the Democrats became such a block to Governor Morton that he had the Republicans boycott legislative sessions to prevent a quorum, and for two years he ran the state without a representative assembly. Vallandigham was arrested on May 5, but no one knew how many followers he had, and when the Great Raid occurred they were still a serious threat to the Northern will to continue the war.[10].

No one despised butternuts more than John Hunt Morgan. He associated them with Kentuckians who betrayed Kentucky by refusing to fight for the South. True Southerners would have actively supported the revolution by joining the Confederate army; these were cowardly traitors, he thought, and he encouraged his men to treat them harshly. In Decatur County, Indiana, the marauders stripped John Clark's store and marched him along for five miles, then gave him an old horse and sent him home "for they did not want any such cowardly villain that was a traitor to their country with them for they had no use for them." In Ohio an old man drove into camp in a farm wagon and asked the raiders to return his three horses. He was a Vallandigham man and was opposed to the war, he said. Morgan had him drive up into the center of the brigade and confiscated his wagon. The man said he could not ride horseback, and Morgan replied that it was all right; he was a prisoner and could walk. The march resumed, and after a few miles the man complained that his boots were blistering his feet and pleaded for his wagon. Morgan had two soldiers pull off his boots, and he walked until night in stocking feet. In camp they forced him to sing a song with the chorus "I'll bet ten cents in specie, that Morgan'll win the race."[11]

Morgan expected Burnside to concentrate in Hamilton, Ohio, a few miles north of Cincinnati on the Hamilton and Dayton Railroad. He believed that once he passed Cincinnati, the danger would be over; all that would be left would be to keep ahead of the pursuing cavalry. Near Hamilton on July 13 he began a thirty-two-hour, ninety-five-mile march around Cincinnati, a pace that historian Robert Henry asserts was never equaled by a cavalry force of this size. It was a dark night, and they moved at the double-quick, with strictly no talking. When a gap developed between the advance brigade and the rear, Duke, leading the rear, had to halt several times to determine the route. He would dismount, light a splinter, and search the road for slaver dropped from the mouths of horses in the advance.[12]

On lengthy forced marches like this, cavalrymen often slept in the saddle —a broken, fitful sleep that only increased the temptation to withdraw from the column and lie down in a fencerow for an hour of uninterrupted, blessed slumber. Officers moved through the ranks arousing the men and, when there was a brief stop, prodding those who had rolled off their horses and lay asleep in the road. "Get up, get up, old man. The Yanks will get you!" they would whisper. One private moaned: "To Hell with the Yanks. I don't care who gets me. I cannot go on any longer!" He and several others were sleeping peacefully when taken prisoner by the Union cavalry.[13]

The rapid marching took a terrible toll on the horses. The Tennessee and Kentucky stock were soon exhausted, and the raiders had to exchange every day or two and sometimes within a few hours. Horse-pressing details combed the countryside; in the words of Maj. Samuel Starling in the Union pursuit force, Morgan "took literally every horse within miles of the road, leaving none for us to recruit from, his way was sprinkled with broken down horses, left on the road." An Ohio woman was plowing corn when a scouting party swept down on the field. As they unhitched her horse, she screamed and danced around, and grabbing a handful of cornstalks, laid it on their shoulders hot and heavy. In Versailles, Indiana, a soldier came in leading a fine pony followed closely by a sixteen-year-old girl. Fright and desperation commingled on her pretty face as she threw her arms around her horse, calling him pet names and saying sadly: "Do not let them part us. I have been faithful and true to you, be ye so to me." Pleading with the soldier's captain, she said she had raised the pony from a foal and they had grown up together, companions and friends. The captain ordered the soldier to look for another mount, and when he handed her the reins the girl burst into tears of gratitude.[14]

They kept moving, twenty-one hours per day, but the farther they went in Ohio the more often they heard the cry, "Halt! Axes to the front!" Over 50,000 Ohio militia had turned out, and many of them were felling trees in the roads ahead, removing planking from bridges, and delaying the column with small skirmishes. The Home Guards of Meigs County set up rifle positions in the precipitous hills that rise eighty feet above the road from Chester to Buffington Island. For the last five miles the road winds through a ravine between the hills, and with the Ohio sharpshooters firing down out of the dense trees with stinging, buzzing frequency, it was like running a gauntlet. By the time the men reached the river bottom, they were worn down and dispirited.[15]

In the end, during the final critical days of the raid, Morgan was overconfident. Early in the morning of July 18, the last day, he was relaxing in a chair on the porch of a crossroads store when Col. Adam R. Johnson rode up. With a wide smile Morgan invited him to dismount and rest: "All our troubles are now over," he said. "The river is only twenty-five miles away, and tomorrow we will be on Southern soil." Daylight was fading that evening when Morgan arrived at Portland, a small village above the ford at Buffington Island. Scouts reported that the ford, which was usually unguarded, was defended by 300 regular infantry and two artillery pieces. Morgan and his staff discussed attacking, but they feared a repulse in the night would scatter and demoralize the exhausted men. They also considered abandoning the wounded, the cannon, and the caravan of loot and going upriver to deeper fords. "But General Morgan was determined," Duke wrote, "(after having already hazarded so much) to save all if possible, at the risk of losing all." Confident that the Union cavalry would not come up, Morgan decided to wait until daylight to attack and clear the ford.[16]

Morgan's overconfidence had also contributed to his unbelievable failure to throw out scouts in all directions. He knew that General Hobson was behind him somewhere, but he had no idea how close; and he had no knowledge that General Judah was anywhere near. The alert reconnaissance he had used on previous raids would have warned him that Hobson's advance was only a few hours behind and Judah's cavalry was marching across the boot-shaped peninsula of Meigs County on Hobson's right flank. When Judah's riflemen attacked from the south the next morning, Morgan's men thought they were seeing ghosts. Judah said Duke told him that he "could not have been more surprised at the presence of my force had it dropped from the clouds."[17]

The Union forces had not come from the sky, however; they had converged on Morgan like a net drawn tighter and tighter by Burnside, coordinating the pursuit in Cincinnati. Postponing preparations for his advance into east Tennessee, he had sent all his cavalry plus a brigade of infantry after the raiders. Hobson's command crossed at Brandenburg and followed in Morgan's rear, usually about twenty-four hours behind. Rebel pressing parties had taken all the fresh horses within five miles of the route, and Hobson was hampered by burned-out bridges. His advance, under Col. August V. Kautz, was delayed over five hours in Jasper, Ohio, while rebuilding a bridge.[18]

On the other hand, the bluecoats were encouraged by the outpouring of love and patriotism that met them at every turn. Women handed them baskets of fried chicken and bread, and stood by the road giving them cool water. Crowds lined the streets of the villages, women gyrating bonnets and handkerchiefs in the air, men and boys waving their hats. "Catch him if you *kin*," they cheered. "Has took every horse I had." "Kill the last one of them." An old Indiana farmer was working in his wheatfield in the remote countryside when the blue cavalry hove into sight. "He stood bareheaded in open-mouthed astonishment until he was able to make out who we were; then dropping his old hat, extending his long arms, and whooping like a comanche, he performed a series of upward leaps in the air, displaying agility that would have made his fortune as an athlete."[19]

What Hobson and Wolford had lacked in courage and determination in Kentucky, they made up for now. The men ate and slept in the saddle, snatching moments of sleep under trees by the road when there was a pause in the relentless marching. When the race ended, they had been rolling in the saddle so many hours that when they dismounted and tried to walk on level ground, they pitched forward like drunk men. Traveling light, besides their weapons some men had only a feed bag and horse brush; others had nothing but a blanket. When the artillery horses broke down on July 14, Hobson detached Kautz's advance brigade and sent it flying forward without wheels. During the last thirty hours, Kautz went nearly seventy miles, from Jackson to Portland, Ohio. Arriving before daybreak and several hours ahead of the main body, Kautz attacked with such aggression as to give the impression that he had the entire force.[20]

With Hobson dogging Morgan's heels, Burnside arranged to head off the raiders and prevent them from crossing back over the Ohio River. He transported a brigade of infantry (1,850 men) to Portsmouth, but realizing they could not capture Morgan, he brought up Judah's cavalry. Judah came by rail to Louisville, then by steamboat to Cincinnati for fresh horses, and up the river to Portsmouth. The timing was right; when Judah disembarked at Portsmouth, he was on Morgan's right flank, between the raiders and the river. Morgan was twenty-five miles north, making his way eastward in a straight line toward Buffington Island. Water transportation had closed the gap; now it was Judah's task to complete on the banks of the Ohio what he had failed to do on the Green River. Advancing to Pomeroy at the top of the Meigs County boot, he wired that Morgan was headed into the peninsula and would be caught: "Moving thus, Morgan is in a trap, from which he can't escape." Judah marched across the ankle of the boot via Racine, and by daybreak on Sunday morning was closing on the ford from the south.[21]

Morgan had neglected to conduct feints to keep Burnside off guard, and once he entered the boot, his options were closed; it was obvious where he was going. On July 16, two days ahead of time, Burnside perceived Morgan's destination and directed a 250-man regiment of state militia in Marietta, Ohio, to come down with two pieces of artillery and guard the ford. They went ashore the next day, threw up earthworks, and were at their post when Morgan's scouts came. They were the force Morgan decided not to assault in the darkness. Later that night, they came to the conclusion that they were all that stood between Morgan and freedom. A steamer had run aground on the sandbar, and they hated to see it fall into Morgan's hands, so after midnight they dumped its cargo of flour in the river and used it to withdraw. No matter—they had done their part by delaying Morgan until morning.[22]

Burnside also coordinated the pursuit with a squadron of navy gunboats commanded by twenty-eight-year-old Lt. Comdr. Leroy Fitch. Assigned to patrol the upper Ohio, Fitch had converted five small steamboats into little fortresses by adding thin armor plating and cannon. His flagship, the USS *Moose*, was a sternwheeler with six 24-pound howitzers, three starboard and three port broadside. The distinguishing feature of the boats was their relatively shallow draft, which enabled them to negotiate the shoals and sandbars on the upper Ohio except during the season of low water in the summer. The *Moose* drew only five feet. Burnside informed Fitch of Morgan's position, and Fitch deployed his squadron along the river on Morgan's right flank and kept moving along, prepared to prevent a crossing. He closed all commercial traffic on the river, and his sailors destroyed all flatboats, skiffs, and scows to deprive Morgan of vessels. In Cincinnati he was reinforced by a sixth boat, the *Alleghany Belle*, a steamboat Burnside had converted by having cotton bales stacked on her deck and a rifled Parrott mounted on her bow. Fitch promised that if Morgan tried a crossing within reach of his gunboats, he could prevent it. His only fear was that Morgan would not turn until he was far upriver where the water was too shallow for navigation.[23]

Morgan had not taken the navy into account, because his scouts had informed him that the upper Ohio was too shallow for gunboats in July. At Buffington, where the head of the island slowed the current and sand and silt were deposited, the water was not boottop high this season. An elderly woman said there had not been high water in July for twenty years and only twice in the last sixty years. On July 9, when the raid began, Pittsburgh reported a depth of only two feet at Buffington—ideal fording conditions and much too shallow for any gunboat. But four days later, heavy rain in the West Virginia mountains raised the river to five and six feet at Buffington. The water was swift and barely deep enough for navigation, but Fitch persisted, warping over rapids and taking great care to avoid being grounded on shoals. "I had determined to cut him off at all hazards," he stated.[24]

With tremendous exertion Fitch and the *Moose* reached Buffington Island at about the same time as Morgan. His other vessels were blockading the fords on a forty-mile stretch around the peninsula, but this, the most likely, was his responsibility. Daylight faded before he could maneuver to the sandbar at the head of the island, so he anchored at the foot, out of range of the ford. This meant that the night Morgan decided not to push across, the ford was clear of naval force. At 2:00 A.M., Fitch became apprehensive; raising steam, he churned slowly into the narrow chute between the island and the Ohio shore. But a dense fog had formed in the valley, and it was so hazardous that he anchored in the chute, still not in range. Shortly after 7:00 A.M. he was feeling his way toward the head of the island when through the white mist he saw a detachment of Morgan's cavalry rushing toward the bar with two pieces of artillery.[25]

Probably no soldiers in the entire war were more startled than that group of Morgan's men. They wheeled, dismounted, and were positioning the cannon to guard the ford when out of the fog came the flash and tremendous roar of the *Moose's* two bow guns. Firing their rifles, they fled, abandoning their artillery to the fiery monster that was not supposed to be there. When Judah and Kautz heard the *Moose*, they began their assault, pouring into the plateau between the river and the high ridges rising a mile from the shoreline, Judah from the south and Kautz from the west and north. If the *Moose* had not been there, Morgan could have organized a rear-guard action and made it over with most of his command. Obviously, he should have escaped before Fitch eased into position.[26]

The lengthy chase had sharpened the appetite of the Union cavalry; the booming of heavy artillery on the river strengthened their courage; and they pitched into the fight with glorious alacrity. The fog had lifted when Hobson came up at midmorning, and one of his brigades charged on horseback, yelling and galloping forward, sabers flashing. Breaking through, they scattered several hundred of Morgan's men into the gullies and ravines at the edge of the valley. Duke rallied sufficient strength to patch the line and hold against Kautz and Hobson, while D. Howard Smith's regiment held against Judah. Leaving 700 men and abandoning the wounded, artillery, and train of spoils, Morgan retreated with most of the command through a deep ravine to the north. Duke and Smith fought until their ammunition ran out at about 4:00 P.M., then surrendered.[27]

Morgan raced fourteen miles to the deep ford at Belleville, West Virginia, and at dusk was swimming the column over the river—he had gained the middle of the stream himself—when the *Moose* hove into view, supported by several civilian steamers pressed into service from near Blennerhassett Island, a few miles upriver from Belleville. The decks of the support boats were crowded with several hundred Union infantry from West Virginia. Morgan had a strong horse and could have easily completed the crossing with the 300 others who did escape, but he turned back. Ellsworth offered to go with him. "No, Lightning," Morgan said, "go on and save yourself if you can do so."[28]

Still trusting Lady Luck to intervene, Morgan led the remnant of his men northward deep into Ohio. At Buffington the next morning, Monday, July 20, Gen. James M. Shackelford asked for volunteers to stay in the saddle continuously without eating or sleeping until Morgan was captured. Everyone stepped forward, but only 500 sound horses could be found, so with that many, plus several hundred mounted Ohio and Pennsylvania militia who joined along the way, Shackelford resumed the chase. For another week Morgan ran, burning bridges behind him, marching in phantomlike silence at night, and slipping through Shackelford's net by ascending precipitous hills where it seemed only a goat could climb. Finally, on Sunday, July 26, he surrendered near West Point, Ohio, less than ninety miles from the shore of Lake Erie.[29]

During the raid and subsequent chase, Morgan's conscious mind apparently shifted into the familiar euphoria. Totally immersed in the activity, he had a greatly exaggerated trust in himself and his luck; it seems likely that the mathematical odds against him did not exist in his perception. Even in surrender he was unrealistically optimistic, believing that his own artful shiftiness would get him paroled immediately. Rather than turning himself in to Shackelford, he negotiated terms with Capt. James Burbick, an officer of the Lisbon militia who was his prisoner at the time. Burbick, in no position to disagree, accepted Morgan's request for immediate parole for himself and his men. When Shackelford's cavalry came up, they ignored Burbick's terms, but Morgan was still convinced that the agreement would be honored by Shackelford's superiors. Shackelford reported that Morgan told him he had never been hunted with such persistence, but "that he himself might have escaped by deserting his men, but that he would not do so." Very likely Morgan could have escaped by separating from the men and assuming one of his many disguises.[30]

The key to the successful Union pursuit was the stronger Union cavalry. Burnside supported the navy gunboat flotilla and used state militia, but basically he relied on his cavalry. Day to day, hardship for hardship, they matched Morgan's men; gaining confidence, they attacked with enthusiasm at Buffington Island and stayed on the trail into northern Ohio with unremitting perseverance. Historians have never given Burnside due credit for his role. He gave priority to the chase and directed it with imagination and precision. After it was over, resuming preparations for the east Tennessee campaign, he told Halleck, "I can now look after the other work you desire done." Less than six weeks later, he marched triumphantly into Knoxville.

Fitch, too, displayed rare determination in his pursuit, overcoming great obstacles and hazards with the tenacity of a bulldog—he was an unrelenting foe. It was Fitch's navy and army task force that prevented Morgan's escape at Belleville; if he had not been there, Morgan would have passed over to safety with more than 1,000 of his force. The water was falling so fast that to anchor for the night of July 19, after turning Morgan from the river the second time, Fitch had to steam south of Buffington Island to prevent being grounded.[31]

The Indiana and Ohio state militias also took their toll, contributing to the debilitated condition of Morgan's men at Buffington and delaying the Rebels long enough for the Union cavalry to catch up.

Yet what was so tantalizing was that the raid almost succeeded. If Morgan had not been delayed at the beginning by the Union expedition against Knoxville, he might have reached Meigs County before the unseasonable rise in the Ohio River. If it had not rained and the river had stayed low, Fitch's gunboats would not have guarded the fords, and Morgan could have held off the Union cavalry with a rear defensive stand while he retreated into West Virginia with most of the division. Or if Morgan had challenged the small militia force manning the breastworks at Buffington, he could have forded before Fitch came into position.

In Kentucky, Morgan had retained the initiative and kept freedom of action, but once he was past Cincinnati, his exaggerated self-confidence led him to relax and underestimate the enemy. This turned out to be his most vital strategic mistake. He allowed the men to cart their loot in a train of slow-moving vehicles, failed to send out scouts, and neglected to post pickets in his rear. In territory where the local masses were hostile, vigilance was more important than ever—in guerrilla warfare it is very difficult to maintain the offensive without the cooperation and support of the populace. Yet what little assistance the Copperheads might have given, Morgan shunned, and there was no Southern grapevine to warn of Fitch's gunboats or Judah's advance, or to advise that the Buffington force was small and inexperienced.

Even though Morgan was captured, however, the raid succeeded in removing from his reputation the tarnish left by six months of reverses, and restored him to the top rank of Confederate heroes. News of his entrance into enemy territory—the only significant raid in Northern territory in the western theater during the Civil War—came when Southern morale desperately needed a boost. Vicksburg and Port Hudson had fallen, and Lee had retreated from Gettysburg. Kate Cumming wrote: "All looks gloomy; there is scarcely one bright spot to be seen." Then, suddenly, "Gen. Morgan, like a comet, has shot out of the beaten track of the army," Jones the Richmond clerk noted, "and after dashing deeply into Indiana, the last heard of him he was in Ohio." The news seemed too fantastic to believe at first, and though people expected him to be captured, they were dazzled. The Richmond *Enquirer* said Southern children would linger over the story and be reassured of the superior equestrianism, unparalleled endurance, and unexampled dash and daring of Southern soldiers.[32]

Editors applauded Morgan as a "Southern Paladin" who went on the offensive, giving Hoosiers and Buckeyes a taste of war: "We have drank [*sic*] of this cup, and we know the sickening, staggering draught that is in it." In New York they were "eating, guzzling, trading, marrying and cheating about as usual, and talking about the war with about as much realization of its actual horrours [*sic*] as of one of Barnum's dioramas," but thanks to Morgan this was not the case in southern Indiana and Ohio. Mentioning that the expedition passed within a few miles of Cincinnati, known as "hogtown" because of its pork industry, a Richmond journalist said: "Could he have reached it, he would certainly have fried it in its own grease." Some voices were raised in criticism of the loss of critical manpower, but people generally concluded that Morgan had exacted a high price in return.[33]

Historians have regarded the raid as a spectacular romantic adventure with almost no military effect. In *How the North Won*, Herman Hattaway and Archer Jones, who have an appreciation for guerrilla warfare, propose that it was Morgan's least productive expedition but did at least delay Burnside's advance into east Tennessee.[34] The delay was of minor significance, however, because Burnside's army reached east Tennessee in time for many of his men to fight at Chickamauga in September.

Like Sherman's march from Atlanta to Savannah, the raid made war on the people of the enemy, albeit in a more limited fashion. After his campaign, Sherman said: "We are not only fighting hostile armies, but a hostile people, and must make old and young, rich and poor, feel the hard hand of war, as well as their organized armies."[35] Sherman's invasion had the desired effect of shattering Confederate morale and weakening the will to resist.

Morgan's raid destroyed several million dollars worth of property; caused the closing of business and the declaration of martial law in Louisville, Indianapolis, Cincinnati, Covington, and Newport; shut down traffic on the Ohio River; and disrupted thousands of lives—but had the opposite effect on enemy morale. It quelled sympathy for the Southern cause in Indiana and Ohio, encouraged Northern enlistment, and stimulated patriotism and support for the United States government. All partisan feelings and prejudices were suspended, and "every heart seemed to be filled with patriotic enthusiasm," said an Indiana newspaper, "an earnest desire to dare and do, in protecting the State, its unsullied honor and fame."[36]

At Mauckport, Jacob Sherman rode horseback up the bank of the Ohio River, warning southbound boats to turn back and avoid being captured by Morgan. A local militia commander in Ohio wired Gov. David Tod, "I am at your service to defend our state and nation." A traveler from Athens to Columbus, Ohio, during the raid reported: "Everywhere one could see the militia flocking in to the various rendezvous. The whole country seemed alive." The Indianapolis *Journal* concluded: "It has evolved our patriotism; it has given us a marvelous unity; it has organized our State forces, and rendered them efficient for any emergency; and it has effectually cowed down sympathy with rebels."[37]

The backlash reinforced the principle that ultimately to win, guerrilla operations must be long-term and widespread or be in conjunction with movements of major armies. Sherman's raid succeeded in lowering Southern morale because it came in conjunction with major victories by regular Northern armies. Morgan's failed because it was an aberration, like lightning on a clear day, a pinprick in a healthy arm—a challenge that tested Northern public will and found it very strong.[38]

From the point of view of the strategy of attrition, the sortie was counterproductive: the property damage was relatively insignificant, given the vast resources of the Union, and only increased the Yankee will to resist. For the Confederate strategy of annihilation, it succeeded in delaying Burnside's invasion of east Tennessee about a month, but when Burnside moved, he did so with greater self-confidence on his own part and that of his staff and his cavalry. Bragg and the other high Confederate decision-makers condemned the expedition as not being worth the cost of Morgan and about 2,100 men;

they considered Morgan more of a maverick than ever. After the early summer of 1863, Morgan was on the wrong side: the Confederate army had repudiated guerrilla warfare, but the Union began extensive use of cavalry raids behind enemy lines. Yet regardless of official criticism, the raid gave a boost to Southern morale when it was greatly needed and reestablished Morgan in the public eye as the great guerrilla chief of the Confederacy. He was a hero again, but still on the horns of the same dilemma he had faced since the wedding: maintaining his status without the driving force he had lost, and doing it without being absent from Mattie.

SIXTEEN

Free Shave and a Haircut

When the three small sternwheel steamers delivering the Confederate raiders captured at Buffington Island arrived at Cincinnati on July 23, they anchored in the middle of the Ohio River all morning. Word spread through the city and over the river in Newport and Covington that Morgan's men had come, and a great crowd gathered on both sides of the river, on the landings and wharves, housetops and balconies. When an adequate guard detachment had been organized, the men were unloaded and placed in railroad cars. General Burnside and Governor Tod extended them the rights of prisoners of war and sent the enlisted men to prison camps in Indianapolis and Chicago, the officers to Johnson's Island in Sandusky Bay on Lake Erie.[1]

But when Morgan himself was taken a few days later, General-in-Chief Halleck began making different arrangements. He had been humiliated too many times by headlines on Morgan's men to allow them regular privileges. Halleck was not generally known as a decisive administrator, but now that he had the man identified by a Southerner as the "longest, sharpest and most lacerating thorn in the sides of the Yankee nation," a man considered by Halleck and his Northern compatriots to be an outlaw leading a band of robbers and murderers, he was resolved to keep him.[2]

Less than twenty-four hours after Morgan surrendered, Halleck asked Governor Tod if he had a vacancy in the state penitentiary for Morgan and the officers with him. The answer was yes, and Halleck immediately ordered them incarcerated in Columbus, with any overflow going to the nearest state prison. He informed Robert Ould, Confederate prisoner exchange agent, that Morgan and his men were to be held as hostages for Col. Abel D. Streight's command, captured in a raid on Rome, Georgia, and imprisoned in Richmond. Streight was actually being treated as a prisoner of war, but Northern newspapers had charged that he was in a common felons' jail in Georgia.[3]

The cartel of prisoner exchange—by which equal numbers of prisoners were traded—had been suspended for officers on May 25, 1863, but officers were still being exchanged through negotiation. Halleck's intervention was unusual. According to international law, fighting for one's country was not a crime, and confinement could not assume a penal character. Halleck considered Morgan an outlaw, but rather than imprison him on that basis, he used the grounds of retaliation and held Morgan as a hostage for reputed Confederate violations.[4]

During his journey to Cincinnati, Morgan was treated as a prisoner of war, and he fully expected to be exchanged soon if not paroled immediately. But when he was locked in the Cincinnati jail and forbidden visitors—including his mother, who came up from Lexington—he protested that his rights were being denied. Nevertheless, he was relaxed and at ease until informed by Union officers that Washington had ordered him held in close confinement in the penitentiary as a hostage. Then Morgan's smile faded, and he became reserved and thoughtful. Going back to his cell, he said to the officer in charge, "General, I wish you would intercede and get a drink of whiskey for me, as I am terribly dry."[5]

The local citizenry became aware that Morgan and the officers captured with him would be transferred the next morning, Thursday, July 30, and a large crowd formed at the Cincinnati jail. Three infantry companies, bayonets fixed, conducted the prisoners two by two down Ninth Street to the Little Miami Railroad depot, where they boarded the train. That afternoon it stopped a few yards from the prison in Columbus, and they were marched under guard to the reception building; there Gen. John S. Mason, commander of Camp Chase, the military prison in Columbus, turned them over one by one to Warden Nathaniel Merion. Each man was searched and taken into the prison. After Mason witnessed the search of the last man, he walked into the prison and observed that they were being given baths and haircuts. Realizing that this was no way to treat prisoners of war, he asked whether the procedure was necessary and was told it was the only way inmates were admitted; that the cells were clean and sweet-smelling, whereas the prisoners were filthy and covered with vermin. Mason agreed that the bath was needed and saw that the trim was in the style of Columbus and no shorter than his own. Most of the Confederates had already been cleaned, and he allowed the process to continue.[6]

Mason was a professional soldier. A native of Steubenville, Ohio, he had graduated from West Point in 1847 and remained in the army continuously, establishing a solid sixteen-year-record. His father had been a surgeon in the War of 1812, and his respectable family had roots back to New England in the early seventeenth century. Deep down, Mason cringed at the unprofessional treatment of the Rebel officers, but his cultural background prevented him from fully understanding just how undignified and degrading the process was to Southern gentlemen and he was mystified when it became a *cause célèbre* in the South.

Each officer was taken to the scouring room and ordered to strip naked. Every article of clothing was searched carefully by trusties and laid aside in a heap. Then the man was ordered into a large hogshead of water and scrubbed with soap and horse brushes by two convicts. A large number of employees and inmates crowded into the room to see the guerrillas, and everyone, including Morgan himself, was subjected to their curious gaze. Then each man was taken to the barber's room, where his beard and mustache were trimmed and his hair cut. Morgan was in the chair when Colonel Cluke and another officer came in, and Cluke exclaimed, "My Heaven, General, what are you having yourself disfigured for?" Morgan replied in a soft voice, "Wait a few moments, gentlemen, and you will see." Several days later, Duke and other officers were brought down from Johnson's Island and welcomed in the same fashion. Col. D. Howard Smith had a magnificent white beard, cultivated since the beginning of the war and reaching to his waist. He wrote: "This morning, as if our degradation and humiliation was not sufficiently complete, we were marched out of our cells to the public wash-room, our persons stripped and washed by a convict, our heads shorn, and our beards taken entirely off." Duke, who had lost his mustache, teased Smith that he could see his handsome face for the first time. "It is no jesting matter, Sir," Smith snapped.[7]

What General Mason did not realize was that personal appearance was related to Southern honor, and to these gentlemen facial hair was a symbol of manhood. As a Richmond humorist had put it:

> Cut off my whiskers? Oh ye Gods!
> I'd rather lose my ears; by odds![8]

It was the kind of insult that inspired more than humorous poetry. Duke wrote "The Rebels' Dream" and smuggled it out to Lexington, where it made the rounds with Southern sympathizers. In the dream a Confederate cavalryman is once again mounted on his charger, attacking in triumph and pride, when he suddenly awakens to the clash of prison bars and hears the warden announce the loss of his "cherished beard & hair."

> Great God! No hope. He must resign
> His youthful pride, his *manhood's sign*.
> Ah! Not that rebel chief, who fell
> From heaven's bright battlements to hell
> Felt degradation more forlorn
> Or knew his honors, *closer shorn*.[9]

The incident captured the imagination of the Southern people and greatly strengthened their identification with Morgan. It gained him much sympathy and wiped away some of the negative feelings about his capture and the loss of manpower. Southern newspapers claimed that the men's faces and heads were shaved: "To this humiliation, this infamy, have the bravest and best champions of the South been brought," an editor cried. Jones the clerk was incredulous: "After all, the enemy did not, durst not, shave the head of Gen. Morgan, and otherwise maltreat him, as was reported." Emma Holmes denounced the brutal Yankees for "*shaving their heads* & treating them like convicts." Kate Cumming declared: "These things seem almost incredible.

Why, savages respect a brave man, and a man like General Morgan, one would think, would gain the admiration of any people who had any sense of chivalry."[10]

Recognizing the humor in it, George Prentice claimed that Morgan's hair had been delivered to him by "Adam's Express" (Adams Express Company was a delivery service) and that he would mail locks of it to every Rebel maid who sent her address. After Morgan escaped, Prentice said that he had given Morgan a wig made from the hair of women admirers, and that if Morgan were ever recaptured, he would place the wig on a figure head outside his office; when male Rebels passed, they could bow, and females could curtsey. And during a later raid, he was curious to know whether Morgan had filled his corps with barbers to shave the hair, whiskers, mustaches, eyebrows, and armpits of prospective prisoners. "John must be careful or, our troops will lather him and his barbers too," he jested. Eventually, Southerners joined the laughter. In February, 1864, giving one of Morgan's officers a saber, a Rebel patriot anticipated that the weapon would retaliate by delivering close shaves to Yankees—a few inches below the scalp.[11]

Including those transferred from Johnson's Island, sixty-eight officers were confined in the Ohio penitentiary. They were segregated from the civil prisoners and assigned to the first and second ranges of a five-tier cellblock, each man occupying a single room seven feet high, three and a half feet wide, and seven feet long. The walls of the tiny cells were of brick, and the only furnishings were a metal bed attached to the wall, a spittoon, and a night bucket. During the day the cells were left open, and they had the freedom of a hallway—160 feet by 11 feet—running the length of the lower tier. At 7:30 A.M. and 3:00 P.M. they were marched to the dining hall for meals, which included sugar and coffee—items denied the convicts. At 4:45 P.M. they were locked in their cells and required to remain silent; at 8:00 P.M. the gaslights in the cells were turned off, but if they had them, they could burn candles an additional hour.[12]

In the daytime they played marbles, checkers, and cards, and during chess tournaments applauded dexterous flanking movements by knights—the favorite piece of cavalrymen. They performed gymnastics on a ladder in the hall and spent hours debating predestination and other topics. One of the best adjustments was made by Lt. Thomas W. Bullitt from Louisville. His desire for knowledge having been kindled at Centre College, he studied law, read Shakespeare, and meditated on the scriptures in the solitude of his cell. He dreaded transfer to a military prison camp where he would lose his "study carrel."[13]

Living conditions were far better than in the military prison camps of either army. As the camps filled up after the total breakdown of exchange, prisoners on both sides suffered from bad water, inadequate sanitation, and disease. In Southern prisons food was less abundant and housing usually deficient; the two largest facilities, Andersonville and Belle Isle, provided no shelter from the elements. In the penitentiary the water was pure, sanitation was up to standard, and the food was so ample that the men gained weight. Ould set to work to schedule their exchange, but before pressing the lesser demand that they be transferred to a military camp, he asked whether it would be wise. "I am sure they are better treated than any of our people elsewhere," he stated. Dick Morgan was being sarcastic, but the truth came through when he wrote: "At first we thought our fate, a hard one, being sent to a Penitentiary in retaliation for the treatment of Col. Streight's men, but experience has taught us to highly appreciate the institution for abundance of *grub*, cleanliness, fine water, and many other privileges which are granted us, for which we are greatly indebted to the hospitable Warden of this institution."[14]

They complained about censorship of their mail—but it was censored in all camps. They bemoaned the regulation that allowed a man to be visited only if he were sick, and then only if the visitor were certified loyal—but that was not unusual either.

Henrietta Morgan had lost one son, and with four of her five remaining boys in prison, she was determined to help them. Right away she sent a box of clothing and two bottles of cordial; Warden Merion delivered the clothes, but as liquor was prohibited, he assigned it to the hospital for dispensation to sick inmates. Then she shipped two large boxes of delicacies. Her sons wrote to thank her, but their letters made clear that she could not visit; nevertheless, on September 6 she appeared and demanded to see her boys. Merion refused but promised to distribute the six hams, seven cakes, and other items she had brought. Through the prison grapevine they heard she was there, and all four tall brothers stood on tiptoe watching eagerly through a window, catching a precious glimpse of her as she rode away in her carriage. When word got around in Kentucky that the prison was accepting gifts, the warden's office was swamped. Inspection of the mountain of packages became so time-consuming that military authorities laid down a new rule: no more edibles or clothing would be received without special permission.[15]

What pressed down upon Morgan and his men—the thought that never left their consciousness—was that they were being held in a maximum security prison for felons. The worst reminder was the method used to discipline anyone who violated prison rules. Like a convict the offender was taken to a range of cells called the "black hole," kept in total darkness and solitary confinement for twenty-four hours, and fed bread and water. The air was stagnant and foul, and strong men returned broken and crying, covered from head to toe with green mold. Maj. W.P. Elliott harassed one of the guards until the man was lying in wait, watching for one more infraction; when Elliott complained that the hominy at dinner was so dark the cook must be in mourning, to the black hole he went. A few others were punished the same way, but Morgan did not complain of that. He wrote Secretary of War Edwin M. Stanton protesting solitary confinement at night and condemning their treatment as criminals when they were admitted. Morgan had been offended when they put him in the Cincinnati jail, but when they told him he was going to the penitentiary, his heart sank. If the Union government violated their rights as military prisoners, there was very little likelihood that they would be exchanged.[16]

Then when he and his men entered the penitentiary, they were overwhelmed with a sense of foreboding. The massive stone walls, twenty-five feet high and four feet thick, the locked iron gates and towering guard posts signaled the abandonment of hope. They struggled against it but were swept under by the conviction that they were in prison for the remainder of the war. The most dreaded event of the day was when the guards bolted the doors for the night—the clashing and banging of metal bars echoed through the cellblock, reminding them of the denial of their rights as military prisoners. The cells had no windows, and the heavy doors were grated with iron bars that left only two-inch-square openings. The stifling sense of cramped confinement was so overwhelming that some men almost fainted when locked in the first time. "The dead weight of the stone prison seemed resting on our breasts," Duke recalled.[17]

These were very active men, and with little time to prepare themselves mentally for indefinite imprisonment, the shock was great. Columbus did not have room for all of them, so seventy from Johnson's Island were taken to the Western Penitentiary of Pennsylvania in Allegheny City on the bank of the Allegheny River opposite Pittsburgh. None of the men in Columbus were treated for mental illness, but in Pittsburgh, H.D. Brown lost touch with reality and had to be watched continually. He was taken to the asylum in Washington, D.C., for several months and returned a mental and physical wreck, a ghost of his former self.[18]

Incarceration is one of the worst things that can happen to a compulsive gambler. Denied euphoria and the revitalization of an ideal self through fantasy, he feels the burden of his deviant identity and is filled with self-pity; his mood sinks to rock bottom. In prison Morgan was deprived of the rituals that had enabled him to cope with the stresses of war. Alone in his dark cell at night—the blackness was total after lights out, except when a guard trudged by and held a lantern near the grating to check the bed—Morgan had no roles to play, no masquerades to transport him into the world of fantasy. He had never enjoyed reading, and all his life he had avoided meditation and solitude. Separated from Mattie, his emotional support and steadying beam, locked in a tiny cell from 4:45 P.M. to 7:30 A.M., he was in unimaginable torment. He suppressed his emotions and was amiable and outwardly cooperative, but it became apparent that confinement was more irksome to him than to any of his companions. He grew restless and impatient, at times almost frantic.[19]

Every night by candlelight he read the prayer book Mattie gave him, but when he prayed to God, his mind filled with thoughts of her. "What a void is the absence of the being who *alone* fills the world!" he wrote. "How true it is that the beloved becomes God! One would think that God would become jealous if the Father of all had not evidently made creation for the Soul, and the Soul for love! What a grand thing to love. The heart becomes heroic through passion. It is no longer composed of any thing but what is pure." Confessing that Mattie was his idol, he told her mother: "I posess [*sic*] your Crown jewel—and she is my religion." John was maintaining his sanity by focusing his thoughts on the love of his wife; and in that love he felt purified and justified—his self-esteem was restored.[20]

He told her that his every thought was of her and his only comfort was in looking forward to their reunion. "My love and adulation of you almost replaces thought, it is a forgetfulness of all else," he said. He wrote her mother: "My separation from her is my greatest trial, everything else is of minor importance. The Universe seems to have fallen out of sight." Opening his pocket daguerreotype of her many times in the day, he would imagine what she was doing and thinking. "You know Darling, that I am a great guesser & can almost tell your thoughts." He wrote her three times a week, the maximum allowed by prison regulations, and watched for her letters with great anticipation. "Another long week passed and nothing from 'My Darling Wife.' Each day [I] feel confident that the next will certainly bring a letter. Without hope what would become of us?" And when one came he was lifted up: "This moment recd. your sweet letter of 22 ult. Have read it twice over. *I am truly happy.*"[21]

Before they parted in McMinnville, they had decided to name the baby John, Jr., if it was a boy and Martha if it was a girl. He frequently mentioned the approaching birth. "Attend to my little namesake, see its mother, see 'My precious Mattie' that they want for nothing." Then, as if his burden were not heavy enough, he received a letter from her stating that she had been indisposed for some time. He realized that if she was ill enough to mention it, her condition must be serious. Was he about to lose his second wife and child to childbirth? "If I can hear from you each week & that you are still blessed with health, then I can be seeming as happy as any, but if a week elapses without a letter, then the little clouds begin to appear & I imagine ten thousand things."[22]

Mattie pleaded with Confederate authorities to do something, as did friends in Richmond. Ould protested the situation vigorously and made it clear that Streight was being treated exactly like other prisoners of war. "Do you wish him shaved and put in a felon's cell?" he asked his Union counterpart. "If you do you are pursuing exactly the course to effect it." After two months Secretary Stanton directed that instead of using Morgan as hostage for Streight, he should be held for Gen. Neal Dow, the famous Maine prohibitionist captured in Alabama and turned over to state authorities on charges of theft of furniture in New Orleans. Mattie heard a rumor that John would be exchanged for Dow, but Ould warned that the North would never agree to trade Morgan for any single general; the only hope was in a restoration of general exchange: "They think him too great a prize and dread him too much in his liberated future."[23]

As Morgan gradually comprehended that he would not be released, he grew more restless every day. When a pathological gambler hits rock bottom, there is great potential for risk taking. In Morgan's case, it took the form of a determination to escape at any cost or hazard. He discussed plans to overpower the guards and break out with force. He offered Capt. L.D. Hockersmith $10,000 for his assistance in making an escape. Hockersmith agreed to help, but not for money. Then Capt. Thomas H. Hines proposed that rather than fighting, they dig a tunnel. Hines and others had discovered an air shaft under the floor of the cells on the lower tier, and Morgan approved a plan to chip through the concrete under Hines's bunk, enter the air chamber, and tunnel through the foundation of the building into the prison yard. From there they would avoid the dogs and guards on the grounds and scale the outer wall. It was an audacious plan, but Morgan was desperate.[24]

The problem with the scheme was that the lengthy hallway outside Hines's cell was guarded constantly by two Union soldiers, and every day each cell was swept out by convicts and inspected by prison guards. The soldiers could be diverted, but as long as civil guards inspected the cells, there was no way to conceal an opening in the floor. They had complained before about being under civilian guard; however, on Friday, October 31, 1863, Morgan wrote to General Mason, requesting him to assume responsibility for them. He reminded Mason that they were in solitary confinement for nearly fifteen hours per day, and on the two previous Sundays they had been locked in their cells all day except for meals and an hour at noon; moreover, it was getting cold in the cells away from the stove in the hallway. Three days later Mason met with Merion and his board of directors, and they agreed to transfer the men to military control immediately: Mason informed Morgan that they would have to obey the rules of the prison, but "as far as practicable," they were to have privileges of prisoners of war.[25]

International law required that military prisoners were to be solely under military guard, and there were no army regulations on housing captives in state penal institutions—Merion and Mason had been feeling their way. Under the initial arrangement, the warden assumed total responsiblity at night, but during the daytime the penitentiary shared control with the army. A prison steward and watchman supervised the cleaning of cells every day, inspected the cells, and assisted in guard duty during the daylight hours. Soldiers from Camp Chase censored correspondence, examined packages, screened visitors, and with a twenty-seven-man guard detail escorted the men to the mess hall for meals. Other than at mealtimes, two soldiers were stationed in the hallway of the cellblock and the remainder positioned in the yard outside the building. After the prisoners were locked up at night, the soldiers marched back to camp.

Under the new system beginning November 4, the prison still guarded the cellblock at night, but during the day the military authorities were in charge exclusively. The civilian steward was replaced by a new military steward, and the day watchman was withdrawn. From the time they were unlocked in the morning to lockup at night, the Rebels were under military guard, as international law provided. Convicts were to empty the night buckets and spittoons, and when one of Mason's officers, Lt. Mark W. Goss, asked who would sweep the cells, one of the directors blurted out, "Let the damn rebels clean their own cells." What was crucial to the escape plan— suspension of the daily cleaning and inspection of cells—had been accomplished.[26]

Meanwhile, to acquire implements for digging, Morgan pretended illness and had his meals brought to his cell. Each time the food tray returned to the dining hall, it was minus a table knife. On November 4, the first day under military guard, the work began and continued for three hours per day. One man would chip away at the eighteen-inch concrete floor under Hines's bunk; another sat on the edge of the bunk at the door, reading and keeping a lookout; and others who were aware of the plan made conversation with the soldiers and kept up a continual clamor in the hallway making handcrafts. Many Northern prison camps permitted men to occupy themselves and earn spending money by manufacturing rings and pins from bones, shells, and buttons, and Morgan's men were allowed to purchase three watch-spring saws and thirty-five blades; these were kept busy during the hours of digging. Dick Morgan made a ring with a cross-shaped setting formed with stones from John's cell, and John mailed a ring to Mattie. The scratching and scraping of the saws covered the digging sounds. Cement fragments were hidden in handkerchiefs, under bunks, and in ashes in the stove until they broke through into the air shaft; then the residue was left there. Hines placed a carpetbag over the hole in the floor.[27]

John's mood brightened as soon as the plan was set in motion—it gave him badly needed action and enabled him to play cat and mouse with the guards. He informed Mattie that ringmaking had become a mania, and he had to force himself to keep silent about the digging. "Would that I could tell you all my thoughts, they would make you happy," he declared, and then remembering the censor, added, "They are all of you, but you Love almost know them." Morgan appeared to be a model prisoner, but at night he would violate the rule of silence and whisper through the bars of his cell door. The night guard was nicknamed "the Spider" because he wore shoes of India rubber and would extinguish his lantern and sneak back in the dark to listen. Morgan said that a certain magnetic shudder invariably warned him of the Spider's approach, but just in case it failed, each morning he sprinkled particles of coal on the walkway near his cell to prevent being surprised.[28]

One morning Hockersmith was down in the air shaft, and Morgan was on the lookout in Hines's cell. The military steward, an army sergeant, asked, "Where is Hockersmith?" Morgan replied, "He is in my room sick," and, taking a document from his pocket, said earnestly, "Here is a memorial I have drawn up to forward to the Government at Washington—what do you think of it?" Flattered by this request from the famous general, the sergeant read the memorandum with grave attention and announced his approval. In the meantime, with tapping signals, Hockersmith was ordered up and presented himself, looking quite unwell indeed.[29]

Once into the air shaft, the conspirators shared the secret with all the men, and crews of two or three worked one- to two-hour shifts, chiseling holes in the underside of the floor of six other cells and chipping through the building foundation at one end of the shaft. Suddenly someone discovered that the tunnel as originally projected would emerge under 20,000 bushels of coal dumped on the ground next to the building. It was necessary to redirect the passageway, but they needed a view of the ground outside in order to do so. A prison rumor spoke of two convicts who had escaped from the cellblock a couple of years before by climbing the narrow iron balconies in front of the five tiers of cells and breaking through a window in the roof. Morgan mentioned this feat to the military guards and boasted that little Capt. Samuel Taylor from Louisville, a nephew of President Zachary Taylor, could duplicate the climb. The guards permitted the experiment, and like a squirrel Taylor sprang from balcony to balcony; at the top he rested, surveying the yard through the windows before his descent. His reconnaissance indicated that they should cut through a side wall twenty-five feet from the end of the building.[30]

Concerned that the thin crust of concrete above the holes chipped in the additional six cells might give way and reveal the plan, the men in the entire lower tier gained permission to lay planks on the floor, ostensibly as protection from dampness. Next, the men in all seven selected cells began sleeping with their heads and hands covered so that the guard would not get suspicious when they left dummies in their bunks. For scaling the outer wall of the penitentiary, a hook was devised from a poker, and a rope ladder was made of bedticking. Each escapee secreted an extra set of clothing to change into after the crawl through the tunnel. The prison prohibited possession of a change of clothing, but the rule had not been enforced since the military took charge.[31]

All of this the prisoners accomplished on their own without outside assistance. Now they needed cash, and military regulations prohibited its possession; when they received gifts of money, it was deposited in a fund for authorized purchases, but cash in hand would be required for railroad tickets—and such expenses as payment of a bribe to a convict for smuggling in a newspaper with a current railroad schedule. In addition they needed connections with the southbound underground railroad through northern Kentucky, and the two men who planned to hide out in Columbus required local assistance. Outside help was readily forthcoming. Hines received money pasted in the back cover of a book, and gold or greenbacks were smuggled in to most of the men; when those left behind were given a shakedown search, many had cash in amounts of less than $50. On the day before the escape, Mrs. Lucy Dorsey of Carlisle, Kentucky, visited her brother Capt. Thomas S. Morgan (no relation to John Hunt Morgan) in the prison hospital. Six days after the escape Lucy wrote a cryptic letter to her grandfather, Henry Bruce in Covington, mentioning that she hoped for an apple butter circumstance—apparently a code phrase for Morgan's safe journey to the Confederacy. There is no proof that Lucy aided the escape, but she may have delivered messages or money through her brother, who was not one of the escapees.[32]

On Thursday morning, November 26, the tunnel was completed and everything was ready; all that was needed was rain to force the dogs that patrolled the yard at night into their kennels. Friday dawned sunny and bright, but Morgan dared not wait another day. General Mason had been transferred to San Francisco and had left on November 25; a new commander might inspect the cells. In fact, Morgan never knew how narrowly an inspection was avoided. The week of November 16, Col. William Hoffman, Commissary-General of Prisoners of the United States, came to Columbus on an inspection tour of military prisons. He visited Camp Chase, but since he had recently received a detailed report from Mason that defended the baths and haircuts, Hoffman saw no need to inspect the penitentiary. If he had, he might have discovered the planks on the floor and the hole under Hines's bunk.[33]

On the last day Morgan knew he was going back into action, and the euphoria returned. Lt. Bullitt recalled:

I shall never forget his appearance as he paced up and down the hall as the sun was almost setting on that beautiful afternoon. While apprehension was felt and depicted on most of the countenances of the prisoners, General Morgan wore a smile which betokened the perfect conviction of success. In my mind he was always a handsome man, and upon this evening his face was lifted with the radiance of hope and the expectation of freedom. His expression it is beyond my power to describe, but a painter who could have caught and reproduced that expression would have been immortalized.[34]

At lockup, Dick Morgan, who was John's size, changed jackets with John and went to John's cell on the second tier; John took Dick's cell, which was one of the seven with holes under the floor. After lights out, sixty-eight prayers rose in unison from sixty-eight bunks deep within the labyrinth of iron gates and gloomy gray walls of the penitentiary. Every man believed that if the general could get free and return to the South, he would somehow free them all—but rain was needed to drive the dogs to shelter. About 9:00 P.M. the wind came up, whistling through the passageways between the massive walls, and then they heard raindrops splashing on the skylights far above. Their prayers were answered; steady rain fell all night.[35]

At midnight the Spider made his regular rounds, and when they were certain he was gone, seven men arose and fashioned dummies in their bunks. Hines crawled through his hole, and the other six stamped through the thin layer of concrete; they met in the air shaft, where Morgan lit a candle and gathered the men around him: Hines, Taylor, Hockersmith, Gustavus McGee, Ralph Sheldon, and Jacob Bennett. Little Taylor the squirrel became a mole and led the way, pushing up the earth at the end of the tunnel and emerging into the yard just twelve inches from the wall of the building. The sky was dark, rain was falling, and the dogs were warm and dry in their kennels. The men boosted Taylor onto a gate connected to the exterior wall; he threw the rope over, and the poker-hook caught. They climbed onto the wall and went into an empty sentry box to change clothing. In descending the rope ladder on the outside, they were all scratched and bruised, and Morgan's hand was skinned severely. The rope would not shake loose so they left it dangling on the wall.[36]

Back in the cellblock Lieutenant Bullitt wrote in his diary: "Nov. 27. At night—the Surprise! Three weeks hard labor, watching & risk. But a worthy & a noble consummation." His next entry was: "Nov. 28 morning. Great God. Be gracious & merciful to us now. Thou has favored us. darkness. Rain. Oh guide the steps of a beloved commander. May he be great in action & in thought. May he gleam—a bright flaming star in the clouded sky of our country. Save him from the enemies who hunt his track."[37]

The seven men had succeeded in breaking out of Ohio's maximum security facility, and it was a fantastic escape, more like a fairytale than reality and dependent on a chain of remarkable circumstances. Being housed over an air shaft, the suspension of cell inspections, Colonel Hoffman's decision not to inspect the prison, and a timely rain all worked in their favor. As Taylor said later, "It seemed as though fate, or providence, or some controlling power, had decreed that we escape, and directed everything to that end." Morgan told an interviewer that Mattie had prayed, and behind prison walls he saw the hands of Providence stretched forth for his safety, for his return to his family and country. Whether or not it was a miracle, the escape was a timeless tribute to ingenuity and the desire for freedom in the human spirit.[38]

The Spider continued his rounds but was fooled by the cloth dummies and did not raise the alarm. At daylight someone saw the rope blowing in the breeze on the southwest wall. At 6:00 A.M. a group of guards and turnkeys rushed into the cellblock, shouting names and frantically running about. "The general's all safe," said the Spider, and they quieted down, assuming the Rebels were secure. Then a convict ran in yelling that a hole had been discovered in the yard, and the hubbub rose again. Unlocking each cell, they discovered the dummies and holes under the seven bunks. Warden Merion first said it must have been bribery, but after inspecting the tunnel, he proclaimed it "head work."[39]

The remaining prisoners were sentenced to two weeks of silent, solitary confinement in their cells, which they considered lenient in light of their complicity. Governor Tod had the militia search every house, cellar, garret, stable, and privy in Columbus. He offered $1,000 reward for Morgan, and Secretary Stanton put up $5,000 from the Federal treasury and armed the Lake Erie shore patrol. An alarm was issued to police and military authorities throughout the Midwest. Four separate investigations were made of the escape—by the prison authorities, the army, Governor Tod, and the Ohio House of Representatives—and they all concluded that the officers had escaped through the ventilation chamber and tunnel without outside aid.[40]

Once outside the prison wall, the escapees separated. Taylor and Sheldon remained hidden by Southern friends in Columbus for a few days and were then recaptured near Louisville, the only ones of the group retaken. Morgan and Hines went together to the depot and boarded the night express to Cincinnati. Wearing green spectacles, Morgan sat down beside a Union colonel and introduced himself as a businessman from Kentucky. At 1:25 A.M. the engine whistled, slowly the wheels turned, and they were headed south. Offering his flask, the colonel remarked, "As the night is damp and chilly, perhaps you will join me in a drink"; Morgan accepted. As the train crossed the Scioto River near the penitentiary, the officer said, "There's the hotel at which Morgan and his officers are spending their leisure," and the "businessman" replied, "Yes, and I sincerely hope he will make up his mind to board there during the balance of the war, for he is a great nuisance."[41]

The train rumbled through the fields and small towns, and Morgan excused himself to speak to a couple of acquaintances a few seats up in the coach. In a manner totally natural and at ease, he shook hands with Hockersmith and Bennett, wished them a safe journey, and returned to his seat. At dawn, when the train came to the suburbs north of Cincinnati, Morgan and Hines jumped off to avoid the chance of being recognized at the terminal. A Union soldier saw them and yelled, "What in the hell do you mean by jumping off the cars here?" John retorted, "What in the Devil is the use of my going into town when I live here? And besides, what business is it of yours?"[42]

Through alleys and back streets they made their way to the Fifth Street ferry, where a boy operating a skiff took them across to Ludlow and pointed out the house they inquired for. Morgan presented his card to the woman who opened the door, and she welcomed them into the first stop on the reverse underground railroad with wildest joy and enthusiasm. After a hasty breakfast her son took them south to the home of William Robinson Thomas in Fort Mitchell. Mrs. Thomas cleaned and dressed Morgan's injured hand, and laundered Hines's trousers, which had gotten muddy in the jump from the train. While the pants dried, she served lunch. Her two young daughters never forgot how Morgan smiled when they asked for a lock of his hair and how afterward he said they were a great improvement over the prison barber. By early afternoon the main roads were blocked by soldiers looking for the escaped prisoners, so Mrs. Thomas furnished them fresh horses and had her twelve-year-old son Will guide them through crosslots and byroads to their next stop.[43]

Traveling by night and resting by day, they made their way through Kentucky. Morgan had a cattle whip and, depending on the situation, posed as a cattle buyer or government mule purchaser. To throw Union soldiers and bounty hunters off the track, they sometimes lay over for as many as four days in one place. Stragglers and escapees from Camp Douglas in Chicago joined them along the way, and Southern friends provided everyone weapons and horses. By the the time they reached the Tennessee border, there were fifty of them, and they pretended to be Union cavalry. On December 18 they were crossing the Tennessee River with a makeshift raft and swimming the horses when they were surprised by a real Union cavalry patrol at their rear, on the northern bank. Morgan's band held them off until he and Hines were over the river, then scattered, the Federals giving chase.[44]

In an interview with a reporter for the Richmond *Examiner*, Morgan said his horse nearly drowned in that crossing. He threw a blanket over the animal and commenced walking him; then suddenly he was seized with a presentiment. Throwing on his saddle he told Hines: "We will be attacked in twenty minutes." He had just tied his girth when minie balls whizzed overhead—a force of enemy cavalry was advancing on their side of the river. Bounding onto his horse, which seemed inspired with new vigor, he separated from Hines and sprang up a mountain like a deer. On the roads below, blueclads established a cordon of pickets, and it was getting dark and beginning to rain.

Coming to a small house, Morgan dismounted and knocked. To the man who answered the door, he introduced himself as a Union regimental quartermaster on his way to Athens, Tennessee, to procure sugar and coffee. The man's wife was in bed, but at the mention of those precious items she sprang out in her nightgown, declaring, "Thank God for that, for we ain't seen any real coffee up here for God knows how long." Delighted with Morgan's offer to share with them and taken by his handsome appearance, she kindled a fire and cooked supper for him. During the meal John said he had heard that some Rebels had tried to cross the river that afternoon. "Yes," she replied, "but our men killed some un um, and driv' the rest back."

"Now, I know that," said Morgan, "but didn't some of them get over?"

"Yes, but they are on the mountain, and can't get down without being killed, as every road is stopped up."

Bestowing his most charming smile, Morgan looked into her eyes and said earnestly, "It is very important for me to get to Athens by tomorrow night, or I may lose that sugar and coffee, and I am afraid to go down any of the roads, for fear my own men will kill me."

"Why Paul," she said, remembering that she had a husband, "can't you show the Captain through our farm, that road down by the field?"

"Of course, Paul," Morgan pleaded, "you can do it, and as the night is very cold, I will give you $10 to help you along." Paul accepted and guided him seven miles to safety.[45]

Throughout the South people gave three cheers at the news of the escape. In Louisville, Coral Owens Hume was beside herself: "Hurrah, Hurrah, Hurrah! I feel like I want to be somewhere, that I can scream as loud as I can. I think I will get into the celler & then no Yankee can hear me. Yes, Hurrah, Hurrah, Hurrah! for John Morgan & 6 of his men have escaped from prison." Then there followed over four weeks of suspense as he made his way through enemy territory with a price on his head. Finally, on Christmas Eve, the announcement came that he was safe. The story was a sensation. Lengthy interviews with Hines and Morgan were published, and their adventure was compared to those from the Arabian Nights and the Count of Monte Cristo. The Richmond *Enquirer* printed "The Leopard—Morgan," a poem glorifying him as a creature too strong and wily to be chained in a felon's prison. "The Leopard is free! is free!" it proclaimed.[46]

Mattie first heard he was safe when she received a telegram from him on December 24 from Columbia, South Carolina: "Just arrived. Will make no stop until I reach you." During the Great Raid she and Alice had left Augusta and migrated to Knoxville to meet John on his return. Then, when Burnside's army pushed into east Tennessee, they fled into Virginia, where Mattie became ill. They went to a mineral spring for therapy and settled down in Danville in the home of Col. Robert W. Withers. It was ironic that Withers was commandant of the Confederate prison camp in Danville; his men guarded 4,000 Union prisoners of war in several tobacco factory buildings. It seemed that Mattie's whole world was dominated by prisons and prisoners. But friends showered her with gifts of fruit, and her lying-in room was always filled with fresh flowers.[47]

On the day of John's escape, November 27, 1863, with great difficulty she had given birth to a daughter. The baby struggled to live, and did until her father was free—she died the next day when he was with friends in northern Kentucky. John arrived in Danville at 6:00 A.M. Christmas day, and he and Mattie had a few precious hours in private. They would have preferred spending the day together in seclusion, but Morgan was a greater hero than ever; he belonged to the nation. At 3:00 P.M., Danville celebrated his homecoming with a military parade and artillery salute. Mayor Thomas P. Atkinson hailed him as the recognized representative of Southern chivalry and declared that the Yankees erred in shearing his hair, for unlike Samson, Morgan's power was in his right arm, not in the covering of his head.[48]

Morgan had learned that the Union government considered him a special enemy who was to be denied the rights of a prisoner of war when captured. The experience had been so traumatic for John that after escaping, he resolved never to be captured again. Northern officials were outraged at the breakout, while Southerners hailed it as further proof that Morgan could always outwit the Yankees. Through the excitement, suspense, and romance of the escape, Morgan became a greater hero than ever.

SEVENTEEN

Deprived of Command

From Christmas to New Year's, John and Mattie stayed in Danville, but he was anxious to go to the capital to press for the release of his men and begin reorganizing his command. They made the trip as soon as Mattie was able to travel, and in Richmond, after a day devoted to receiving the public, John initiated his efforts on Saturday, January 9. He hoped to get the officers transferred to military prisons first; then work on their exchange. The Union War Department still maintained that Morgan's men were hostages for Neal Dow and his command. Therefore, Morgan visited Dow in Libby Prison. When introduced, Morgan smiled and said: "General Dow, I am very happy to see you here; or, rather I should say, since you are here, I am happy to see you looking so well."

"General Morgan," Dow replied, "I congratulate you on your escape; I cannot say that I am glad you did escape, but since you did, I am pleased to see you here."

They engaged in friendly conversation for a few minutes, and Morgan was also introduced to Colonel Streight and greeted warmly by the Union prisoners from Kentucky. Morgan did not mention it, but living conditions were much worse than where he had been. In this drafty tobacco warehouse, the officers had shivered for several days with no fuel for fires.[1]

Next, Morgan met with Secretary of War James A. Seddon and Commissioner Ould. They explained that the government had adopted the policy of retaliation, and an equal number of Union prisoners should be placed in penal institutions in the South. The only problem was where—the state prisons in Georgia and Virginia were full, so the military prison in Salisbury, North Carolina, was being furnished with penitentiary facilities, but until that was finished, nothing could be done other than protest. Over the next few weeks Morgan conferred with Ould several times and on one occasion requested authority to build a penitentiary himself. He said he could construct wooden cells in a vacant building and have Yankee officers in them in no time. But Ould's threats finally bore fruit. Since they no longer had Morgan, the Union authorities were more flexible about keeping his command, and in March, 1864, all the officers were transferred to military prisons. Several were then exchanged, although some of the officers and men were still prisoners when peace came.[2]

On Sunday morning, January 10, Mattie felt strong enough to leave the suite in the Ballard House to attend St. Paul's Episcopal Church, opposite Capitol Square. It was the church that President and Mrs. Davis attended, but this day John and Mattie were "the observed of all observers."[3]

Mattie spent the next day resting in the hotel, and John attended his formal reception at the Virginia legislature. Immediately afterward, he kept an appointment with President Davis at the executive mansion. Davis was cordial—he appreciated Morgan's contribution to Southern morale and to the war effort—yet it made him uncomfortable that Morgan inspired the people as he had never been able to do. Davis's political supporters and friends in the press still lauded him, but the ranks of his critics had grown, and the people of Richmond had come to ignore him. In January, 1863, coming home from his first major tour of the western Confederacy, he was greeted with a brass band; eleven months later, when he returned from the second such trip, no one noticed his arrival. On the morning of Morgan's great public reception, he had called for his horse and had ridden off alone into the suburbs, allowing the people the unencumbered pleasure of their hero worship. There is no record of their conversation, but most likely Morgan requested continued efforts to free his men and support in reorganizing his command.[4]

During the next several days Morgan met frequently with other members of the Kentucky bloc, who were in the capital in unusual numbers that winter. "These huge Kentuckians fill the town," observed Mrs. Chesnut. In addition to three generals—John C. Breckinridge, Simon B. Buckner, and Joseph Lewis—the Confederate governor of Kentucky, Richard Hawes, was present, as was Gen. John Bell Hood, convalescing from amputation of his right leg at Chickamauga and seriously courting Sally Buchanan "Buck" Preston from South Carolina. They enlivened the social scene with a round of dinners and receptions; they toured the fort at Drewry's Bluff; and Hood, Breckinridge, and Morgan were formally presented to the Confederate House of Representatives.[5]

The dream of liberating Kentucky was still alive, and out of these gatherings came a formal proposal for a grand western strategy. On January 15, Morgan, Buckner, Breckinridge, and Lewis proposed a spring offensive to President Davis. Gen. Joseph E. Johnston's army would advance from Dalton, Georgia, against Union forces in Chattanooga. Simultaneously, 8,000 Kentuckians drawn from infantry and cavalry commands throughout the Confederate army and concentrated in eastern Tennessee, would march on horseback through Cumberland Gap into Kentucky. This part of the plan had Morgan written all over it, including the projected results: Federal supply lines would be disrupted; Union troops would be diverted from Johnston's front; and the people of Kentucky would arise and join the Confederacy. Davis liked the plan and agreed to suggest it to Johnston as one possibility among several. Johnston turned it down, declaring that turning good infantry into bad cavalry would be a mistake.[6]

Morgan's fellow Kentuckians were aware of his considerable informal power in Richmond. The Richmond *Enquirer* noted that the city was "rendered starry" by the presence of such heroes as Hardee, Breckinridge, Morgan, and Stuart (and in that list Morgan's rank was given as major general when he was only a brigadier). On the streets a rumor said that Morgan would be named commander of all the cavalry in the Department of Tennessee. Mattie received the highest public honor of her life when both houses of the Confederate Congress formally received her. One evening a handsome young officer who said his name was John Bull was arrested in the lounge of the Ballard House for being drunk and disorderly. The mayor dismissed the charges when Bull claimed that he had overindulged during a lengthy wait to catch a glimpse of Morgan.[7]

Morgan attempted to harness his informal power in reorganizing his command. Approximately three-fourths of his men were in Northern prisons, and several hundred were scattered. Some had not gone on the Great Raid; others had separated during the raid and avoided capture; and several had escaped from prison camps. Remnants had united with the Confederate army under Joseph Johnston, who had replaced Bragg; they were organized as an identifiable regiment and two separate battalions stationed in Decatur, Georgia—but they called themselves Morgan's men and longed to return to his command. As soon as Morgan's homecoming was announced, one of his officers in Decatur ordered absentees to report to camp immediately.[8]

On January 1, Morgan had issued an emotional call to his men, summoning them to rendezvous in Decatur. The notice was published widely and reverberated throughout the Confederate army: soldiers in every branch of service read it and assumed Morgan was beckoning them.

SOLDIERS,—I am once more among you, after a long and painful imprisonment.

I am anxious to be again in the field. I, therefore, call on all the soldiers of my command to assemble at once at the rendezvous which has been established at this place.

Your country needs your services, the field of operation is wide, and the future glorious, if we only deserve it.

Remember how many of your brave comrades are still pining in a felon's cell. They call loudly on you for help. They expect it of you. Will you disappoint them?

Come at once and come cheerfully, for I want no man in my command who has to be sent to his duty by a provost marshal.

The work before us will be arduous, and will require brave hearts and willing hands. Let no man falter or delay, for no time is to be lost. Every one must bring his horse and gun who can. Those who cannot will have them furnished.[9]

Morgan was surprised at the response. He did not comprehend how deeply the Southern people identified with him, and he had no idea that he had such a hold on their emotions. Applications for transfer flooded into his temporary headquarters in the basement of the Varieties Theater in Richmond, over 14,000 in three weeks; they came from men in every department and every branch of service, including seasoned veterans of infantry and artillery, men who had fought at Bull Run, Antietam Creek, Chancellorsville, Vicksburg, and Gettysburg. The ground swell was partly due to weariness and boredom, to the need for a break in the routine. But, like the partisan ranger act in 1862, Morgan's announcement touched the hearts of Southerners, appealing to the romantic hope that a knight on a white horse could lead mounted men to victory. Morgan promised adventure, romance, and success, all of which were woefully missing in regular service.[10]

Eighteen-year-old Harry D. Burr of Richmond, a veteran of Gettysburg, said he preferred "an active cavalry service, where strong souls, and willing hands are needed, to the inactive drone-life of artilery [*sic*]." Two sailors on the CSS *Charleston* complained that when they transferred from the infantry, they had applied for privateering duty but were assigned to the ship, "which is almost a prison—entirely to inaction, to say nothing the menial & disagreeable duties to be performed here." To a twenty-two-year-old in Chapel Hill, North Carolina, Morgan's proclamation was more personal: "I have read accounts of your adventures, which has [*sic*] thrilled me through and through, and caused me to like your kind of service, and more especially to have you as a leader."[11]

Applications for transfer had come to Morgan before, and the problem was widespread in the Confederate army. Departmental commanders often complained that demoralized infantrymen sought what was considered lighter, less tedious assignment to the cavalry, especially the partisans. In April, 1862, fifteen Mississippi infantrymen stationed in Savannah had wanted to join Morgan; they hoped to get ahead of other applicants by mentioning that "one of our number, E.W. Maulding, has served as a Commanche [*sic*] hunter in Texas, is A#1 with a lasso and if you can not immediately supply us with horses will soon rope in enough of them from the Yankees to mount us." Later that year a battalion of partisan rangers in Macon, Georgia, offered themselves: "The record of your chivalry and daring has fired our enthusiasm and awakened a most anxious desire to share the peril and the glory of 'Morgan's Men'. . . . We are Georgians anxious to be led by you to the Banks of the Ohio." From 1862 on, high-ranking Confederate officers had complained to the War Department that troops wanted to go with Morgan for "brisk adventures and active movement."[12]

This latest demand for transfers became a storm that seemed to threaten discipline and order in the whole Confederate army. An infantryman in Charleston lamented that his commander dared not approve his reassignment because others would insist on the same, and the regiment would be greatly reduced. Six men in Gen. Richard S. Ewell's corps near Orange Court House, Virginia, wrote: "We have not been able to find out the *Red Tape* manner, of accomplishing this," but "our whole company would join you in a moment." From Chaffin's Farm, Virginia, one of Lee's soldiers stated: "The men of this Brigade are mad to join you, and if the law would allow it you could raise a good regiment here." And J. Porter Hamilton, one of Lee's officers, offered to transfer his entire infantry regiment to Morgan's cavalry.[13]

A canard spread through the hospitals that Morgan was accepting disabled men. One man wrote from his bed: "I have been wounded in the hip. Can get a surgeon's certificate that I am unfit for Infantry service. I would prefer being with your command because I am a lover of an active and hazardous life." A Tennessee private claimed: "By exposure I am rendered unable to perform infantry service having contracted chronic rheumatism. However, I feel sufficiently able to perform cavalry service, and I am anxious to join your command." Five men wrote from the Richmond city jail, pointing out that their charges were slight, and a word from Morgan would certainly produce their immediate release.[14]

Morgan's staff answered the requests with a polite form letter in which the general stated that he would accept with pleasure, but army regulations required the approval of the applicant's commanding officer. At his headquarters everything was handled through formal channels, but in Decatur, Col. Adam R. Johnson sent out officers to recruit for the division—"More Men for Morgan!" read the headline in one of their advertisements—and unscrupulous men traveled through the country claiming authority to recruit for Morgan. They told stirring tales about raids they never went on, and drank round after round of free drinks offered in toasts to the great chief. Right and left they approved transfers and signed up men who were subject to conscription. After he was arrested and sobered up, Jon F. Andrews apologized: "Attribute it to whiskey, as I have been on a spree for the last three weeks and do not know what I said."[15]

General Johnston complained to President Davis that recruiting agents were enticing his infantry to desert: "I therefore earnestly beg Your Excellency to annul all these authorities and forbid them for the future." General Lee told Davis that he was certain Morgan had not approved, but Morgan's recruiters were enticing his convalescents from Richmond hospitals: "You will see if this conduct is allowed that all discipline is destroyed & our armies will be ruined," he wrote. Davis forwarded Lee's letter to Morgan, who replied that he had given no authority to recruit and knew nothing about Lee's complaint.[16]

The South was nearing exhaustion, and men and equipment were increasingly difficult to replace. Colonel Johnson had repeatedly applied through channels for uniforms and horses, to no avail. When Morgan returned, therefore, Johnson authorized the division surgeon, the chaplain, and other staff members to solicit contributions of cash for horses, clothing, and blankets. As soon as Morgan heard about this, he wired Johnson from Danville, ordering such solicitation to halt immediately, but he was too late. Within six days the citizens of Augusta, Georgia, donated $10,000. Savannah responded liberally, as did Macon, where fund raisers lauded Morgan as a cavalryman without parallel, combining "craft and audacity and intimate knowledge of the topography of the country." In Atlanta wealthy citizens gave $10,000, and the Refugee and Resident Ladies Society raised $4,000 by staging two soirees of tableaux, pantomimes, and music. The Richmond *Whig* announced on January 15: "The liberal spirit in which the people throughout the country are responding to the call upon them encourages us with the hope that Morgan and his men will be again very soon in the saddle and on the war path."[17]

The students at Columbia Female College in South Carolina collected $454: "It is a simple offering, but it testifies the universal admiration and esteem due to such men; and allow me, sir, in the name of all Southern women, to express to you, in these words, the undying love and pride which each one of us bears, in her innermost heart, for the name of '*Morgan.*'" In an open letter Morgan respectfully declined the donation, pointing out that the War Department had agreed to equip and supply his command and provide everything needed to place him in the field immediately. The women of Chester, South Carolina, sent $475 they had collected before word came that Morgan was not receiving cash. They promised that in the future all that was needed to resume collections was mention of the name of Morgan.[18]

When word got around that Morgan was not accepting cash donations, people sent equipment and personal gifts instead. From Charleston came seven imported saddles and bridles; from Columbia six fine English saddles; from Lynchburg a bridle, martingale, and spurs of Southern manufacture; and from Danville a saddle, bridle, and spurs: "You have fairly won the Spurs by your many Knightly tills against the enemies of your country." And L. Loeser & Co. of Augusta, Georgia, gave him a general's cap made in record time because the ladies in the factory fought over the honor of making part of it.[19]

Morgan applied to the War Department for authority to assemble his command at Abingdon, Virginia, where horses could be impressed for his dismounted men, recruits could be raised, and he would be in a position to raid behind enemy lines in Kentucky. In a follow-up letter the next day, endorsed by four members of the Confederate Congress, he proposed a three-pronged Kentucky raid. He would march to Lexington via Pound Gap; another column would go through Cumberland Gap, and a third through Burkesville. He promised to demonstrate that the vigor of Southern cavalry was undiminished.[20]

Gen. Samuel Cooper, adjutant and inspector general, turned down the request, recommending that Morgan be assigned to Johnston's army defending Atlanta. Secretary Seddon overruled Cooper and approved, explaining that in southwest Virginia, Morgan would be better able to fill his ranks. Seddon ordered that individuals who had originally enlisted under Morgan and had been subsequently attached to other units now be transferred to Morgan. The reassignment of the still-organized Morgan entities was left to the discretion of General Johnston, but Seddon recommended that Johnston restore them to Morgan if possible.[21]

For the time being, Morgan had done all he could in Richmond, and as Mattie had regained her strength, they departed for Atlanta on January 27. In Atlanta it was announced that they would arrive on Saturday, February 6, and long before the designated hour several thousand people gathered at the huge "car shed" of the Western & Atlantic Railroad terminal. It was a wide, sweeping, block-long, structure, the symbol of Atlanta as the industrial hub and gateway to the deep South. The crowd filled the shed and the spacious switching tracks east of it, every heart anxious to fling an ovation at the hero's feet. There was no human being they would rather have seen at that moment, no person alive.

At ten o'clock a whistle sounded down the track, the smoke of the engine appeared above the rooftops, and the train lumbered into view. The mass of people came alive and pushed forward, preventing the train from entering the shed. It stopped and they surrounded it—a sea of heads, a crushing multitude encompassing the cars and making it impossible for Morgan to leave the train. Presently a way was opened, and as he appeared on the platform between two cars, a scream went up, peal upon peal, filling the air and echoing through the streets in one continuous, deafening cheer.

John and Martha were taken through the crowd to a carriage, and once they were seated, men spontaneously unhitched the horses from the shafts and seized the honor of drawing Morgan's coach through the city. They were followed by a line of carriages bearing dignitaries, a battalion of infantry, a band, and a mob of boys chanting "Morgan! Morgan!" To young Sally Clayton, who was there, it was "about the greatest day ever seen in Atlanta."[22]

Taking the hero worship in stride, Mattie wrote: "Johnny & myself are now in excellent health, and he stands prominent in the hearts of the people." They stayed in the same hotel as John's sister, Tommy Duke; if they were separated for a few minutes, Mattie would inquire: "Tommy, where is the General?" and John would ask: "Tommy, where is Mattie?"

Morgan met with Johnston, a dapper gray-haired man, and persuaded him to give back all of his units. Johnston directed the commanders to prepare the men but to remain in position until Morgan gave the order to leave for southwest Virginia.[23] But the more he thought about it, the more reluctant Johnston was to lose Morgan's men. His 50,000-man army was outnumbered two to one, and he had only 4,200 cavalry present for duty. On February 17, a portion of those had left when he had to send most of Hardee's corps to reinforce the Mississippi-Alabama department. They had not gone far, however, when skirmishing broke out on the left flank, and fearing a general advance, he had ordered Hardee back to Atlanta. It turned out to be not an attack in force, but the crisis left Johnston in no mood to follow through on the transfer; therefore, he asked Seddon to leave him the regiment and the best battalion and give Morgan the battalion commanded by Capt. J.D. Kirkpatrick.[24]

Morgan refused to accept this decision. Leaving directions with Kirkpatrick to march through Georgia and the Carolinas and meet him in western Virginia, he and Mattie went back to Richmond to resume lobbying for all of his men. He pleaded with the Kentucky bloc, met personally with Davis again and with Bragg, who had become a special adviser to the president. George Grenfell had joined Morgan's headquarters staff temporarily, and he twisted arms with vigor. But it was no use; their only gain was the assignment of two Kentucky cavalry brigades already stationed in southwest Virginia, men who had never served under Morgan. The government had given him the assignment he wanted and had returned one of his old battalions, but he was greatly disappointed.[25]

Before leaving Richmond, Morgan wrote a lengthy letter to Samuel Cooper detailing the history of his orphaned commands and how each had volunteered to join him. He protested that to deprive him of most of his troops was to deprive him of his command: "We have fought together on many a hard field and have suffered the same privations, they are endeared to me by every tie which binds a Commanding Officer to his men, and I am proud to know that the same attachment exists in their breasts for me." He was deeply hurt; when a company volunteered to join him, he considered it a sacred bond that the government had no right to sever. Nevertheless, when he and Mattie departed from Richmond on March 21, the nearest he had come to winning a concession was a promise from Bragg that the units would be restored at the earliest opportunity.[26]

For nearly three months Morgan had campaigned to reorganize a command with which he could resume guerrilla raids into Kentucky, and in his estimation he had failed. The contrast between the public's adoration and support and the army's refusal to reassign his men led Morgan's friends to assume that Bragg was conspiring against him.[27] But Bragg had bent further than anyone by agreeing to assist in the transfer if it became feasible, and strategists in the high command believed they had been generous. In spite of the fact that Morgan lost most of his troops on an unauthorized raid, his request for assignment in southwest Virginia was approved, he was handed two brigades of cavalry already on that front, and he was allowed a battalion of cavalry from the thin forces in Atlanta.

Davis and Seddon, puzzled at Morgan's intransigence, breathed a sigh of relief when he finally left Richmond. No matter how many times they had explained the vital significance of Atlanta to the survival of the Confederacy, and no matter how they had stressed Johnston's desperate scarcity of cavalry, he had refused to be reconciled. They had witnessed firsthand the independent attitude that characterized Morgan's war. But Morgan knew that to be successful, he needed soldiers who were highly motivated and self-disciplined enough to work as a team. In this sense he truly had no command. Without Duke's assistance, he faced the almost impossible challenge of shaping some of the worst soldiers in the Confederacy into an efficient guerrilla force.

EIGHTEEN

The Last Kentucky Raid

Describing the guerrilla army of young David, the Hebrew chronicler wrote: "And every one that was in distress, and every one that was in debt, and every one that was discontented, gathered themselves unto him; and he became a captain over them." Guerrilla movements tend to attract individuals from the criminal fringe, and Morgan's had done so all along but never to so great an extent as in early 1864. In Decatur, Kirkpatrick's battalion had been the dumping ground for volunteers who swarmed in, responding to Morgan's call in the newspapers. Some were former Morgan's men; others were loafers, bummers, and thieves—riffraff more eager for plunder than for legitimate warfare. Concerning this battalion of about 800, Morgan complained, "I have nothing left but a disorganized body of men." He instructed Kirkpatrick to organize them in companies before beginning the march to southwest Virginia.[1]

Once Kirkpatrick set out, it would have been superfluous for him to report on their progress, for Morgan traced the line of march by the almost daily complaints of "outrageous conduct" he received. For example, in Greenville, South Carolina, Lt. James F. Witherspoon and a companion were arrested for violating curfew. An argument broke out, and Witherspoon drew his pistol and struck the corporal of the guard. He was court-martialed and discharged, but upon appeal was eventually restored to rank and resumed active duty. Others took horses, broke into corncribs and smokehouses, and plundered private property. Some posed as Morgan and gave orders on the quartermaster general in his name. Before they left South Carolina, Morgan instructed Kirkpatrick to arrest men guilty of crime, dismount them, and send them under guard to Richmond. But he had not heard the last of this unrestrained trek of his men.[2]

Wars have a brutalizing influence, and the longer fighting continues, the more inhumane people become. The Civil War provided a golden opportunity for the lowest order on both sides to commit savage criminal acts. By 1864 lawless violence was pervasive in parts of Missouri, Kentucky, Tennessee, and North Carolina. In the mountains of eastern Kentucky, military authorities despaired of restoring order and opened refugee camps to give people sanctuary from outlaws. Among men in active service in the armies, cases of sexual molestation and rape were rare, at least; when they did occur, the other men reacted with abhorrence. A Texas cavalryman apprehended in the act of rape was lynched by fellow soldiers. A Union officer charged with attempted rape in Rock Castle Creek, Kentucky, was court-martialed and sentenced to three years' hard labor with a ball-and-chain attached to his leg. Sherman knew of only two cases of rape in his large army in 1864 and 1865.[3]

But in Allegheny County, North Carolina, deep among the high ridges and isolated valleys of the Blue Ridge Mountains and far away from the marching men and exploding shells, violence came on horseback, bringing the crimes of indecent exposure, attempted rape, and murder. The people in the county were predominantly small farmers, growing corn, beans, and sweet potatoes and raising cattle on open grassland within dense forests where laurel bushes tangled around tall locust, oak, hickory, and pine. The people were strong yeomen stock, thrifty and hardy, with a highly developed sense of justice and an intense attachment to place. They loved the land and were at one with the earth, taking their babies to the fields and encouraging them to roll in the dirt and crawl on the ground. Unfortunately, the isolation and broken terrain provided sanctuary for deserters, robbers, and bush-whackers, heavily armed and on the alert, in their eyes the wariness of hunted men. Local militiamen fought them in pitched battle, and early in 1863 Confederate soldiers were sent in to restore law and order.[4]

The seasons passed, and the mountain people hunted and tended their gardens; the sows had pigs in the woods; and the cattle survived on patches of grass in remote coves. On Friday morning, April 29, 1864, bright sun-shine was drying the dew on the laurels when Martha Cheek and Mary Carpenter, women in their early twenties, walked the narrow road to Martha's small patch of corn, Martha carrying her baby in her arms. The birds flut-tered about, cardinals busily feeding their young and mockingbirds singing in the tulip poplar trees. Martha placed the baby in the dirt at the edge of the field, and she and Mary talked as they worked with sprouting hoes, breaking the crust so the tender shoots could push through. Martha's hus-band Richard was fighting in the Confederate army, and she and Mary worked together frequently.

Suddenly, four soldiers on horseback approached on the road and stopped at the field, dismounting and tying their bridle reins to low hanging tree limbs. Two of the strangers sauntered over to Mary, one grasped her arm and said; "You are a pretty lass. Let's talk."

"Leave me alone," she demanded, jerking her arm away. But the other man grabbed her, pulled her down, and attempted to rape her. She wrestled free and ran. He drew his revolver and yelled: "Halt or I'll shoot," but Mary disappeared into the woods. Meanwhile, the other two troopers approached Martha, who had snatched up her baby on one arm and stood defiantly hold-ing her hoe in the other hand. The first man seized the hoe and flung it into the bushes; the other grabbed her around the waist and held her. She dropped the baby, and it began to cry; Martha kicked and screamed at the top of her voice. They placed their hands under her clothing and repeatedly threatened to kill her unless she submitted. She broke away, but one of the men who had attacked Mary tackled her and attempted to run his hands inside her dress. She fought tooth and nail, and when he finally realized she would not be intimidated, he unbuttoned his trousers and exposed himself. "My name is Edwards," he snarled. Then all four men returned to their horses, mounted and left.[5]

Martha fastened her clothing and was calming the baby when several friends in the local militia, heavily armed, rushed into the field, responding to Mary's alarm. Martha quickly told them what had happened, and then two other horsemen appeared, headed along the road in the same direction as the first four. One of them, R.M. Burbridge, stopped and identified himself as a cavalryman in Company G of Kirkpatrick's battalion, Morgan's cavalry. He condemned the behavior of the four men, agreed they should be punished, and rode away. A few minutes later the four attackers returned with a squad of men and accused the local militia of being bushwhackers. They demanded that the mountaineers lay down their arms; when they refused, firing broke out, and Chesley Cheek—Martha's father-in-law—was killed, along with one of Morgan's men.[6]

Martha and Mary gave depositions to John Gambill, Allegheny County justice of the peace, and he turned the documents over to Lt. J.R. Burke, Confederate conscript officer for the district. Pleading for justice, Burke forwarded the affidavits to the North Carolina conscript office: "We have often heard it said & seen it published that *Yankees* had been guilty of such conduct towards defenseless women but I am loath to believe that a *Confederate* soldier could *so far* forget themselves and so near imitate Yankee *meanness* and *Cowardice* as to stoop to such as this." The records eventually came to Morgan, but there is no record that justice was done.[7] If he had ordered an investigation, it would have been very difficult to identify the guilty individuals; yet in the interest of justice he should have made an attempt. Morgan had been negligent in dispatching such a loosely organized group across the country. Most were law-abiding men, but the incident indicates what kind of human beings had attached themselves to the core of real soldiers. Nevertheless, this is the only incident of sexual crime in the command revealed in documentary records.

Morgan, with Mattie and eighteen-year-old Key, his youngest brother, arrived in Abingdon from Richmond on March 27. Key was attached to headquarters, and John and Mattie assumed the role of surrogate parents for him. "I have never seen a youth grow so rapidly," Mattie told his mother. "He begins to look quite like a man." Living at Acklin, the stately brick mansion built by wealthy merchant James Greenway and currently the residence of John Campbell, the Morgans continued their close companionship, remaining together constantly except when he took the field for a few days. Keeping her apprised of his whereabouts, one night he wired: "Always keep my promises to you. The train is behind time. May not reach Abingdon before daylight." Worrying about her safety, on another occasion he warned: "Be prepared to move at any time."[8]

During Morgan's first brief inspection of outposts, Mattie wrote his mother: "I feel perfectly lost when separated from him, and my most earnest prayer is, that I may never have to endure his absence again for as great a length of time as when he was in prison." Indeed, they agreed that his imprisonment was the worst calamity either of them had ever experienced, and time and time again Morgan talked about how it could have been avoided if only he had left his men and cut off alone disguised as a businessman or Yankee officer. The discussion culminated in a covenant: she promised to be vigilant in fleeing from enemy advances on headquarters, and he vowed never to surrender but rather, when surrounded, to separate from his command and escape like a lone wolf. He told his staff many times that Union forces would never take him alive, that he would never surrender and be incarcerated in a felon's cell again. The covenant with Mattie is the ultimate symbol of Morgan's personal approach to the war. His deep psychological needs had priority as always, and henceforth he would risk being killed rather than raise his hands in surrender.[9]

Morgan's independent attitude was still manifest in his prosecution of the war as well. Southwest Virginia was strategically significant because of the lead mines at Wytheville, which yielded as much as 150,000 pounds per month, and the saltworks at Saltville, which provided a large portion of the Confederacy's salt (essential in preserving pork, a staple of the Southern diet). Morgan's assignment included responsibility for the defense of the region, but as a guerrilla his goal was to prepare his disorganized command for a raid into Kentucky. He had about 2,000 men, of whom 800 were without horses and at least 500 unarmed. He requisitioned 500 Enfield rifles and 500 saddles and bridles from the ordnance department, and established a factory to make saddles and a large blacksmith shop to produce horseshoes.[10]

Preparations for the raid were interrupted by the great Union offensive launched by General Grant, Lincoln's newly appointed general-in-chief. One of Grant's diversionary thrusts, a cavalry raid by a force of 2,500 men under Gen. William Averell, attempted to destroy the Virginia and Tennessee Railroad and interrupt the flow of salt and lead into eastern Virginia. Morgan joined forces with Gen. William E. Jones, a West Point graduate who at the beginning of the war had been secluded in the Virginia mountains, mourning the death of his wife at sea. Training a regiment of volunteers he had recruited, Jones was so gruff that his men named him "Grumble." But he was an able officer, and Morgan willingly served as his subordinate during the Union threat.[11]

With a combined force of 4,500 men, Jones and Morgan marched from Saltville to Wytheville, where a crowd of women welcomed them joyfully. Advancing to Crockett's Gap near the town, they made contact with Averell on the afternoon of May 11. Averell's men were dismounted and drawn up in defensive line on a hill facing a large open field. Jones ordered a dismounted frontal assault, and giving a tremendous shout, the Rebels charged up the hill, driving the outnumbered blueclads from their position. Morgan led a force around the right flank, and Averell retreated again and again until Jones called a halt at sunset. Morgan wrote Mattie: "If we had 2 more hours of daylight would have captured the entire force. My men fought magnificently driving them from hill to hill, it was certainly the grandest sight I ever witnessed, to see a handful of men driving such masses before them. Averell fought his men elegantly, tried time again to get them to charge, but our boys gave them no time to form."[12]

Jones and Morgan had successfully defended their sector of the front, and Morgan regained confidence in this, his first combat since his capture. It was one of the few times in his career that he fought in a subordinate role, but he did not hesitate to publicize his contribution. Before the smoke cleared, he dispatched a courier to Wytheville to report the victory to Mattie and to department headquarters. The skirmish attracted little attention in the press, yet one article was headlined: "Gen. Morgan's Defeat of Averell."[13]

Mattie wired congratulations, and the next day John wrote: "Am perfectly lost without you 'My Sweet One' & if I only knew how long we will remain here would send for you, but my movements are so very uncertain that I should be compelled to stand it a little longer." After describing the skirmish, he inquired: "How are you my Love? Telegraphed you last night asking how you were, but received no reply. I am so very curious to know. . . . Shall be with you as soon as I can get off but you well know that."[14]

Averell's defeat was duly noted in Washington by General Halleck, who, in his new position as chief of staff, was as interested in Morgan as ever. When intelligence reports indicated that Morgan was shoeing his horses and arming his men for a raid through Pound Gap into Kentucky, Halleck forwarded the information to the commander of the district of Kentucky, Gen. Stephen G. Burbridge, in Louisville. Burbridge, who succeeded General Boyle in February, was a man who took his duty very seriously, as the people of Kentucky were learning. A farmer and lawyer from Scott County, Kentucky, he had attended Georgetown College and Kentucky Military Institute, and had seen action at Shiloh. He was an extremist who expressed himself through action. Ignoring public opinion and refusing to temper his enthusiasm with wisdom or mercy, he ruled Kentucky with a provocative, arbitrary hand; to Kentuckians he became one of the most detested individuals in the war.[15]

Burbridge reacted to the serious depredations of outlaw guerrillas by proclaiming a policy of retaliation. When a Union citizen was killed by outlaws, four Confederate prisoners in the custody of the military authorities were to be shot to death. The resulting reign of terror was one of the bloodiest violations of human rights in the Civil War. Some of the Confederate civilians and soldiers executed were guilty of no crime. The correspondence relating to these summary shootings is among the most chilling in the documentary record of the war, and Burbridge's hand was ever present. "Have the men been shot that I ordered?" he telegraphed to Munfordville. "If not, have them shot at once, except Goulder. Send him to Lexington." The executions were carried out in public and left courthouse lawns throughout the state stained with blood.[16]

During previous Morgan raids in Kentucky, General Boyle had quivered and quaked at his headquarters, frantically organizing forces to defend Louisville, Frankfort, and other points. Burbridge, however, as soon as he received Halleck's telegram, attempted to prevent Morgan's raid before it started by opening an offensive aimed at destroying the raiders in their base camp in southwest Virginia. Embarking on steamboats, he and General Hobson took separate forces up the Ohio to Catlettsburg and down the Big Sandy River to Louisa, where they proceeded overland to the mouth of Beaver Creek near Pikeville. Together they had about 2,100 men, all mounted— some as cavalry, others as mounted infantry and artillery.

They arrived at Beaver Creek on May 28, two days before Morgan left camp in Virginia. If they had continued at the same pace, they would have intercepted him before he passed through Pound Gap. But Burbridge's advance had failed to collect supplies at the rendezvous as he had directed, and an inventory revealed that he had rations and forage to last only two days. Rather than going forward and living off the country, he halted, sent a detachment to Louisa for provisions, and waited at Beaver Creek one full week for their return on June 4. A scouting party sent ahead to Pound Gap skirmished briefly with Morgan's videttes when Morgan came through at sundown on June 1, but Burbridge's strategic offensive had bogged down in the mountains long enough for Morgan to break through and seize the initiative.[17]

Morgan was counting on the raid itself to provide horses and equipment for his command. Previously, he had managed to scratch up enough horses to mount the men beforehand, but this time 800 of his 2,000 cavalrymen had to walk and run to Kentucky. Commissary stores were scarce, and the men were tired of "blue beef," which soaked up the brine it was preserved in worse than pork did; it smelled and tasted terrible. Another serious insufficiency was a lack of artillery; cannon were simply unavailable. Everyone did have a rifle, but many had no cartridge box, and what boxes they had were too shallow for the cartridges used in their Enfield rifles. Moreover, Morgan's inspector general reported on May 23: "I would earnestly call your attention to the fact that hundreds of your men are absolutely *naked*. Some are in their shirts and drawers, while others are compelled to remain in camp and cover their nakedness with blankets. Over five hundred are barefooted. It is most shocking in what want and destitution these men are reduced. You can not look at their evolutions in drill without seeing, in many cases, their privates

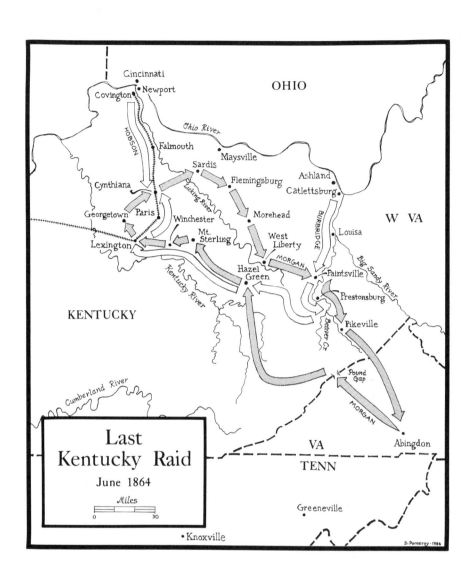

OHIO

Cincinnati
• Newport
Covington •

Ohio River

HOBSON

Falmouth

Maysville

Sardis

Flemingsburg

Ashland •

Catlettsburg •

Cynthiana

Licking River

Morehead

BURBRIDGE

Louisa •

W VA

Georgetown   Paris

Winchester

Mt.
Sterling

West
Liberty

Paintsville

Big Sandy River

Lexington •

MORGAN

Prestonsburg

Hazel
Green

Beaver Cr.

Pikeville •

Kentucky River

KENTUCKY

Pound
Gap

Cumberland River

MORGAN

VA

Abingdon •

Last
Kentucky Raid

June 1864

Miles

0   30

TENN

Greeneville •

• Knoxville

D. Pomeroy · 1986

exposed! I see men here wearing pieces of blankets to prevent the exhibition of their persons to the public gaze." In Kentucky they could take clothing, boots, and food from the Yankees, and just talking about it accomplished Morgan's goal of lifting morale. If the officers will perform their duty, he said, "we shall do our Country great service & cover ourselves with honors."[18]

Morgan used scouting reports of Burbridge's campaign as justification to begin his raid. He suggested to his superiors that the way to defend the lead and salt mines was by advancing into Kentucky and forcing Burbridge to withdraw to defend his district. Like his opponent, Morgan proposed an imaginative strategic offensive, but his plans totally disregarded the fact that the Union offensive in the Shenandoah Valley was resuming and that his command was needed in Virginia to fight forces much more powerful than Burbridge's. Gen. David Hunter was marching up the valley with 8,500 Union men, and without Morgan, Grumble Jones would face them with only 5,600. Jones, realizing that he would be in dire straits if Morgan left, was reluctant to give his consent. But the command structure was extremely confusing, and it was not certain that he possessed the authority to disapprove.

Morgan dispatched his command, then asked for Jones's approval. To Mattie he wrote: "Had some difficulty in getting off on yesterday but talked Genl. J. into it. He had received a telegram from Gen. Lee to send all his troops from this Dept. to Staunton, Va. to assist Gen. Imboden who is threatened by Gen. Hunter from the Valley. So you see 'Love' I was fortunate in having sent off my comd. when I did." Two days into the expedition, Morgan informed the War Department that Jones had approved and that he was on his way. He gave the Richmond strategists no opportunity to order him back: the letter went eastward as he marched into Kentucky. The Confederate high command was dismayed. Bragg endorsed Morgan's letter: "It is a most unfortunate withdrawal of forces from an important position at a very critical moment," and Seddon wrote under that: "Noted. Unfortunately, I see no remedy for this movement now."[19]

As far as Morgan was concerned, he was fighting as he always had, with a guerrilla raid behind enemy lines. He was following his own rules; this time, though, his insistence on independent raiding endangered the Confederate war effort in his section of the front, and what is most condemning is that he fully realized it. He warned Mattie to beware of capture by the Union army bearing down upon her and cautioned her to keep the ambulance standing by ready to transport her to safety in the mountains of North Carolina.

The raiders were predominantly Kentuckians; about half of them had been with Morgan before, and most were honorable men. Thomas J. McElrath was a classical scholar; William J. Bohon wore a fine uniform and quoted poetry. Two sons of Confederate Gen. Humphrey Marshall were along: Capt. John J. Marshall, with black beard, curly black hair, and dark flashing eyes, carrying a saber and looking as proud as a knight; and his seventeen-year-old brother Humphrey, Jr., a cavalryman who hated horses and horseback riding, and walked with the dismounted contingent at every opportunity.

Even so, discipline was a problem throughout the command and especially among the wild characters who had wandered in from all over the country. Morgan placed one battalion of this motley crew under the command of Col. Clarence J. Prentice, son of George Prentice, the Louisville editor. Clarence had drifted into camp one night after the raid began, coming out of the Kentucky mountains with his mascot, "Baby Bates," a young giant from eastern Kentucky. Bates's huge size attracted attention; after the war, Prentice took him to Louisville from eastern Kentucky and made a show of him in saloons on Fifth Street. Clarence addressed his men by their first names and held them in line with his pistol, training them to give the Rebel yell every time he raised his gold-braided cap.[20]

Morgan realized that his most serious deficiency was his officer corps. His style of leadership and tactics demanded efficient, dedicated subordinates, but most of his experienced officers were still in prison camps, including Duke. Cal had been exchanged and went along on the raid, but he was the only brother present. One of the three brigade commanders, Col. Henry L. Giltner, 4th Kentucky Cavalry, had never before been on a raid with Morgan. His best brigade commander was Col. D. Howard Smith, who had been exchanged. But Smith complained that some of his men were accustomed to being handled very loosely, and that when he attempted to instill a modicum of discipline, they became his bitter enemies. On earlier raids Morgan had had a harmonious team of handpicked officers, and the enlisted men had generally volunteered in companies with friends from the same locality. They were acquainted with each other and were dedicated and loyal to Morgan. On this raid, he was less able to weld his troops into a finely honed fighting machine. This deficiency was especially felt on the company commander level and among the scouts.[21]

The second night on the trail, Morgan slept in a comfortable mountain home. "All in fine condition and spirits," he wrote Mattie, "feel confident of success & hope 'My Precious One' to be enabled to send you news soon that will gladden your 'dear heart.'" On the back he wrote a postscript: "Since writing the within My 'Darling' have recd. your sweet acceptable letter. also Map. How did I forget it. It is invaluable. I could not have done without it. You are the dearest & best wife in the '*World*.' Shall say my prayers each night & you my Love shall be remembered in all. *All* your wishes shall be gratified. I am *ever* & entirely your devoted Husband." The next evening he said the time was dragging and his only pleasure was writing her. "When I am with you, 'My Own Darling' I am satisfied that I do not appreciate you as you deserve but when separated I feel my *entire* dependence upon *you* for happiness."

Passing through gloomy mountain ravines and moving farther from her, his old temptations and repressed guilt surfaced, moving him to swear faithfulness. "Do not 'Love' think that I will forget you for a moment. It is *impossible*. Your dear image is ever before me & never poses less." Reading the Bible and praying, he promised to "try & be better & hope to be enabled at no distant period to accompany you to Communion. We must be alike in all things. Except Love, it is utterly impossible for you to equal me in that."[22]

Morgan should have left the 800 dismounted men in Abingdon. They were heroic—walking up steep mountains and straining over tremendous rocks and rugged ravines; they made 230 miles in ten days, leaving their shoes in tatters and their feet raw and bleeding—but they slowed down the march. On June 7, Morgan wrote: "Today made but little progress owing to the condition of the dismounted men. Their feet are nearly worn out, having to wade streams for the last seven days & climb very precipitous mountains, reached 'Hazel Green' at 6 o'clock."[23]

That morning of June 7, southeast of Hazel Green near Quicksand Creek, Morgan had dispatched several advance detachments to confuse the enemy, magnify estimates of his strength, and destroy communications around Lexington to prevent reinforcements from reaching there. Five companies were detached, and they succeeded in isolating Lexington. Capt. Peter Everett was sent to Maysville, where he was to turn and feint on Newport. Another company halted communication from Mount Sterling to Paris, and one cut off travel from Winchester to Lexington. Most strategic was the work of the company that burned bridges on the Louisville and Frankfort Railroad, preventing Indiana militia from coming from Louisville by train. Morgan directed still another company to destroy bridges on the Kentucky Central Railroad—the line from Cincinnati to Lexington—between Paris and Cynthiana. They did, but the attack should have been duplicated north of Cynthiana. The sixty miles of railroad from Cincinnati to Cynthiana was left open, and that subsequently proved to be important.[24]

In Hazel Green, Morgan left the dismounted men behind and pushed ahead all night, reaching Mount Sterling at daybreak on June 8. He surprised the Federal garrison in the town and took 380 prisoners. His men celebrated with a beggar's revel in the captured camp. Ravenously hungry, they breakfasted on coffee with sugar, meat, and fresh-baked bread. George Mosgrove recalled: "In the tents we found a number of officer's trunks filled with 'biled shirts,' fine clothing, etc. In common with others, I found a trunk, and without any conscientious scruples jumped upon it with both feet and smashed the top into smithereens. That was the only way to get into it, and of course I was bound to 'get there.' The owner had the key in his pocket and was probably miles away with General Burbridge. The officer who owned the trunk must have been a dandy, a gentleman of exquisite fancy. I forthwith discarded my 'old clothes' and 'dressed up' in elegant habliments [*sic*] found in the trunk, and, as luck would have it, they fitted me to a t-y ty." Helping themselves to Federal supplies, all the men acquired boots, and what they could not wear or carry they destroyed. Forty Union commissary wagons were sent back down the road to give the dismounted brigade a ride.[25]

Some of the raiders swaggered to the business district and began plundering retail stores, strewing dry goods, broken furniture, and other items in the street, and robbing citizens of jewelry, clothing, and money. In Indiana and Ohio, Morgan had authorized his officers to search banks and courthouses for United States government funds, which was legal confiscation if the money was transferred to the Confederate treasury. On this raid he gave the same authority, and an officer and two enlisted men proceeded to the Mount Sterling branch of the Farmer's Bank of Kentucky. Finding it closed, they went to the home of cashier William Mitchell and at gunpoint forced him to open the walk-in vault and the safe. There were no government deposits, but they took $59,057.33 in gold and silver coins and banknotes, along with several thousand dollars belonging to individual citizens. They violated international law by stealing these private funds and distributing the loot among themselves.[26]

There is no evidence that Morgan specifically approved the taking of non-government funds or the pillage and robbery of private property; in fact, before the raid he issued General Orders no. 4, demanding strict prosecution of men caught pillaging. But he failed to take action against the thieves. He should have ordered the arrest of the culprits and forced them to restore the stolen property, as he had done in Columbia before the death of Tom Morgan. When Colonel Smith heard about the bank robbery and requested him to investigate immediately, Morgan replied that he would when he had time. He was making his own rules, and in his mind the bank robbery was justified under the policy of retaliation, as was the armed robbery of private citizens on the street. Once his personal war had escalated to this level of violence, his men rightly interpreted his inaction as approval, and those who were so inclined looked forward to the next town and the next bank.[27]

On earlier Kentucky raids, Morgan's scouts had been successful in providing accurate, updated intelligence. On this raid he ordered the scouts stationed in his rear to stay in contact with Burbridge and report by courier; instead, they all came riding into Mount Sterling with the news that Burbridge's entire force had gone into Virginia to attack the salt mines. As far as Morgan knew, therefore, no Federal force of strength was in Kentucky, and Burbridge would not be a threat for at least two days. By midafternoon everything was accomplished in Mount Sterling and it was time to move; Morgan needed to go swiftly into the raid, as was his practice. Furthermore, if he remained in Mount Sterling overnight it would be difficult to justify not investigating the bank robbery. To move out immediately would place the issue behind him; in the glory of victory it would shrink into insignificance, Morgan probably thought. Later, his official defense for not investigating on the scene was the necessity of conquering Lexington before it could be reinforced.[28]

All available horses had been rounded up, including family buggy ponies, but the difficult march had killed over 200 horses, and after they were replaced, there were not enough to mount all of the dismounted brigade. The primary objective of this raid was Lexington, where the Union army was keeping several hundred fine horses in government stables. Seizure of the jewel of the Bluegrass would shed luster on Morgan's men and prove that the Southern cavalry was still vigorous. On his own, Morgan had occupied Lexington only once, when attention had been diverted by Bragg's invasion and retreat, and now he needed to take it quickly before reinforcements arrived. Again he left the dismounted men behind and proceeded toward Lexington with one mounted brigade. He perceived no danger; they would all be reunited in the Lexington area, where he would have horses waiting. This decision, based as it was on inaccurate intelligence, was a serious mistake.[29]

When Burbridge's advance detachment returned to Beaver Creek from Pound Gap, he sent Hobson and forty men backtracking through Louisa and Catlettsburg to Cincinnati. In the Queen City, Hobson was to organize the Home Guards and press southward on the railroad toward Lexington. With the main body, Burbridge set out in direct pursuit of Morgan. On June 8 he marched all day and all night, and in the predawn hours of June 9, near Mount Sterling, an informer told him that the Rebel pickets were posted carelessly and in close, on the verge of the camp. At 4:00 A.M., with 1,600 men and two twelve-pound howitzers, Burbridge fell upon the two brigades Morgan had left behind. They were asleep, and the Yankees rode over them as they lay in their blankets. Morgan's men withdrew, counterattacked, and finally retreated toward Lexington. They had inflicted enough damage on Burbridge to delay him for several days, but their own losses were 51 dead, 83 wounded, 100 captured, and 100 missing.[30]

The two brigade commanders, Colonel Giltner and Col. Robert M. Martin, were embittered by their defeat. They felt that Morgan had left them exposed in the rear, and they shifted the blame for their surprise to him. For the first time there was disharmony between Morgan and his commanders. Early in the raid he had quarreled with Col. Robert A. Alston, and Alston had resigned his brigade command and left in a huff. After the raid Giltner and Martin united with Alston in demanding an investigation of bank robbery and other depredations. In the postwar years Giltner operated the leading hotel in Mount Sterling, and when he told his guests about his humiliating defeat, he declared that he would never forgive Morgan for leaving him exposed.[31]

Morgan and the advance brigade had spent the night of June 8 in Winchester, where he made his headquarters in a beautiful mansion. Before retiring he wrote Mattie; "My bedroom is elegant. Am living in grand style, but am not happy. My Idol is not with me, but her image is ever before me."

The next morning a courier brought word that Mount Sterling was under attack, and he remained stationary all day, allowing the two battered brigades to come up and deciding that it was not a good idea to divide his column after all. The delay gave some of his men in Winchester time to rob the bank of Simpson and Winn that day; they took an undetermined sum, along with securities left there for safekeeping by citizens. Charlotte F. Buckner, for example, lost $2,500 in bonds.[32]

By then, bank robbery had become a characteristic of the expedition. The day before (June 8), the detached company under Captain Everett had attempted to rob the Maysville Branch of the Northern Bank of Kentucky but found nothing, because the cash and securities had been loaded in a wagon and taken under guard to Hillsboro, Ohio. They impressed every horse they could find; broke into the post office and telegraph office; and looted a shoe-store and several other retail businesses; and robbed citizens of watches, clothing and cash. They intercepted Richard Deacon, who was on his way to Ohio, and relieved him of $500.[33]

During the night of June 9, after Giltner and Martin had caught up, Morgan left Winchester with his entire command, reaching Lexington at dawn. Following a brief skirmish with a small Union force, his men seized hundreds of valuable thoroughbreds, more than enough to mount every raider on a fresh horse. Most of the animals belonged to the Union cavalry, but some were blooded horses that wealthy breeders had left in government stables for safekeeping. The instant the large barns were cleared of horses, the Rebels fired them, filling the morning sky with dark clouds of heavy smoke, which obscured the sun and excited fear in the county that the entire city was burning.[34]

The visit was brief, only a few hours, but long enough to relieve residents of their hats, boots, watches, and money. And a few men robbed the Lexington Branch of the Bank of Kentucky of between $9,000 and $10,000 in gold, silver, and greenbacks. (One of the thieves, weighted down with more specie than he could carry, summoned George W. McCullough, who happened to be riding by; he inquired his name and company, and handed him a bag containing $650 in silver coins, directing him to keep it until further notice. McCullough brought the money safely to Abingdon and turned it over to a prominent citizen there.) Morgan detached one company on a scout to Frankfort, where it pinned down 183 Union troops; he reorganized the remaining 1,200 men into two brigades commanded by Smith and Giltner.[35]

At 11:00 A.M. the column rode into Georgetown, where Morgan's command had been welcomed so warmly two years before. Southern sympathizers filled the streets again, but this time they saw Confederate soldiers breaking down the doors of businesses and stealing private property. The people huddled in groups on the sidewalk, shaking their heads in disapprobation. When Mosgrove saw a group of young women from a local school standing on a corner watching several of Morgan's men going in and out of a clothing store and loading their horses with plunder, he felt ashamed for the Confederacy. This was Colonel Smith's hometown, and Smith did not want it on the record that he was present when its bank was robbed. He quickly surrounded the local branch of the Farmer's Bank of Kentucky with his men, and accompanied by the cashier, he personally examined the accounts and determined that no government deposits were on hand. Then he stationed a guard around the bank and went home to see his eighteen-year-old son Howard, who was seriously ill with typhoid fever. Constantly throughout the afternoon his visit at Howard's bedside was interrupted by merchants requesting guards, and before it was over, Smith's brigade was protecting the bank, the post office, and several businesses.[36]

Departing Georgetown in the night, the raiders invaded Cynthiana at daylight on Saturday, June 11, and after a brief skirmish the small Federal garrison took shelter in stores and houses. Morgan had no artillery, so he ordered his men to begin burning the town. Several dwelling houses and businesses were afire when the bluecoats surrendered. At 2:00 P.M. pickets north of town sounded the alarm that an enemy force was approaching along the railroad from Cincinnati. It was General Hobson, who had recruited 600 militia in Cincinnati and brought them down on three trains. Hobson attacked with vigor but surrendered when Morgan came charging along the dry railroad ditches in his rear, leading a mounted flanking attack in person. But Hobson knew that if he could detain Morgan, Burbridge might have an opportunity to strike again; therefore, for four hours he negotiated an offer to present himself and his staff to the Union government in exchange for Morgan's officers in prison camps. By the time agreement was reached, the afternoon was far spent, and Hobson assumed that he had significantly delayed Morgan.[37]

The men destroyed Hobson's three trains, and stacked the infantry rifles and ammunition captured from his volunteers. At first these captured munitions seemed a godsend because Morgan's men were running out of Enfield cartridges. He ordered Giltner's brigade to exchange their Enfield rifles for the infantry weapons and turn their Enfield ammunition over to Smith. But they refused; the Enfields were handier to carry on horseback, and they were reluctant to part with them. Morgan hesitated to force the issue and found himself suffering from scarcity in the presence of abundance.[38]

But it seems probable that he was not worried about being delayed by Hobson or about insufficiency of ammunition or anything else that Saturday afternoon. The record does not indicate his exact thoughts, but it may be that, elated by the successful attack on Cynthiana and the capture of Hobson's entire force, he shifted to the conscious state of euphoria, power, control, and triumph. If so, he became lost in a world of his own where he was the master of his fate and outside reality did not exist. In his own inner world the odds did not apply to him, and he was unable to evaluate his behavior to adapt to reality. Perhaps the excitement of this mood inspired him to sit down and with his own hand write his first official report of the raid.

He announced the conquest of Mount Sterling, Lexington, Maysville, and Cynthiana, the feint on Frankfort, the burning of railroad bridges around Lexington, and the capture of Hobson's "entire Brigade—numbering 2000 men. Himself & Staff. Three RR Trains with Baggage & Horses &c. &c." But there was one problem: "Fear if attacked before I can obtain ammunition to fit my guns that I will have to fall back (the enemy are armed with the old Musket, mine being Enfields). . . . All is working well. The people are ready and anxious to strike for the South, if they can be supported. My only fear is that my ammunition will fail." Finally, he wrote a postscript: "Since the above I learn that the force which entered Va. under Gen'l Burbridge to attack the salt works & lead mines has returned and is moving to attack me."[39]

Handing the report to a courier, Morgan told his adjutant to call a meeting of the staff and brigade commanders. He informed them that scouting reports placed Burbridge and a large force fifteen miles down the road at Paris, and he asked their opinion as to whether they should withdraw and be satisfied with their fruits of victory or stand and fight Burbridge. Most of the officers favored withdrawal—but Morgan directed them to form lines two miles south of town and prepare to give battle the next day.[40]

Giltner returned to his brigade with grave apprehension. After the prescribed deployment had been made, he asked his aide, G.D. Ewing, to accompany him on a ride out to the picket line. "Ewing," he said, "I very much fear there is a serious disaster ahead. General Morgan is a very likable man, and a genius in raiding; but he is such an optimist. I have advised him to leave at once but he persists in remaining and fighting Burbridge's command with near-empty guns. In all probability he will attack us at daylight tomorrow." They finished making the rounds and had dismounted when Morgan and some of his staff officers rode up and asked if Giltner had inspected his guard lines. Morgan said that he expected Burbridge would attack by early morning. Giltner answered that his command had only two rounds of ammunition per man and that they would be unable to withstand an attack, to which Morgan replied in a tone of asperity: "It is my order that you hold your position at all hazards; we can whip him with empty guns."[41]

Morgan was caught up in the same kind of overconfidence that he had displayed during the last days of the Great Raid. After the war Ewing concluded that Morgan was "one oversanguine commander," and "an optimist and somewhat intoxicated with excessive enthusiasm."[42] As at Buffington Island, Morgan decided to risk all rather than fleeing with what he had. On this occasion his high-risk taking did not correspond with the principles of guerrilla warfare. Guerrilla strategy dictated flight, but he chose to stay in the game and risk his men. In the enigmatic mind of John Morgan, the gambler overcame the guerrilla, and he turned himself and his command over to the goddess of chance. Later he told Duke that "he could have achieved success unparalleled in his entire career, if fortune had favored him" at Cynthiana.[43]

Sure enough, at two-thirty the next morning, Sunday, June 12, Burbridge's force of 2,400 mounted soldiers fell upon Morgan's encampment. Giltner's brigade, defending the center of the line, ran out of cartridges, threw down their empty Enfields, swam the Licking River, and fled through the fields and byways. Smith's brigade followed and it was every man for himself. No one was more speedy in flight than Morgan. Fulfilling the covenant with Mattie, he galloped north toward Falmouth at the head of the retreat. Mosgrove reflected: "I was glad to see him getting away, for had he been captured he would have fared badly—as the Federals had not forgiven him for his daring escape from the Ohio prison." In the panic, Pvt. Mark L. Dismukes lost the plunder he meant to share with his brother: "I got nothing at all on this trip, that is I didn't get out on account of my horse being captured and every thing I had in my saddlebags things which would have been of great value to us. . . . lost all my clothes but those I wore on my back."[44]

At Sardis, a small town south of Maysville, several Confederates recouped their losses by breaking into a general store reputedly owned by a Union man. The entire column halted, and officers attempted to prod the looters back into line, but company after company dissolved as men saw that "everything was going," and they wanted a share. Horses were loaded with domestic cotton, bolts of calico, muslin, boots, shoes, baby shoes, and various other items. "It was enough to bring the blush of shame to the cheek of any honest cavalier," Mosgrove said, "and was especially mortifying and humiliating to all proud Kentuckians, and more's the pity we were nearly all Kentuckians."[45]

Morgan still maintained that Kentucky was pro-Southern, and he never gave up the idea. Back in Abingdon on August 3, he insisted that if a Confederate army could occupy the state for sixty days, 25,000 recruits would be gained. But his own reputation in Kentucky was tarnished by the depredations of his men. Prentice accused him of inaugurating widespread outlaw guerrilla violence in the state, and in the editor's view, the armed robbery and looting confirmed it. "At one time," Duke wrote, "an avowal of 'belonging to Morgan' was thought, even in Kentucky, tantamount to a confession to murder and highway robbery." A man who deserted after Mount Sterling declared: "I would almost as soon have been killed as caught in such company." He and a good many others turned the other way and stayed in Kentucky to join outlaw bands.[46]

Meanwhile, Lee's Army of Northern Virginia was defending Richmond against the main thrust of Grant's offensive. As the large Union Army of the Potomac settled down to lay seige on Petersburg, Southerners prepared for a lengthy campaign of defensive warfare. Then came the news of Morgan's raid and many were inspired anew. J.B. Jones, the war clerk in Richmond, predicted that Morgan would soon be invading Maryland and Pennsylvania. Kate Cumming was thrilled: "Morgan is again in the saddle, bringing dismay to the *loyal* Kentuckians." One commentator hailed the moral profit derived from Morgan's display of vitality at a time when the North was assuring the world that the South was disabled and on its last legs. Another compared it to Scipio's invasion of Africa in the second Punic War and hoped Morgan's raid would relieve the Confederacy as Scipio had delivered Italy. Morgan was congratulated for preventing Burbridge's invasion of Virginia, destroying Union property, capturing Union soldiers (including Hobson), and acquiring fresh horses. One admiring editor proclaimed that Morgan did more with a handful of men than the cavalry of Virginia had done in the entire war.[47]

The reaction of the Confederate high commanders was not so generous. Bragg and Seddon had condemned the expedition when it began. In separate reports to Davis, Bragg and General Hood predicted that Morgan would return with a handful of disorganized men unfit for service until disciplined and reequipped. They were right, but it was a harsh condemnation, given the fact that on most previous forays except the Great Raid, he had captured large quantities of munitions and supplies and the time required to regroup had been brief and worthwhile considering the benefits gained.[48]

The strident criticism stemmed from the high command's concern with Morgan's abandonment of the southwest Virginia front at a critical juncture. While Morgan was gone, Grumble Jones was overrun and killed by Hunter's army on June 5. The next day General Breckinridge, desperately facing the onslaught at Lynchburg, requested that Morgan give relief with an attack on the enemy flank at Staunton. Col. George B. Crittenden, temporary department commander, replied that he would forward the message to Morgan at once, but "I do not think his command can be made available toward Staunton, as he passed through Pound Gap six or seven days since, intending to move to the interior of Kentucky." The Union invaders seized Staunton and burned the railroad depot, several factories, and some railroad bridges. They destroyed many miles of the Virginia and Tennessee and the Virginia Central railroads, and on Sunday, June 12—the day Morgan was defeated at Cynthiana—they burned the Virginia Military Institute. The campaign ended before Morgan returned, but only after Lee diverted Jubal A. Early's command from Richmond to the valley.[49]

Morgan had used the same guerrilla tactics as before, conducting night marches, surprising the enemy, destroying communications, causing confusion with detachments, and striking behind the lines where opposition was weak. His scouts shared the blame for the defeat at Mount Sterling, but they performed adequately otherwise, and the far-flung detachments had been effective.[50]

But Morgan, with the same overconfidence that had frustrated the Great Raid in Ohio, had ignored the basic principles of hit-and-run. On June 11 he had accomplished his objectives and had written his report; it was time to withdraw. Instead, with unreasonable optimism, he prepared to combat Burbridge's force, which was twice as strong, and he proposed to do it when his ammunition was running dangerously low. Many of the men had robbed and looted; his silence had given them approval and created hostility between him and his immediate subordinate—three of whom united in petitioning the Confederate government to investigate the depredations.

NINETEEN

The Final Gamble

On his way back to Abingdon from the Last Kentucky Raid, John wrote to Mattie: "How very anxious I am to see you & to hold you in my arms. Do not think I shall permit myself to be separated from you again." Upon his return he learned that he had been named commander of the Department of Western Virginia and East Tennessee, his first and only departmental command, and one of the least desirable assignments in the entire army. There was overlapping jurisdiction and great confusion; the position was a revolving chair in which, in less than a year, nine men had served. Everything was so disjointed that when Crittenden had taken over, he had asked Richmond: "What are the geographical limits of my command?"[1]

The War Department probably meant for the appointment to be temporary, and Morgan hoped it would be. He had never sought such responsibility; it was too confining and involved such administrative duties as discipline and logistics—activities he despised—and defense of territory rather than independent raiding. But administrative duties were pressing, and since there was no one else to turn to, he took action. A vital lead ore shipment at the mines was being delayed because the rail lines had not been restored since Hunter's offensive. Morgan had the consignment loaded on a wagon train, transported to the nearest open railhead, and delivered to Richmond. Then his men took the empty wagons into North Carolina for corn. At the same time he applied to the War Department for commissary funds, shoes and uniforms.[2]

More persistent was the problem of discipline. About 700 of the men who went into Kentucky eventually drifted back, and many of them refused to report for duty. Styling themselves "independent scouts," they wandered through the valleys committing larceny on the private property of citizens. The situation required action, and in spite of his aversion to discipline, he ordered the arrest of men absent without leave and promised speedy courts-martial. Soon the jails were crowded, and military courts were meeting day and night. But as soon as the bummers were released, they repeated their offenses. Their baneful influence festered and spread in the command. On July 2, Morgan requested authority to transfer them to the infantry, where "they could be brought under the rigid discipline of an infantry command in a large Army." Richmond denied the petition. Then, attempting to strengthen his ranks with men of the quality he had had before, Morgan proposed granting amnesty to those who had deserted and returned home to Kentucky and Tennessee. He stated that he was aware it was an irregular suggestion, but one which would benefit the country. Jefferson Davis turned it down, declaring that under no conditions could terms be made with deserters at large.[3]

Morgan's department came under the jurisdiction of Robert E. Lee, and Lee's first instructions were for Morgan to collect his troops, watch the enemy, and defend the saltworks. Morgan promised to comply, at the same time proposing a raid by a small body of cavalry on enemy supply lines in the direction of Charleston, West Virginia. Lee approved, while reemphasizing the importance of defending the department. Two weeks later, Morgan asked: "Where must I strike the enemy?" Lee responded by ordering a raid on the Baltimore and Ohio Railroad west of Cumberland, Maryland, and encouraging Morgan to proceed from there into Pennsylvania. At that moment Jubal Early and 14,000 Confederate cavalry were withdrawing from a spectacular raid on the outskirts of Washington, D.C., and Chambersburg, Pennsylvania. Early had relieved some of the pressure in the Shenandoah Valley and on Lee's army defending Petersburg, and Lee hoped a diversion by Morgan would do the same.[4]

Lee's suggestion was an excellent projected use of Morgan's ability. Lee was attempting not to stifle him but to use his strength as a partisan raider— warning him, however, to place priority on the defense of the lead and salt and to leave only if prudent. Morgan told Lee that he was sick and could not go. About a week later, when Lee was informed that Morgan had recovered, he inquired what operation Morgan could take with advantage.[5]

Morgan did not reply. Instead, he went over Lee's head, applying directly to Bragg in Richmond for authority to lead 500 to 600 men on a great sweeping raid southward through North Carolina against the supply lines of Sherman's army, which was investing Atlanta. Bragg forwarded the request to Seddon, who wired Lee: "If he could be safely spared for such an enterprise as he proposes it might prove advantageous, but he is only too apt to be seduced off by the prospect of an independent and adventurous expedition." The secretary left the decision to Lee, who answered that the raid would leave the upper valley of Virginia open to attack. Once again, this time to Seddon, Lee suggested a diversion in West Virginia and Pennsylvania: "He would not then be out of reach of the interests with the defense of which he is specially charged." Seddon and Davis agreed to leave it up to Lee and support whatever he decided.[6]

That was where matters stood on August 4, and that was where they remained—Morgan led no raid in support of Lee. He had not meant to conduct a raid or he would have done it. His command was in a state of dissension and demoralization, and he was not ready to leave Mattie's side, but he wanted to test the water and keep his options open for independent operations in the future. Lee must have learned what Morgan's western commanders had known for a long time, that Morgan was not a good team player.

Food for men and horses being continually scarce, Morgan's foraging parties ranged farther and farther to the southwest, into the east Tennessee valley between the Cumberland Plateau and the Unaka Mountains. Supply wagons rolled along level roads, over the hills and gentle slopes through Washington County into Greene County, gathering hay and oats from the open, sweeping farms where tobacco ripened in the sun. Greeneville, the county seat of Greene County and hometown of Andrew Johnson, was occupied mostly by yeomen who had few slaves and shared Johnson's dislike for the aristocrats of the Nashville basin and the cotton region of west Tennessee. Johnson had risen from success in tailoring to mayor, governor, United States senator, and military governor. When secession was debated in Greeneville, he and other leaders addressed great rallies in opposition. The town was the site of the convention in June, 1861, that attempted to separate east Tennessee from the rest of the state and have it remain loyal to the Union.

Greeneville had seceded with Tennessee, but Confederate soldiers on duty there stared into hostile eyes and unfriendly faces. Kirby Smith said it was enemy country where the people were ready to rise for the Union and were always eager to spy for the Union army. Much of east Tennessee had been terrorized by vigilante committees and bushwhacking societies from both sides, and there was great bitterness. In Nashville, Johnson considered it his responsibility to provide security to the citizens and encourage their loyalty to the Union cause. He was sensitive to the political ramifications of depredations in the state and was particularly offended by Morgan.

Johnson recognized that Morgan was a hero of Southern sympathizers in Tennessee. Not only had Morgan's raid on Cave City spoiled his great Union rally two years before, but Morgan had followed through with a telegram to Johnson, printed in a Knoxville newspaper on July 4, 1862, boasting that he had burned Federal cotton, smashed a train, and torn up a railroad within Johnson's jurisdiction. At that time Johnson could do nothing but fume, but now he had his own soldiers, the "Governor's Guard," a cavalry brigade reporting directly to him. The brigade was commanded by Johnson's adjutant general, Alvan C. Gillem, a native of middle Tennessee and graduate of West Point who had established a career in the army serving on the frontier in Florida and Texas. Johnson had offered the outfit to Sherman for his Atlanta campaign, but Sherman had declined, styling the brigade a political unit, "a refugee hospital for indolent Tennesseans," good for nothing except drawing pay and rations.[7]

Rebuffed by Sherman, Johnson prepared to attack Morgan. Gillem sent scouts into east Tennessee to gather intelligence, and Johnson directed him to "kill or drive out all marauders [*sic*]" in the region. He gave specific permission to pursue enemy bands across state borders into neighboring states, thus authorizing Gillem to attack Morgan's headquarters in Abingdon. With 1,200 men Gillem proceeded to Knoxville, marched through Strawberry Plains, and advanced on Morgan's pickets; he captured a few men and, according to one of his official reports, a black horse with a white-blaze face belonging to one of Morgan's officers. With several small skirmishes, he drove Morgan's men out of Rogersville, Bulls Gap, and Greeneville, totally clearing Greene County of Rebel forces. Morgan's advance pickets fell back to Jonesboro in Washington County.[8]

But after a successful initial phase, Gillem's campaign bogged down in eleven days of marching and countermarching in Greene County. Once he backtracked nearly twenty miles in a futile attempt to intercept Wheeler's cavalry, passing through on their lengthy raid in Sherman's rear. Many of Gillem's troops were from Washington County and Johnson County to the east, and they were puzzled as to why they were covering the same ground and never advancing toward the enemy. Among themselves they said that Gillem was afraid; Gillem claimed that he was maintaining contact with his supply line to Knoxville. Whatever his reasons, in no rush to advance, he bivouacked at Bulls Gap on August 30, sent a detail to Knoxville for fresh commissary stores, and settled down to shoe the horses, repair the wagons, and rest.[9]

Morgan's response to the incursion was to strike Gillem and attempt to drive him back to Knoxville. He welcomed the opportunity to fight because he was in desperate need of a victory. His disgruntled brigade commanders had persistently demanded an investigation of the allegations of depredations on the Last Kentucky Raid. On July 3, Morgan notified them that his inspector general, Capt. B.H. Allen, had inquired into the matter and found rumors but no tangible evidence. Alston and Martin responded with a lengthy letter to Allen furnishing abundant evidence, including the fact that McCullough had brought out the bag of silver coins. At that point Morgan gave Allen thirty days' disability leave and did not appoint a replacement. In effect, he had suspended the investigation, and Alston and Giltner were enraged. They said Morgan was being very high-handed and that he was delaying to protect the offenders. Deciding that their only alternative was to go over Morgan's head, they wrote to Confederate Governor Hawes of Kentucky and to Secretary Seddon demanding an inquiry. Giltner signed the letter to Seddon, and in it he explained that he was sending a duplicate directly to Seddon because he feared the one going through channels would be delayed by Morgan.

Morgan studied Giltner's letter for seven days, carefully drafted a cover letter, and forwarded the correspondence to Seddon. He admitted that soldiers from his command had robbed the bank at Mount Sterling but argued that the exigencies of the raid had prevented an investigation on the scene. He claimed that even though Allen was on leave, he was making progress; he just needed more time to sift the facts and obtain answers to correspondence he had initiated with witnesses in Kentucky. Morgan emphasized that since returning from the raid, Giltner had been insubordinate and that his complaint derived "more from personal pique toward me than indignation at my delay."[10]

By that time, rumors were circulating in Richmond that if Morgan had not incited the thieves, he had connived with them and was shielding them from discovery and prosecution. Morgan dispatched officers to plead his case at the War Department, but when finally admitted after first getting a cold shoulder, they heard the command "abused, & misrepresented in the bitterest terms." On August 22, Seddon relieved Morgan of his departmental command, and on August 30 suspended him from command of his men and appointed a court of inquiry to meet in Abingdon on September 10 to consider his authority for the Last Kentucky Raid and "excesses and irregularities, amounting in many instances to depredations and spoliations."[11]

At last Morgan's independence in making his own rules and fighting the war in his own personal way had caught up with him. His policy of retaliation had gotten out of hand and escalated to armed robbery of Union citizens and financial institutions, and by neglecting to take disciplinary action, he had given de facto approval. His reputation was tarnished, and he could not bring himself to investigate because he knew that the Pandora's box of depredations would be opened. Realizing, however, that he could not be an effective leader again until the matter was cleared up and discipline was restored, he pleaded with his friend Eli Bruce to encourage the government to begin with the inquiry as soon as possible. "Why is it that the Authorities at Richmond do not send forward the members of the Court of Inquiry?" he asked.[12]

When Duke, having been exchanged, arrived in Abingdon and saw Morgan for the first time since the prison escape, "he was greatly changed," Duke noticed. "His face wore a weary, care-worn expression, and his manner was totally destitute of its former ardor and enthusiasm. He spoke bitterly, but with no impatience, of the clamor against him, and seemed saddest about the condition of his command."[13]

In his letter to Bruce, written on August 31, Morgan complained bitterly that it was impossible to maintain discipline when the War Department was receiving and giving official recognition to dissidents who had gone to Richmond without his permission. Concerning his own involvement in the charges, he did not state that he was innocent. Instead, he attacked the character of two of the witnesses against him: he alleged that surgeon James F. Keiser was a liar and thief and had gone to Richmond without leave, and that Colonel Martin had received payment fraudulently for horses reportedly killed in Kentucky: "I am not *alone* responsible, for all the irregularities." And despite Seddon's order relieving him of command, he added, "I have been & am still in comd. of my troops, trying to do my duty to my Country."[14]

In Abingdon, when the court of inquiry was announced on August 30, there was great excitement, and the townspeople awaited the arrival of members of the court with anticipation. But Morgan had silenced his critics in the past with spectacular success in the field; in this crisis, too, he reacted by taking action, hoping that a headlining victory over Gillem would renew his support among the people and give him and his men a better chance at the hearing. Disobeying his suspension order, he rendezvoused his troops at Johnson City, thirty miles east of Greeneville, and marched down the valley with about 1,500 men and two pieces of artillery. A few miles south of Johnson City, at Jonesboro, he telegraphed Mattie on Friday, September 2: "Arrived here at one o'clock. Command has been moved forward." He left Jonesboro that afternoon and marched all night.[15]

Taking the advance was Capt. James E. Cantrill's company of men who, having been forced out of Greene County by Gillem, were familiar with the roads. On Saturday morning, several miles from Greeneville, Morgan sent a courier to Cantrill, directing him to halt; the general and his staff would lead the column. The thought of General Morgan riding the point through hills rife with bushwhackers astounded Cantrill. It seemed foolhardy and unreasonable. He sent a lieutenant to warn the general that they had been fired on in this area just a few days before. Morgan thanked Cantrill for the information but said he did not apprehend any danger. When he rode through the column to the advance position, a tremendous cheer went up— the last ovation Morgan's men would ever give their beloved chief.[16]

Morgan and his staff, still riding as videttes, reached Greeneville at about 2:00 P.M. on Saturday and prepared to spend the night, setting up headquarters in the largest house in town—the elegant mansion of Mrs. Catherine Williams, wealthy widow of Dr. Alexander Williams. A slaveowner and Southern sympathizer, Mrs. Williams had three sons: Thomas, a Confederate officer; William, a major on Morgan's staff and present with the command in Greeneville; and Joseph, a Union officer. Joseph's wife Lucy, a local woman, was living with Catherine.

When an aide came to Catherine requesting hospitality, she insisted on speaking in person with Morgan. She had a special interest in his command, not only because William was a member but also because she was connected to Mattie's family by marriage. She told Morgan that he would always be welcome, but she feared that if he stayed in the house away from his men, he would be in great danger. Nine days before, Gillem had been in Greeneville overnight, and his cavalrymen were well armed and well mounted. For the last thirty-six hours the townspeople had been expecting the Federals to return. Morgan insisted, nevertheless, and ordered an early breakfast so that he could be off at daybreak for Bulls Gap.[17]

At the telegraph office he sent Mattie the last message she would receive from him:

Mrs. Gen. Jno. H. Morgan   Greeneville, 3rd Sept., 1864
Abingdon

Arrived here to day. Find that Enemy have not been this side of Bull Gap & none
there. 'Mizpah.'

Jno. H. Morgan
Brig. Genl.[18]

Mizpah was the location in ancient Israel where Jacob and Laban erected an
altar as a sign of the covenant between them; John used it to renew his covenant with Mattie never to surrender.

At about 4:00 P.M. the main body of the command began coming into
town. Cantrill rode up to Morgan, who was standing on Main Street in front
of the Williams house. He looked rested: "His conversation was cordial and
he seemed in splendid spirits. He told me that from the best information he
could get there was no enemy nearer than Knoxville or at Strawberry Plains
at the nearest." Cantrill begged to disagree; reliable scouts from his company
had reported a regiment at Bulls Gap and one at Morristown. Cantrill was
only slightly in error—the regiment near Morristown had moved to Bulls
Gap, and Gillem's entire force was eighteen miles away. Unshaken, Morgan
replied that if they had been there, they had left, and as his brigades came
in he deployed them on the outskirts of town a mile and a half toward Bulls
Gap. Col. W.E. Bradford's detachment was on the left, Colonel Giltner in
the center, and Colonel Smith on the right, forming an arc about one-half of
the distance around Greeneville.[19]

Later in the evening, Lucy Williams's father, Jacob Rumbough, came to
the Williams house and warned Morgan that he should not sleep away from
his command. But it would have been highly unusual for him and his staff
to bivouac in the field, and he said that he did not perceive any danger. In
subjecting his command once again to the perils of headquarterism, he was
only following customary procedures.[20]

Headquarterism was widespread, but not every commander had the mis-
chievous infirmity. A courier with an important dispatch for Stonewall Jackson searched throughout the camp one night and finally found the general,
rolled up in his cloak, fast asleep among his men. And a member of Lee's
staff who asked which local mansion he preferred was told, "Pitch our *tents*
here." Lee's men admired him for sleeping in an ambulance on the march
and in a tent in camp.[21]

But Morgan enjoyed brushing his teeth and washing his hands—he had
small hands for a six-foot general and was preoccupied with keeping them
clean. He took pleasure in changing into clean clothing and eating with aristocratic women in a comfortable dining room supplied with a tablecloth and
napkins. And he loved sleeping in a private room on a featherbed. It would
have been demoralizing to him to sleep in the field with the men.

The Williams mansion, built in 1821, was designed like an Irish country
manor, three stories high with double chimneys at each end. Situated on a

slight rise at the rear of a large lot on Main Street, the house dominated an entire block, which it shared with a small hotel and other buildings on the opposite corner and the Episcopal Church midway in the square, facing Church Street. Guests approached on a walkway from Main Street and passed through a formal garden landscaped with boxwood, violets, ivy, and fruitbearing grapevines. Inside was a circular staircase, rising three full flights, its intricately carved walnut railing finely crafted with wooden pegs and not a single nail. The parlor, which had seen many balls and receptions, occupied one side of the main floor and featured two huge fireplaces and an elegantly decorated ceiling. At different times Union Generals Burnside and Gillem and Confederate Gen. James Longstreet had stayed there.[22]

The staff shared bedrooms on the third floor, two to a room except for Morgan, who had privacy in the front room on the Church Street side, with a window overlooking the garden and Main Street. He brushed his teeth, changed uniforms, and went to dinner. Catherine hosted, along with Nancy Scott, granddaughter of Hugh L. White, the prominent Knoxville banker and political associate of Andrew Jackson. "We spent the evening pleasantly," Nancy wrote, "it being the first time I had ever been in Gen. Morgan's company." Someone noticed that Lucy was missing, but Catherine explained that she had gone for watermelons to College Farm, about four miles south of town, and might be staying with the overseer's family. Lucy was a tall woman with dark hair and strong, even features; she walked with a masculine gait and loved to ride horseback. Catherine was right; she was at the farm. She had intended to return, but the overseer refused to escort her because he did not want trouble with the Confederates.[23]

What Morgan and his aides did not know was that while they dined, James Leahy, a boy about twelve years of age, was racing the eighteen miles of good road to Bulls Gap on his little mare. Leahy lived with his widowed mother in a small house two miles west of Greeneville, and late Saturday afternoon he had come home from the mill with a bag of meal and had fallen into the hands of James M. Fry, a Morgan scout on picket duty. Fry seized Jimmy's bag of meal and his horse, but as Fry and his comrades ate supper, the boy led his mare through a cornfield and got away. When Gillem's men were in Greeneville, they had been friendly with him, and he determined to inform them that the Rebels had come. Jim had no idea that Morgan himself was in town. All he had seen was part of Bradford's brigade on the left, and he estimated that the entire force was between 200 and 300.[24]

After dinner and just before sundown, while the men in the field were eating supper, Morgan and an aide rode into the camp on the Rogersville Road north of town. Looking confident and cheerful in an immaculate uniform with no insignia of rank, well-fitting black cavalry boots, and silver spurs, he sat comfortably on "Sir Oliver," a chestnut sorrel thoroughbred, a horse of great power and beauty given to him by an admirer after his escape from prison. It was a striking scene, the well-poised man and horse moving between tents and pausing to exchange pleasantries with groups of men, their figures outlined by the light thrown out by the bright cooking fires. Just before leaving, he called Captain Cantrill aside and said he was satisfied there was no enemy near except a few bushwhackers quartered in a cove three or four miles away. Then, with a genial smile, he wished everyone a pleasant evening, and gliding down a slope toward the road, he disappeared in the gathering twilight.[25]

Between 8:00 and 9:00 P.M., Jim Leahy rode into the Federal camp at Bulls Gap. Col. John K. Miller, one of Gillem's brigade commanders, cross-examined him, but he would not deviate from his simple, straightforward report. Miller took the boy to Gillem, and the tall West Point general listened intently and asked questions. After dismissing Jim, Gillem and Miller discussed the situation. Miller insisted upon attacking, but Gillem objected strenuously, arguing that a night movement was unconventional and dangerous. Miller reminded him that many of the men had grown up in this area and were as familiar with the roads and paths as with the hallways of their own homes. Finally, after Miller accepted responsibility for the decision, Gillem consented.[26]

They decided to divide into two columns and surround the Morgan force. At 10:00 P.M. the first column of 500 men, commanded by Lt. Col. William H. Ingerton, 13th Tennessee Cavalry, headed toward Greeneville with the object of slipping through obscure bridle paths and trails to come into position between the enemy and Greeneville. Gillem and Miller followed an hour later with the main body of over 600, advancing on the direct road. At daybreak Gillem's column was to open fire, signaling the beginning of the surprise pincers assault. The Union commanders had no idea whatsoever that Morgan's entire command of 1,500 was at Greeneville, and as far as Gillem knew, Morgan was still at his headquarters in Abingdon. If he had known the facts he would never have moved—at least not in the direction of Greeneville. This was one situation when by chance Morgan's reputation failed to intimidate his opponent and shield him from attack.[27]

At 11:00 P.M., Morgan sent out aides to inspect the picket lines. They reported all quiet, and he went to bed at midnight. Less than an hour later, a thunderstorm rolled up the valley, and rain fell in torrents. Thinking of his men in their tents and remembering the headquarters guards just outside the house, he went down and moved them inside the lower hall, where it was dry.[28]

Gillem's men were on their way when the storm began, and the night turned so dark that they had to rely on flashes of lightning to locate the road. The horses kept bumping into each other and falling in ditches; during one dark spell a lieutenant on Gillem's staff rode off a bridge and was seriously injured. No light or frolicsome conversation was heard, and as Gillem rode between two staff members, he suddenly shouted: "It is a wild-goose chase, I told you gentlemen, and Colonel Miller is responsible for it, and not me!"

They pleaded with him to lower his voice lest the men hear and become discouraged.[29]

Toward morning the rain slackened, and about seven miles from Greeneville, Gillem's videttes saw a man running from his house toward the woods. "Halt or we shoot," they screamed, and he stopped, throwing his hands in the air. When they asked where he was going at this hour, he explained that he was a Union man and had assumed they were a Confederate conscript party. He said that he had been in Greeneville the day before and learned that Morgan was at the Williams house. This was the first news Gillem's column had of Morgan's presence. Three miles from town, Mary Keenan, a black woman, hailed them from in front of her cabin with the same message. Gillem and his staff discounted both reports as rumors and proceeded as planned.[30]

In the Williams house, Maj. Charles Albert Withers, Morgan's assistant adjutant general, went into Morgan's room at 4:00 A.M. and awakened him. "It is raining, is it not?" Morgan said.

"Yes."

"Then countermand my order to move at daylight. Let the boys have time to get their guns dry. Better say seven o'clock."

Withers sent couriers with written orders to the three field commanders; in a few minutes they returned with initialed receipts, and Withers went back to bed.[31] Downstairs, Catherine had gotten up before the house servants and had breakfast underway when they awoke. When it was ready, she called at Morgan's door.

"It looks so cloudy and misty," he answered, "I think I'll wait a while, Mrs. Williams." Catherine went back to the kitchen to tell the servants the meal would be delayed.[32]

Just before daybreak, Colonel Ingerton's men moved quietly into position between Bradford's command and Greeneville, and dismounted to listen for the opening volley from the main column. Suddenly a young black man rushed up from the direction of Greeneville and demanded to see the commander. Escorted along the line to Ingerton, he said: "For God's sake get out of here as quickly as possible. General Morgan is in town, and has a force of 5,000 men, and if you do not retreat at once every one of you will be killed or captured." But instead of thinking retreat, Ingerton asked where Morgan was. "The general and his staff are sleeping at Mrs. Williams' house." Ingerton immediately sent for his best company commander, Capt. C.C. Wilcox, and ordered him to take two companies and "dash into town, surround the Williams residence and bring Morgan out dead or alive." Taking his own company and that of Capt. S.E. Northington, Wilcox galloped into town.[33]

Sunday morning was dawning, and daylight was glimmering through the drizzle and gray haze when Wilcox's blitz force charged into town in columns of four. Near the Williams house they divided, and he led twenty-five men up Main Street in front, sent another squad up Irish Street behind the house,

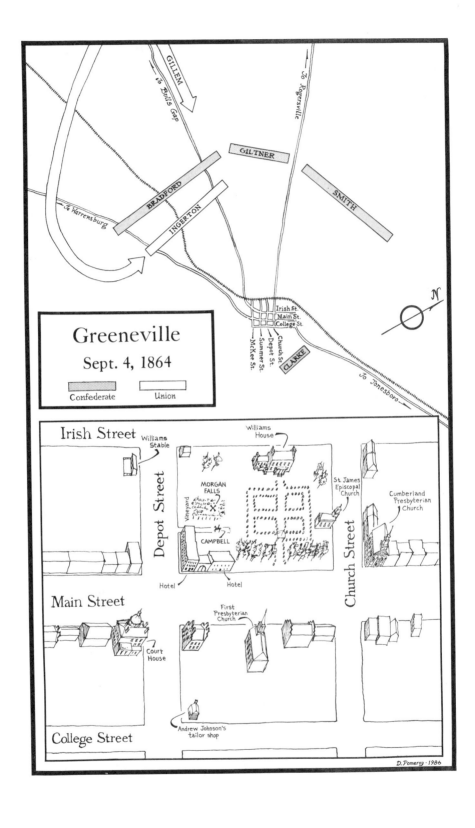

Greeneville

Sept. 4, 1864

Confederate   Union

D. Pomeroy · 1986

and another against the Williams stables on Depot Street across from the mansion. Main Street was crowded with cavalry horses, their heads turned toward the sidewalks, where their masters were asleep under porches and in doorways. Wilcox's men yelled and fired at the sleeping Rebels. Scrambling to their feet, Morgan's men shouted, "Bushwhackers! Bushwhackers! Save yourselves!" and grabbed for their horses. Some jumped on and raced away bareback; others were killed, wounded, or captured by the Federals, who turned back and began taking prisoners.

Morgan, wearing his well-worn blue overcoat, was the last one to come bounding down the stairs. Near the bottom he asked, "Where are they?"

"Everywhere," Mrs. Williams replied in despair.[34]

Pausing at the front door with his entire staff gathered around, he asked for their help in escaping. Capt. James T. Rogers said it looked impossible, as they were surrounded. "We must do it if possible," Morgan said. They ran into the front yard and scattered helter-skelter, several diving under the church building with their chief. Unable to see what was happening, he sent Withers back in the house to view the situation from the top windows. Withers soon returned, declaring that the Federals were surrounding the block as thick as they could sit on their horses. He tried to persuade Morgan to go back to the house and barricade it until the command came. "It's no use," Morgan said. "The boys can not get here in time. The Yankees will never take me prisoner again."[35]

He and three others ran across the garden to the rear of the basement of the old hotel facing Main Street, and Morgan sent Maj. C.W. Gassett to the front to reconnoiter. Suddenly a squad of Federals rode through the alley behind the hotel, and Morgan, Captain Rogers and L.T. Johnson, a clerk, ran into the vineyard to avoid being trapped in the cellar. Gassett went out the front, grabbed a stray horse, and rode away—the only staff member to escape. Withers and other aides were surrendering in different locations in the garden, but Morgan and his two companions lay motionless, concealed in the vines.[36]

Then a soldier wearing a brown jeans jacket rode up to the white picket fence around the garden. Assuming that he was a Confederate coming to the rescue, they stepped out—and to their surprise he demanded their surrender. At that moment Captain Wilcox and several others rode up. Rogers and Johnson threw up their hands and walked toward Wilcox. Morgan turned and walked the other way.[37]

The soldier in the brown jacket was Pvt. Andrew J. Campbell, now one of Wilcox's men. His evidence later described what happened next: "I, in a loud tone, ordered him to halt, but instead of obeying he started into a run. I then repeated the order, and at the same time brought my gun to my shoulder so as to cover him, when seeing that he still disregarded me, I deliberately aimed at and shot him. He dropped in his tracks and died in a few minutes. But I did not know at that time, nor even had the least idea of, who it was I had shot." Questioned as to whether Morgan returned fire or resisted in any manner, Campbell said: "To my order to halt he made no reply whatever, and seemed only intent on getting away."[38]

"Oh God!" Morgan gasped, and throwing both arms in the air, fell forward. The ball entered his back, just to the inside of the left shoulder blade, and passed through his heart and out through his left breast. In addition to his blue overcoat, he was wearing parlor slippers, blue trousers, and a white shirt with blue polkadots, a Masonic pin on the front. Suspecting from his clothing that he was an officer, Wilcox asked one of the captured staff members, Capt. Henry B. Clay (a grandson of Henry Clay, the statesman), to identify the body. Clay dropped to his knees beside Morgan, crying, "You have just killed the best man in the Confederacy."

"Who is it?" asked Wilcox.

"It is General Morgan."

"Load him on Private Campbell's horse, boys," Wilcox ordered.

"No, take him in the Williams house," Clay protested.

"My orders are to take him out, dead or alive, and as he is dead, I have no other way to take him," said the captain.[39]

The body was thrown on Campbell's horse in front of Campbell, and he rode through the streets toward Gillem's lines. By then Gillem's column and Ingerton's force had routed Bradford's brigade. Smith's and Giltner's brigades heard the firing and at first assumed that pickets were shooting their wet guns after being called in from duty. When the firing became general, however, the bugler blew "saddle up" and "assembly," and they raced to town double-quick. Coming over a rise, they saw the streets of Greeneville filled with blue uniforms, and on the hill west of town they saw Gillem's main body in a long, well-displayed battle line. One company circled to the right toward Gillem, halted, and were observing the enemy when something happened which, when they later realized what it was, chilled them to the bone every time they remembered it. Over the sound of sporadic rifle fire there arose in Gillem's line a tremendous cheer that sounded through the damp streets and wet shingles of the rooftops in the Sunday morning air. It was the greeting the Union troops gave Campbell as they made way for him, bearing Morgan's body to Gillem.[40]

Smith and Giltner veered to their left and combined with the artillery battery stationed on the Jonesboro Road, and Smith ordered the artillery, commanded by Capt. Jerome Clarke, to open on the Federals in the streets around the Williams house. Clarke, a tall, seasoned veteran at nineteen years of age, had fought bravely at Stones River, Vicksburg, and Chickamauga before wandering into camp at Decatur, Georgia, in response to Morgan's summons. In a few weeks he would desert the army and sweep across Kentucky, robbing trains and holding up stagecoaches in the most famous crime spree in the state during the war. His boyish, clean-shaven face and long, curly, reddish-brown hair contributed to the legend that he was female;

thrilled with the notoriety, he accepted the alias "Sue Mundy." A little over six months after Morgan's death, he was hanged in Louisville before a large crowd of spectators.

But all that lay in the future—in Greeneville, Clarke's battery elevated its guns and commenced throwing shells in a high arc toward the Williams house. One flew over the rooftops and hit the Cumberland Presbyterian Church on the corner just north of the Williams lot. The cannonball is still embedded in the brick above the front door of the church, and today parishioners congregating on the beautiful antique brick sidewalks of Main Street can look up and see it there, a vivid reminder of the death of the Confederate hero.

Smith ordered a mounted assault on Gillem's force, but it was quickly repulsed. Then Gillem advanced on Smith's position, and what remained of Morgan's division retreated to Jonesboro, assuming that Morgan had been captured. The Confederates had over 75 casualties and 106 taken prisoner; Gillem had 9 wounded (only one mortally) and none captured.[41]

News passed through the Union lines ahead of Campbell that Morgan was dead. "The killing of Morgan! Who told you that grapevine story?" Gillem asked. When Campbell rode up, however, Gillem congratulated him but denounced his treatment of the body. Campbell pointed out that Captain Wilcox had ordered it, based on directions from Colonel Ingerton. As it turned out, Wilcox and Ingerton, who had taken the initiative resulting in Morgan's death, were not rewarded by promotion, whereas Gillem and Campbell were. Union officials were reluctant to decorate the officers responsible for treating the dead general's body with disrespect.[42]

Gillem had the body placed on a saddle blanket under a cluster of cedar trees three-fourths of a mile from town. When the skirmishing ceased, he had it put on an artillery caisson and escorted to the Williams house, where it was laid on Lucy's bed. Lucy returned from the farm a few minutes later and helped clean the body. She went to the room Morgan had occupied and fetched a clean shirt and uniform and his ceremonial sword. "I did not know until I reached home that Gen. Morgan was killed; then the servants told me," she wrote. "God only knows how I felt when I entered my room and saw all that remained earthly of Gen. Morgan. I gazed on the calm face of the sleeper for an instant, a prayer surged from my heart to heaven, to spare my darling soldier brother from such a fate. How innocent I was that I'd be the principal sufferer. God knows my soul is not guilty, and all the malicious falsehoods of my enemies cannot make it so."[43]

Only later did Lucy become aware of how her life was changed by Morgan's death, and hers was not the only one. "How are the mighty fallen in the midst of battle," David lamented for Saul. When a famous hero like Morgan is killed, the emotional repercussions can be great. Tales went throughout the land that Lucy had betrayed Morgan by riding to Bulls Gap that Saturday afternoon to inform Gillem. "Betrayed by a Woman," the headlines read, and the emotional intensity was heightened by reports that Morgan was murdered after he surrendered, and that before he died he was dragged through the mud, placed on a mule, and paraded around town, wringing his hands and clutching his hair in pain while his captors screamed, "Here's the Kentucky horse thief."[44]

Morgan's family believed for the remainder of their lives that Lucy betrayed him and that his body was desecrated. Uncle Tom Hunt, who had retired from the service, said Morgan's death made him feel "a very strong inclination to go into Kentucky to raise troops." Eli Bruce told Mattie's father, "Suffice to say he was betrayed by a woman, and was really and truly murdered." Henrietta wrote Mattie three years after the war: "I can never be reconciled to the betrayal and a woman. Is it possible such acts of infamy are permitted to pass unpunished in this world? God grant the fiend may come to an untimely end. She has made the remnant of my days gloomy, gloomy." When Mattie mentioned that Lucy's husband had visited the Ready family, Henrietta said: "I should think Williams would be ashamed to show his face before your family. I am thoroughly disgusted with the rascality of the age."[45]

Duke visited Greeneville soon after the shooting and interviewed soldiers and citizens, but admitted in his history of the command that he could not determine the facts. He intimated that Lucy might have been involved and wrote that Morgan's friends believed he was murdered after he surrendered. Duke himself was convinced that the body was handled with shameful disrespect. Every few years during the remainder of Duke's life, the controversy was revived by publication of a fresh "eye-witness" account. In 1905 he wrote to Dick Morgan that he believed Lucy was capable of the betrayal, but he had never seen positive proof of her guilt. "I have never met any one who professed to have witnessed the actual killing, and although some have in recent years, claimed to have been ocular witnesses of it, I do not credit such statements; I believe that no one saw the death shots fired except the men who fired them."[46]

Lucy, convicted without a hearing, was ostracized from society in Greeneville. She moved to Knoxville, was divorced from her husband, and went into exile in Fort Worth, Texas. A shadow fell over the house of Catherine Williams as well. One ridiculous canard said that John and Catherine, who was old enough to be his mother, had been lovers, and when his ardor cooled and his attention shifted to another beautiful buxom widow of Greeneville, Catherine betrayed him out of jealousy. Attempting to clear her reputation, her friends wrote letters to the editors of prominent newspapers and submitted handwritten accounts to libraries.[47]

Another Greeneville woman benefited by the death. Sarah Thompson, a widow, supported herself and three children after the war by lecturing in the North on how she passed through Morgan's picket lines pursuing her milk cow and sent a boy to Bulls Gap to report Morgan's location. She claimed that her motive was vengeance—her husband J.H. Thompson had been killed on duty with the Union cavalry. It is possible that she did attempt to send word to Gillem, but at different times she contradicted herself, and supporting testimony is lacking.[48]

Gillem categorically denied that any female brought word to Bulls Gap, and he protected Leahy by never identifying him as the informant. He took Jim to Nashville and enrolled him in school at his own expense; when Jim tired of it, he was able to return home to Greeneville and live a normal life—something that would have been impossible if he had been identified in his lifetime.[49]

One mysterious fact in Morgan's death was that he was the only head-quarters officer killed. Reacting to accusations that it was murder after surrender, Gillem ordered an investigation. On the Confederate side, Gen. John Echols conducted an inquiry to ascertain whether there was misconduct or neglect on the part of Morgan's officers. Both results were negative.[50] The death was unusual not because of murder or betrayal or undue negligence, but because Morgan took an unreasonable gamble, his highest risk. At least it is satisfying to realize that he did it his way—he preferred the chance of being shot to the torment of being incarcerated and separated from Mattie for the duration, which would have been seven months.

The Federal attack was successful for several reasons. Total surprise was accomplished because the men were familiar with the terrain, made an ally of the stormy weather, used a night march for concealment, and attacked at dawn. The political sentiment of local residents encouraged civilians to inform the Federals of Morgan's location. The intelligence delivered by Leahy set the raid in motion, and its inaccuracy gave the attackers false confidence. Colonel Ingerton, acting on information provided by a citizen, modified his troop disposition in response to the enemy situation and sent the strike force to capture or kill Morgan. The surprise was complete and the expedition successful far beyond Gillem's hopes.

Morgan apparently discounted the intelligence of an experienced captain who was familiar with local conditions and had recent scouting reports. He also disregarded the pleadings of civilian friends that he spend the night in camp surrounded by his men. The major roads leading into Greeneville were picketed, and he had a small contingent at headquarters, but years of experience had demonstrated that Civil War pickets slept at their posts in the early morning hours, giving great advantage to the audacious night raider. Mosby captured Union Gen. Edwin H. Stoughton in his bedroom at Fairfax Court House. Forrest raided Gen. Stephen A. Hurlbut's headquarters in the Gayoso Hotel in Memphis and would have seized the general if he had not spent the night elsewhere. In the same raid a separate detachment attempted to capture Gen. Cadwallader C. Washburn at his mansion headquarters in the suburbs. The men became excited and broke Forrest's command of silence, alerting the general and enabling him to escape in his nightshirt, abandoning his uniform, papers, and personal effects. And Morgan had captured Colonel Boone in his hotel room and had been surprised himself at Lebanon, Tennessee.

Gillem's pending appointment as brigadier general of volunteers was immediately confirmed, and soon he was promoted to brevet major general, and later from captain to colonel in the regular army. Remaining in the military, he served in the occupation force during Reconstruction, then in Texas and California.

Three days after Morgan was killed, Andrew Campbell was promoted to first sergeant of Company G for gallantry and "success in arresting, by an accurate shot, the flight of Gen. John H. Morgan, one of our country's most prominent enemies." A month later he was commissioned first lieutenant. But he paid a price for these rewards. Not only had he deserted the Confederate army, but he had killed one of the heroes of the revolution. In May, 1865, the war was over and his old Confederate brigade came through Tennessee on the way home. With an escort he rode into their bivouac just north of Greeneville, and they hissed him out of camp. He soon mustered out, then volunteered for infantry service in Arkansas during Reconstruction. Stationed near Madison, Arkansas, he came into contact with many men from his former Confederate regiment, and they greatly resented him.[51]

One day he and other blueclad officers were drinking at a saloon in Madison when a former Rebel officer, heavier and taller than Campbell, challenged him to a wrestling match. Campbell rose to the occasion: before his antagonist realized what was happening, he was lying on his back on the floor with Campbell towering over him. Humiliated, the Rebel rose to his feet and drew a Derringer. Campbell quickly sprang on him and was wrenching the pistol from his hand when it went off, the bullet striking the Confederate's forehead. There was much bleeding, but to Campbell's relief it was only a scalp wound, and the man recovered. On May 14, 1868, Campbell resigned from the army; at last report he was living in Madison.[52]

Morgan was dead before the date set for his court of inquiry. It was postponed until September 20, when it convened in Abingdon. The transcripts were later destroyed, but extant documents reveal that some of the witnesses screened Morgan's reputation. After hearing many witnesses and compiling a large collection of documents, the three officers appointed to the court determined that several of Morgan's commissioned officers should be tried. President Davis ordered the accused to be brought before the special military court for the Department of East Tennessee, one of the tribunals established under a Confederate law passed October 9, 1862. These courts were given jurisdiction over offenses defined as crimes by civil legislation.[53]

On November 4, General Breckinridge, as departmental commander, approved the trials, and the accused came from Wytheville with their witnesses, wagons, servants, and baggage. Some time after November 19, the proceedings began. On trial the defendants no longer protected their chief but, in the words of Judge-Advocate Milton P. Jarnagin, "did not hesitate to claim unanimity under his alleged orders." In other words, they laid all the blame on Morgan. Many of the men in Morgan's command, now led by Duke, greatly resented these attacks on his reputation, and the military court incurred much ill will from local citizens and soldiers. Several individuals were found guilty and sentenced, but the trials were interrupted when Union Gen. George Stoneman's army came charging through the valley, wreaking havoc on the lead mines and saltworks, occupying Abingdon on December 14, and scattering the court, thus enabling the prisoners to escape. They had gone to Kentucky, people said. On March 20, 1865, Jarnagin turned over the records of the court of inquiry and the transcripts of the trials to General Echols, and they were filed among Confederate government papers in Salisbury, North Carolina. Almost as if he meant to disrupt investigation of the bank robberies and prevent future historians from knowing about them, Stoneman on April 12 raided Salisbury, burning several cotton factories and Confederate warehouses, one of which contained these documents.[54]

In the North, news of Morgan's death circulated widely in bold headlines. The Unionist Knoxville *Whig* screamed: "John Morgan is no more! And when he died a Thief and Coward expired." The Chicago *Tribune* stated: "John Morgan has suddenly passed unto death, much to the regret of associate horse thieves and peace sneaks." Sherman replied to the telegram informing him: "Yours with dispatch received. Good!" In Washington, a courier from the War Department rushed to the White House with the news that Morgan had been killed by Andrew Johnson's bodyguards.[55]

In the South the news of Morgan's death was overshadowed by Sherman's occupation of Atlanta two days earlier. Mrs. Chesnut was already numb: "They say General Morgan has been killed. We are hard as stones. We sit unmoved and hear any bad news change may bring. Are we stupefied?" Several published eulogies emphasized his role as a representative of chivalry and reminded everyone of the public's identification with him. "His knightly and heroic deeds will live freshly in the memories of his admiring countrymen and glow brightly on the historic page," one proclaimed. The Abingdon *Virginian* asserted: "The Confederate States have not produced a purer patriot or a more gallant and fearless leader. . . . no name will shine brighter in the glorious galaxy, as no patriot has sacrificed or suffered more."[56]

The Richmond *Enquirer* agreed: "This war has not developed a military character more complete than that of John H. Morgan, nor one who had won more upon the affectionate confidence of the great body of the people." His contribution "is familiar to the country, and will form part of the history of the war with which his name and fame have become imperishably intertwined and identified." The Richmond *Whig* also extolled the hero: "Another brave, daring and chivalric cavalier has sealed his devotion to his beloved South with his heart's blood. First Ashby, then Stuart, and now the dashing

Kentuckian, whose name was known and cherished in every clime where his country or liberty had a friend." He has "been placed upon the retired list with the heroes whose deeds of chivalry have made them immortal."[57]

A poem in the *Whig* recalled that Southern hopes had ridden with Morgan; in the future, it said, when the finger moves down the list of dead Southern heroes, "T'will pause at Morgan's first."[58] Kate Cumming wrote in her diary:

Alas! how fleeting is every thing in this world; it seems but yesterday that he took for his bride one of Tennessee's fairest daughters. She is now bereft of her all, and, like the bride of Glenullen,

> "Shall await,
> Like a love-lighted watch-fire, all night at the gate;
> A steed comes at morning; no rider is there;
> But its bridle is red with the sign of despair."

He was brave, chivalrous, and patriotic. He will never die in the hearts of his countrymen. He has fallen in a great cause—a nobler death he could not have wished for. "His spirit will walk abroad, and never rest till the great cause triumph.

Perhaps it was symbolic of Morgan's renegade independence that he was killed while leading an offensive at a time when he had been suspended from command. His disregard for military regulations and international law had contributed to demoralization and dissension in his division. One of his field commanders at Greeneville, Colonel Giltner, was among the group of officers demanding an investigation. Jim Leahy's report to Gillem set in motion the chain of events leading to Morgan's death. Fortunately for Gillem, Jim's report underestimated the Rebel force and did not include the news that Morgan was present; therefore, the Morgan legend did not come into play, and Gillem was spared the Morgan jitters. But the foray would probably not have resulted in Morgan's death without the young black man's warning to Colonel Ingerton that Morgan and his entire force was in town.

Still, after all was said and done, the surprise encroachment at headquarters did not mean that John had to die. The key to the mystery of his death is that he gambled his life on escape, rather than surrender and risk being returned to a felon's cell and separated indefinitely from Mattie.

TWENTY

Hero of the Lost Cause

The undertaker in Greeneville embalmed Morgan's body, but it would not come to rest in the Lexington Cemetery for nearly four years. Meanwhile, as a Southern folk hero, he was honored with three funerals: one in Abingdon for Mattie and his men, another in Richmond for the Confederate nation, and a third in Lexington for his hometown and the state of Kentucky. By the time he was laid under the bluegrass, he was being deified as a local symbol of the Lost Cause, uniting more Kentuckians under a banner of nostalgic hero worship than he was able to do in life.

Mattie first learned of John's death in the afternoon of the day he was killed, when she received the following telegram:

Headquarters Brigade, Near Rheatown, Tenn., September 4, 1864.

Mrs. General Morgan, Abingdon, Va.

With deep sorrow I have to announce the sad intelligence of your husband's death. He fell by the hands of the enemy, at Greenville [*sic*], this morning. His remains are being brought away under flag of truce. We all mourn with you in this great affliction. Most respectfully,

H.L. Giltner,
Colonel Commanding Brigade.[1]

The next day it was confirmed when Maj. D.H. Llewellyn called at Acklin in person with a wire he had received from Duke: "The General is dead. His body is being brought in by Flag of Truce Party. Break the news to his wife."[2]

In Greeneville, Catherine and Lucy Williams and their servants clothed Morgan's body in his dress uniform and placed it in a walnut coffin in the Williams parlor. Confederate Capt. John J. McAfee found the room filled with women, both Union and Confederate, "all very deeply affected, and seeming, without distinction, to deplore his fall." This was something people noticed wherever Morgan's body was displayed; a remarkable number of women came to mourn his death. A crowd of spectators stood in front of the house and lined both sides of Main Street as McAfee's men carried the coffin out the front door and put it on a small one-horse wagon. As the procession slowly started off, a woman stepped out and handed McAfee a beautiful black velvet drape to cover the coffin.[3]

A few miles east of Greeneville the escort reunited with Morgan's command, and they fell in column and trudged along in double file, with leaden gait. When they reached the railroad station in Jonesboro, the coffin was opened for Basil Duke to view the body. Looking down at the earthly remains of his beloved brother-in-law and best friend, countless memories of generosity, kindness, and warm friendship filled his mind, and he burst into tears, weeping openly. Men who had suppressed their emotions thus far were overcome and gave vent to their grief. "Surely men never grieved for a leader as Morgan's men sorrowed for him," Duke wrote. "The tears which scalded the cheeks of hardy and rugged veterans, who had witnessed all the terrible scenes of four years of war, attested it, and the sad faces told of the aching hearts within."[4]

After dark on Monday, September 5, the little wagon bearing Morgan's body turned from the macadam road into the lane in the expansive front lawn of Acklin. His coffin was set in the parlor, and hundreds of people came through to gaze upon his face and offer condolences to Mattie, Tommy and Basil Duke, and Key Morgan.[5]

The next afternoon at four o'clock Morgan's chaplain, S.P. Cameron, officiated at funeral services held at Saint Thomas Episcopal Church, and Gen. George B. Crittenden directed the largest and most imposing funeral procession there had ever been in southwest Virginia. Unarmed honor guards on horseback rode on each side of the hearse, and behind the family carriage Morgan's men followed in a long-mounted train, two by two. Dark masses of clouds rose in the west and darkened the sun just as the coffin was being placed in an above ground vault in Sinking Spring Cemetery.[6]

As far as Mattie was concerned, John had been given a proper burial, and she would not attend the other two funerals. But she agreed that the identification of the people of the South with John was so powerful the nation should have the opportunity of giving him a state funeral. The body would be laid in a vault in Hollywood Cemetery in Richmond until peacetime, when it could be returned to Kentucky. Nevertheless, even if she had wanted to accompany Morgan's body to Richmond, she was physically unable. She was two months pregnant, and the shock and grief of John's death threatened her health. The priority was to save John's precious baby.[7]

Cal Morgan assumed the responsibility of escorting the remains to Richmond, and nine days later he made the journey. He meant to reach the city in the early evening that Thursday and have the body lie in state overnight in the capitol. But an accident on the Danville Railroad delayed the train, and it did not arrive until ten o'clock Friday morning. At the depot was a band, a battalion of State Guard troops, a fire brigade, the Kentucky delegation in Congress, and Mayor Mayo. A hearse drawn by four gray horses led the procession to the Confederate House of Representatives, where Morgan lay in state for two hours, his coffin draped with a Confederate flag. A multitude of citizens and soldiers congregated in the rotunda, and when the doors were opened, they filed by slowly. An unusual number of women came; many brought wreaths and fresh cut flowers and laid them on the casket as they passed.[8]

The Hustings Court of Richmond adjourned for the day and gathered at the capitol wearing the customary badge of mourning over the loss of a man who "after filling numerous and arduous posts of duty to his country, has fallen as became a valiant soldier in the Country's cause." They joined Secretary Seddon, Governor William Smith, Mayor Mayo, the city council, and the honor guard in the procession to Hollywood Cemetery. President Davis was conspicuous by his absence, but he was certainly consistent: he had missed Morgan's wedding, his reception in Richmond, and now his funeral. Before they reached the burial ground, the soldiers were withdrawn to reinforce pickets driven in by a Yankee incursion at Chaffin's Farm. The rear of the column closed up; under the grand oak trees overlooking the James River, with Rev. George Patterson, army chaplain and Episcopal minister, officiating, the body was placed in the vault of W.W. Dunnavant of Richmond.[9]

About that time, in Lexington, Henrietta Morgan sat at her writing table with a heavy heart. "The blow seemed, for a time, more than I could bear up under, cut off as I was, from all my props," she wrote Cal. "God seems to have fitted our backs to the burdens, the weight of mine is getting very heavy." With one son buried in a garden in Lebanon, another lying in a tomb in Richmond, and the rest in prison camps and scattered abroad, her motherly love swelled up: "I wish I could gather you all up and away to some far off place, where there was no wars or rumors of wars. Excuse me, my dear boy, my heart is nearly broken. I live in hourly dread of some other calamity."[10]

Mattie sojourned in Augusta, Georgia, for her lying-in, and the baby was a healthy girl who was named Johnnie, for her father. Several months later, after the war ended and they went home to Murfreesboro, Mattie wrote: "She has indeed proved a blessing to me direct from God, and the only happiness I look forward to in future is that of rearing her. She is said to be a perfect little Morgan in appearance." In December, 1865, she took Johnnie to Lexington for a visit and for the next several years corresponded regularly with Henrietta.[11]

In the fall of 1867, the Morgan family began making plans to remove the bodies of John and Tom to Lexington. Henrietta was particularly bothered by the fact that Tom was lying in the private property of a stranger, but she wanted both of them buried in the Hunt-Morgan plot, side by side, at the same time. They talked it over and decided that since John had been buried with all rites and honors performed by Confederate friends and was in a proper cemetery, they would not move him until spring. His many admirers would want to pay their respects, and if the ceremonies were scheduled in the winter, inclement weather might preclude that. Tom was brought to

Lexington on March 21, 1868, and placed temporarily in a vault, and Cal began making arrangements to move John in April.[12]

On schedule, Cal went to Richmond and at noon on Saturday, April 11, 1868, met at City Hall with Kentuckians who agreed to form a committee of escort. He went to the cemetery with a local undertaker, and they transferred the body to a metallic case in a new walnut casket. Cal commented that the body was well preserved and looked perfectly natural.[13]

Morgan's women admirers in Richmond had visited his vault regularly, keeping it decorated with fresh flowers. When the remains were borne away on Wednesday morning, April 15, his friends were saddened that "all that remains of the most attractive tenant of Hollywood" was leaving. Nature seemed to join in the final tribute, the trees assuming their new green livery, the grass growing, and the spring flowers adding color to the scene in honor of the "knightliest horseman who ever drew sword to guard his own and his country's honor," said a reporter for the Richmond *Enquirer and Examiner.*[14]

Draped in black velvet, the bier was taken by the committee of Kentuckians by water to Washington, D.C., where the Kentucky delegation in Congress received them at the wharf. Fortunately, the news was filled with the impeachment trial of President Andrew Johnson in the Senate and with Johnson's dedication of a new statue of Lincoln on this third anniversary of Lincoln's death; Cal and the Kentuckians were able to honor John without causing an incident or producing controversial publicity. The body was quietly escorted to the depot of the Baltimore and Ohio Railroad and placed on a train, generating only brief notices in the local newspapers.[15]

When the train arrived at the Little Miami Railroad depot in Cincinnati at 7:00 A.M. the next day, a committee of northern Kentuckians was waiting on the platform. Several former members of Morgan's staff lived in northern Kentucky, and plans had been made to give them and other friends of Morgan an opportunity to pay their respects. Cal had insisted that a private residence be used to display the body because a public exhibition might stir up controversy. Local Confederate veterans selected Landford Place, the Covington home of Mrs. Charles Albert Withers, Sr., the mother of Morgan's last adjutant.

At Landford Place on Sanford Street, between Sixth and Seventh Streets, the coffin was placed in the parlor on an elaborate catafalque under a tent of black material, but when they opened it, the smell forced them to close it immediately. It was covered with flowers, and friends came throughout the day, greatly disappointed at not being able to see the remains. Albert Withers and seven other former staff members sat up all night with the body, and at 6:00 A.M., Friday, April 17, the casket was removed to the Kentucky Central Railroad depot and put on display in a baggage car. Pausing at stations along the route to Lexington, the conductor waited for crowds of spectators to view the bier, wreathed with flowers and crowned with crossed swords.[16]

At an early hour, Lexington was crowded with people from Fayette and surrounding counties, and strangers who had arrived on trains throughout the night. Between eighty and ninety of Morgan's "Old Squadron" were present and delegations came from Indiana, Ohio, and Virginia. The hotels were full, carriages lined the principal streets, and business was brisk in the shops. Not since Morgan's triumphal entry in September, 1862, had the city been this congested—the charm of the Morgan legend still had the power to attract the multitudes.[17]

Mattie and Johnnie were not present, but Henrietta and her family accompanied the Lexington committee of arrangements to the station to meet the train at 11:10 A.M. Charlton's wife, Nellie, stepped forward and laid a cross-shaped spray of red and white carnations on the coffin, which was then placed in a black-plumed hearse garlanded with evergreens and drawn by two gray horses. Meanwhile, on Main Street in front of the Phoenix Hotel, the Old Squadron formed in double file. Tom Quirk and Tom Hines were present, as were D. Howard Smith and W.C.P. Breckinridge. They marched to Christ Church and at the entrance welcomed their commander.[18]

Long before the service was to begin, groups of women, accompanied by an occasional man, started filing into the church. By 11:00 A.M. all the pews, except those reserved, were filled to utmost capacity. Hardly one-tenth of the gathering throng gained entrance; the remainder stood outside, clogging the streets and making them almost impassable. Duke and his wife Tommy came in with Henrietta and the family. Kirby Smith and William Preston were among the pallbearers who brought the coffin down the lengthy center aisle and posited it in the chancel before the altar. The people seemed to join in a spirit of unity in which even the historic rivalry between Lexington and Louisville was laid aside for a moment: from a front pew six young girls stepped out and placed six wreaths on top of the many arrangements already in place; one of the wreaths was from the city of Louisville and one from Lexington. The chaste beauty of the sanctuary, with its graceful stained glass windows and simple, wide ceiling lent Gothic elegance to the occasion—on one level a funeral for Morgan, but in a broader sense a romantic farewell to a lost world gone forever, the civilization of the Old South.[19]

Henrietta was greatly impressed with the large number of bouquets from distant friends she had never seen. The Southern women of Lexington had welcomed Morgan in 1862 with red and white ribbons on their bonnets; now they decorated his flower arrangements with red and white streamers. Henrietta was particularly moved by the devotion of the mother of one of Morgan's men who took two weeks from teaching school to make a cross of wax flowers, "the most superb" Henrietta had ever seen.[20]

The choir sang "Guide Me, O Thou Great Jehovah"; then, following a brief oration by Rector Jacob Shipman, the body was borne out during the singing of "Peace Troubled Soul." Outside, the mass of spectators watched the cortege form in front of the church on Market Street at noon. First came the committee of arrangements, then a brass band, followed by the Masonic fraternity, clergy, pallbearers, hearse, family carriages, the Old Squadron walking two by two, other members of Morgan's cavalry in double file on horseback, and about 2,000 citizens in carriages and on foot. Along the route down Limestone to Main and west on Main, many of the stores were closed, and the streets were filled with sad-faced people closely packed on every sidewalk, in each window and doorway, and on the balconies.[21]

Henrietta thought of Mattie: "Your heart would have been satisfied with the spontaneous manifestations of love and respect," she wrote. "His blessed spirit seemed to preside over the weather. Since April it was boisterous. Friday was a heavenly day. The sun shone out in all his glory. All nature seemed in repose. Occasionally the wind would wail as if in lamentation over the departed."[22]

The solemn parade turned into the cemetery, already green with grass and gemmed here and there with the first frail spring flowers. At one of the winding drives they met pallbearers with Tom's body, and the two brothers were reunited after nearly four years and borne side by side to their double grave. Passing near the monument of Henry Clay, the procession moved quietly to the Hunt-Morgan section, where the graves of children and grand-children were gathered in neat circles around Catherine and John Wesley Hunt. The crowd closed around, almost extending across the narrow lane to the Bruce plot, where Becky Morgan and her son were buried. The mounted cavalry from Morgan's command sat their horses in a circle at the back of the throng, and when the choir sang "I Heard a Voice from Heaven," accompanied by a cornet from the band, men who had never wept in battle sobbed openly over their dead chief.[23]

Rector Shipman spoke briefly, followed by the Baptist minister, and the Masons performed their burial rite. Finally, several women heaped wreaths on the two mounds of fresh earth, and on top of John's someone laid an arrangement with a small Confederate flag attached. It was the only obvious display of Rebel sentiment all day. Some out-of-state newsmen had expected a "vehement and rebellious demonstration," but all was tranquil—no cat-calls, taunts, or yells; no bitterness or bravado. Many Union veterans, some of whom had fought Morgan, marched in the cortege. Everyone seemed bound together in sincere regret, and it was as if the dreadful years of conflict had never occurred; "all is changed," wrote a reporter, "and it appears as if he had lived in another country." Another said: "Even now an air of romance surrounds his forays, and friend and foe begin to speak softly and gently of Morgan."[24]

And another commentator was certain that "whatever may be said of the right or wrong of the 'Lost Cause,'" no one could question the motives of those who carried its banner. The phrase "Lost Cause," which had come into use soon after Appomattox, was used to perpetuate the Confederate ideal. It was apparently an identification with the lost cause of Scotland in its struggle for independence, as described in the romantic writing of Sir Walter Scott.

Edward Pollard's 1866 history of the war from the Southern view used the title *The Lost Cause*.[25]

The meaning of the term has always been nebulous. In *God and General Longstreet: The Lost Cause and the Southern Mind*, Thomas L. Connelly and Barbara L. Bellows distinguish between the Inner Lost Cause and the National Lost Cause. The former represents the efforts of diehard former Rebels to justify secession and rationalize Confederate defeat. The latter is the timeless identification with the romantic legend on the Old South and the perpetuation of the memory of Southern defeat.[26]

Proponents of the Inner Lost Cause held reunions, published veterans' magazines, and erected monuments in courthouse squares. Seeking to appease their frustrations and adjust to the calamity and alienation of defeat, they asserted their moral superiority. Their basic theme was that Southerners, as Christian knights, never departed from the tactics of chivalrous gentlemen in fighting the churlish Yankee hordes; the South had had the morally superior leaders, as symbolized by the number one hero of the Inner Lost Cause—the saintly Robert E. Lee.[27]

Basil Duke was a prominent spokesman of the Inner Lost Cause movement. In his *History of Morgan's Cavalry* (1867) he blamed the Confederate defeat on Davis's defensive strategy and failure to inspire the people. Duke condemned Bragg for losing the best opportunity to liberate Kentucky during the 1862 invasion of the state. Kentuckians who had fought for either side had emerged with honor, he wrote, but the dignity of the Commonwealth had been sacrificed by the avarice and cowardice of those who remained uncommitted and fought for neither side.

Duke admitted that Morgan was no saint, that some of his men committed inexcusable excesses on the Last Kentucky Raid, and that some deserted to become outlaws at the close of the expedition. He conceded that Morgan's men shot pickets early in the war and mentioned double-quicking the prisoners of war from Lebanon to Springfield on the Great Raid. He discussed at least ten occasions when Morgan deceived the enemy by masquerading as a Union officer. But Duke's popular and influential book omitted the atrocities on the prisoners of war in Gallatin in 1862 and the robbery of prisoners and civilians on the Great Raid. It described the pillage in Indiana and Ohio but left out the search of banks and courthouses for government funds and the ransom of gristmills. Neither did Duke discuss the bank robberies on the Last Kentucky Raid, or Morgan's policy of retaliation, or the decoying of the steamboat on the Ohio River at Brandenburg.

Duke deflected charges that Morgan's men committed atrocities and stole from Union prisoners as unfounded wartime accusations. He denied that the bummers in the command were characteristic of the men in general, and he refused to admit that the command violated flags of truce. Duke denounced what he called the Yankee accusation that Morgan was a guerrilla chief whose men committed "Guerilla outrages." "Guerrilla" had become a very unpopular expression in Kentucky; it had come to mean the lowest form of cowardly deserter, villain, and marauder. To be called a guerrilla in the post–Civil War era was to be associated with the despicable jetsam of the war who specialized in the depravity of intimidation, whipping, robbing, raping, and murdering.[28]

Understandably, then, Duke stressed that Morgan was a regularly commissioned officer and avoided interpreting Morgan's strategy and tactics from the point of view of classic guerrilla warfare. Furthermore, Duke did not understand the strategy of attrition. He believed in Morgan's attempts to stir revolution in Kentucky and his pacification of Union provost marshals, and in describing Morgan's tactics and strategy he defined the pattern of partisan or guerrilla warfare, but he evaluated Morgan's contribution from the viewpoint of the strategy of annihilation. He was in the mainstream of Civil War strategists, but it caused him to fall short of a full and realistic appreciation of Morgan's role. To interpret Morgan strictly in terms of the strategy of annihilation was to isolate much of his contribution and make him seem far less significant than he was. Subsequent biographers followed Duke's leadership, and the prejudice against the term "guerrilla" precluded meaningful and comprehensive evaluation of Morgan's role.

Duke's book is significant as well in that, like Morgan's funeral, it reflected and contributed to the spirit of reconciliation in Kentucky at the close of the war. During the final months of fighting, a majority of the people became greatly disaffected with the Union and in sympathy turned to the South. Slaveowners despised Burbridge's successor, John M. Palmer, for using his authority to free the slaves in Kentucky. Many opposed the Thirteenth Amendment, which the General Assembly rejected, and citizens protested continuing violations of their constitutional rights and the enlistment of blacks in the Union army. Once peace came, Kentuckians who had been unwilling to fight for the Confederacy felt most comfortable uniting with the South in the Inner Lost Cause. Morgan had always over-estimated Southern sentiment in the state, but in truth this feeling was gaining strength by the time of the Last Kentucky Raid. Most of the voters went Democratic in the election of 1864, when McClellan carried Kentucky 61,478 votes to Lincoln's 26,592. The Democratic Party had gained control of the state by the end of the war, and when the Confederate veterans came home, they seized control of the party.[29]

The state legislature quickly removed restrictions on former Rebels, and the majority of citizens supported them for political office. D. Howard Smith wrote on December 26, 1865: "Indeed the feeling is so strong where I have been with all *true* Democrats, that a large majority of them, or at least of those I have heard talk, say that they will not vote for any man, for the future, if they can help it, who has not seen service in the Confederate army." In many communities former Confederates were glorified. "Any one can discover," a pundit wrote, "with half an eye, that the returned rebels are the pets of the people—are the elite, the lions." D. Howard Smith was elected state auditor on the Democratic ticket, and during his campaign a diehard Unionist protested: "Everywhere avowed rebels are elected to office, and they even propose now to give to one of Morgan's men the most lucrative office in the state, in consideration, we suppose, of his distinguished services in tearing up our railroads, burning our property, and killing men who were defending the State Government under which he proposes to hold office."[30]

Thomas Hines was elected county judge in Warren County and eventually justice of the state supreme court. W.C.P. Breckinridge and other Morgan veterans openly appealed to the voters on the basis of having served as Morgan's men. Ralph Sheldon, one of the escapees from the Columbus penitentiary, was elected registrar of the land office. William J. Stone, who lost a leg fighting under Morgan, was elected speaker of the state House of Representatives, and served in the United States House of Representatives. James B. McCreary, an officer on Morgan's staff from Madison County, was elected to the Kentucky house in 1869, served as house speaker (1871–74), and in 1875 defeated Union veteran John M. Harlan for governor. Then he served as United States congressman and senator, and in 1911 was elected governor for a second time.[31]

Having failed to liberate Kentucky from the Yankee Republican Party with minie balls and artillery shells, Morgan's men had taken the state by storm with ballots.

Cal and Dick Morgan opened a hemp factory in Lexington; Charlton Morgan moved from job to job in government and business; Key Morgan became a clerk for grain dealers and other wholesale merchants in Lexington. Ironically, Basil Duke became the chief counsel and lobbyist for the L&N, which was attempting to achieve a monopoly in the South and needed a symbol of the Inner Lost Cause for public relations with former Confederates. With his goatee and mustache, magnetic charm, gracious manners, and reputation as second in command to Morgan, he succeeded marvelously in the role for twenty years.[32]

Thus, in politics and business Morgan's men were beneficiaries of Kentucky's identification with the Inner Lost Cause. Southerners in general created the nostalgic cult of the heroic Confederate soldier. "Every boy growing up in this land now had continually before his eyes the vision," wrote W.J. Cash, "and heard always in his ears the clamorous hoofbeats, of a glorious swashbuckler, compounded of Jeb Stuart, the golden-locked Pickett, and the sudden and terrible Forrest . . . forever charging the cannon's mouth with the Southern battle flag."[33]

Many adherents of the Inner Lost Cause idolized Morgan. Annie Barnwell Morton of Beaufort, South Carolina, published a poem elevating "The Old Jacket of Gray" of one of Morgan's men to the status of holy relic. In one verse she declared:

Though the cause we loved is a "Lost Cause" still
It lives in hearts that will ever thrill
At sight of the gray, though no more will
John Morgan be leading the way.[34]

When the young boys of Lexington played war, they pretended to fight Morgan raids. On one July 4th evening soon after the war, a squad of little tykes marched by Hopemont bearing a flag with a single star, and as they passed, Henrietta heard them giving three cheers for Jeff Davis and three for John Morgan. A Louisville reporter at Morgan's funeral predicted that his name would rise from the grave and be perpetuated in sweetest song from the lips of children: "The knightly horseman will be the first picture which the father will paint for his boy, and the strongest example to urge manhood to honorable action."[35]

A Lexington journalist repeated the chivalrous refrain: "He rides down into history a knight of noblest mien and knightliest grace, an equal and worthy companion of Sidney, Bayard, Harry Lee, Stuart," and other heroes. Morgan was portrayed as a great man whose courage had rarely been equaled and who was never surpassed in the history of chivalrous warfare.[36] A citizen of Louisville published a poem lauding him as the most noble knight in history and forecasting his immortality:

Although no marble column rise,
    Above the hero's bed,
To mark the spot where Morgan lies,
    Among the honored dead;
Although no sculptured stone shall tell,
    The stranger passing by
The mournful story how he fell,
    His name will never die;
For glory with a jealous care,
Shall guard the hero resting there.[37]

Southerners proclaimed their view in magazines such as the *Southern Bivouac* (1885–87), edited by Duke, and in eloquent addresses delivered at countless local reunions of their old brigades. The first encampment for the entire South was the 1889 organizational meeting of the United Confederate Veterans, held in New Orleans. In 1895 the United Daughters of the Confederacy was established at a convention in Atlanta. The first reunion of Morgan's men was held at the Phoenix Hotel on the evening of his burial. The men pledged fidelity and affection for each other for as long as they lived and resolved "that the memory of our illustrious and beloved leader shall ever be as indelibly stamped upon the tablets of our hearts as his name is written on the undying page of History."[38]

They met thereafter every few years, at least until 1927. In 1871, the year Smith was reelected state auditor the first time, he invited them to Frankfort and served as chairman. In 1898 they gathered in Cincinnati as guests of the 7th Ohio Cavalry. But the most memorable of all was the camp in Lexington in 1883 on the twentieth anniversary of the Great Raid. For three days (July 24-26) 300 delegates met at Woodland Park. They had a band, and from the state arsenal they requisitioned two cannon to fire salutes at sunrise and sunset. On Friday, July 24, at 2:00 P.M., the public attended a grand ceremony and heard speeches by Duke, William Preston, and former Governor McCreary. The center of attention, however, was Morgan's eighteen-year-old daugher, Johnnie.[39]

Mattie had eventually married Judge James Williamson of Lebanon, Tennessee, and they reared Johnnie and their own two sons and two daughters. During the reunion Johnnie stayed at Hopemont with her grandmother, and at the meetings she was the pet of the command. "She is a very beautiful girl, sprightly and accomplished," a reporter said. The men gave her a gold watch, and at the public ceremony, when McCreary asked if she had anything to say, she whispered, "Governor, just tell them I love them, and how glad I am to see them." He asked if she would enjoy shaking hands with the men, and with tears in her eyes, she exclaimed, "Indeed I would."[40]

The occasion was a highlight in Johnnie's life. Four years later, when she was twenty-two, her mother became seriously ill, and for several months Johnnie remained by her side, tenderly caring for her until her death in the fall of 1887 at the age of forty-six. On May 1, 1888, when she was twenty-three, Johnnie married Rev. Joseph W. Caldwell, a Presbyterian minister from Selma, Alabama. A few weeks after the wedding, Caldwell went to London, England, as a delegate to the Pan-Presbyterian Council, and about the first of July Johnnie died of typhoid fever—leaving no direct descendants of John Hunt Morgan.[41]

Morgan's men collected postcards of his portrait, of Henrietta's photograph in front of Hopemont, and of a reprint of Paul Hamilton Hayne's poem, "The Kentucky Partisan." When they marched through the cemetery to bury a comrade in the Confederate section, they would bare their heads as they passed Morgan's grave. Friends and family kept the grave covered with fresh flowers for several years. The cemetery, with a steady succession of flowering cherry trees, magnolias, crab apples, and dogwood, followed by various shrubs and flowers, is one of the most beautiful in the United States. "My graves," wrote Henrietta, "are all the while covered with beautiful flowers. I was out last evening. It is the loveliest spot on earth. Everything is beautiful perfection." When Johnnie was still a young child, Henrietta invited her for a visit: "We can go to the beautiful cemetery so full of bloom and see where your precious father and dear Uncle rest, all covered with sweet flowers. You must have a little basket to carry your blossoms to strew on the graves."[42]

By the turn of the century the frustrations of the Confederate veterans had lessened and their attitudes softened. Their hair turned white, the Rebel yell at the encampments grew hoarse and weak, and many were tottering around with walking canes. The generation of the Inner Lost Cause was passing; the movement was fading into the National Lost Cause. The latter includes such manifestations as the popularity of the Confederate flag, the playing of "Dixie" at high school and university athletic contests, and Grandpa Jones singing "Are You from Dixie?" at the Grand Ole Opry.[43]

When Frank G. Rankin was growing up in Louisville early in the twentieth century, his father introduced him to Basil Duke and other veterans. "I was a boy at the time that John Hunt Morgan still lived fresh in the memory of the Morgan men," Rankin said. "Confederate reunions were the most exciting occasions that an impressionable boy could conjure up in the wildest flights of imagination." To young Frank, Morgan was a "peerless cavalier," third only to Lee and George Washington. He eagerly memorized a verse his Aunt Priscilla taught him:

> I wanted to be a cavalryman
> And with John Hunt Morgan ride,
> A Colt revolver in my belt
> A sabre by my side.
> I wanted a pair of epaulets
> To match my suit of gray,
> The uniform my mother made
> And lettered C.S.A.[44]

And countless other schoolboys stood at the front of their class proclaiming from memory:

> I'm sent to warn the neighbors, he's only
> a mile behind;
> He's sweeping up the horses, every horse
> that he can find.
> Morgan, Morgan, the raider, and Morgan's
> terrible men,
> With Bowie knives and pistols are galloping
> up the glen.[45]

People never forgot that Morgan's men took their horses, but upon the passing of the Civil War generation, the robbing of banks and other depredations were seldom mentioned—it was as if they had never happened. Along with other Lost Cause apologists throughout the South, Southerners in Lexington took it upon themselves to see that the children were taught properly. In 1908 the Lexington school board gave in to the pressure of Confederate veterans and censored a sixth-grade history textbook because it described looting of private property on the Great Raid. Duke published a second edition of his history in 1906, a third in 1909, and by popular demand, *Reminiscences of General Basil W. Duke, C.S.A.* in 1911.[46]

In 1906 the Kentucky United Daughters of the Confederacy resolved to erect an equestrian statue of Morgan in Lexington. A committee was appointed to raise funds and select a sculptor. After reviewing models by fourteen artists, they commissioned Pompeo Coppini, an Italian-born sculptor living in San Antonio. Coppini erected a studio on Bellaire Avenue off West Sixth Street and visited Fayette County horse farms to study Kentucky thoroughbreds. The committee made it clear that Morgan's most famous horse was Black Bess, a mare. But Coppini convinced the committee that a mare would appear too small for a statue of heroic proportions and reminded them that after Morgan lost Bess in the Lebanon Races, he had ridden a stallion or a gelding. The statue cost over $15,000, and when the Daughters were unable to raise it all, the Kentucky legislature appropriated $7,500 to complete the work.

The unveiling on October 18, 1911, was a gala event, complete with a parade on Main Street with Duke and other men on horseback, marching bands from Lexington and Louisville, and Union and Confederate veterans and their sons and daughters walking and riding in nearly a hundred carriages and automobiles. The procession ended at the courthouse, where a raised platform had been built and bleachers erected on Upper Street for the family and special guests. Some 10,000 people jammed the square, and spectators leaned from the windows and stood on top of buildings to view the unveiling. Duke presided, and Dick and Charlton Morgan were present, as were Tommy and Kitty. Gov. Augustus E. Willson was among the speakers. Large Confederate flags were carried in the parade, and a chorus of school children arranged in the shape of the Stars and Bars sang "Dixie" and the "Star-Spangled Banner." When the ribbons were cut and the statue revealed, the enthusiastic crowd gave a mighty cheer.

But over the years fans of Black Bess refused to be comforted. A legend developed that the public had expected a mare and that at the unveiling the crowd reacted with groans and curses. For many years Lexington college students have sneaked onto the courthouse lawn late at night to paint the offending portion of the horse's anatomy in outlandish colors.[47]

Morgan's pistols, razor, and other personal effects became collector's items. Mattie tried for months to retrieve his toothbrush, Masonic pin, and boots; all she found were the boots, defiled by the feet of some Union soldier who had worn them. When Morgan surrendered on the Great Raid, he gave his fancy bridle to Charley Maus of the Ohio militia. It passed down in the family to Alice Burnett, who gave it to President Franklin D. Roosevelt for his birthday in 1934. In August, 1959, a towboat broke apart Dam 44 at Leavenworth on the Ohio River, causing the water to drop about five feet and exposing part of the hull of the *Alice Dean*. Morgan buffs from Harrison County, Indiana, went out with axes, collected several pieces of the white oak hull, and made them into attractive little plaques, authentic relics of the Great Raid.[48]

During World War II a reader of the Lexington *Herald* wrote the editor that since, in his opinion, Morgan fought for the same kind of slavery as Hitler, the statue at the courthouse should be melted down for scrap metal. A flurry of rebuttals came in: one said the statue "stands as a symbol of those intrepid heros who fought and died, or suffered worse, for the 'native green hills of their Fatherland'; theirs alone is 'the Bivouac of the Dead.' Take away the symbol of the hero of the past and there is no incentive for the future. When did we ever need it more than today?"[49]

During the Korean War, WLW Radio in Cincinnati featured Morgan in a broadcast of its *Our America* series of dramatizations. On the battlefields of South Korea, the 623rd Field Artillery Battalion of the Kentucky National Guard bore a coat of arms from the army's heraldic branch identifying it as Morgan's Men. Their official motto, "Seize the Opportunity," indicated their determination to perform feats like Morgan's raiders.[50]

The Kentucky Historical Society began its popular program of erecting highway markers in 1949. As of 1983 approximately 1,420 sites had been marked, and people were so interested in identifying locations relating to Morgan's raids that his name appears more often than any other—at least seventy times, twice as many as Abraham Lincoln or Daniel Boone. East of Abingdon the overpass crossing the Norfolk-Southern Railway is named the John Hunt Morgan Memorial Bridge. The Red Mile harness racing track in Lexington has a John Hunt Morgan race. John B. Jett of Taylor Mill, Kentucky, dresses as Morgan and leads the Second Kentucky Cavalry Civil War Reenactment group on parades and displays each summer.[51]

In the mid-1950s Don D. John, proprietor of a bookshop in Louisville, collected information for his proposed five volumes of the annals of Morgan and his men. He dreamed of publishing a day-by-day account of Morgan's career and a brief biographical sketch of every man who served under him. Probably not more than 6,000 men actually fought with Morgan, but John's mailbox was flooded with over 12,000 names; it seemed that nearly everyone wanted to nominate his grandfather as one of Morgan's raiders. In May, 1983, Mark Harris, director of the Kentucky division of the Louisville Free Public Library, commented in an interview that many whose kinsmen fought for the Confederacy believe that Morgan was their leader. "If everybody's granddaddy who fought with Morgan really did, the South would have won the war," Harris remarked.[52]

It was truly remarkable that Morgan's funeral in Lexington, only three years after the war, occurred without a single unpleasant incident. Less than six years before, when his command was bearing down on the city during the First Kentucky Raid, he was such a threatening and divisive figure that Henrietta had to be evacuated for her safety. The funeral was a unity feast, symbolizing the reuniting of families torn asunder by the issue of secession and signifying that the bitter heritage of the past was blotted from memory. In a spirit of conciliation and forgiveness, both Union and Confederate veterans marched in the funeral cortege; the people united under the banner of the Lost Cause; and Morgan's men and other Confederate veterans seized political control of the state, twice electing one of Morgan's officers governor.

In Virginia and throughout the nation, the cult of the Lost Cause canonized Robert E. Lee as the perfect symbol of the supposed moral superiority of Confederate leadership. In Kentucky, admirers of Morgan transformed him into a conventional cavalry officer and a gallant, intrepid cavalier.

Actually, the Morgan legend current in the Civil War, with all its mythical embellishments, was closer to the truth. In Morgan's character several of the weaknesses and strengths of the Old South civilization stood out in exaggerated relief, probably as clearly as in any other individual. To the people of the Confederacy, he was always John Hunt Morgan, folk hero and great revolutionary guerrilla chief.

NOTES

Abbreviations

Manuscript Collections

BGTHP-HMH	Blue Grass Trust for Historic Preservation, Hunt-Morgan House, Lexington
CCMC-FC	Calvin C. Morgan & Co. Papers, Filson Club Library, Louisville
DMFP-SHC	Duke-Morgan Families Papers, Southern Historical Collection, University of North Carolina Library, Chapel Hill
HMP-UK	Hunt-Morgan Papers, University of Kentucky Library, Lexington
JHMP-FC	John Hunt Morgan Papers, Filson Club Library, Louisville
JHMP-SHC	John Hunt Morgan Papers, Southern Historical Collection, University of North Carolina Library, Chapel Hill
JHMP-TU	John Hunt Morgan Papers, Transylvania University Library, Lexington
JHMP-WKU	John Hunt Morgan Papers, Kentucky Library, Western Kentucky University, Bowling Green
JMP-DU	John M. McCalla Papers, William R. Perkins Library, Duke University
M-KHS	Collection on the death of Morgan, Kentucky Historical Society Library, Frankfort
MBF-KHS	Morgan biographical file, Kentucky Historical Society, Frankfort
MBS-NKU	Mary Bruce Sharon Collection, oral history archive, Northern Kentucky University, Highland Heights
MCP-MC	Morgan and Cogswell Families Papers, McClung Collection, Lawson-McGhee Library, Knoxville, Tennessee
MDFP-FC	Morgan and Duke Families Papers, Filson Club Library, Louisville
MFF-KHS	Morgan Family File, Kentucky Historical Society Library, Frankfort
MFP-TSLA	Miller Family Papers, Tennessee State Library and Archives, Nashville
MRF-KHS	Map Room File, Kentucky Historical Society Library, Frankfort
SP-KHS	D. Howard Smith Papers, Kentucky Historical Society Library, Frankfort
THHP-UK	Thomas H. Hines Papers, University of Kentucky Library, Lexington
WP-SHC	Charles A. Withers Papers, Southern Historical Collection, University of North Carolina Library, Chapel Hill

People

CM	Calvin Morgan
CCM	Calvin C. Morgan
HM	Henrietta Morgan
JHM	John Hunt Morgan
MM	Mattie Morgan
RCM	Richard C. Morgan

1. Folk Hero of the Revolution

1. Richmond *Enquirer*, January 9, 1864; Richmond *Examiner*, January 9, 1864; Richmond *Whig*, January 9, 1864; Willis F. Jones to Mrs. Basil Duke, December 28, 1863, DMFP-SHC. On New Year's Day, John B. Jones, a clerk in the War Department, wrote in his diary: "If he comes, he will be the hero, and will have a larger crowd of admirers around him than the President." John B. Jones, *A Rebel War Clerk's Diary*, 2 vols. (Philadelphia, 1866), II, 122.

2. Richmond *Examiner*, January 9, 1864; Richmond *Enquirer*, January 9, 1864; unidentified, undated typed copy of clipping, John Hunt Morgan Papers, Kentucky Library, Western Kentucky University, Bowling Green (hereafter JHMP-WKU); Robert Manson Myers, ed., *The Children of Pride: A True Story of Georgia and the Civil War* (New Haven, Conn., 1972), 1142; Basil W. Duke, *History of Morgan's Cavalry* (Cincinnati, Ohio, 1867), 29, 162. Morgan dyed his hair, mustache, and beard; the natural color was light brown.

3. Richmond *Examiner*, January 9, 1864; Richmond *Enquirer*, January 11, 1864; lecture by J.D. Kirkpatrick, typed copy, JHMP-WKU (hereafter Kirkpatrick lecture); L. Virginia (Smith) French diary, March 22, 1863, typed copy, Tennessee State Library and Archives, Nashville (hereafter French diary).

4. Richmond *Enquirer*, Richmond *Examiner*, Richmond *Whig*, January 9, 1864.

5. Richmond *Whig*, January 9, 1864.

6. Ibid.

7. Richmond *Enquirer*, Richmond *Examiner*, Richmond *Whig*, January 9, 1864; Jones, *Diary*, II, 125.

8. Richmond *Examiner*, January 12, 1864; Richmond *Enquirer*, January 19, 1864.

9. Undated article, Columbia *South Carolinian*, reprinted in Atlanta *Intelligencer*, January 27, 1864, and Richmond *Enquirer*, January 27, 1864.

10. Undated article, Atlanta *Confederacy*, reprinted in unidentified newspaper, April 8, 1862, Hunt-Morgan Papers, University of Kentucky Library, Lexington (hereafter HMP-UK).

11. Richmond *Whig*, May 21, 22, 1862; Atlanta *Intelligencer*, April 4, 6, 8 (3 articles), 10, 11, 1862, May 8, 1862; Mobile *Register and Advertiser*, March 25, 27, 29, 1862, April 3, 19, 24, 1862.

12. Richmond *Examiner*, March 17, 1862; Richmond *Whig*, May 20, 1862; Richmond *Dispatch*, August 1, 1862; unidentified, undated clipping, typed copy, JHMP-WKU.

13. Unsigned note on back of JHM to MM, May 31, 1864, JHMP-SHC.

14. Knoxville *Register*, July 4, 1862.

15. May Wheat-Shobus to MM, January 18, 1864, Malinda (no surname) to JHM, December 28, 1862, Mrs. William Clark to JHM, August 19, 1862, JHMP-SHC; John F. Marszalek, ed., *The Diary of Miss Emma Holmes: 1861-1866* (Baton Rouge, La., 1979), 262.

16. French diary, January 19, 1863; genealogical data, MFP-TSLA; Richmond *Enquirer*, August 11, 1862; Duke, *History*, 136; note on the back of JHM to Mrs. Charles Ready, November 9, 1863, JHMP-SHC.

17. Knoxville *Register*, July 4, 1862.

18. Anna L. Sanders to JHM, January 20, 1864, JHMP-SHC.

19. Genealogical data, MFP-TSLA; Charles A. Withers journal, typed copy, Charles A. Withers Papers, Southern Historical Collection, University of North Carolina Library, Chapel Hill (hereafter WP-SHC); Clement Eaton, *A History of the Southern Confederacy* (rpt., New York, 1961), 204-08; Ann Firor Scott, *The Southern Lady: From Pedestal to Politics, 1830-1930* (Chicago, 1970), 80-102, 110-12.

20. Eaton, *Confederacy*, 205; *Southern Literary Messenger* (February, 1863), 125.

21. John David Smith and William Cooper, eds., *Window on the War: Frances Dallam Peter's Lexington Civil War Diary* (Lexington, Ky., 1976), 47; Junius Henri Browne, *Four Years in Secessia: Adventures Within and Beyond the Union Lines* . . . (Hartford, Conn., 1865), 211-12; undated Louisville *Journal* article reprinted in Richmond *Enquirer*, April 6, 1864;

Myers, *Georgia*, 1142. An experienced reporter in Atlanta wrote that Morgan's reception there in February, 1864, reminded him of the welcome extended the Marquis de Lafayette in 1824-25. Unidentified clipping, February 6, 1864, typed copy, JHMP-WKU.

22. *Vidette*, August 19, 1862.

23. Marszalek, *Holmes*, 164; Belle McDowell to CM, October 12, 1862, HMP-UK.

24. French diary, January 19, 1863.

25. Lucy Jennings to Mrs. Basil Duke, August 3, 1862, MDFP-FC; G. Glenn Clift, ed., *The Private War of Lizzie Hardin* (Frankfort, Ky., 1963), 86.

2. Patriarchs and Southern Honor

1. Unsigned letter fragment to Thomas Morgan, n.d., HMP-UK; Lexington *Argonaut*, May 9, 1897; Bertram Wyatt-Brown, *Southern Honor: Ethics and Behavior in the Old South* (New York, 1982), 14, 118-19.

2. Thomas J. Taylor, "Early History of Madison County," *Alabama Historical Quarterly* (Winter, 1930), 500; Madison County Circuit Court, Minute Book 12, May session, 1824; Lexington *Kentucky Statesman*, April 2, 1861; Mobile *Register and Advertiser*, April 24, 1862; undated clipping, Knoxville *Register*, Tennessee State Library and Archives, Nashville. Street affrays were common in frontier Huntsville, and a man increased in stature by participating. St. Clair was a son of John's uncle Samuel D. Morgan. Samuel Dold Morgan Papers, Tennessee State Library and Archives, Nashville. Charles Douglas was slightly wounded, and a bystander was seriously hurt; "Wash" was unscathed.

3. MCP-MC; genealogical notes, HMP-UK; typed note, April 15, 1829, JHMP-FC.

4. Gideon Morgan to Andrew Jackson, November 23, 1813, Gideon Morgan Papers, Tennessee State Library and Archives, Nashville; Thurman Wilkins, *Cherokee Tragedy: The Story of the Ridge Family and the Decimation of a People* (New York, 1970), 67, 72; John P. Brown, *Old Frontiers* (rpt., New York, 1971), 462.

5. Robert V. Remini, *Andrew Jackson and the Course of American Empire 1767-1821* (New York, 1977), 214-15; Brown, *Old Frontiers*, 464; S.G. Heiskell, *Andrew Jackson and Early Tennessee History*, 3 vols. (Nashville, Tenn., 1920-21), I, 505. The 39th Regiment, commanded by Col. John Williams, was the first to reach the breastworks.

6. Huntsville *Alabama Republican*, June 11, 1824; Mississippi Territory Tax Records, Madison County, 1812, 1813, 1815; Madison County Court, Indirect Property Records, Deed Book A, 250-52, Deed Book B, 204-07, Deed Book E, 146-47, 403-04, 447, Deed Book I/J, 105-06, 134-35.

7. Huntsville *Alabama Republican*, October 9, 1819, July 26, August 16, October 4, 1822, June 6, July 4, 1823, January 23, October 29, 1824.

8. See James A. Ramage, *John Wesley Hunt: Pioneer Merchant, Manufacturer and Financier* (Lexington, Ky., 1974). Hunt's reputation as Kentucky's first millionaire seems justified. His estate was valued at $886,989.28; his two executors were bonded for $1,300,000 each. Fayette County Circuit Court Records, September, 1849.

9. Basil W. Duke, *Morgan's Cavalry* (New York, 1906), 15; Parish Records, Christ Church Episcopal, Lexington; unknown author, *Glimpses into Ante-Bellum Homes* (Huntsville, Ala., n.d.), 18-19; Lexington *Leader*, June 1, 1973; Madison County Court, Deed Book E, 447.

10. Madison County Court, Deed Book I/J, 297-303; Huntsville *Alabama Republican*, January 16, 23, February 20, 1824; Huntsville *Southern Advocate*, July 1, August 26, 1825.

11. Personal interview, Roy Cochran, April 21, 1983, Huntsville, Ala.

12. Huntsville *Southern Advocate*, May 26, 1826.

13. Ibid., March 30, May 25, August 24, 1827, January 25, 1828.

14. Madison County Court, Deed Book L, 163-64, 248-49.

15. Samuel D. Morgan to James W. McClung, January 8, 1828, Septimus D. Cabaniss Papers, McClung Collection, Lawson McGhee Library, Knoxville; Huntsville *Alabama*

Republican, February 11, 1825; Huntsville *Southern Advocate*, February 8, April 18, 1828; Madison County Court, Deed Book M, 314-15, 317-19, Deed Book O, 18-19.

16. Huntsville *Southern Advocate*, July 11, October 3, December 24, 1828, October 16, 1829, December 11, 1830; Madison County Court, deed book M, 537. Charlton Hunt was Lexington's first mayor.

17. CCM to John Wesley Hunt, February 14, 1831, HMP-UK.

18. Fayette County Court, Deed Book 8, 82; Huntsville *Southern Advocate*, May 28, 1833. After they moved, Hunt sold the house in Huntsville for $2,500. Madison County Court, Deed Book N, 343. Luther reestablished himself in business in Huntsville but never on the same scale as before. Samuel moved to Nashville, and Alexander went to Kansas. Louise Barry to Frances Coleman, February 17, 1962, MFF-KHS.

19. CCM to JHM and CM, December 13, 1838, HMP-UK.

20. Ibid.; CCM to HM, May 17, 1839, HMP-UK.

21. Fayette County Court, Deed Book 20, 1; CCM to JHM and CM, February 27, 1839, MDFP-FC.

22. James A. Ramage, "The Hunts and Morgans: A Study of a Prominent Kentucky Family" (Ph.D. dissertation, University of Kentucky, 1972), 175; Christ Church Records; Huntsville *Southern Advocate*, May 28, 1833.

23. CCM to JHM and CM, December 13, 1838, HMP-UK.

24. *Lexington City Directory* (Lexington, Ky., 1838), 130; Kentucky State Tax Records, Fayette County, 1833, 1839, 1840, 1845, 1848, 1849, 1850, 1851.

25. CCM to JHM and CM, February 27, 1839, MDFP-FC.

26. Charlton Morgan to HM, June 23, no year, Kitty Morgan to HM, December 23, 1855, HMP-UK; Thomas Morgan to HM, August 4, 1862, JHMP-SHC; RCM to HM, April 15, 1855, BGTHP-HMH.

27. CCM to HM, May 17, 1839, HMP-UK.

28. CCM to JHM and CM, February 27, 1839, MDFP-FC; CCM to HM, May 17, 1839, HMP-UK.

29. CCM account book, 1847-58, MDFP-FC; CCM to Samuel Morgan, April 10, 1847, Abraham D. Hunt to John Wesley Hunt, August 20, 1838, HMP-UK; Fayette County Tax Records, 1853.

30. CCM to JHM and CM, n.d., HMP-UK; Christ Church Records. Calvin and Henrietta were married in Christ Church, and his funeral was there. He was apparently not a church member. She was a communicant at times and had the four youngest children baptized.

31. CCM to Samuel Morgan, April 10, 1847, HMP-UK.

3. The Quest for Honor

1. Kenneth Keniston, "Social Change and Youth in America," *Daedalus* (Winter, 1962), 162-63; Erik H. Erikson, "Youth: Fidelity and Diversity," *Daedalus* (Winter, 1962), 15; Ruth Benedict, "Continuities and Discontinuities in Cultural Conditioning," *Psychiatry*, 1 (May, 1938), 161-67; Wyatt-Brown, *Honor*, 120-22, 132.

2. Adelphi Society Minute Book, September 9, 1842-June 28, 1844 (Transylvania University Library, Lexington); Transylvania University, *Catalogue* (Lexington, Ky., 1844), 14; Transylvania University, Adelphi Society treasurer's book, September 16, 1842; John D. Wright to author, April 6, 1983; John D. Wright, *Transylvania: Tutor to the West* (Lexington, Ky., 1975), 95-97.

3. Adelphi Minute Book, June 14, 21, 1844; unidentified clipping, March 19, 1862, THHP-UK. Blanchard was from Washington, Kentucky.

4. Duke, *History*, 19; Transylvania University, Minute Book of Trustees, July 4, 5, 1844.

5. Wyatt-Brown, *Honor*, 175, 186, 191.

6. Richard M. Johnson to James K. Polk, September 2, 1845, Miscellaneous Papers,

Filson Club Library, Louisville. Johnson's influence in the Democratic Party and with President Polk was slight.

7. William M. Pratt diary, May 20, 1846, University of Kentucky Library, Lexington; H. Edward Richardson, *Cassius Marcellus Clay: Firebrand of Freedom* (Lexington, Ky., 1976), 57-59. I am grateful to the Kentucky Historical Society for permission to include information published in "John Hunt Morgan and the Kentucky Cavalry Volunteers in the Mexican War," *Register of the Kentucky Historical Society*, 81 (Autumn, 1983), 343-65.

8. Kentucky Adjutant General's Office, *Report of the Adjutant-General of the State of Kentucky, Mexican War Veterans* (Frankfort, Ky., 1889), 26-27; Lexington *Observer and Reporter*, May 27, June 3, 1846. Beard was a carpenter in Fayette County.

9. Lexington *Observer and Reporter*, June 6, 1846.

10. Ibid., June 6, 1846, April 10, 1847; CCM to Samuel D. Morgan, April 10, 1847, typed copy, HMP-UK; Louise Barry to Frances Coleman, February 17, 1962, MFF-KHS; Fayette Tax Records, 1845.

11. Lexington *Observer and Reporter*, July 15, November 18, 1846; Kentucky Adjutant General, *Report*, 26-27; U.S. House of Representatives, *Executive Documents*, 30th Cong., 1st sess. (1848), Doc. 62, 36-37. Marshall had graduated from West Point and had resigned from the army to practice law in Louisville.

12. Lexington *Observer and Reporter*, July 1, 8, 15, 1846; Cassius M. Clay, *The Life of Cassius Marcellus Clay* (Cincinnati, Ohio, 1886), 119.

13. Lew Wallace, *An Autobiography*, 2 vols. (New York, 1906), I, 124; Robert S. Henry, *The Story of the Mexican War* (Indianapolis, Ind., 1950), 86-88, 241-42; Richard G. Stone, Jr., *A Brittle Sword: The Kentucky Militia, 1776-1912* (Lexington, Ky., 1977), 57.

14. Lexington *Observer and Reporter*, July 22, 1846; Temple Bodley and Samuel M. Wilson, *History of Kentucky*, 4 vols. (Chicago, 1928), II, 197; Otis A. Singletary, *The Mexican War* (Chicago, 1960), 20.

15. Lexington *Observer and Reporter*, September 2, 5, December 23, 1846.

16. William A. McClintock, "Journal of a Soldier of the Second Kentucky Regiment: Trip through Texas and Northern Mexico, in 1846-1847," typescript, William Alexander McClintock Papers, Historical Manuscript Collection, University of Texas Archives, Austin; Kentucky Adjutant General, *Report*, 10.

17. Bodley and Wilson, *Kentucky*, II, 198; McClintock, "Journal."

18. Lexington *Observer and Reporter*, September 2, October 14, November 12, 1846; Bodley and Wilson, *Kentucky*, II, 195.

19. McClintock, "Journal."

20. Ibid.; Seymour V. Connor and Odie B. Faulk, *North America Divided: The Mexican War, 1846-1848* (New York, 1971), 44; Henry, *Mexican War*, 139.

21. Holman Hamilton, *Zachary Taylor: Soldier of the Republic* (Indianapolis, Ind., 1941), 219-32; Singletary, *Mexican War*, 28-48.

22. William S. Henry, *Campaign Sketches of the War with Mexico* (New York, 1847), 270-75.

23. James H. Carleton, *The Battle of Buena Vista* (New York, 1848), 24-26; Henry, *Mexican War*, 243-47; David Lavender, *Climax at Buena Vista* (Philadelphia, 1966), 172; Lowry J. Beard journal, typed copy, Kentucky Military History Museum, Frankfort.

24. Edward J. Nichols, *Zach Taylor's Little Army* (Garden City, N.Y.: 1963), 214-15; Lavender, *Buena Vista*, 149-50; Hamilton, *Zachary Taylor*, 234; Henry, *Mexican War*, 245-47.

25. Justin H. Smith, *The War with Mexico*, 2 vols. (New York, 1919), I, 388-89.

26. U.S. House of Representatives, *Executive Documents*, 30th Cong., 1st sess. (1848), Doc. 8, 132-33, 145-46, 163-65 (hereafter *House Exec. Doc. 8*); Carleton, *Buena Vista*, 39; Lavender, *Buena Vista*, 182-86; Smith, *War with Mexico*, I, 388. Seven Americans were wounded on the slopes; none was killed. *House Exec. Doc. 8*, 165.

27. *House Exec. Doc. 8*, 166-67; Hamilton, *Zachary Taylor*, 236; Lavender, *Buena Vista*, 192-93.

28. CCM to Samuel D. Morgan, April 10, 1847, typed copy, HMP-UK; Lexington *Observer and Reporter*, April 14, 1847.

29. *House Exec. Doc. 8*, 134-35, 139, 148, 150-51, 167-68; Carleton, *Buena Vista*, 91-94; Lavender, *Buena Vista*, 204. In the American army 267 men were killed, 456 wounded, and 23 missing. Mexican casualties may have approached five times that rate. Henry, *Mexican War*, 253.

30. Carleton, *Buena Vista*, 129-32; Henry, *Mexican War*, 253.

31. *House Exec. Doc. 8*, 139, 142-43, 168; Lavender, *Buena Vista*, 209; Kentucky Adjutant General, *Report*, 11.

32. Kentucky Adjutant General *Report*, 26-27; Lexington *Observer and Reporter*, June 23, 1847.

33. Lexington *Observer and Reporter*, August 4, 1847.

34. Ibid.

35. Ibid.; Pratt Diary, July 31, 1847.

36. JHM to John M. McCalla, October 25, 1847, JMP-DU.

37. JHM to John M. McCalla, October 25, 1847, JMP-DU.

38. JHM to John M. McCalla, January 3, 1848, JMP-DU.

39. Samuel D. Morgan to MM, January 4, 1867, JHMP-SHC.

4. Honor Gained

1. Thomas Hart, a wealthy entrepreneur like Hunt, was the father of Lucretia Clay, Henry Clay's wife. Benjamin Gratz was a prominent manufacturer and trustee of Transylvania University. Today his house on North Mill Street faces Gratz Park, which bears his name.

2. CCM, account book, 1848-57, Miscellaneous Papers, MDFP-FC; Ramage, "Hunts and Morgans," 206; Christ Church Records; *Lexington City Directory* (1859), 85. Rebecca was named after Gratz's sister Rebecca, who was said to appear as the noble Jewess Rebecca in Sir Walter Scott's *Ivanhoe*.

3. Calvin M. McClung to HM, October 27, 1856, HMP-UK. The unnamed son was buried near his maternal grandfather, John Bruce, in the Bruce family plot in Lexington Cemetery. The location of the grave did not reflect estrangement from the Morgans but harmony on John's part with the Bruces.

4. Rebecca Morgan to HM, April 15, no year, HMP-UK.

5. Rebecca Morgan to HM, n.d., HMP-UK; Edward Shorter, *A History of Women's Bodies* (New York, 1982), 108-15.

6. Mary Hunt Hanna to HM, n.d., HMP-UK; Christ Church Records.

7. CCM, account book, 1848-57, MDFP-FC; Fayette County Tax Records, 1850, 1851, 1852, 1853.

8. JHM to CM, April 18, 21, 1859, HMP-UK.

9. Memorandum, "Total Amount of Wool Sheared," 1860, accounts of sale and bills of lading, 1860, HMP-UK; accounts of sale and bills of lading, 1859-61, CCMC-FC; Thomas H. Hunt to Calvin C. Morgan & Co., June 8, 1861, HMP-UK. Dick Morgan had studied engineering at Kentucky Military Institute and had worked as a civil engineer.

10. Wright, *Transylvania*, 166; John D. Wright, *Lexington: Heart of the Bluegrass* (Lexington, Ky., 1982), 75.

11. J. Winston Coleman, *Slavery Times in Kentucky* (Chapel Hill, N.C., 1940), 115-41.

12. Ibid., 121, 158-59; Fayette Circuit Court Records, March 11, 1856, Index Books, File 1196, File 1308; Ramage, "Hunts and Morgans," 196-97.

13. Wyatt-Brown, *Honor*, 73-74, 373; W.J. Cash, *The Mind of the South* (New York, 1941), 82-83.

14. Robert S. Starobin, *Industrial Slavery in the Old South* (New York, 1970), 43-44, 134; James E. Newton and Ronald L. Lewis, *The Other Slaves: Mechanics, Artisans and Craftsmen* (Boston, 1978), x, xiii; Richard C. Wade, *Slavery in the Cities: The South, 1820-1860* (New York, 1964), 38-48; Louis C. Hunter, *Steamboats on the Western Rivers* (rpt., New York,

1969), 271-304, 442-54; Claudia Dale Goldin, *Urban Slavery in the American South, 1820-1860: A Quantitative History* (Chicago, 1976), xi-xiv, 1-2, 9, 124-28.

15. C.C. Cole to JHM and CM, January 22, 1857, HMP-UK; JHM to CM, penciled note on Oglesby & McCaulay to JHM and CM, April 27, 1857, CCMC-FC. The owners of the *Belfast* paid the full amount. Steamer *Belfast* Account, May 21, 1857, HMP-UK.

16. Lunsford P. Yandell to CM, April 5, 1861, Rodes Woods to JHM, February 18, 1857, HMP-UK; Rodes Woods to JHM, March 22, 1857, typed copy, in possession of Burton Milward, Lexington.

17. Kentucky militia bond, February 16, 1852, Kentucky Military History Museum, Frankfort; Kentucky *Acts* (1854), 85.

18. Kentucky *Senate Journal* (1857), 37; Lexington *Observer and Reporter*, September 16, 1857; Lexington *Kentucky Statesman*, September 15, 1857; Wright, *Lexington*, 82, 86. The Kentucky Military History Museum has a Lexington Rifles shako on display.

19. Kentucky militia bond, October 8, 1858, Kentucky State Guard photographs, Kentucky Military History Museum, Frankfort; Kentucky *Senate Journal* (1859), 59; Lexington *Observer and Reporter*, September 16, 1857; Lexington *Kentucky Statesman*, September 15, 1857; J. Winston Coleman, *The Springs of Kentucky* (Lexington, Ky., 1955), 75-76; Duke, *History*, 88.

20. Cash, *Mind*, 45, 50-51, 61; Wyatt-Brown, *Honor*, 23-24, 361.

21. Duke, *History*, 20.

22. JHM to CM, May 19, 1857, HMP-UK; Kentucky *Acts* (1854), 72-73; Kentucky *Senate Journal* (1857), 29, (1859), 30; Wright, *Lexington*, 40-41. The revenue from the law to suppress betting was to be divided between the public schools (two-thirds) and the successful prosecuting attorney (one-third).

23. JHM to CM, August 1, 3, 1860, CCMC-FC; Lowell H. Harrison, *The Civil War in Kentucky* (Lexington, Ky., 1975), 4-5; Thomas D. Clark, *A History of Kentucky* (Lexington, Ky., 1960), 312.

24. JHM to CM, August 1, 1860, CCMC-FC; John W. George to CM, November 13, 1860, HMP-UK; undated memorandums, typed copies, Blanton Duncan to JHM, November 12, 14, 1860, typed copies, in possession of Burton Milward, Lexington. Breckinridge won 72 electoral votes to 39 for Bell; Breckinridge carried eleven Southern states.

25. Burton Milward, address to the Lexington Rotary Club, October 13, 1960, in possession of Burton Milward, Lexington; Richard C. Curd to CM, April 22, 1856, Maggie Simpkins to CM, June 29, 1859; R.T. Morrison to CM, April 7, 1860, HMP-UK.

26. Rodes Woods to JHM and CM, November 5, 1857, J.C. Hensley to CM, June 25, 1859, HMP-UK; J.C. Hawkins to CM, August 4, 1859, CCMC-FC; Blanton Duncan to JHM, December 13, 1860, typed copy, Blanton Duncan file, Kentucky Historical Society, Frankfort.

27. Smith and Cooper, *Diary*, 47; Pratt diary, March 21, 1858; Mary Hunt Hanna to HM, March 4, 1862, HMP-UK; Duke, *History*, 20.

28. MM to HM, June 25, 1865, HMP-UK; Duke, *History*, 21; Richmond *Whig*, September 7, 1864.

5. The State Guard

1. Meriam Gratz diary, July 21, 1861, Catherine (Peter) and Howard Evans Papers, University of Kentucky Library, Lexington; Lexington *Kentucky Statesman*, July 26, 1861.

2. Harrison, *Kentucky*, 1-2; Thomas Lawrence Connelly, *Army of the Heartland: The Army of Tennessee, 1861-1862* (Baton Rouge, La., 1967), 274; Lexington *Kentucky Statesman*, June 18, September 17, 1861; Pratt diary, April 13, 1861, quoted in Wright, *Lexington*, 87.

3. John H. DeBerry, "Confederate Tennessee" (Ph.D. dissertation, University of Kentucky, 1967), 37; Sally Rochester Ford, *Raids and Romance of Morgan and His Men* (rpt., Owensboro, Ky., 1980), 15.

4. Lexington *Kentucky Statesman*, January 25, February 5, 8, 1861.

5. Lexington *Kentucky Statesman*, January 25, 29, February 22, 26, 1861. In the battle of Raisin River in 1813, 100 Kentucky soldiers were scalped and "Remember the Raisin" became a battle cry. The Old Infantry identified themselves as the reorganization of a company that was called into service for defense against the Indians in the 1780s and was active in the War of 1812, participating in the battle of Raisin River. Lexington *Kentucky Statesman*, April 3, August 21, October 30, 1860; Program, January 18, 1861, photographic negative in possession of Burton Milward, Lexington.

6. William C. Harris to RCM, April 15, 1913, in Lexington *Leader*, May 11, 1913; J. Winston Coleman, *The Squire's Sketches of Lexington* (Lexington, Ky., 1972), 47; *Lexington City Directory* (1859), 108.

7. Harris to RCM, April 15, 1913.

8. *The War of the Rebellion: A Compilation of the Official Records of the Union and Confederate Armies*, 73 vols., (Washington, D.C. 1880-1901), (ser. 1) 52(2): 49-50 (hereafter *OR*). In respect of the state's noncommitted position, Confederate recruiting was being conducted quietly. Later, when Kentucky declared neutrality, the Confederacy withdrew its enrolling agents and encouraged volunteers to gather at the Camp Boone, Tennessee, recruiting center. E. Merton Coulter, *The Civil War and Readjustment in Kentucky* (rpt., Gloucester, Mass. 1966), 104.

9. C.M. Taylor to JHM, March 28, 1860, HMP-UK; Lexington *Kentucky Statesman*, April 23, 30, September 3, 1861.

10. Harrison, *Kentucky*, 9-10.

11. James A. Ramage, "Thomas Hunt Morgan: Family Influences in the Making of a Great Scientist," *Filson Club History Quarterly*, 53 (1979), 8-9; Lexington *Kentucky Statesman*, January 25, February 22, May 10, July 9, 1861; Thomas H. Morgan to JHM, July 5, 1861, HMP-UK.

12. Coulter, *Kentucky*, 89; Lexington *Kentucky Statesman*, August 23, 1861.

13. Lexington *Kentucky Statesman*, August 23, 1861; William C. Davis, *Breckinridge: Statesman, Soldier, Symbol* (Baton Rouge, La., 1974), 280-81; Daniel Stevenson, "General Nelson, Kentucky, and Lincoln Guns," *Magazine of American History*, 10 (1883), 136-37.

14. *OR* (ser. 1) 7:116-17; Coulter, *Kentucky*, 67-76, 77-80.

15. Davis, *Breckinridge*, 285-86; Duke, *History*, 89.

16. Duke, *History*, 89-90; Richmond *Whig*, September 7, 1864.

17. Undated article in Atlanta *Commonwealth*, reprinted in Richmond *Enquirer*, April 1, 1862; Duke, *History*, 89; James Chowning Davies, "The J-Curve of Rising and Declining Satisfactions as a Cause of Revolution and Rebellion," in Hugh Davis Graham and Ted Robert Gurr, eds., *Violence in America: Historical & Comparative Perspectives* (Beverly Hills, Calif., 1979), 415-18.

6. Gambler and Guerrilla

1. John S. Mosby, *The Memoirs of Colonel John S. Mosby*, ed. Charles Wells Russell (Boston, 1917), 23; Duke, *History*, 94.

2. Walter Laqueur, *The Guerrilla Leader: A Historical Anthology* (Philadelphia, 1977), 3-12, 18-22, 29-41; Che Guevara, *Che Guevara on Guerrilla Warfare*, introduction Harries-Clichy Peterson (New York, 1961), 8-9; Russell F. Weigley, *The Partisan War: The South Carolina Campaign of 1780-1782* (Columbia, S.C., 1970), 3; Mao Tse-Tung, *Mao Tse-Tung on Guerrilla Warfare*, trans. Samuel B. Griffith (Garden City, N.Y., 1978), 17-28; Robert B. Asprey, *War in the Shadows: The Guerrilla in History*, 2 vols. (Garden City, N.Y., 1975), xi-xii.

3. George B. Davis, *The Elements of International Law* (New York, 1903), 290; Henry W. Halleck, *Halleck's International Law*, 2 vols., (rpt., London, 1878), II, 44. In Europe strategists had used words such as *guerrilla*, *partisan*, and *irregular* to refer to warfare conducted by small units, usually composed of amateur soldiers devising their own fighting techniques. Don Higginbotham, "Reflections on the War of Independence, Modern Guerrilla

Warfare, and the War in Vietnam," in Ronald Hoffman and Peter J. Albert, eds., *Arms and Independence: The Military Character of the American Revolution* (Charlottesville, Va., 1984), 3.

4. Richmond *Dispatch*, April 9, 1863; Louisville *Journal*, March 20, 1862; *OR* (ser. 1) 20(2): 165, 10(1): 4-7; Bell I. Wiley, *The Life of Johnny Reb: The Common Soldier of the Confederacy* (Indianapolis, Ind., 1943), 108-19; Halleck, *Law*, II, 30-34, 42-44; Davis, *Law*, 321, 511-12. Indication of how notorious Morgan was for wearing the enemy uniform is revealed in an event that occurred in April, 1862. Dressed in civilian clothing, a party of Union guerrillas under J.J. Andrews raided the Georgia State Railroad between Atlanta and Chattanooga. When captured, they justified being out of uniform by pointing out that Morgan had dressed in blue and passed into Federal lines disguised as Pennsylvania cavalry. Their defense was rejected: seven were hanged, and fourteen imprisoned. *OR* (ser. 1) 10(1): 632-34.

5. William R. Eadington, Introduction, in Eadington, ed., *Gambling and Society: Interdisciplinary Studies on the Subject of Gambling* (Springfield, Ill., 1976), 253; David P. Campbell, "Who Wants to Be a Professional Gambler?" in Eadington, *Gambling*, 274-75; Tomas Martinez, "Compulsive Gambling and the Conscious Mood Perspective," in Eadington, *Gambling*, 354-59; William H. Boyd, "Excitement: The Gambler's Drug," in Eadington, *Gambling*, 371-73; Kirkpatrick lecture; Duke, *History*, 94, 98.

6. Duke, *History*, 301-02; Kirkpatrick lecture; William G. Stevenson, *Thirteen Months in the Rebel Army* (New York, 1864), 116.

7. Basil W. Duke, *Reminiscences of General Basil W. Duke, C.S.A.* (Garden City, N.Y., 1911), 95.

8. Stevenson, *Army*, 113, 117; Duke, *History*, 96-98. There is no record of whether the officer was killed.

9. Lexington *Leader*, September 27, 1972; Edison H. Thomas, *John Hunt Morgan and His Raiders* (Lexington, Ky., 1975), 19; Duke, *History*, 101; *OR* (ser. 1) 52(2): 199, 7: 714, 724-25; bills and receipts, November 2-26, 1861, JHMP-SHC. On Duke, see Lowell H. Harrison, "General Basil W. Duke, C.S.A.," *Filson Club History Quarterly*, 54 (January, 1980), 5-6.

10. Maria I. Knott diary, December 4, 1861, Knott Collection, Kentucky Library, Western Kentucky University, Bowling Green.

11. *OR* (ser. 1) 7: 12-13, 745-46; *Frank Leslie's Illustrated Newspaper*, January 25, 1862.

12. George W. Johnson to Ann Johnson, December 16, 1861, January 23, 1862, "Letters of George W. Johnson," *Register of the Kentucky Historical Society*, 40 (October, 1942), 343-45; *OR* (ser. 1) 7: 761-62. It is ironic that George Johnson pointed out the danger of guerrilla service. About four months later he was killed himself, serving in the enlisted ranks at Shiloh.

13. William R. Plum, *The Military Telegraph during the Civil War in the United States*, 2 vols., (1-vol. rpt., New York, 1974), I, intro.

14. Plum, *Telegraph*, I, 189-90.

15. *OR* (ser. 1) 7: 116-17; Plum, *Telegraph*, I, 189.

16. *OR* (ser. 1) 7: 116-17; Duke, *History*, 107-08.

17. Plum, *Telegraph*, I, 190-91.

18. Unidentified clipping, December 11, 1861, reprinted from Cincinnati *Gazette*, HMP-UK; unidentified, undated clipping, reprinted from Cincinnati *Times*, HMP-UK; Cincinnati *Gazette*, December 16, 1861; *OR* (ser. 1) 7: 508.

19. Connelly, *Heartland*, 10; Duke, *History*, 113-18.

20. United States War Department, General Orders no. 100, April 24, 1863, in Halleck, *Law*, II, 43; Duke, *History*, 105; Richmond *Whig*, October 1, 1861; R. Lockwood Tower, ed., *A Carolinian Goes to War: The Civil War Narrative of Arthur Middleton Manigault* (Columbia, S.C., 1983), 239.

21. Duke, *History*, 129.

22. Ibid., 121-24.

23. Atlanta *Intelligencer*, April 2, 1862; undated New York *Times* article reprinted in Atlanta *Southern Confederacy*, April 2, 1862; undated, unidentified clipping, JHMP-WKU.

24. Cincinnati *Gazette*, March 14, 1862.

25. Lynchburg *Virginian*, April 12, 1862; unidentified clipping, March 19, 1862, HMP-UK; unidentified, undated clipping, DMFP-SHC.

26. Unidentified, undated clipping, DMFP-SHC.

27. Richmond *Whig*, June 16, 1862; Richmond *Enquirer*, June 16, 1862.

28. Unidentified clipping, March 18, 1862, HMP-UK; unidentified clipping, December 30, 1862, JHMP-WKU.

29. *OR* (ser. 1) 16(1): 254.

30. *OR* (ser. 1) 7: 433-34.

31. Thomas L. Connelly, *Civil War Tennessee: Battles and Leaders* (Knoxville, Tenn., 1979), 13, 34; Lot D. Young, *Reminiscences of a Soldier of the Orphan Brigade* (Paris, Ky., n.d.), 52.

32. Rutherford, Tennessee *Courier*, December 4, 1955; Alice Ready journal, February 13, 1862, Southern Historical Collection, University of North Carolina Library, Chapel Hill.

33. Charles Ready to Robert L. Caruthers, January 15, 1843, Robert L. Caruthers Papers, Southern Historical Collection, University of North Carolina Library, Chapel Hill.

34. Kate S. Carney diary, January 1-August 26, 1859, Southern Historical Collection, University of North Carolina Library, Chapel Hill; Berta McGavock to Martha Ready, n.d., JHMP-SHC.

35. Ready journal, May 28, 1860; Virginia Clay-Clopton, *A Belle of the Fifties: Memoirs of Mrs. Clay of Alabama* (rpt., New York, 1969), 169; Martha Ready to Mrs. Martha Ready, July 30, 1862, JHMP-WKU.

36. Mary Cheatham to Martha Ready, April 25, 1858, JHMP-SHC.

37. Ready journal, April 20, 1860; Cecil F. Holland, *Morgan and His Raiders: A Biography of the Confederate General* (New York, 1942), 62.

38. Ready journal, February 11, March 3, 1862; Holland, *Morgan*, 68; James A. Ramage, "Civil War Romance: The Influence of Wartime Marriage on the Life and Career of John Hunt Morgan," in James C. Klotter and Peter J. Sehlinger, eds., *Kentucky Profiles: Biographical Essays in Honor of Holman Hamilton* (Frankfort, Ky., 1982), 102, 106.

39. Ready journal, March 3, 11, 15, 1862.

40. Ibid., March 8, 1862. Buckner was exchanged in August, 1862.

41. Huntsville *Democrat*, April 2, 1862.

42. Richmond *Whig*, April 15, 1862; Atlanta *Southern Confederacy*, April 12, 1862; French diary, March 22, 1863.

43. Richmond *Enquirer*, April 28, 1862.

44. Ready journal, March 9, 1862; *OR* (ser. 1) 10(1): 4-7.

45. Ready journal, March 9, 1862.

46. Connelly, *Heartland*, 135; *OR* (ser. 1) 10(1): 6-7.

47. Richmond *Whig*, April 7, 1862; Ezra J. Warner, *Generals in Blue: Lives of the Union Commanders* (Baton Rouge, La., 1964), 327. International law provided that the flag of truce was to be used sparingly, particularly during an engagement. Halleck, *Law*, II, 47; Henry Wheaton, *Elements of International Law*, 6th ed. (Boston, 1855), 470-72.

48. Richmond *Whig*, April 7, 1862.

49. Ready journal, March 15, 1862; *OR* (ser. 1) 10(1): 31.

50. Richmond *Enquirer*, April 2, 1862, *OR* (ser. 1) 10(1): 31-32; Charles P. Roland, *Albert Sidney Johnston: Soldier of Three Republics* (Austin, Tex., 1964), 304. Wood, of the First Mississippi Cavalry, outranked Morgan but chose to serve under him as aide nevertheless.

51. Martinez, "Compulsive Gambling," 359-60.

52. Betty Carolyn Congleton, "George D. Prentice: Nineteenth Century Southern Editor," *Register of the Kentucky Historical Society*, 65 (April, 1967), 94, 111-13.

53. Holland, *Morgan*, 78-79; Louisville *Journal*, March 25, 1862.

54. Genealogical notes, Miller Family Papers; Richmond *Enquirer*, April 2, 1862; *OR* (ser. 1) 10(1): 31-32.

55. Ready journal, March 15, 19, 1862; Holland, *Morgan*, 79-83. Later that day Union troops occupied Murfreesboro.

7. "O! For a Dozen Morgans"

1. Richmond *Enquirer*, April 4, 1862; Mobile *Register and Advertiser*, April 1, 1862; unidentified clipping, April 8, 1862, HMP-UK; Atlanta *Confederacy*, March 19, 1862.

2. Peter Horry and Mason L. Weems, *The Life of General Francis Marion, A Celebrated Partisan Officer* . . . (rpt., Philadelphia, 1881); William Gilmore Simms, *The Life of Francis Marion* (rpt., New York, 1971).

3. Paul H. Hayne, "The Kentucky Partisan," *Southern Literary Magazine* (April, 1862), 229.

4. Ibid.

5. J. V. Ridgely, *Nineteenth-Century Southern Literature* (Lexington, Ky., 1980), 2, 32-35; Rollin G. Osterweis, *Romanticism and Nationalism in the Old South* (New Haven, Conn., 1949), 19, 41, 43, 45, 109; Michael C.C. Adams, *Our Masters the Rebels: A Speculation on Union Military Failure in the East, 1861-1865* (Cambridge, Mass., 1978), 3-10.

6. Ridgely, *Literature*, 32-35, 42-43, 48; Nathaniel Beverley Tucker, *The Partisan Leader: A Tale of the Future* (rpt., Chapel Hill, N.C., 1971).

7. Ridgely, *Literature*, 50-52.

8. Ibid., 53-69.

9. Ideally, according to the cult of the Southern gentleman, Morgan would have been a planter, lawyer, politician, or professional soldier. Instead, he was a businessman, and some regarded that profession with disdain. The mythmakers emphasized his aristocratic breeding, wealth, and noble appearance and manners.

10. Richmond *Whig*, April 7, 1862; G.T. Goode to JHM, August 24, 1862, Hugh (illegible) to MM, February 28, 1863, JHMP-SHC; Kate Cumming, *A Journal of Hospital Life in the Confederate Army of Tennessee* (Louisville, Ky., 1866), 149; Duke, *History*, 29.

11. Mobile *Advertiser and Register*, May 24, 1862; Richmond *Enquirer*, January 12, 1864; unidentified, undated clipping, JHMP-SHC.

12. Richmond *Whig*, October 9, 1861.

13. Ibid., February 24, 1862.

14. Russell F. Weigley, *The American Way of War: A History of United States Military Strategy and Policy* (New York, 1973), 102.

15. Richmond *Whig*, March 12, 1862; Richmond *Examiner*, March 17, 1862.

16. Phillip Shaw Paludan, *Victims: A True Story of the Civil War* (Knoxville, Tenn., 1981), 51-52; Virgil Carrington Jones, *Gray Ghosts and Rebel Raiders* (New York, 1956), 92; Ethelbert Courtland Barksdale, "Semi-regular and Irregular Warfare in the Civil War" (Ph.D. dissertation, University of Texas, Austin, 1941), 68; *OR* (ser. 1) 4: 1008.

17. Ready journal, March 12, 15, 1862; Richmond *Examiner*, March 17, 1862; undated article in Atlanta *Confederacy*, reprinted in Richmond *Whig*, March 20, 1862; Huntsville *Democrat*, April 2, 1862.

18. Richmond *Whig*, April 2, 1862.

19. Undated article in New Orleans *Crescent*, reprinted in Richmond *Enquirer*, April 5, 1862; Atlanta *Confederacy*, April 12, 1862; Knoxville *Register*, April 19, 1862; Lynchburg *Virginian*, April 21, 1862.

20. Richmond *Enquirer*, March 27, 1862; *Southern Literary Messenger* (April, 1862).

21. *DeBow's Review* (May, 1862); Richmond *Examiner*, March 24, 1862; Richmond *Enquirer*, March 17, 27, April 1, 1862. The Richmond *Examiner*, April 29, 1863, pointed out that subjection of the South was "simply impossible, if only the people resolve to resist to the end."

22. Richmond *Whig*, April 14, 1862; Atlanta *Intelligencer*, April 20, 22, 1862; Eaton, *Confederacy*, 90; Richmond *Enquirer*, April 18, 1862.

23. Richmond *Whig*, April 17, 22, 1862; Eaton, *Confederacy*, 112; Richmond *Examiner*, March 17, 1862; Richmond *Enquirer*, April 4, 1862.

24. Richmond *Whig*, April 22, 1862.

25. *Journal of the Congress of the Confederate States of America, 1861-1865*, 8 vols. (New York, 1904-05), II, 195, 220, V, 193, 261-62 (hereafter *Journal of Congress*); James M. Matthews, ed., *The Statutes at Large of the Confederate States of America*, 1st Cong., 1st sess., 48; Andrew

Brown, "The First Mississippi Partisan Rangers, C.S.A.," *Civil War History*, 1 (December, 1955), 371-72; Weigley, *Partisan*, 55. A general order by the War Department stipulated that authority to recruit had to be approved by the commanding general of the local department and the President, but in practice the permission of a departmental commander was sufficient.

26. *Civil War Times Illustrated* (October, 1974), 9-10; Jones, *Ghosts*, viii; Virgil Carrington Jones, *Ranger Mosby* (Chapel Hill, N.C., 1944), 172; Richmond *Whig*, May 7, 1862; Brown, "Partisan Rangers," 372; Atlanta *Intelligencer*, May 2, 1862; Mobile *Advertiser and Register*, May 22, 1862.

27. Atlanta *Intelligencer*, January 20, 1864.

28. *Southern Literary Messenger* (July-August, 1862); Richmond *Enquirer*, August 18, 1862; Richmond *Examiner*, December 25, 29, 1862.

29. Paludan, *Victims*, 31; Richmond *Whig*, May 22, 29, 1862; Jones, *Mosby*, 89-93. One Union official pointed out that the Union army had one partisan unit—the Independent Loudon County Rangers.

30. Henry W. Halleck, *International Law, or Rules Regulating the Intercourse of States in Peace and War* (San Francisco, 1861), 386 (hereafter *International Law*); Barksdale, "Irregular Warfare," 365.

31. Richard Shelly Hartigan, *Lieber's Code and the Law of War* (Chicago, 1983), 2, 9-12.

32. Ibid., 35-36.

33. *OR* (ser. 2) 4: 739.

34. Jones, *Mosby*, 93, 95; *OR* (ser. 1) 43(1): 811, (ser. 2) 4: 913. After Lieber wrote the essay on guerrillas, Halleck appointed him to a special board to study military law; out of that came General Orders, no. 100. Known as Lieber's Code, the document was a landmark in the law of land warfare. Hartigan, *Lieber's Code*, 14-22.

35. Jones, *Ghosts*, 89; Herman Hattaway and Archer Jones, *How the North Won: A Military History of the Civil War* (Urbana, Ill., 1983), 357-58; Weigley, *War*, 132.

36. Knoxville *Register*, August 14, 1862; Barksdale, "Irregular Warfare," 122-24, 126; William C. Davis, *The Battle of New Market* (Garden City, N.Y., 1975), 18-19, 35-39, 51, 58, 61-70.

37. Jones, *Mosby*, 13, 56-79; Hattaway and Jones, *History*, 446, 622.

38. Jones, *Mosby*, 20-28, 33, 45-56, 89-97.

39. Ibid., viii, 244.

40. Brown, "Partisan Rangers," 372-99; Wyatt-Brown, *Honor*, 351.

41. Brown, "Partisan Rangers," 372; Jones, *Mosby*, 173.

42. Knoxville *Register*, October 19, 1862, March 19, 1863; William D. Cotton, "Appalachian North Carolina: A Political Study, 1860-1889," (Ph.D. dissertation, University of North Carolina, 1954), 118; John G. Barrett, *The Civil War in North Carolina* (Chapel Hill, N.C., 1963), 188.

43. Wiley, *Johnny Reb*, 45, 142; *OR* (ser. 1) 33: 1081.

44. Richmond *Examiner*, July 10, 1862; *OR* (ser. 4) 2: 26, 48; Brown, "Partisan Rangers," 381. On September 29, 1862, Congress concurred with removal of draft exemption for partisans. *Journal of Congress*, II, 230, 251, 255, 377-78.

45. *OR* (ser. 4) 2: 289, 1003, (ser. 1) 33: 1082, 1252; *Statutes at Large*, 1st Cong., 4th sess., 202. Lee stated that the system gave license to deserters who committed depredations on friends and foes, and discipline was undermined in that men had a constant desire to leave the regular army for the freedom of the rangers. *OR* (ser. 1) 33: 1252.

46. Weigley, *War*, 3-5, 13; Emory M. Thomas, *The Confederacy as a Revolutionary Experience* (Englewood Cliffs, N.J., 1971), 45-46.

47. Weigley, *War*, 15, 25-26.

48. Ibid., 35; Weigley, *Partisan*, 2, 16-17, 24, 46; Higginbotham, "Reflections," 23-24.

49. Weigley, *War*, 93, 96-97.

50. Guevara, *Guerrilla*, 11; Weigley, *War*, 92-93; Barksdale, "Irregular Warfare," 61.

51. James D. Richardson, ed., *The Messages and Papers of Jefferson Davis and the Confederacy*, 2 vols. (rpt., New York, 1966), I, xviii-xix; Don C. Seitz, *Braxton Bragg: General of the Confederacy* (rpt., Freeport, N.Y. 1971), 142.

52. Weigley, *War*, 123; Tower, *Manigault*, 201.

53. Weigley, *War*, 128, 132; Hattaway and Jones, *History*, 2; Adams, *Masters*, 148; Charles H. Wesley, *The Collapse of the Confederacy* (Washington, D.C., 1937), ix.

54. Grady McWhiney and Perry D. Jamieson, *Attack and Die: Civil War Military Tactics and the Southern Heritage* (University, Ala., 1982), xiii-xv.

55. Edward A. Pollard, *The Lost Cause: A New Southern History of the War of the Confederates* (New York, 1866), 727-29.

56. Charles Royster, *A Revolutionary People at War: The Continental Army and American Character, 1775-1783* (Chapel Hill, N.C., 1979), 7, 152-58.

57. *OR* (ser. 1) 17(2): 310; Hattaway and Jones, *History*, 662.

58. Richmond *Examiner*, May 11, 1863; Richmond *Whig*, May 21, 1863, March 7, 1864; Knoxville *Southern Chronicle*, June 28, 1863.

8. From Shiloh to Cave City

1. Holland, *Morgan*, 89; Mobile *Advertiser and Register*, March 25, 1862.

2. Richmond *Examiner*, February 2, June 23, 1862; Richmond *Whig*, May 14, 1863; Lynchburg *Virginian*, March 27, 1862; Stamley Kimmel, *Mr. Davis's Richmond* (Toronto, 1958), 106; Duke, *History*, 261.

3. Lynchburg *Republican*, April 3, 1862, reprinted in Richmond *Enquirer*, April 4, 1862, and Atlanta *Intelligencer*, April 9, 1862; Richmond *Whig*, April 5, 1862; Charleston *Mercury*, undated, reprinted in Atlanta *Intelligencer*, April 10, 1862.

4. Knoxville *Register*, July 4, 1862.

5. Duke, *History*, 143.

6. Duke, *Cavalry*, 84-85.

7. Duke, *History*, 148-49. Duke did not mention Morgan's trip to Richmond or his absence on Sunday morning. It is a measure of his love for his brother-in-law that he "covered" for him in writing of these events. In his description of the time Morgan was absent, he mentioned "Morgan's squadron" but never Morgan himself in an active sense or even by name until early Sunday afternoon, April 6. Then all of a sudden Morgan is there, leading the men, with no mention that he had been gone. Duke emphasized that Johnston's offensive was a total surprise, completely unexpected. Duke, *History*, 138-48. Also see Basil W. Duke, "Personal Recollections of Shiloh," paper read before the Filson Club, April 6, 1914.

8. Duke, *History*, 148-50; Nathaniel C. Hughes, *General William J. Hardee: Old Reliable* (Baton Rouge, La., 1965), 107.

9. Duke, *History*, 150.

10. *OR* (ser. 1) 10(1): 613; Connelly, *Heartland*, 166-69.

11. Robert S. Henry, *"First With The Most" Forrest* (Indianapolis, Ind., 1944), 75, 77-79, 81. Forrest never had Morgan's reputation of running from a fight, but he reacted to the accusation that Morgan's men were not fighters: at Chickamauga in November, 1863, when Morgan was in prison, a remnant of his command served under Forrest, and Forrest proclaimed them excellent soldiers. At Shiloh, Forrest commanded a regiment with a few hundred more men than Morgan's squadron.

12. Barksdale, "Irregular Warfare," 169, 185; Henry, *Forrest*, 16, 19; Walter Laqueur, *Guerrilla: A Historical and Critical Study* (Boston, 1976), 68.

13. Henry, *Forrest*, 80–81; John Allan Wyeth, *That Devil Forrest: Life of General Nathan Bedford Forrest* (New York, 1959), 64; Richmond *Whig*, April 11, 1862; Richmond *Enquirer*, April 14, 1862; Lynchburg *Virginian*, April 16, 1862; Atlanta *Intelligencer*, April 18, 1862.

14. *OR* (ser. 1) 10(1): 569, 620. John's brother Charlton, an aide to Trabue, was wounded on Sunday at Shiloh.

15. *OR* (ser. 1) 10(2): 437; Duke, *History*, 156.

16. Duke, *History*, 157-58; Atlanta *Southern Confederacy*, May 13, 1862; *OR* (ser. 1) 10(1): 876, 10(2): 162. Among the captives was Lt. E.M. Mitchel, son of Gen. Ormsby Mitchel,

whose command had occupied Huntsville and taken Charlton Morgan prisoner. Charlton was there convalescing from his wound at Shiloh. Morgan paroled the lieutenant in exchange for Charlton.

17. Richmond *Enquirer*, May 19, 1862.

18. Atlanta *Southern Confederacy*, May 13, 1862. This operator was not the famous George A. Ellsworth, who tapped his first Yankee wire on July 9, 1862.

19. Richmond *Enquirer*, May 22, 1862.

20. French diary, March 13, 1863.

21. Ibid., March 22, 1863; Knott diary, June 12, 1862; *OR* (ser. 1) 10(1): 891.

22. Tall hats decorated with artificial flowers, bows, and ribbons were in fashion. Wags derided them as "coal-scuttles" and "sky-scrapers." *Southern Literary Messenger* (June, 1863), 377.

23. French diary, March 22, 1863.

24. *OR* (ser. 1) 10(1): 891, 10(2): 184.

25. *OR* (ser. 1) 10(2): 180-83; Holland, *Morgan*, 106; Louisville *Journal*, January 6, 1863.

26. *OR* (ser. 1) 10(2): 56, 110-11, 118, 128, 180-81; Holland, *Morgan*, 106-07.

27. Ramage, "Hunts and Morgans," 236; Richmond *Enquirer*, June 17, 1862; Atlanta *Southern Confederacy*, May 20, 1862; Holland, *Morgan*, 110.

28. JHM to F.L. Childs, July 1, 1862, William N. Tillinghast Papers, Duke University Library, Durham. Before he was wounded, Bee had given Jackson the sobriquet "Stonewall."

29. Richmond *Whig*, May 7, 19, 20, 21, 22, 1862; Richmond *Enquirer*, May 26, 27, 1862; Edward A. Pollard, *Southern History of the War*, 2 vols. (rpt., New York, 1977), I, 404.

30. Richmond *Enquirer*, May 24, 26, 1862; Richmond *Whig*, May 26, 1862; Atlanta *Southern Confederacy*, May 20, 21, 1862.

31. Richmond *Enquirer*, May 27, 1862.

32. Atlanta *Southern Confederacy*, June 1, 1862.

33. Holland, *Morgan*, 110.

34. Cumming, *Journal*, 28.

35. Duke, *History*, 171.

36. Mobile *Register*, undated article reprinted in Richmond *Whig*, June 19, 1862. Wash Morgan was the son of John's great uncle Gideon, brother of Luther Morgan. Genealogical notes, MCP-MC. On Grenfell, see Stephen Z. Starr, *Colonel Grenfell's Wars: The Life of a Soldier of Fortune* (Baton Rouge, La., 1971).

9. The First Kentucky Raid

1. Duke, *History*, 181-83; Seitz, *Bragg*, 138; Richmond *Dispatch*, August 1, 1862; Richmond *Enquirer*, August 9, 1862.

2. Duke, *History*, 157.

3. Max R. Williams, ed., "An Awful Affair" by Joseph Graham, *Civil War Times Illustrated* (April, 1984), 51.

4. Stephen Z. Starr, *The Union Cavalry in the Civil War*, 3 vols. (Baton Rouge, La., 1979-85), I, 220, II, 33; Duke, *History*, 176-79. Morgan used the howitzers until just prior to the Great Raid in Indiana and Ohio.

5. Weigley, *Partisan*, 16; Hattaway and Jones, *History*, 324; Richard M. McMurry, *John Bell Hood and the War for Southern Independence* (Lexington, Ky., 1982), 26.

6. Duke, *History*, 320; unidentified clipping, January 7, 1883, THHP-UK.

7. *Southern Literary Messenger* (June, 1863), 383.

8. Duke, *History*, 186-89.

9. Ibid., 190, 197. The brigade took the garrisons at Tompkinsville (which they outnumbered 2 to 1), Lebanon (4 to 1), and Cynthiana (about 2 to 1).

10. *OR* (ser. 1) 16(1): 774-75; Hammond *Times*, December 4, 1960; *Confederate Veteran*, 1 (1900), 35-36; Plum, *Telegraph*, I, 193-94; Duke, *Reminiscences*, 126. The first message Ells-

worth intercepted was a telegram to Col. Sanders Bruce, Union commander of the garrison at Bowling Green and John's brother-in-law; it ordered Bruce to pursue Morgan. George A. Ellsworth to Charlton Morgan, n.d., printed in unidentified, undated clipping, MBF-KHS.

11. Plum, *Telegraph*, I, 194-96. "Z" was W.H. Drake, and the Lebanon operator hiding in the willows was D.E. Martyn.

12. Ibid., I, 196-97; Duke, *History*, 192-94.

13. Plum, *Telegraph*, I, 198.

14. Ibid., I, 200.

15. London *Times*, September 12, 1862; Duke, *Reminiscences*, 128; Duke, *History*, 212-13. Ellsworth's rank was private.

16. Duke, *History*, 184, 186, 199-202; Richard H. Collins, *History of Kentucky . . . ,* 2 vols. (Kentucky Historical Society rpt., Frankfort, Ky., 1966), I, 103-04; *OR* (ser. 1) 16(1): 756-59; Richmond *Enquirer*, August 26, 1862.

17. Duke, *History*, 199-202.

18. Nashville *Dispatch*, August 26, 1862; Duke, *History*, 187, 205.

19. Thomas L. Connelly and Archer Jones, *The Politics of Command: Factions and Ideas in Confederate Strategy* (Baton Rouge, La., 1973), 74-75. Frank G. Rankin emphasized Morgan's campaign to liberate Kentucky in "The Saga of Morgan and His Men," address before the Chicago Civil War Round Table, March 12, 1971, Confederate Sketches Papers, Southern Historical Collection, University of North Carolina Library, Chapel Hill.

20. Handwritten lyrics, July 4, 1862, DMFP-SHC.

21. Duke, *Reminiscences*, 22.

22. Connelly and Jones, *Politics of Command*, 74; Richmond *Enquirer*, August 9, 1862; Richmond *Dispatch*, August 1, 1862; Duke, *History*, 72, 74.

23. Clift, *Lizzie Hardin*, 87-88.

24. *OR* (ser. 1) 52(2): 309; Coulter, *Kentucky*, 149-51.

25. Richmond *Enquirer*, August 9, 1862; Duke, *History*, 206.

26. Duke, *History*, 279, 285; Nashville *News*, June 14, 1904; unidentified, undated clipping, JHMP-TU, Starr, *Grenfell's Wars*, 51.

27. RCM to JHM, May 4, 1863, JHMP-SHC; Duke, *Reminiscences*, 124-25.

28. Ibid.

29. *OR* (ser. 1) 16(2): 733-34.

30. Connelly, *Heartland*, 200-01; *OR* (ser. 1) 39(2): 750.

31. Duke, *History*, 196.

32. Lucy Jennings to Tommy Duke, August 3, 1862, MDFP-FC.

33. Smith and Cooper, *Diary*, intro.; "Gratz Park: A Walking Tour," pamphlet by Blue Grass Automobile Club (Lexington, Ky., 1982). Kitty had married Calvin M. McClung, and they lived in St. Louis. After he died she married Ambrose P. Hill, who became a lieutenant general in the Army of Northern Virginia and commanded a corps at Gettysburg and the Wilderness. Tommy was the wife of Basil Duke and was still in Lexington; later she would join her husband in Tennessee. Burton Milward, *The Hunt-Morgan House* (Lexington, Ky., 1979), 12. Key turned seventeen on September 1, 1862, and on September 10 enlisted in John's command.

34. Smith and Cooper, *Diary*, 1-2.

35. Ibid., 4; HM to Basil Duke, December 1, 1862, HMP-UK.

36. Lucy Jennings to Tommy Duke, August 3, 1862, MDFP-FC. Tommy Morgan Duke's name was often spelled Tommie.

37. *OR* (ser. 1) 16(1): 745, 747, 759-62, 16(2): 143, 239, 52(1): 480.

38. Connelly, *Tennessee*, 54; Hattaway and Jones, *History*, 216; *OR* (ser. 1) 16(2): 143, 226-27, 300-301, 319, 325, 339-40. President Davis suggested that Gen. Humphrey Marshall, in command of the West Virginia department, launch a fourth raid across the mountains into Kentucky, but it failed to develop. *OR* (ser. 1) 12(3):922; Connelly, *Heartland*, 207.

39. Starr, *Union Cavalry*, I, xii, II, 506; Hattaway and Jones, *History*, 323; *OR* (ser. 1) 16(2): 159, 234, 360-61; John W. Rowell, *Yankee Cavalrymen: Through the Civil War with the Ninth Pennsylvania Cavalry* (Knoxville, Tenn., 1971), 71.

40. Unidentified, undated clipping, DMFP-SHC; Richmond *Enquirer*, August 26, 1862; *OR* (ser. 1) 16(2): 301, 314-15, 322.

41. Jones, *Diary*, I, 142; Richmond *Enquirer*, July 19, July 26, August 1, 1862; Richmond *Examiner*, July 28, 1862; Richmond *Dispatch*, August 1, 1862.

42. Richmond *Enquirer*, August 18, 1862.

43. Knoxville *Register*, July 22, 1862; Richmond *Dispatch*, July 21, 1862.

44. Richmond *Whig*, September 7, 1864.

10. The Gallatin Raid

1. Duke, *History*, 206-07; unidentified clipping, June 1, 1866, THHP-UK. The Georgia regiment and the Tennessee company departed at the conclusion of the raid.

2. Duke, *History*, 208-09; John M. Porter memoir, Confederate Collection, Tennessee State Library and Archives, Nashville; Wiley, *Johnny Reb*, 143, 243.

3. Wiley, *Johnny Reb*, 234-35, 242; Henry, *Forrest*, 15; A.D. Kirwan, ed., *Johnny Green of the Orphan Brigade: The Journal of a Confederate Soldier* (Lexington, Ky., 1956), xiii; Duke *History*, 92-94.

4. Fritz M. Marx, ed., *Elements of Public Administration* (Englewood Cliffs, N.J., 1959), 83, 437, 445-48; Mao Tse-Tung, *Guerrilla*, 27, 81; unidentified clipping, June 1, 1866, THHP-UK.

5. Edward G. Longacre, *Mounted Raids of the Civil War* (New York, 1975), 184; Duke, *Reminiscences*, 278; Starr, *Union Cavalry*, I, 225.

6. Duke, *History*, 28; Ramage, "Hunts and Morgans," 239; JHM to Adam R. Johnson, April 2, 1864, JHMP-SHC.

7. Unidentified clipping, June 1, 1866, THHP-UK; Lexington *Herald*, June 25, 1904; Leland Hathaway journal, 39, typed copy in possession of John Marshall Prewitt, Mount Sterling, Kentucky; Guevara, *Guerrilla*, 33; Duke, *History*, 203-04.

8. JHM to MM, March 21, 1863, JHMP-SHC. Morgan's men were usually diligent in caring for their horses and weapons. Duke, *History*, 208.

9. Unidentified, undated clipping, JHMP-WKU; Delegates of 2nd Kentucky Cavalry Battalion to Samuel Cooper, n.d., JHMP-SHC. The young man died six hours later.

10. Duke, *Reminiscences*, 281-82.

11. Ibid., 279-80. When Morgan disciplined a soldier, the punishment was usually mild. One method was to forbid the offender to participate in the next raid; another was to transfer the man to the infantry. At least one man was blown out of the command: that is, dishonorably discharged by being marched in front of his regiment and blown out of camp by the screech of the bugle. Kirkpatrick lecture; Duke, *History*, 207.

12. *OR* (ser. 1) 16(1): 846; Thomas, *Morgan*, 48. Boone's unit was the 28th Kentucky Infantry regiment.

13. T.R. Love account, Samuel Robert Simpson Papers, Tennessee State Library and Archives, Nashville; Duke, *History*, 210-12; French diary, March 22, 1863.

14. *OR* (ser. 1) 16(1): 844, 846-49.

15. Plum, *Telegraph*, I, 275-77.

16. Thomas, *Morgan*, 48-49; Kirkpatrick lecture; Duke, *History*, 214-15; *OR* (ser. 1) 20(1): 189. The tunnel reopened on November 26, 1862.

17. *OR* (ser. 1) 16(1): 271; Warner, *Generals in Blue*, 51-52. Buell was born in Lowell, Ohio, and spent his childhood in Lawrenceburg, Indiana. He graduated from West Point, was wounded in the Mexican War, and stayed in the army as an able administrator.

18. *OR* (ser. 1) 16(2): 324-25, 330, 336, 339-40, 360-62; Louisville *Journal*, January 6, 1863. When Buell learned of Morgan's raid, he assumed that Morgan was headed to Kentucky and alerted Ohio and Indiana to send men there.

19. *OR* (ser. 1) 16(2): 361; Connelly, *Heartland*, 202-03; Duke, *History*, 223.

20. *OR* (ser. 1) 16(1):857, 16(2): 748-49, 753; Seitz, *Bragg*, 150; Hattaway and Jones, *History*, 220; Connelly, *Tennessee*, 54-55.

21. *OR* (ser. 1) 16(1): 843-44, 16(2): 329-30, 334; James W. King to Jimmy King, August 15, 1862, Federal Collection, Letters, 1862-63, Tennessee State Library and Archives, Nashville; Duke, *History*, 215.

22. Duke, *History*, 215; French diary, November 22, 1862.

23. Duke, *Reminiscences*, 160-61; Duke, *History*, 226; Wiley, *Johnny Reb*, 170-71.

24. *Vidette*, August 19, 1862. John signed the document on August 18.

25. Davis, *Law*, 325-26.

26. *OR* (ser. 1) 16(1): 878-79; Love account; George B. Guild memoir, Confederate Collection, Tennessee State Library and Archives, Nashville.

27. Duke, *Reminiscences*, 256-57.

28. French diary, March 22, 1863; Duke, *History*, 216.

29. French diary, March 22, 1863; unidentified clipping, June 1, 1866, THHP-UK.

30. *OR* (ser. 1) 16(1): 879; Duke, *History*, 216-17; Guild memoir. There was a widespread belief in the Union army that Duke was the manager and driving force of Morgan's command. Lowell Harrison concluded correctly that Duke served as a counterbalance to Morgan's impulsiveness and made a major contribution to the success of Morgan's men. Harrison, "Duke," 14, 20, 25.

31. Harrison, "Duke," 14, 20, 25; unidentified clipping, June 1, 1866, THHP-UK; Duke, *History*, 218.

32. Duke, *History*, 218-21.

33. Ibid., 221-23; *OR* (ser. 1) 16(1): 872, 875-76, 878, 881.

34. *OR* (ser. 1) 16(1): 882.

11. Bragg's Kentucky Invasion

1. *OR* (ser. 1) 16(2): 733-34; Connelly and Jones, *Politics of Command*, 74; Connelly, *Heartland*, 200-201, 209; Richmond *Whig*, October 8, 19, 1861, October 4, 1862; Richmond *Enquirer*, January 9, 1864; Richmond *Examiner*, June 25, 1862; *Southern Literary* Messenger (February-March, 1862).

2. Undated article from Savannah *Republican*, reprinted in Richmond *Whig*, May 22, 1862; Atlanta *Southern Confederacy*, July 24, 1862; *OR* (ser. 1) 16(2): 741; Seitz, *Bragg*, 154.

3. Connelly, *Heartland*, 208-09; Connelly, *Tennessee*, 57; Harrison, *Kentucky*, 21, 34, 41; *OR* (ser. 1) 16(2): 771. When Gov. George Johnson was killed at Shiloh, the Provisional Council elected Hawes.

4. Handwritten song lyrics, JHMP-SHC.

5. Printed broadside, August 22, 1862, copy in possession of author.

6. Unidentified, undated clipping, DMFP-SHC; Halleck, *Law*, II, 103. Morgan's command burned the Marion County courthouse in Lebanon on July 5, 1863.

7. Holland, *Morgan*, 146; J. Winston Coleman, *Lexington during the Civil War* (Lexington, Ky., 1938), 25; Smith and Cooper, *Diary*, 7-10.

8. Smith and Cooper, *Diary*, 7-10; HM to CM, n.d., handwritten copy in possession of Burton Milward, Lexington.

9. Holland, *Morgan*, 148, illus. following 150; Duke, *History*, 233.

10. Unidentified clipping, August 1, 1866, THHP-UK; Duke, *History*, 257-58.

11. Porter memoir; *OR* (ser. 1) 16(1): 991-92, 995.

12. *OR* (ser. 1) 16(2): 822; Tower, *Manigault*, 37.

13. Harrison, *Kentucky*, 42-48; Connelly, *Heartland*, 274, 276-77.

14. Harrison, *Kentucky*, 48-49; Connelly, *Tennessee*, 54-57.

15. Morgan approved of Bragg's retreat; when a commander is demoralized, he should not lead a fight, he believed. Duke, *History*, 261.

16. Duke, *History*, 282-85; *OR* (ser. 1) 16(2): 985; Holland, *Morgan*, 155-56.

17. Duke, *History*, 288-89; William A. Milton account, MRF-KHS.

18. Duke, *Reminiscences*, 174-75; *Vidette*, November 2, 1862. See Thomas, *Morgan*, 57, for a description of the destruction of the railroad.

19. Richmond *Dispatch*, November 3, 1862; Charleston *Courier*, December 20, 1862.

20. Duke, *History*, 293, 295-99.

21. Ibid., 300; Milton account.

22. Duke, *History*, 300-301; *OR* (ser. 1) 16(2): 596. Morgan reunited with his main body about an hour later.

23. Duke, *History*, 304; Holland, *Morgan*, 163-64; *OR* (ser. 1) 20(2): 417-18, 421-23. Bragg's general headquarters staff began addressing Morgan as a general in official correspondence. Edwin C. Bearss, "The Battle of Hartsville and Morgan's Second Kentucky Raid" (Research Project No. 4, Stones River National Military Park, 1960). Bragg wrote Davis that Forrest and Morgan were useful only in partisan service. *OR* (ser. 1) 16(2): 996. He was correct about Morgan; less so about Forrest.

24. *OR* (ser. 1) 20(2): 417-18, 421-23.

25. *OR* (ser. 1) 20(1): 63-64.

26. *OR* (ser. 1) 20(1): 62, 63; Seitz, *Bragg*, 218; Duke, *History*, 308; Burton Milward, *Tom Quirk—'Our Tom'*," *Newsletter of the Kentucky Civil War Round Table*, May 11, 1981, 2-4.

27. *OR* (ser. 1) 20(1): 63; Seitz, *Bragg*, 218; Ed Porter Thompson, *History of the Orphan Brigade* (Louisville, Ky., *1898*), *429-33*.

28. Kirwan, *Green*, 54-55; Duke, *History*, 309-10.

29. Kirwan, *Green*, 55. Johnny Green, born in Henderson County, Kentucky, grew up in Louisville and graduated from Louisville Male High School. He enlisted in Bowling Green on October 7, 1861, and eventually rose to sergeant major.

30. Hathaway journal; Duke, *History*, 310.

31. *OR* (ser. 1) 20(1): 43-44, 59-61, 66; Duke, *History*, 311; Bearss, "Battle of Hartsville," appendix.

32. *OR* (ser. 1) 20(1): 54, 58, 69-70; Kirwan, *Green*, 56; Duke, *History*, 312; Henry Lane Stone narrative, map room file, Kentucky Historical Society Library, Frankfort (hereafter MRF-KHS).

33. Kirwan, *Green*, 57.

34. Stone narrative.

35. French diary, March 22, 1863; *OR* (ser. 1) 20(1): 48; Kirwan, *Green*, 58.

36. George Winchester diary, December 8, 1862, Winchester Papers, Tennessee State Library and Archives, Nashville; *OR* (ser. 1) 20(2): 68; Seitz, *Bragg*, 218; Bearss, "Battle of Hartsville," appendix. In his official report Morgan declared that Duke "was, as he always has been, 'the right man in the right place.' Wise in counsel, gallant in the field, his services have ever been invaluable to me." *OR* (ser. 1) 20(1): 67.

37. Hathaway journal; *OR* (ser. 1) 20(1): 41-45.

38. *OR* (ser. 1) 20(1): 64, 20(2): 445; McWhiney and Jamieson, *Attack*, xiv; James M. McPherson, *Ordeal by Fire: The Civil War and Reconstruction* (New York, 1982), 288, 292, 387-88; Jones, *Diary*, I, 226; Charleston *Courier*, December 10, 1862; Richmond *Dispatch*, December 10, 1862; Knoxville *Register*, December 14, 1862.

39. Kenneth P. Williams, *Lincoln Finds a General*, 4 vols. (New York, 1949-59), IV, 245-47.

12. Wedding Bells and the Christmas Raid

1. Nashville *Banner*, n.d., clipping, JHMP-TU; Stanley F. Horn, *Tennessee's War, 1861-1865: Described by Participants* (Nashville, Tenn., 1965), 129.

2. C.B. Hilliard to MM, December 18, 1862, JHMP-SHC.

3. Tower, *Manigault*, 158; unidentified, undated clipping, Morgan Family Papers, University of Kentucky Library, Lexington.

4. James Lee McDonough, *Stones River—Bloody Winter in Tennessee* (Knoxville, Tenn., 1980), 47, 49; Samuel W. Scott and Samuel P. Angel, *History of the Thirteenth Regiment, Tennessee Volunteer Cavalry, U.S.A.* (rpt., Blountville, Tenn. 1973), 135, 184-85, illus. following 384, 451, 464, 471; unidentified, undated clipping, reprint from Philadelphia

Weekly Times, MBF-KHS; Francis B. Heitman, ed., *Historical Register and Dictionary of the United States Army* (Washington, D.C., 1903), 276.

5. Dance invitation, December 15, 1862, JHMP-SHC; James B. McCreary journal, December 21, 1862, carbon of typed copy, Duke University Library, Durham.

6. Hattaway and Jones, *History*, 317; McPherson, *Ordeal*, 308; Connelly, *Tennessee*, 59; Thomas L. Connelly, *Autumn of Glory: The Army of Tennessee, 1862-1865* (Baton Rouge, La., 1971), 25-26; *OR* (ser. 1) 20(1): 189.

7. *OR* (ser. 1) 20(1): 189, 20(2): 28-29, 43, 58, 77, 117-18; Warner, *Generals in Blue*, 410-11.

8. *OR* (ser. 1) 20(2): 50-51, 77, 144, 147, 185.

9. Ibid., 20(1): 189, 20(2): 31, 75, 135.

10. Ibid., 20(2): 462; JHM to MM, January 2, 1863, JHMP-SHC.

11. Thomas, *Morgan*, 71: Ramage, "Hunts and Morgans," 255.

12. *OR* (ser. 1) 20(1): 140.

13. Ibid., 147; Louisville *Journal*, January 14, 1863; John Allan Wyeth, *With Sabre and Scalpel: The Autobiography of a Soldier and Surgeon* (New York, 1914), 179.

14. Duke, *History*, 327; *OR* (ser. 1) 20(1): 152, 154-57, 52(1): 55-56.

15. Duke, *History*, 328, 330; Wyeth, *Sabre*, 182.

16. John Allan Wyeth, "Morgan's Christmas Raid, 1862-63," in Francis T. Miller, ed., *The Photographic History of the Civil War*, 10 vols. (New York, 1911-12), IV, 148, 150; Wyeth, *Sabre*, 184; Plum, *Telegraph*, I, 303; *OR* (ser. 1) 20(1): 153; Louisville *Courier Journal*, September 27, 1936; Louisville *Journal*, January 3, 1863; Davis, *Law*, 297.

17. Louisville *Courier Journal*, September 27, 1936.

18. Thomas, *Morgan*, 68; Duke, *History*, 335; *OR* (ser. 1) 20(1): 138, 155-57; Edwin C. Bearss, "General John Hunt Morgan's Second Kentucky Raid," *Register of the Kentucky Historical Society*, 71 (January, 1973), 177-78, 187; Wyeth, *Sabre*, 185. The 71st Indiana were first captured by Kirby Smith in Richmond, Kentucky, on August 30, 1862. After their second capture Governor Morton placed them on guard duty in Indianapolis. *OR* (ser. 2) 4: 701, 717, 5: 391.

19. *OR* (ser. 1) 20(2): 176-77, 180, 194, 201, 222.

20. Ibid., 185-86, 238.

21. Ibid., 20(1): 142, 145-47, 20(2): 174, 188, 225, 236, 251, 284, 291.

22. Ibid., 20(2): 236-38.

23. Ibid., 20(1): 137. The passenger train with the intractable conductor was prevented from going beyond Munfordville.

24. Ibid., 138-40.

25. Wyeth, *Sabre*, 186-87; Holland, *Morgan*, 186.

26. Louisville *Journal*, January 8, 1863; Wyeth, *Sabre*, 187-88.

27. Duke, *Reminiscences*, 124-25; Louisville *Journal*, January 8, 12, 1863.

28. *OR* (ser. 1) 20(1): 157; Duke, *History*, 340-41; Thomas, *Morgan*, 70; Wyeth, *Sabre*, 189-90; Porter memoir.

29. *OR* (ser. 1) 20(1): 143-46.

30. Ibid., 145; Sidney P. Cunningham, handwritten account, JHMP-TU.

31. *OR* (ser. 1) 20(1): 134; Duke, *History*, 342; McDonough, *Stones River*, 166-71.

32. *OR* (ser. 1) 20(1): 176, 371-72, 20(2): 62-63, 144, 185, 272, 287, 289; McDonough, *Stones River*, 65-66. Gen. Jeremiah T. Boyle in Louisville was commander of 17,488 men in the western district of Kentucky. He reported to General Wright, commander of the Department of the Ohio, with headquarters in Cincinnati. Rosecrans had a brigade of 2,969 men under Gen. James B. Steedman guarding the L&N in southern Kentucky and northern Tennessee.

33. JHM to MM, January 2, 1863, JHMP-SHC. Morgan had 3,900 men, and Forrest had 2,100.

34. *OR* (ser. 1) 23(2): 14, 49.

35. Ibid., 20(1): 672, 20(2): 504; Richmond *Examiner*, December 30, 1862; Richmond *Whig*, January 16, 1863; Richmond *Dispatch*, December 30, 1862, January 5, 31, 1863.

36. Starr, *Grenfell's Wars*, 86; Duke, *History*, 321-22; Mary Cahal to MM, December 16, 1862, JHMP-SHC.

37. JHM to MM, December 23, 1862, January 2, 1863, JHMP-SHC.

38. JHM to MM, January 2, 1863, JHMP-SHC.

39. Tower, *Manigault*, 54; MM to JHM, January 6, 1863, JHMP-SHC.

40. MM to JHM, January 6, 1863, JHMP-SHC; Holland, *Morgan*, 187.

13. The Winter of Romance

1. Connelly, *Autumn of Glory*, 69; Duke, *History*, 351; JHM to MM, January 17, 1863, quoted in Holland, *Morgan*, 203; MM to Mary Cheatham, February (no day), 1863, JHMP-SHC.

2. Duke, *History*, 29; Withers journal, WP-SHC; Holland, *Morgan*, 195; JHM to MM, March 21, 1863, JHMP-SHC.

3. JHM to MM, March 21, August 10, 1863, JHMP-SHC; Francis Key Morgan to HM, September 20, 1864, HMP-UK.

4. Tower, *Manigault*, 72; Hathaway journal; Basil W. Duke, *Morgan's Cavalry* (New York, 1909), 256; Duke, *History*, 346-47, 400-401.

5. French diary, February 15, 1863; MM to Mary Cheatham, February (no day), 1863; unidentified, undated clipping, typed copy, JHMP-WKU. Richmond *Enquirer*, April 1, 7, 1863, quoted in J. Cutler Andrews, *The South Reports the Civil War* (Princeton, N.J., 1970), 340.

6. French diary, February 15, 1863.

7. Ibid.; MM to Mary Cheatham, February (no day), 1863; unidentified, undated clipping, typed copy, JHMP-WKU.

8. Duke, *History*, 354-55; unidentified clipping, September 19, 1866, THHP-UK. There was no "Captain Johnson" in the Fifth Kentucky Cavalry—apparently Morgan created the name.

9. *OR* (ser. 2) 5: 188-89, 192; Milton account.

10. Duke, *History*, 404-05.

11. *OR* (ser. 1) 23(2): 656; Horace Ready to MM, undated, JHMP-SHC.

12. Duke, *History*, 376-77; Hathaway Journal; *OR* (ser. 1) 23(1): 155.

13. *OR* (ser. 1) 23(1): 157; Duke, *History*, 375-80; Hathaway Journal. Union Col. Robert H.G. Minty's cavalry linked up with Hall at 7:00 P.M. *OR* (ser. 1) 23(1): 157.

14. Duke, *History*, 380; JHM to MM, March 21, 1863, JHMP-SHC; *OR* (ser. 1) 23(1): 153.

15. *OR* (ser. 1) 23(1): 153; Richmond *Dispatch*, March 30, 1863; JHM to MM, March 21, 1863, JHMP-SHC.

16. JHM to MM, March 21, 1863 (2nd letter), JHMP-SHC.

17. *OR* (ser. 1) 23(1): 207-14; Duke, *History*, 382-87.

18. JHM to MM, April 4, 1863, JHMP-SHC; Duke, *History*, 389; *OR* (ser. 1) 23(1): 207.

19. Samuel D. Morgan to MM, April 17, 1863, JHMP-SHC; Nashville *Daily Union*, April 14, 1863.

20. *OR* (ser. 1) 23(1): 267, 23(2): 263, 248-49.

21. Ibid. 23(1): 267; 23(2): 783; French diary, April 26, 1863. Duke was at Liberty, twenty-five miles along the front to the right of Woodbury, and was therefore not involved in the action.

22. Louisville *Courier Journal*, January 12, 1901; French diary, April 26, 1863.

23. Duke, *History*, 295.

24. *OR* (ser. 1) 23(1): 268; French diary, April 26, 1863.

25. French diary, April 26, 1863; *OR* (ser. 1) 23(1): 269, 23(2): 785.

26. Chattanooga *Rebel*, undated article reprinted in Richmond *Whig*, April 29, 1863, and Richmond *Dispatch*, April 30, 1863; *OR* (ser. 1) 23(2): 824; Marszalek, *Holmes*, 261.

27. Duke *History*, 390-92; *OR* (ser. 1) 23(1): 269.

28. Duke, *History*, 391-94; Richmond *Dispatch*, May 21, June 1, 1863; Richmond *Whig*, May 21, 1863; Marszalek, *Holmes*, 261.

29. Duke, *History*, 403-06; Braxton Bragg to JHM, June 6, 1863, JHMP-SHC.

14. The Great Raid: Through Kentucky

1. *OR* (ser. 1) 23(1): 705; Howard Swiggett, *The Rebel Raider* (Indianapolis, Ind., 1934); Connelly, *Tennessee*, 66; Starr, *Union Cavalry*, I, 273; Robert S. Henry, *The Story of the Confederacy* (Garden City, N.Y., 1931), 296; Lowell H. Harrison, "The Civil War in Kentucky: Some Persistent Questions," *Register of the Kentucky Historical Society*, 76 (January, 1978), 21.

2. Duke, *History*, 411; Samuel D. Morgan to JHM, June 11, 1863, JHMP-SHC.

3. Duke, *History*, 411; 440. All five of John's brothers had joined the Confederate army, and all except Key, the youngest, went on the raid. Calvin was a captain on John's staff. Dick had been adjutant in Col. Roger W. Hanson's First Regiment of the Kentucky State Guard and had served as aide de camp to Gen. John C. Breckinridge and assistant adjutant general to Kitty's husband, Gen. A.P. Hill; he transferred to John's command in early 1863 and became commander of a newly created regiment. Charlton, who was wounded at Shiloh, was captured three times: in Huntsville, Alabama, recuperating from his Shiloh wound; during Cluke's thrust against Lexington in early 1863; and on the Great Raid, when he was an aide to John. Thomas was a first lieutenant on Duke's staff.

4. JHM to H.W. Walter, June 2, 1863, JHMP-WKU; Joseph Wheeler to H.W. Walter, June 5, 1863, Kinloch Falconer to Joesph Wheeler, June 5, 1863, Mrs. C.S.W. Fleming to MM, January 4, 1864, JHMP-SHC.

5. JHM to MM, June 12, 13, 1863, quoted in Holland, *Morgan*, 222.

6. *OR* (ser. 1) 23(1): 817. Louisville had about 2,000 Home Guards and 1,600 soldiers, many of them convalescents. *OR* (ser. 1) 23(1): 691; Louisville *Journal*, July 10, 1863. But what protected the city from cavalry raids throughout the war was its location on the Ohio River. In Paris or Georgetown or other towns, a raider could head in any direction and keep the opposition off balance; in Louisville the options were reduced and the chance of being captured much greater.

7. *OR* (ser. 1) 23(1): 817-18; Duke, *History*, 321.

8. *OR* (ser. 1) 23(2): 442; Duke, *History*, 415; JHM to MM, June 20, 1863, JHMP-SHC.

9. *OR* (ser. 1) 23(1): 384-93; Duke, *History*, 414; Warner, *Generals in Blue*, 57.

10. *OR* (ser. 1) 23(1): 655, 23(2): 392, 417, 447, 469; James R. Bentley, ed., "The Civil War Memoirs of Captain Thomas Speed," *Filson Club History Quarterly*, 44 (July, 1970), 241; Warner, *Generals in Blue*, 255-56; John L. Blair, "Morgan's Ohio Raid," *Filson Club History Quarterly*, 36 (July, 1962), 245-49; Lowell H. Harrison, "A Federal Officer Pursues John Hunt Morgan," *Filson Club History Quarterly*, 48 (April, 1974), 133.

11. *OR* (ser. 1) 23(1): 679-80, 23(2): 469.

12. Duke, *History*, 419-20; *OR* (ser. 1) 23(1): 646.

13. Duke, *History*, 424-27; *OR* (ser. 1) 23(1): 648-49. Tom was first lieutenant of Company I of the 2nd Kentucky, but John had transferred him to Duke's staff to prevent him from placing himself in line where the fire was hottest.

14. *OR* (ser. 1) 23(1): 648-49; Charlton Morgan to HM, July 6, 1863, HMP-UK; Lexington *Herald-Leader*, August 2, 1960; Maria Knott to Samuel C. Knott, August 5, 1863, Knott Collection, Kentucky Library, Western Kentucky University, Bowling Green; Charles A. Johnston, "Lebanon as I Have Known It: Recollections," 111, copy of typed mss., Filson Club Library, Louisville. After a simple rite, Tom was buried in the flower garden of Rev. Thomas H. Cleland, where his body remained until 1868.

15. Louisville *Journal*, July 11, 13, 1863; *OR* (ser. 1) 23(1): 649; Hathaway journal; Duke, *History*, 427.

16. *OR* (ser. 1) 23(1): 652-53; Louisville *Journal*, July 13, 1863.

17. Plum, *Telegraph*, II, 58; *OR* (ser. 1) 23(1): 702; Knoxville *Southern Chronicle*, August

8, 1863. Ellsworth knew the operators would be suspicious if he took the key, so he had them transmit for him. This was the second passenger train Ellsworth had decoyed on the raid. On July 4, on the Lebanon branch line, he had lured a train from Louisville into an ambush five miles west of Lebanon. The detachment with him tore up the track, burned a culvert, and derailed the engine and several cars, killing a Union soldier and wounding a male passenger. Plum, *Telegraph*, II, 55-57.

18. Knoxville *Southern Chronicle*, August 8, 1863; Richmond *Examiner*, July 21, 1863; Louisville *Journal*, July 8, 1863.

19. Duke, *History*, 428-30; *OR* (ser. 1) 27(1): 684, 703, 706, 714; Indiana W.P. Logan, *Kelion Franklin Peddicord* (New York, 1908), 124.

20. Byron (no surname) to Hattie (no surname), June 28, 1863, individual letter, ALS, University of Kentucky Library, Lexington; *OR* (ser. 1) 23(2): 663-67, 688, 692, 694-96, 701. There were about 2,000 men in the Michigan regiments.

21. *OR* (ser. 1) 23(1): 655-56.

22. *OR* (ser. 1) 23(1): 628, 655, 658; Hambleton Tapp, "Incidents in the Life of Colonel Frank Wolford, Colonel of the First Kentucky Cavalry," *Filson Club History Quarterly*, 10 (April, 1936), 82-99.

23. Warner, *Generals in Blue*, 231-32; *OR* (ser. 1) 23(1): 695-96; Harrison, "Morgan," 133.

24. *OR* (ser. 1) 23(1): 659, 717.

25. Louisville *Journal*, July 9, 10, 1863. Decoying the *Alice Dean* with fake distress signals violated international law. Halleck, *Law*, II, 26-27.

26. *Official Records of the Union and Confederate Navies in the War of the Rebellion*, 31 vols. (Washington, D.C., 1894-1922), (ser. 1) 25: 243, 245 (hereafter *ORN*); Duke, *History*, 432-33; J.D. Sprakes diary, July 8, 1863, J.D. Sprakes Collection, Filson Club Library, Louisville; Louisville *Journal*, July 10, 1863; *OR* (ser. 1) 23(1): 659; Arville L. Funk, *The Morgan Raid in Indiana and Ohio (1863)* (Mentone, Ind., 1971), 5.

15. The Great Raid: Indiana and Ohio

1. Basil W. Duke, *The Great Indiana-Ohio Raid* (Louisville, Ky., n.d.), 16.

2. Henry L. Stone to his father, July 8, 1863, typed copy, Henry L. Stone Papers, Indiana Historical Society Library, Indianapolis; unidentified, undated clipping, JHMP-WKU.

3. Milton account.

4. History of Jennings County, typed copy, Alice Ann Bundy Papers, Indiana Division, Indiana State Library, Indianapolis; Kate Starks to Leander Starks, July 15, 1863, Kate Starks letters, Indiana Division, Indiana State Library, Indianapolis; Duke, *Raid*, 22.

5. Pamela J. Bennett, "Curtis R. Burke's Civil War Journal," *Indiana Magazine of History*, 65 (1969), 310.

6. *ORN* (ser. 1) 25: 254; Milton account; *Harper's Magazine* (August, 1865); Richmond *Dispatch*, July 28, 1863; Knightstown *Tri-State Trader*, November 21, 1970; Seymour *Times*, July 15, 1863; Duke, *History*, 437.

7. Arville L. Funk, *The Battle of Corydon* (Corydon, Ind., 1976), 13, 19; Funk, *Raid*, 29; Corydon *Weekly Democrat*, July 14, 1863; Aurora *Commercial*, July 30, 1863; Davis, *Law*, 306; Arville L. Funk to author, March 27, 1984; Hathaway journal. On Buck Creek in Harrison County, Indiana, Peter Lopp refused to pay, and his mill was destroyed. Funk, *Corydon*, 11. It should be noted that Duke was present and unable to deter the looting. He probably would have failed to prevent depredations on the Last Kentucky Raid as well.

8. *OR* (ser. 1) 23(1): 644; Ramage, "Indiana's Response to John Hunt Morgan's Raid," *Journal of the Jackson Purchase Historical Society*, 8 (June, 1980), 1-9.

9. *OR* (ser. 1) 23(1): 749; Duke, *History*, 446. On the skirmish at Corydon, the only significant action in Indiana during the raid, see Funk, *Corydon*.

10. McPherson, *Ordeal*, 345-47. Swiggett's *Rebel Raider* has the thesis that Morgan was involved with the Copperheads. James D. Horan described how Morgan's friend and of-

ficer, Thomas H. Hines, conspired with them in 1864-65, after he left Morgan's command. See Horan, *Confederate Agent: A Discovery in History* (New York, 1954).

11. Kate Starks to Leander Starks, July 15, 1863; Jeremiah H. Simms, *Last Night and Last Day of John Morgan's Raid* (n.p., 1913), 12.

12. Duke, *History*, 440-43; Henry, *Confederacy*, 297; Sprakes diary, July 13, 1863.

13. Duke, *History*, 444; Milton account.

14. Milton account; Hathaway journal.

15. Unidentified, undated clipping, DMFP-SHC; Hathaway journal; *OR* (ser. 1) 23(1): 658.

16. Adam R. Johnson, *The Partisan Rangers of the Confederate States Army* (Louisville, Ky., 1904), 146-47; Duke, *History*, 448.

17. *OR* (ser. 1) 23(1): 657.

18. Ibid., 645, 662.

19. Ibid., 640; Harrison, "Morgan," 134; Aurora *Commercial*, July 23, 1863.

20. Harrison, "Morgan," 135, 138; *OR* (ser. 1) 23(1): 660-63.

21. *OR* (ser. 1) 23(1): 655-56, 711, 770, 781.

22. Ibid., 737, 760-61, 766; *Harper's Magazine* (August, 1865), 294.

23. Myron J. Smith, "Gunboats at Buffington: The U.S. Navy and Morgan's Raid, 1863," *West Virginia History*, 44 (Winter, 1983), 97-98; *ORN* (ser. 1) 25: 243-44, 250-56. The *Springfield*, which delayed the crossing at Brandenburg, was one of Fitch's boats.

24. Myron J. Smith, "An Indiana Sailor Scuttles Morgan's Raid," *Indiana History Bulletin*, 48 (June, 1971), 92; Smith, "Raid," 105; *ORN* (ser. 1) 25: 253-54; Hathaway journal; Duke, *History*, 460. Warping involved fastening a line to a tree or anchoring it upriver and having the crew tug on the line, dragging the boat over the bar.

25. Smith, "Raid," 106: *ORN* (ser. 1) 25: 243.

26. *ORN* (ser. 1) 25: 243-44.

27. Harrison, "Morgan," 137; *OR* (ser. 1) 23(1): 641, 656; Hathaway journal.

28. George A. Ellsworth to Charlton Morgan, August 20 (no year), in unidentified, undated clipping, MBF-KHS; *OR* (ser. 1) 23(1): 769.

29. *OR* (ser. 1) 23(1): 642-44; Ramage, "Hunts and Morgans," 267. Commander of the 8th Kentucky Cavalry, Shackelford was from Lincoln County, Kentucky. Warner, *Generals in Blue*, 433-34.

30. *ORN* (ser. 1) 23: 644; Ramage, "Hunts and Morgans," 267-68. After the war there was considerable controversy over who should have credit for receiving Morgan's unorthodox surrender. Clearly, Morgan gave up when Maj. George W. Rue's force, under General Shackelford's command, was closing in on him. Morgan was only using Burbick to gain lenient terms.

31. *OR* (ser. 1) 25(1): 245.

32. Cumming, *Journal*, 75; Jones, *Diary*, I, 384; Robert G.H. Kean, *Inside the Confederate Government: The Diary of Robert Garlick Hill Kean*, ed. Edward Younger (New York, 1957), 81-82; Richmond *Enquirer*, July 31, 1863.

33. Richmond *Enquirer*, July 27, 1863; Richmond *Examiner*, July 27, 28, 1863; unidentified, undated clipping, JHMP-WKU.

34. Hattaway and Jones, *History*, 444-45.

35. Ibid., 655.

36. Indianapolis *Gazette*, July 13, 1863.

37. *Harrison County Agricultural Society Centennial Program* (1959), 53; P.W. Taylor to Adjutant General's Office, July 13, 1863, correspondence of the Ohio Adjutant General, Ohio Historical Society, Columbus; Indianapolis *Journal*, July 15, 1863. The Louisville & Evansville Mail Co. presented a bell to the citizens of Mauckport in gratitude for Sherman's saving one of their boats.

38. If the guerrillas organized under the partisan act had widely raided Union regions, they would probably have produced the same result. Their best chance was to fight on the defensive in the Confederacy and hope to wear down Northern resolve with a lengthy war.

16. Free Shave and a Haircut

1. Sprakes diary, July 23, 1863; *OR* (ser. 1) 23(1): 14; Duke, *History*, 464.

2. Huntsville *Confederate*, printed in Marietta, Ga., December 18, 1863.

3. *OR* (ser. 1) 23(1): 6, (ser. 2) 6: 153, 156-57. The enlisted men were kept in military prisons.

4. William B. Hesseltine, *Civil War Prisons: A Study in War Psychology*, American Classics Series (New York, 1964), 96; Davis, *Law*, 315.

5. *OR* (ser. 2) 6: 495-96; Richmond *Enquirer*, August 8, 1863.

6. Richmond *Enquirer*, August 8, 1863; *OR* (ser. 1) 6: 420.

7. Richmond *Enquirer*, January 5, 1864; Duke, *History*, 271, 469. Morgan's money belt was stuffed with gold coins and greenbacks, which, presumably, he would have deposited in the Confederate treasury.

8. *Southern Literary Messenger* (February, 1863).

9. Poem, September 10, 1863, MBS-NKU.

10. Jones, *Diary*, II, 17; Cumming, *Journal*, 86; Marszalek, *Holmes*, 293-94; unidentified, undated clipping, JHMP-WKU. With romantic fascination, Jones read all the mail coming into the department from the West and finally determined for himself the truth that nobody was shaved. Jones, *Diary*, II, 22, 26, 89.

11. Louisville *Journal*, June 11, 13, 1864; Richmond *Enquirer*, February 6, 1864; unidentified, undated clipping, JHMP-WKU.

12. *OR* (ser. 2) 6: 421, 448, 724-26.

13. Cincinnati *Enquirer*, January 7, 1883; "Reminiscences and Prison Journal of Thomas Walker Bullitt," typed copy, Bullitt Family Papers, Southern Historical Collection, University of North Carolina Library, Chapel Hill (hereafter Bullitt journal).

14. Robert Ould to Preston Johnston, September 19, 1863, Richard C. Morgan to Preston Johnston, August 29, 1863, JHMP-SHC.

15. *OR* (ser. 1) 6: 668-70; Hesseltine, *Prisons*, 42-51; JHM to MM, August 10, 1863, JHMP-SHC; CM to HM, September 7, 1863, BGTHP-HMH.

16. *OR* (ser. 2) 6: 158, 733; Duke, *History*, 492-93; Thomas W. Bullitt, "More of General Morgan's Escape," *Southern Bivouac*, 1 (July, 1885), 119.

17. Duke, *History*, 468.

18. *OR* (ser. 1) 6: 478, 841-42; Hathaway journal.

19. Martinez, "Compulsive Gambling," 365-67.

20. JHM to MM, October 12, 1863, JHM to Mrs. Charles Ready, November 9, 1863, JHMP-SHC.

21. JHM to MM, September 13, October 12, November 18, 1863, JHM to Mrs. Charles Ready, November 9, 1863, JHMP-SHC.

22. JHM to MM, August 30, November 10, 18, 1863, JHMP-SHC.

23. William P. Johnston to MM, September 30, 1863, Robert Ould to MM, October 30, 1863, JHMP-SHC; *OR* (ser. 2) 6: 229, 237; Hesseltine, *Prisons*, 104. Alabama courts ruled that they lacked jurisdiction over Dow and transferred his case back to the military authorities.

24. Martinez, "Compulsive Gambling," 365-67; Richmond *Enquirer*, January 5, 1864; Bullitt, "Escape," 116; Hopkins County *Gleaner*, undated clipping, HMP-UK; *OR* (ser. 2) 6: 725.

25. *OR* (ser. 2) 6: 448, 461, 675, 725.

26. Hesseltine, *Prisons*, 1; *OR* (ser. 2) 6: 448, 461, 672, 675, 677, 725.

27. Richmond *Enquirer*, January 5, 1864; Columbus *Ohio State Journal*, November 30, 1863; Hesseltine, *Prisons*, 50; JHM to MM, November 18, 1863, JHMP-SHC. The saws were capable of cutting through the prison bars. By penitentiary standards, the military authorities were being unduly lax.

28. JHM to MM, November 18, 1863, JHMP-SHC; Bullitt journal; Richmond *Enquirer*, January 5, 1864.

29. Richmond *Enquirer*, January 5, 1864.

30. Duke, *History*, 481-83; Richmond *Enquirer*, January 5, 1864.

31. *OR* (ser. 2) 6: 666, 726, 731; Duke, *History*, 483-84.

32. *OR* (ser. 2) 6: 667, 669, 728, 731; Thomas H. Hines, "General Morgan's Escape," *Southern Bivouac*, 1 (June, 1885), 53; Lucy Dorsey to Henry Bruce, Jr., December 3, 1863, MBS-NKU.

33. Bullitt, "Escape," 117; *OR* (ser. 2) 6: 636. Orders dated November 17 assigned Mason to duty as acting assistant provost marshal general in San Francisco, where he served until March 10, 1865. He remained in the army after the war, serving a total of forty-one years. He retired in 1888 and died in Washington, D.C., in 1897.

34. Bullitt, "Escape," 117-18.

35. Ibid., 118; Hines, "Escape," 54.

36. Richmond *Whig*, January 5, 1864; Hines, "Escape," 54; *OR* (ser. 2) 6: 733; Duke, *History*, 485, 487.

37. Bullitt journal.

38. Lexington *Kentucky Leader*, October 28, 1894; unidentified, undated clipping, JHMP-WKU.

39. *OR* (ser. 2) 6: 666; Bullitt journal.

40. *OR* (ser. 2) 6: 632, 670-71, 724; Columbus *Crisis*, December 2, 1863.

41. Richmond *Enquirer*, January 5, 1864; Richmond *Whig*, January 15, 1864; Columbus *Ohio Statesman*, November 27, 1863.

42. Richmond *Enquirer*, January 5, 1864; L.D. Hockersmith, *Morgan's Escape* (Madisonville, Ky., 1903), 49.

43. Caroline S. Cunningham, typed account, JHMP-TU. Morgan and Hines identified the woman who befriended them in Ludlow as Mrs. Ludlow. She may have been Helen A. Ludlow, widow of Israel Ludlow for whom Ludlow is named. Israel was the son of one of the founders of Cincinnati; before Ludlow was incorporated he owned all the land within its borders. Helen was a native of Alexandria, Virginia. She lived near the Ohio River on River Road, which connected Ludlow and Covington. C. Vann Woodward, ed., *Mary Chestnut's Civil War* (New Haven, Conn., 1981), 536.

44. Richmond *Examiner*, January 5, 1864; Hines, "Escape," 55-59; Richmond *Whig*, January 15, 1864.

45. Richmond *Examiner*, January 5, 1864. Hines was guided across the mountains by a ten-year-old boy. Richmond *Whig*, January 15, 1864.

46. Louisville *Courier-Journal*, October 18, 1936; Richmond *Enquirer*, December 25, 1863, January 5, 14, 1864; Marszalek, *Holmes*, 334.

47. JHM to MM, December 24, 1863, Mrs. C.S.W. Fleming to MM, January 4, 1864, JHMP-SHC; Richmond *Enquirer*, January 19, 1864; unidentified, undated clipping, JHMP-WKU.

48. Gwyn A. Parry to G. Glenn Clift, September 28, 1958, MFF-KHS; Richmond *Enquirer*, January 12, 1862; unidentified, undated clipping, JHMP-WKU.

17. Deprived of Command

1. Richmond *Enquirer*, January 11, 1864.

2. Holland, *Morgan*, 297; William P. Johnston to JHM, April 12, 1864, Charlton Morgan to MM, March 30, 1864, JHMP-SHC; *OR* (ser. 2) 6: 1055, 1076.

3. Richmond *Examiner*, January 11, 1864.

4. Emory M. Thomas, *The Confederate State of Richmond: A Biography of the Capital* (Austin, Tex., 1971), 143; Hudson Strode, *Jefferson Davis*, 3 vols. (New York, 1955-64), II. 6.

5. Connelly and Jones, *Politics of Command*, 79-80; Davis, *Breckinridge*, 403; McMurry, *Hood*, 83; Woodward, *Chesnut's Civil War*, 534; Richmond *Whig*, January 18, 1864.

6. Connelly and Jones, *Politics of Command*, 80.

7. Richmond *Examiner*, January 9, 15, 1864; Richmond *Enquirer*, January 12, 27, 1864.

8. Duke, *History*, 507-11; Richmond *Enquirer*, December 25, 1863.

9. Richmond *Examiner*, January 9, 1864; Charleston *Mercury*, January 13, 1864.

10. Richmond *Examiner*, January 14, 15, February 5, 1864; Fitzgerald Ross, *Cities and Camps of the Confederate States*, ed. Richard B. Harwell, (Urbana, Ill., 1958), 175; applications for transfer, January, 1864, JHMP-SHC.

11. Harry D. Burr to JHM, January 10, 1864, H.C. Moore and E.H. Keasler to JHM, January 15, 1864, James M. Cox to JHM, January 21, 1864, JHMP-SHC.

12. Wiley, *Johnny Reb*, 142; Allen D. Carpenter, et al. to JHM, April 29, 1862, HMP-UK; G.T. Goode to JHM, August 24, 1862, John Wharton to JHM, March 5, 1863, JHMP-SHC; *OR* (ser. 1) 20(2): 391.

13. J.P. Bland to JHM, January 14, 1864, H.I. Jasper, et al. to JHM, January 14, 1864, Charles F. James to JHM, January 15, 1864, J. Porter Hamilton to JHM, January 17, 1864, JHMP-SHC.

14. Philip W. Alexander to JHM, January 18, 1864, A.J. Swinebroad to JHM, January 9, 1864, Robert Burch, et al. to JHM, January 8, 1864, JHMP-SHC.

15. Form letter, n.d., Opie Starte to JHM, May 18, 1864, JHMP-SHC; Atlanta *Intelligencer*, January 22, 1864; W.S. Bacon to JHM, January 25, 1864, quoted in Holland, *Morgan*, 302.

16. Robert E. Lee to Jefferson Davis, January 20, 1864, JHMP-SHC; *OR* (ser. 1) 32(2): 604.

17. Richmond *Enquirer*, January 1, 9, 1864; Richmond *Whig*, January 1, 15, 1864; Adam R. Johnson to JHM, January 5, 1864, William H. Barnes to JHM, February 12, 1864, JHMP-SHC; Macon *Telegraph*, undated clipping, HMP-UK; Atlanta *Intelligencer*, January 13, 23, 24, 1864.

18. Richmond *Examiner*, January 21, 1864; William H. Orchard to JHM, February 3, 1864, Mrs. John A. Bradley to JHM, January 27, 1864, JHMP-SHC. After Morgan returned their donation, the student body at Columbia offered to give him a reception. Apparently, Morgan refunded all donations.

19. Richmond *Examiner*, January 20, February 18, 1864; B. Mordecai to JHM, February 1, 1864, L.H. Locker to JHM, April 6, 1864, L. Loeser & Co. to JHM, February 5, 1864, JHMP-SHC.

20. *OR* (ser. 1) 32(2): 602, 619, 621-22. In a letter to Breckinridge requesting assignment to his department in southwest Virginia Morgan estimated that in Kentucky there were nearly 50,000 horses belonging to the Union government. JHM to John C. Breckinridge, February 13, 1864, in possession of Frank G. Rankin, Louisville.

21. *OR* (ser. 1) 32(2): 602-03, 619, 621-22.

22. Samuel Carter, *The Siege of Atlanta, 1864* (New York, 1973), 34, 91; unidentified clipping, February 6, 1864, typed copy, JHMP-WKU; Atlanta *Intelligencer*, February 7, 9, 1864.

23. MM to Charlton Morgan, February 14, 1864, George W. Morgan to HM, February 24, 1864, HMP-UK; *OR* (ser. 1) 32(2): 743.

24. Connelly, *Autumn of Glory*, 292-95; *OR* (ser. 1) 32(2): 788-89, 811-12, 818, 820. Morgan's remnant in Johnston's army was in Joseph Wheeler's cavalry, in a brigade commanded by Col. Warren Grigsby. It consisted of the 9th Kentucky Cavalry regiment, commanded by W.C.P. Breckinridge, a battalion commanded by Captain Dortch, and a battalion under Captain Kirkpatrick. William F. Bell to JHM, January 12, 1864, W.C.P. Breckinridge to JHM, February 11, 1864, JHMP-SHC.

25. Duke, *History*, 514-15; *OR* (ser. 1) 52(2): 651-52; Connelly and Jones, *Politics of Command*, 79.

26. JHM to Samuel Cooper, March 16, 1864, typed copy, MRF-KHS; Duke, *History*, 514.

27. Holland, *Morgan*, 298; Connelly and Jones, *Politics of Command*, 79; William E. Metzler, *Morgan and His Dixie Cavaliers* (Columbus, Ohio, 1976), 84.

18. The Last Kentucky Raid

1. JHM to William E. Simms, April 19, 1864, Robert A. Alston to J.D. Kirkpatrick, April 3, 1864, JHM to J.D. Kirkpatrick, April 12, 1864, JHMP-SHC; W. Buck Yearns

and John G. Barrett, eds., *North Carolina Civil War Documentary* (Chapel Hill, N.C., 1980), 200-203.

2. Robert A. Alston to J.D. Kirkpatrick, April 3, 1864, JHMP-SHC; Yearns and Barrett, *North Carolina*, 200-203; James F. Corn, *Jim Witherspoon: A Soldier of the South, 1862-1865* (Cleveland, Tenn., 1962), 1-15.

3. Richard M. Brown, "Historical Patterns of American Violence," in Graham and Gurr, *Violence in America*, 21-22; Wiley, *Johnny Reb*, 234; General Orders no. 89, October 20, 1864; Thomas E. Bramlette Papers, Kentucky State Library and Archives, Frankfort; Lloyd Lewis, *Sherman: Fighting Prophet* (New York, 1932), 452, 454.

4. Cotton, "North Carolina," 3-4, 31-33, 55-56, 97-98; Paludan, *Victims*, 3, 10, 23; Barrett, *North Carolina*, 240.

5. Affidavits, May 3, 1864, sworn before John Gambill, justice of the peace, Allegheny County, North Carolina, JHMP-SHC.

6. David Edwards to J.R. Burke, May 6, 1864, JHMP-SHC.

7. J.R. Burke to Ninth District Enlistment Officer, May 12, 1864, Peter Mollett to Bureau of Conscripts, May 19, 1864, Bureau of Conscription to JHM, May 27, 1864, JHMP-SHC.

8. MM to HM, February 25, 1864, HMP-UK; JHM to MM, undated, and March 29, 1864, unidentified, undated clipping, JHMP-SHC; Walter H. Hendricks to author, September 29, October 5, 1984; L.C. Angle to author, October 8, 10, 1984; Abingdon *Washington County News*, January 31, 1974.

9. MM to HM, March 29, 1864, HMP-UK; JHM to MM, June 1, 27, 1864, unidentified, undated clipping, JHMP-SHC; Charles A. Withers to D. Howard Smith, September 27, 1883, M-KHS; James M. Fry, *The Death of General John H. Morgan and What Led Up to It* (Wills Point, Tex., n.d.), 10; Scott and Angel, *Thirteenth Regiment*, 181.

10. Richmond *Enquirer*, April 23, 1864; JHM to Chief of Ordnance, Longstreet's Corps, April 5, 1864, JHMP-SHC; *OR* (ser. 1) 37(1): 66-68, 39(1): 76.

11. Kevin H. Siepel, *Rebel: The Life and Times of John Singleton Mosby* (New York, 1983), 11.

12. JHM to MM, May 11, 1864, JHMP-SHC.

13. Unidentified, undated clipping, JHMP-WKU; Withers account.

14. JHM to MM, May 11, 1864, JHMP-SHC.

15. *OR* (ser. 1) 39(2): 36, 39.

16. Ibid., 174, 203.

17. Ibid., 39(1): 22, 24, 33, 39, 68.

18. Ibid., 39, 76; George Dallas Mosgrove, *Kentucky Cavaliers in Dixie: Reminiscences of a Confederate Cavalryman*, ed. Bell I. Wiley, (Jackson, Tenn., 1957), 136; Bryan H. Allen to JHM, May 23, 1864, JHM to James W. Bowles, May 23, 1864, JHMP-SHC.

19. JHM to MM, May 31, 1864, JHM to Samuel Cooper, May 31, 1864, JHMP-SHC; *OR* (ser. 1) 39(1): 66.

20. Mosgrove, *Cavaliers*, 118-19, 249-50, 253-55.

21. JHM to James W. Bowles, May 23, 1864, JHM to W.E. Simms, June 25, 1864, JHMP-SHC; Duke, *History*, 520; D. Howard Smith to James F. Robinson, February 1, 1869, M-KHS.

22. JHM to MM, May 31, June 1, 1864, JHMP-SHC.

23. JHM to MM, June 7, 1864, JHMP-SHC.

24. JHM official report, July 20, 1864, JHMP-SHC; *OR* (ser. 1) 39(1): 34, 68, 39(2): 88.

25. JHM official report, July 20, 1864, JHMP-SHC; *OR* (ser. 1) 39(1): 68; JHM to MM, June 8, 1864, JHMP-SHC; Mosgrove, *Cavaliers*, 140.

26. *OR* (ser. 1) 39(1): 74, 77, 80-81, 83; *Kentucky Reports*, Vol 63, Pt. 2, 496-99; Davis, *Law*, 306, 311; D. Howard Smith memo, June 25, 1865, M-KHS.

27. E.C. Barlow to D.H. Smith, July 3, 1865, M-KHS; Patrick Michael McCoy, "John Hunt Morgan: A Reevaluation of His Military Career" (master's thesis, Southern Illinois University, 1981), 74; *Kentucky Court of Appeals Reports*, (Frankfort, Ky., 1867), Vol. 63, Pt. 2, 496-99 (hereafter *Kentucky Reports*).

28. *OR* (ser. 1) 39(1): 68, 72-73.

29. JHM official report, July 20, 1864, JHMP-SHC; JHM to MM, June 7, 1864, JHMP-SHC.

30. *OR* (ser. 1) 39(1): 23-24, 28, 44, 79.

31. Mount Sterling *Sentinel Democrat*, June 28, 1961.

32. JHM to MM, June 8, 1864, JHMP-SHC; *OR* (ser. 1) 39(1): 77; Lexington *Observer and Reporter*, June 15, 1864.

33. G. Glenn Clift, *History of Maysville and Mason County* (Lexington, Ky., 1936), 179-80, 234-35; Maysville *Bulletin*, June 9, 1864.

34. JHM official report, July 20, 1864, JHMP-SHC; Duke, *History*, 526.

35. *OR* (ser. 1) 39(1): 24, 52, 78; Lexington *Observer and Reporter*, June 11, 15, 1864.

36. Mosgrove, *Cavaliers*, 149; D. Howard Smith to James F. Robinson, February 1, 1869, M-KHS; Lexington *Observer and Reporter*, June 15, 1864.

37. JHM official reports, July 20, 1864, June 11, 1864, JHMP-SHC; Duke, *History*, 526-27; *OR* (ser. 1) 39(1): 28, 34-36. Morgan and Hobson came to the unorthodox agreement that Hobson and his officers would be paroled and sent under escort of Cal Morgan and two other Confederate officers to Cincinnati, where they were to offer themselves in exchange for Morgan's imprisoned officers. If the Union army rejected the bargain, Hobson was to report as a prisoner of war within Confederate lines. Refusing to recognize the deal, Union authorities detained the escort for several weeks.

38. Mosgrove, *Cavaliers*, 157; Duke, *History*, 527; JHM official report, June 11, 1864, JHMP-SHC.

39. JHM official report, June 11, 1864, JHMP-SHC.

40. G.D. Ewing, "Morgan's Last Raid into Kentucky," *Confederate Veteran*, 31 (July, 1923), 254-56.

41. Ibid.

42. Ibid., 256.

43. Duke, *History*, 532.

44. Mosgrove, *Cavaliers*, 160-61; D. Howard Smith official report, July 19, 1864, Mark L. Dismukes to John Dismukes, July 17, 1864, JHMP-SHC; *OR* (ser. 1) 39(1): 25-26, 28. Burbridge was rewarded with personal congratulations from Lincoln and promotion to brevet major general.

45. Mosgrove, *Cavaliers*, 163.

46. JHM official report, June 11, 1864, JHMP-SHC; *OR* (ser. 1) 39(2): 750; Richmond *Enquirer*, April 6, 1864; Duke, *History*, 12, 530; Louisville *Courier-Journal*, November 20, 1960; unidentified, undated clipping, JHMP-WKU.

47. Jones, *Diary*, II, 239-42; Cumming, *Journal*, 133; Richmond *Enquirer*, July 4, 7, 1864; unidentified, undated clipping, JHMP-WKU.

48. *OR* (ser. 1) 39(1): 66, 76. Jones, *Diary*, II, 284.

49. *OR* (ser. 1) 37(1): 160, 39(2): 616, 635, 638-39. Jones had assumed command of the department on May 23 because nobody was in charge. On May 31 he turned it over to Crittenden.

50. Quirk was present on the expedition. Lexington *Herald*, June 25, 1904.

19. The Final Gamble

1. JHM to MM, June 27, 1864, JHMP-SHC; *OR* (ser. 1) 39(2): 635, 657; Paludan, *Victims*, 55, 103-04.

2. JHM to William E. Simms, June 23, 1864, JHMP-SHC; *OR* (ser. 1) 39(2): 722-23.

3. *OR* (ser. 1) 39(2): 664-65, 698-99; JHM to Samuel Cooper, July 2, 1864, JHMP-SHC.

4. *OR* (ser. 1) 39(2): 701, 733, 735; JHM to Robert E. Lee, June 30, 1864, Robert E. Lee to JHM, June 30, 1864, JHMP-SHC; Douglas S. Freeman, *R.E. Lee: A Biography*, 4 vols. (New York, 1934-35), III, 460.

5. *OR* (ser. 1) 39(2): 733.

6. Ibid., 735, 640-41, 746-47.

7. Knoxville *Register,* July 4, 1862; *OR* (ser. 1) 39(2): 80.

8. Alvan C. Gillem to John K. Miller, June 9, 1864, Federal Collection, Tennessee State Library and Archives, Nashville; Leroy P. Graf and Ralph W. Haskins, eds., *The Papers of Andrew Johnson,* 6 vols. to date (Knoxville, Tenn., 1967-), VI, 199; Scott and Angel, *Thirteenth Regiment,* 151, 158.

9. Connelly, *Autumn of Glory,* 434-35; McMurry, *Hood,* 144; Scott and Angel, *Thirteenth Regiment,* 153, 160-61; *OR* (ser. 1) 39(1): 160, 489. Hood, in command of Confederate forces in Atlanta, ordered Wheeler to raid Sherman's communications. Wheeler swept westward into middle Tennessee, and Gillem did not come close to making contact.

10. *OR* (ser. 1) 39(1): 73-80.

11. Ibid., 80, 39(2): 804; JHM to Eli M. Bruce, August 31, 1864, JHMP-SHC. Gen. John Echols succeeded Morgan as departmental commander.

12. JHM to Eli M. Bruce, August 31, 1864, JHMP-SHC.

13. Duke, *History,* 532.

14. JHM to Eli M. Bruce, August 31, 1864, JHMP-SHC. Duke published a letter Morgan wrote to Seddon on September 1 but apparently never mailed. In it he said the allegations were false and demanded an immediate investigation. Duke, *History,* 535-36.

15. Duke, *History,* 532; D. Howard Smith memorandum, September 21, 1866, M-KHS; JHM to MM, September 2, 1864, JHMP-SHC.

16. James E. Cantrill to D. Howard Smith, September 22, 1883, M-KHS; Duke, *History,* 537.

17. Richard H. Doughty, *Greeneville: One Hundred Year Portrait, 1775-1875* (Greeneville, Tenn., 1975), 222, 227, 237; unidentified, undated clipping, Jonathan M. Orr account, JHMP-SHC; Scott and Angel, *Thirteenth Regiment,* 159-60; French diary, April 23, 1865.

18. JHM to MM, September 3, 1864, JHMP-SHC.

19. James E. Cantrill to D. Howard Smith, September 22, 1883, M-KHS; Scott and Angel, *Thirteenth Regiment,* 160-61; Sydney K. Smith, *Life, Army Record, and Public Services of D. Howard Smith* (Louisville, Ky., 1890), 126.

20. Orr account.

21. Richmond *Enquirer,* September 10, 1864; *Southern Literary Messenger* (January, 1863); Freeman, *Lee,* II, 484-85.

22. Doughty, *Greeneville,* 277-79.

23. Unidentified, undated clipping, JHMP-SHC; George W. Hunt to D. Howard Smith, September 24, 1883, M-KHS; Orr account; Doughty, *Greeneville,* 237-38.

24. Fry, *Death,* 7-8; Doughty, *Greeneville,* 230-31; J.W. Scully, "General John Morgan . . . Account of His Death," reprint of a letter to the editor, New Orleans *Picayune,* July 5, 1903, *Southern Historical Society Papers,* 31 (1903), 126; W.A. Smith and Wallace Milam, "The Death of John Hunt Morgan: A Memoir of James M. Fry," *Tennessee Historical Quarterly,* 19 (March, 1960), 58-60; John B. Brownlow to D. Howard Smith, July 10, 1885, D. Howard Smith Papers, Kentucky Historical Society Library, Frankfort (hereafter SP-KHS); unidentified, undated clipping, M-KHS; James F. Corn, *Death in a Garden: A Civil War Chronicle* (Cleveland, Tenn., n.d.), 9-12.

25. James E. Cantrill to D. Howard Smith, September 22, 1883, M-KHS; *National Tribune,* January 12, 1939; Mosgrove, *Cavaliers,* 181.

26. Scott and Angel, *Thirteenth Regiment,* 166-67; Doughty, *Greeneville,* 230-31.

27. Scott and Angel, *Thirteenth Regiment,* 165-67; Doughty, *Greeneville,* 232; *OR* (ser. 1) 39(1): 489.

28. Charles A. Withers to D. Howard Smith, September 27, 1883, M-KHS; Greenwood *Index,* March 26, 1908.

29. *OR* (ser. 1) 39(1): 490; Doughty, *Greeneville,* 232; Scott and Angel, *Thirteenth Regiment,* 167.

30. John B. Brownlow to D. Howard Smith, July 10, 1885, SP-KHS; Smith, *Smith,* 143-44, 187-88; Doughty, *Greeneville,* 232.

31. Withers to Smith, September 27, 1883, Smith memo, September 21, 1866, M-KHS.

32. Orr account.

33. Scott and Angel, *Thirteenth Regiment*, 169; Scully, "Morgan," 126, 128.

34. Scott and Angel, *Thirteenth Regiment*, 173-74.

35. *OR* (ser. 1) 39(1): 492; Withers to Smith, September 27, 1883, M-KHS; Smith, *Smith*, 128.

36. Orr account; unidentified, undated clipping, JHMP-SHC; Smith, *Smith*, 128.

37. *OR* (ser. 1) 39(1): 492; Fry, *Death*, 11-12.

38. Unidentified, undated clipping, reprinted in Philadelphia *Weekly Times*, undated, MBF-KHS.

39. Scott and Angel, *Thirteenth Regiment*, 175-76; Doughty, *Greeneville*, 234; Fry, *Death*, 11-13. Henry "Harry" Boyle Clay was the son of Thomas H. Clay and Marie Mentelle of Lexington, Kentucky.

40. *National Tribune*, January 12, 1939; Smith memo, September 21, 1866; George W. Hunt to ed., Philadelphia *Weekly Times*, n.d., M-KHS.

41. Smith, *Smith*, 138; *OR* (ser. 1) 39(1): 490.

42. Scully, "Morgan," 127; Scott and Angel, *Thirteenth Regiment*, 181-83.

43. Scott and Angel, *Thirteenth Regiment*, 177; Orr account; Fry, *Death*, 18. Lucy's brother, Thomas S. Rumbough, was a captain in the Confederate cavalry and was killed a week later in a skirmish near Morristown, Tennessee.

44. Richmond *Whig*, September 13, 20, 1864; Smith, *Smith*, 129.

45. Thomas Hunt to Cal Morgan, September 26, 1864, HMP-UK; Eli M. Bruce to Charles Ready, September 11, 1864, HM to MM, n.d., August 28 (no year), JHMP-SHC.

46. Duke, *History*, 531-32, 538-40; Basil Duke to Richard C. Morgan, April 16, 1905, James L. Norris Papers, Southern Historical Collection, University of North Carolina Library, Chapel Hill.

47. Doughty, *Greeneville*, 238-39; unidentified, undated clipping, MBF-KHS; Richmond *Enquirer*, September 14, 1864; Orr account.

48. Handwritten manuscript by Sarah E. Thompson, Sarah Thompson to "Sister," May 19, 1865, letter fragment, September 19, 1864, Sarah E. Thompson Papers, William R. Perkins Library, Duke University. In one version she claimed that she rode to Bulls Gap herself rather than sending a boy. In reconstructing the killing of Morgan, the key was an understanding of his personality and life experiences. The rule the author followed in evaluating evidence in the many accounts was to depend upon the testimony of two or more reliable witnesses. For example, Jim Leahy's role is documented from both the Union and Confederate sides, as is testimony that Morgan fled when ordered to surrender.

49. Scully, "Morgan," 128.

50. *OR* (ser. 1) 39(1): 491-92.

51. Scott and Angel, *Thirteenth Regiment*, 184-85; Heitman, *Historical Register*, 276; Fry, *Death*, 15. In Madison, Campbell served in the 19th Infantry regiment commanded by Gen. Charles H. Smith.

52. Unidentified, undated clipping, reprinted in the Philadelphia *Weekly Times*, undated, MBF-KHS; Heitman, *Historical Register*, 276.

53. *OR* (ser. 1) 39(1): 81; Milton P. Jarnagin memoir, Confederate Collection, Tennessee State Library, Nashville.

54. *OR* (ser. 1) 39(1): 81-83, 49(1): 324; Jarnagin memoir; unsigned letter, November 19, 1864, JHMP-SHC; Davis, *Breckinridge*, 470-78. In 1866 in Anderson County Circuit Court, the Farmer's Bank of Kentucky sued James F. Witherspoon, who had been court-martialed for resisting arrest in Greenville, South Carolina, for damages in the robbery. The circuit court rendered judgment against Witherspoon and ordered sale of a tract of land belonging to him. He appealed, and the state Court of Appeals overturned the circuit court and found Witherspoon innocent. The high court ruled that the robbery was a great outrage, and the loss was heavy and should be repaired. They were unable to determine whether Morgan sanctioned or ordered the robbery. Referring to General Orders no. 4, they pointed out that there was evidence that Morgan had attempted to prevent depredations. Regardless, Witherspoon neither "counseled, aided, or even approved, the robbery," the judges determined. Subsequently, Witherspoon distilled whiskey and engaged in other

business in Harrodsburg. He died in 1921 at eighty-one years of age and was buried in his gray uniform in Spring Hill Cemetery in Harrodsburg. *Kentucky Reports*, Vol. 63, Pt. 2, 496-99; Corn, *Witherspoon*, 24-25.

55. Metzler, *Morgan*, 107; *OR* (ser. 1) 38(5): 812.

56. Woodward, *Chesnut's Civil War*, 643; unidentified, undated clipping, Abingdon *Virginian*, undated article reprinted in unidentified, undated clipping, JHMP-SHC.

57. Richmond *Enquirer*, September 7, 1864; Richmond *Whig*, September 6, 1864.

58. Richmond *Whig*, September 8, 1864.

59. Cumming, *Journal*, 149.

20. Hero of the Lost Cause

1. Mosgrove, *Cavaliers*, 176.

2. Basil W. Duke to MM, September 5, 1864, JHMP-SHC.

3. Richmond *Whig*, September 20, 1864; *Confederate Veteran*, 9 (August, 1901), 381.

4. Richmond *Whig*, September 13, 1864; Duke, *History*, 540.

5. Abingdon *Washington County News*, January 31, 1974: unidentified, undated clipping, JHMP-SHC.

6. Unidentified, undated clipping, JHMP-SHC; Thomas, *Morgan*, 114.

7. Francis Key Morgan to HM, September 20, 1864, MM to HM, June 20, 1865, HMP-UK; unidentified, undated clipping, JHMP-SHC.

8. Jones, *Diary*, II, 284; Richmond *Whig*, September 17, 1864; Richmond *Enquirer*, September 16, 17, 1864; unidentified, undated clipping, JHMP-SHC.

9. Richmond *Dispatch*, April 13, 1868; unidentified, undated clipping, JHMP-SHC.

10. HM to CM, October 29, 1864, copy in possession of Burton Milward.

11. MM to HM, July 24, 1865, December 5, 1866, HMP-UK; HM to MM and MM to HM, various undated letters, JHMP-SHC.

12. Richard C. Morgan to MM, December 10, 1867, JHMP-SHC; Lexington *Tri-Weekly Statesman*, March 24, 1868.

13. Richmond *Enquirer and Examiner*, April 11, 1868; Mary Zalinda Morse to Nina Withers, April 19, 1868, typed copy, BGTHP-HMH.

14. Richmond *Enquirer and Examiner*, April 16, 24, 1865; Richmond *Dispatch*, April 13, 1868.

15. Richmond *Dispatch*, April 16, 1868; Washington *National Intelligencer*, April 16, 1868; Washingion *Evening Star*, April 17, 1868; Cincinnati *Commercial*, April 17, 1868. The statue of Lincoln was designed by Lot Flannery and erected in front of City Hall. Washington *National Intelligencer*, April 16, 1868.

16. Cincinnati *Commercial*, April 16, 17, 1868; Cincinnati *Enquirer*, April 14, 1868; Cincinnati *Gazette*, April 13, 1868; Richmond *Enquirer and Examiner*, April 17, 1868; Mary Zalinda Morse to Nina Withers, April 19, 1868, in possession of the family of Mrs. Frank C. Biddle, Cincinnati.

17. Cincinnati *Enquirer*, April 18, 1868; Cincinnati *Commercial*, April 18, 1868; Lexington *Observer and Reporter*, April 18, 1868.

18. Cincinnati *Enquirer*, April 18, 1868; Cincinnati *Commercial*, April 18, 1868; Richmond *Enquirer and Examiner*, April 25, 1868; Nellie Morgan to MM, April 19, 1868, JHMP-SHC.

19. Lexington *Observer and Reporter*, April 18, 1868; Lexington *Kentucky Gazette*, April 18, 1868; Cincinnati *Enquirer*, April 18, 1868; Cincinnati *Commercial*, April 18, 1868; Richmond *Enquirer and Examiner*, April 25, 1868; Nellie Morgan to MM, April 19, 1868, JHMP-SHC.

20. HM to MM, April 19, 1868, JHMP-SHC.

21. Nellie Morgan to MM, April 19, 1868, JHMP-SHC; Richmond *Enquirer and Examiner*, April 25, 1864; Lexington *Kentucky Gazette*, April 18, 1868.

22. HM to MM, April 19, 1868, JHMP-SHC.

23. Lexington *Observer and Reporter*, April 18, 1868; Richmond *Enquirer and Examiner*, April 25, 1868; Mary Zalinda Morse to Nina Withers, April 19, 1868, typed copy, BGTHP-HMH.

24. Cincinnati *Commercial*, April 18, 1868; Lexington *Kentucky Gazette*, April 18, 1868; unidentified, undated clipping, JHMP-WKU.

25. Lexington *Observer and Reporter*, April 18, 1868; Thomas L. Connelly and Barbara L. Bellows, *God and General Longstreet: The Lost Cause and the Southern Mind* (Baton Rouge, La., 1982), 2-3.

26. Connelly and Bellows, *Lost Cause*, 1-4.

27. Ibid., 1-2, 6-82; Charles R. Wilson, *Baptized in Blood: The Religion of the Lost Cause, 1865-1920* (Athens, Ga., 1980), 1-57.

28. Duke, *History*, 13-15, 55-56, 85, 262-76; Hambleton Tapp and James C. Klotter, *Kentucky: Decades of Discord, 1865-1900* (Frankfort, Ky., 1977), 2.

29. Duke, *History*, 2-3, 11, 28; Harrison, *Kentucky*, 102, 106; Coulter, *Kentucky*, 187, 296-311.

30. Tapp and Klotter, *Kentucky*, 14; Coulter, *Kentucky*, 285-96, 300-301.

31. Tapp and Klotter, *Kentucky*, 163, 170, 415, 461, 465; Coulter, *Kentucky*, 285-96, 300-01; James C. Klotter, "Sex, Scandal, and Suffrage in the Gilded Age," *Historian*, 42 (February, 1980), 239. Breckinridge ran for the United States House of Representatives in 1894 and lost by only 255 votes out of about 19,000.

32. James A. Ramage, "Thomas Hunt Morgan: Family Influences in the Making of a Great Scientist." *Filson Club History Quarterly*, 53 (January, 1979), 8.

33. Cash, *Mind*, 124, 127-28.

34. Cited in Fry, *Death*.

35. HM to MM, n.d., JHMP-SHC; Richmond *Enquirer and Examiner*, April 24, 1868.

36. Lexington *Observer and Reporter*, April 18, 22, 1868.

37. Ibid., April 25, 1868.

38. Connelly and Bellows, *Lost Cause*, 5-6; minutes, Morgan's Old Squadron, April 17, 1868, JHMP-SHC.

39. Unidentified, undated clipping, JHMP-TU; printed invitation, M-KHS; photo, September 7, 1899, MDFP-FC; unidentified, undated clipping, DMFP-SHC.

40. Unidentified, undated clipping, HMP-UK; unidentified, undated clipping, DMFP-SHC; HM to Johnnie Morgan, n.d., JHMP-SHC; unidentified, undated clipping, JHMP-WKU.

41. Unidentified, undated clippings, HMP-UK; Thomas, *Morgan*, 90-91; Holland, *Morgan*, vii; unidentified, undated clipping, JHMP-WKU.

42. Postcards, JHMP-TU; postcard, BGTHP-HMH; *Newsletter of the Lexington Civil War Round Table*, 16 (September, 1972), 3; HM to MM, May 21 (no year), HM to Johnnie Morgan, n.d., JHMP-SHC.

43. Connelly and Bellows, *Lost Cause*, 3-4, 86.

44. Rankin, "Saga of Morgan."

45. Ramage, "Hunts and Morgans," 304.

46. Lexington *Herald*, April 5, 1908.

47. Lexington *Leader*, October 16, 1961, October 23, 1972, April 12, 1981; Lexington *Herald*, September 17, 1911; Burton Milward, "The Unveiling of the Morgan Statue," in Barbara Sutton, ed., *Lexington—As It Was: A Memento* (Lexington, Ky., 1981), 52-56.

48. R. Max Gard, *The End of the Morgan Raid* (Lisbon, Ohio, 1963), 20; interview with Arville Funk, July 7, 1984, Corydon.

49. Lexington *Herald*, undated clippings, MRF-KHS.

50. Broadcast transcript, JHMP-TU; Louisville *Courier-Journal*, April 22, 1952.

51. Dianne Wells and Mary Lou S. Madigan, comps., *Update: Guide to Kentucky Historical Highway Markers* (Frankfort, Ky., 1983), n.p.; Walter H. Hendricks to the author, September 29, 1984; telephone interview, John B. Jett, September 23, 1984; Lexington *Herald-Leader*, June 23, 1983.

52. Don D. John, *The Great Indiana-Ohio Raid* (Louisville, Ky., n.d.); Don D. John to Mrs. George Morgenstern, February 14, 1956, MRF-KHS.

BIBLIOGRAPHICAL NOTE

The Hunt-Morgan Papers at the University of Kentucky provide documents on John Hunt Morgan's family, business career, and marriages. The Morgan and Duke Families Papers and the Calvin C. Morgan & Co. Papers in the Filson Club Library have business records and family correspondence. Manuscript collections at Transylvania University illuminate Morgan's youth. The Blue Grass Trust for Historic Preservation collection has letters written by the Morgan brothers while prisoners in the Ohio state prison and other prison camps.

Most helpful on Morgan's second marriage are the John Hunt Morgan Papers, the Alice Ready Journal, and other sources in the Southern Historical Collection at the University of North Carolina in Chapel Hill. The collection on the death of Morgan included in the D. Howard Smith Collection at the Kentucky Historical Society has firsthand accounts of Morgan's death; and the Map Room File, catalogued as the Don John Civil War Collection, has details on the Great Raid.

The L. Virginia (Smith) French diary and other manuscripts at the Tennessee State Library and Archives have eyewitness accounts of Morgan in middle Tennessee. Published Civil War diaries furnish evidence of his popularity and contemporary newspapers are a rich source on the movement for guerrilla warfare and Morgan as a folk hero. *The War of the Rebellion: A Compilation of the Official Records of the Union and Confederate Armies* (1880-1901) discloses information on his Union opposition, the triad system, and Morgan's personal relations with Bragg, Lee, and others.

Basil W. Duke's *History of Morgan's Cavalry* (1867) is an invaluable account. *The Civil War in Kentucky* (1975) by Lowell H. Harrison has an excellent brief overview of Morgan's career. In *John Hunt Morgan and His Raiders* (1975), Edison H. Thomas effectively analyzes attacks on the L&N; and in *The Military Telegraph . . .* (rpt., 1974), William R. Plum recounts disruption of the Union telegraph. The most detailed biography, Cecil F. Holland's *Morgan and His Raiders* (1942), has a great deal of information on Morgan's second marriage. Thomas L. Connelly's *Army of the Heartland: The Army of Tennessee, 1861-1862* (1967) and *Autumn of Glory: The Army of Tennessee, 1862-1865* (1971) provide perspective on Morgan's role in the western campaign. On Morgan's family background see the author's *John Wesley Hunt: Pioneer Merchant, Manufacturer and Financier.*

INDEX

WINNERS OF THE
Douglas Southall Freeman History Award

Five Tragic Hours: The Battle of Franklin
James L. McDonough and Thomas Connelly
1984

The Last Review: The Confederate Reunion,
Richmond, 1932: An Album
Virginius Dabney
1985

Rebel Raider: The Life of
General John Hunt Morgan
James A. Ramage
1986